MW01004883

ADVANCE PRAISE FOR

ENDLESS ENDLESS

"Elephant 6 stormed Athens and breathed new energy into an already stratospherically creative scene. Their love of music was and is remarkable."

—Michael Stipe

"One person thinks Elephant 6 is a tree. Another thinks it is a snake. One person thinks it is an art commune. Another thinks it is a record label. Taken together, all the different perspectives build up to a thoughtful and authoritative account of our collective."

—Robert Schneider,
Elephant 6 cofounder (The Apples in Stereo)

"A thorough and accurate look at Elephant 6! It's wild that I played music with some of these people for around twenty years and didn't know some of this stuff. A fascinating read!"

—John Kiran Fernandes (The Olivia Tremor Control,
Circulatory System, Cloud Recordings)

"The Elephant 6 collective stands as part of and apart from the wonderful and world-class music scene of Athens, Georgia. *Endless Endless* provides an in-depth look at wonders and mysteries of its creation and lasting impact. It's also a great read."

—Patterson Hood, writer and artist (The Drive-By Truckers)

"It's the ultimate dream for any musician throughout their career to be surrounded by a community full of geniuses and freaks supporting and contributing to each other's art, and that's exactly what E6 was. *Endless Endless* perfectly captures the beautiful and complex dynamics between the longtime friends and bandmates involved in E6, and it left me longing for the era of four-track recording, mixtapes, and the inspiration that is so powerfully fostered by close-knit, small-town communities. Indie music truly would not be where it is today without all of these artists paving the way!"

—Julia Shapiro (Chastity Belt)

"*Endless Endless* is an intimate portrait of a small, out-of-the-way scene touched by magic. It captures the raw thrill of creative discovery in the time before digital culture took over our lives, and it's a testament to the power of friendship, showing what can happen when you find your people and make your own world."

—Mark Richardson, rock and pop critic for the *Wall Street Journal* and former editor-in-chief of *Pitchfork*

"Part oral history, part celebration, part mystery, *Endless Endless* is a lovely, compulsively readable book about a musical movement that was as important and lasting as it was humble and modest. Adam Clair clearly adores this world and draws us into it with deep research and sharp perspective, but, more than anything, with laid-back, endearing prose that draws you in and lets you be a part. Reading this book makes you feel like you're listening to the music it chronicles, which might be the best compliment, among many, that I can give it."

—Will Leitch, author of *How Lucky*

"Everyone who listened to (and became obsessed with) *In the Aeroplane Over the Sea* has wondered, at some point, how the hell such a masterwork could've emerged, seemingly out of nowhere. *Endless Endless* answers that question by meticulously tracking the artists and themes and magic that led to the seminal indie rock album of our generation. I still regret that I missed a Neutral Milk Hotel concert in Boston in 1997. I thought they'd be around forever, that there was no rush. Adam Clair has given me the next best thing: the definitive story of who they were, where they came from, and how they assembled one of the greatest indie rock records of all time."

—Michael Schur, TV writer/producer and creator of *The Good Place*

ENDLESS ENDLESS

Endless Endless

A Lo-Fi History of the Elephant 6 Mystery

Adam Clair

New York

Hachette Books
Hachette Book Group
1290 Avenue of the Americas
New York, NY 10104
HachetteBooks.com
Twitter.com/HachetteBooks
Instagram.com/HachetteBooks

First Edition: January 2022

Published by Hachette Books, an imprint of Perseus Books, LLC, a subsidiary of Hachette Book Group, Inc. The Hachette Books name and logo is a trademark of the Hachette Book Group.

Print book interior design by Linda Mark

Library of Congress Control Number: 2021949028

ISBNs: 9780306923944 (hardcover); 9780306923968 (ebook)

Printed in the United States of America

LSC-C

Printing 1, 2021

For Marc

Contents

Introduction

In a *Pitchfork* interview published in 2002, Jeff Mangum spoke with his friend Marci Fierman about what he had been up to in the four years since his band Neutral Milk Hotel released *In the Aeroplane Over the Sea*, one of dozens of records released by the amorphous, distributed collective of musicians and other artists known as the Elephant 6 Recording Company and, of those records, the one that has found the largest audience by far.

The piece is interesting not just because Mangum is thoughtful and eloquent and philosophical throughout, but also because it was the first interview he had granted in more than three years. It was the first interview he'd done since the end of the tour supporting *Aeroplane*, when he, Fierman writes, "seemed not only to have ducked the spotlight, but perhaps to have stepped inadvertently into some negative-matter black hole."

It was also the last time *anybody* has interviewed him. He has given this book his blessing but politely declined requests to speak on the record for it.

Jeff's conversation with Fierman is largely about what he'd been up to since the brief set he'd played on New Year's Eve a few years earlier, the final night of 1998, after which he did one of the most radical things an ascendant rock star can do: nothing. He stopped performing. He released no more music and participated in no more interviews. He never even said goodbye.

In the interview, Jeff recounts a dream he had had about a year prior:

> I was standing on the ocean. I saw a blur come around, from my right side to my left. It was a hand putting something next to me. When I looked closer I saw that what the hand had put there was a little sea turtle. . . . I picked up the sea turtle and put [it] in my hand and it turned into a butterfly. And then it turned into a black spider. It kept turning into a butterfly, a spider, a butterfly, a spider. It would pulsate between the two. I put my hands around it to grasp it and blood ran out of my hands and fell into the sand. Then as I let go of it, the blood rose up from the sand and turned again into the butterfly/spider. It hovered about a foot above my hand, and turned into a little ball of light. So that whole sequence repeated two or three times: it would land back in my hand, turn into a creature, and when I tried to hold it, it would crush again into blood, and when I would let go the blood would rise back up and turn into a ball of light . . .
>
> I didn't have to analyze it afterwards. The butterfly and the spider represented two opposing sides: all the things that I love and consider to be beautiful and gentle and wonderful, and all the things that threaten me[,] the things about life that I can't come to terms with because they don't fit into my nice, happy picture of the way I want the world to be. It kept morphing back and forth to show me that they're both one and the same; they're dependent on one another to exist. When I tried to grasp at either what I love or what I hate, I destroyed the very ability of being able to really penetrate the essence of either. By trying to understand it, I would just crush it. But when I let go and let it be what it was, it would turn into light to show me that both sides come from the same source. I think the vision was trying to tell me to just live and be joyful and stop creating these internal wars over all the pain that is within myself and that I see all around me . . .

Records like *In the Aeroplane Over the Sea* are extraordinarily difficult to talk or write about. Perhaps that's a defeatist way to start a book about people who made *Aeroplane* and records like it, but what Jeff took from his dream applies here, too. The harder one tries to understand it, the more difficult to understand it can become. The very act of *trying* to understand it can destroy whatever it is that eludes us. To investigate something like this is to kill it, like pinning a butterfly in a shadow box, preserving the brilliance of its wings by ensuring they never flap again.

Everybody listens to music, and so everybody has opinions about music, and we mostly consume it on such a visceral level that words tend to be insufficient for expressing those opinions. Our appreciation can be reflexive and instantaneous, or it can be cultivated over years of listening, but rarely is it *rational*. If we could express in words exactly what a piece of music does for us, we likely wouldn't need that piece of music—or music at all, for that matter. Words are, at their absolute best, an approximation, regardless of what they describe. There is always a gap between signifier and signified, and so writing about the experiential frequently boils down to some prolix version of "You had to be there." Music writing is thus not a mimetic attempt to replace the experience of listening to music, any more than the million billion poems written about love are about replicating the actual feeling of being in love.

"Show, don't tell" is as common a dictum as you'll find in writing classes. It would be banal if it weren't such good advice. If art has an essence, it is the act of showing rather than telling. The art that really sticks with us, though, is the art that shows by necessity rather than by choice: the work that seems at once monolithic and irreducibly complex, pieces we carry around with us as they alternately mystify and clarify, beckoning us to look deeper and deeper and deeper and deeper and deeper without any promise of a way out on the other side. That is, art endures not when it shows *instead* of telling, but rather when it *shows what could not otherwise be told.* It communicates what only it can, such that we can't really explain what we just experienced, and the only meaningful thing you can say about it is: go check it out for yourself.

There's no answer key in the pages that follow, no glossary, no annotated explanation of what Jeff or anybody else meant by this or that lyric or setlist or recording decision. This music—and most transcendent art, really—is powerful because it is interpretive, and in celebrating and exploring that work, hard explanation would only serve to destroy it. This, ultimately, is what makes records like *Aeroplane* and other great Elephant 6 works so difficult to talk about: every attempt to really understand it on a more-than-personal level serves only to undermine its power, until that power is completely drained and there's nothing even worth trying to understand. Everyone has their own reasons for loving it, drawn from their own unique set of experiences. To even attempt to discuss that power in a book is to universalize those experiences, to pile up the craggy raw materials of our individual lives and then flatten them with a steamroller.

Allow me to explain what I tried to do instead, because there's room for only so much. There are more than a few legitimate Elephant 6 bands that get no mention at all in the pages that follow, and though I conducted more than one hundred interviews for this book, there are still plenty of people whom I didn't speak with. The details of this story are infinite, and this book is merely an approximation of the spirit that runs through it.

* * *

FEW PIECES OF TECHNOLOGY HAVE ALTERED THE HISTORY OF MUSIC like the cassette tape. Would-be rock stars no longer needed a studio to record their work, which also meant they didn't need the backing of a label or an independent source of wealth. They could do it anywhere, and with minimal investment. The cassette democratized home recording in such a profound way that the clicking, squealing, and hissing artifacts of the medium itself have become aesthetic affectations on even purely digital works. Home-burned CDs, DJ sets, YouTube and Spotify playlists, and official hip-hop releases often bear the name "mixtape," generations removed from any analog medium.

Just as transformative as the ability for artists to record and reproduce their music independently was the freedom for anyone to compile their own mixtapes, curating a listening experience for themselves or sharing the music they love with others. The cassette tape meant you could share the songs you wrote with your friends, but even if you couldn't play a note, you could share the music you *liked* with your friends just by dubbing it from the radio or your personal collection. Suddenly, anyone could be a DJ. Tape trading like that had two major effects. First, by allowing people to share their music this way, music could spread at a velocity it never had before. So rather than saying, "Hey, here's a cool song, you should [come to my house/go to a record store/wait for it to maybe come on the radio] so you can hear it," you could just hand someone a cassette, which shifted some of the power from radio DJs, glossy music magazines, and record store clerks (who were themselves all beholden to label influences in some unsavory ways). But second and at least as important is the connection that emerges when one person gives a tape to another person. Beyond the gesture of the transaction itself, the recipient must put themselves in the giver's headphones as they listen, forging a deeply empathetic bond. To share art, as both currency and communication, is to understand one another.

Another overlooked aspect of lo-fi music ("low-fidelity," an epithet of pride)—whether recorded to tape originally or just copied that way—is that it is often quieter. Even when turned up loud, it can sound almost like a whispered secret meant only for you or like eavesdropping on one meant for someone else, something you're not supposed to share or something you're not supposed to hear, or both. Our brains are wired to interpret this quality of sound as intimate, fragile, precious.

The cassette tape formed and strengthened communities of musicians and music lovers and allowed them to flourish. In the ensuing pages, the importance of this technology arises again and again. Without it, the story of the Elephant 6 and of contemporary music in general would be vastly different. So, both structurally and conceptually, I tried to approach this book with the same sensibilities: I wrote this book as a sort of mixtape. I hope whatever afore-, un-, and still-to-be-mentioned shortcomings in fidelity or continuity or anything else are at least excusable in light of that framework, and may be even part of the charm.

Everything in this world is a metaphor. Whole galaxies mimic the behaviors of subatomic particles, and there are trend lines through everything in between. People who make lo-fi music—namely, the people this book is about—often take a similarly fuzzy approach to many things in their lives. As such, not everyone interviewed for this project has a particularly sharp memory, and very few of them documented anything as it was happening. Which is to say, aside from interviews, there are only so many primary sources from this era, a time just before camera phones and social media so dramatically expanded the way we catalog the minutiae of our lives into hard drives and hashtags. The timelines and anecdotes presented to me in interviews often contradicted themselves, even within one source's telling. These same sources, however, were also supremely generous in sharing their thoughts. As if I were making a mixtape, I consider my authorial role on the ensuing pages primarily to be one of curation and sequencing, though the process has usually felt collaborative, cowritten by everyone quoted herein.

Analog means palimpsestic. Prior to digital technology, copying always meant degradation, a loss of fidelity. That loss has a sound of its own, filling in whatever fidelity might be missing. Just as sediment petrifies rotting wood, other stuff can seep in where fidelity is lost. Bootlegs and mixtapes are rife with this extra sound, the sound of duplication, the sound of transmission, the sound of human connection. The mixtape you dub for someone contains not just the songs you wanted to share but a hum from spinning reels, decay from the heat of your hatchback, abrasion from a cassette player's sullied heads, maybe even music you had previously dubbed on the same cassette. But if the songs are curated and sequenced in just the right way, these are aleatoric footprints to be treasured, not blemishes that invalidate.

To the recipient, it's both a burdensome assignment—please listen to this, thoughtfully, and tell me what you think—and an act of charity. It's a gesture that can indicate and/or accelerate intimacy between parties. A good mixtape can be a little hazy and distorted, and it absolutely *should be* eclectic, jumping around chronologically and stylistically and emotionally but cohering into an evocative piece of collage art that's greater (or at least a little different) than the sum of its carefully selected parts. It can draw equally from the obscure and the popular and be crafted for an audience of one billion or just one, but it should always come from somewhere intimate, personal. The essence of a mixtape is something unique, something potentially challenging and horizon-broadening and soul-connecting, but still something comforting and familiar. At its core, it's simply a way for one person to gather and share something they value.

I approached this book as if I were making a mixtape of the story of the Elephant 6, to show what I cannot otherwise tell—how one group of people gathered and shared what it valued most—with a welcome layer of room tone. It's mostly chronological, but chronology was of no higher priority than expressing something abstract that runs through this collective. To do that required some variance in style and perspective. A multifaceted thing demands different lenses for different facets. What I've included is sequenced as it is to convey that maximally. A good mixtape is about letting the music speak for itself: arranging it such that it can speak loudest and most clearly, and then getting out of the way. The curator defers to the artists. In the same tradition, I have avoided my own interpolation except where narratively necessary, letting the people of the Elephant 6 tell their stories in their own words.

One more thing, and then we'll get into it. Among the reasons people connect so deeply with *In the Aeroplane Over the Sea* seems to be the negative space created by impossibly abstract lyrics, unfamiliar instrumentation, and other bits of psychedelic mystique. What's most interesting is also the toughest to describe,* and Jeff's refusal to explain turns any critical examination of the album into a solipsistic exercise that tells you more about the critic than about the record itself. Most of our universe is empty, of course. Shaping that emptiness is an act very similar to filling it.

The vast negative space creates a blankness onto which the listener projects their deepest anxieties and scars. The album becomes an anthem for the damaged, agnostic toward the particulars of a given listener's trauma, with both arms outstretched to console. No matter the intensity of your troubles, *Aeroplane* can refract them through its many facets into something jarring, comforting, terrifying, and enlightening. It's an album that feels not just alive, but able to *listen back.*

Neutral Milk Hotel—loosely, Jeff Mangum, Julian Koster, Jeremy Barnes, and Scott Spillane, though Robert Schneider played on both albums (and was an early member of the live band), and other musicians contributed to the record and played shows with them—released *In the Aeroplane Over the Sea* in February 1998. Critics loved it from the start and only more so as time went on,† and after playing nearly one hundred raucous shows that year in the United States and Europe, Jeff and his band stopped cold. After a show at the 40 Watt Club in Athens, Georgia, on December 31, 1998, Mangum hid from the public eye for more than a decade, releasing no new music, refusing interviews (with the exception of the conversation mentioned earlier), and performing in public only once

* Part of why this album continues to be so popular is that instead of explaining why it's so good, people tend to insist that someone listen to it themselves, if not giving them a copy or playing it for them right then and there.

† *Pitchfork*, for example, awarded the album a stout 8.7 out of 10 when the album first came out and revised it to a 10 upon its re-release just a few years later, one of only a handful of albums the site has ever awarded a perfect score.

in that span.* There wasn't a press release announcing a breakup, and neither Jeff nor any of his bandmates ever offered any sort of explanation or even an acknowledgment of the hiatus. He just went silent. Where once stood a shambolic indie rock quartet, there was now only space.

Then something weird happened. Neutral Milk Hotel's popularity was on an upward trajectory while the band was active, but it shot up much more sharply when the band disappeared. Even if the band was no longer active, fans kept sharing and evangelizing about it, and despite hearing the band only in the past tense, those new fans were just as enamored and likely to keep sharing. The album has become iconic, the band legendary, and the collective from which it emerged a scene worthy of study. All after they stopped, despite frequent cries for them to start again.

What's missing—or at least what's not immediately apparent—from both the album and the public understanding of Mangum himself becomes just as compelling as what is actually there. I began researching this book in 2008 and spent an awful lot of time with Elephant 6 folks, even living with a few of them at different junctures. This book is composed largely of the interviews I conducted with them, but it's also informed by my time hanging out with them, between sets at a show, over a plate of nachos, or on someone's back porch. If I learned one thing from our time together, it's this: art is not a thing or a category but rather a means of analysis.† The question "Is it art?" is premised on a false binary. Regardless of intent or skill or authorship, absolutely anything can be viewed through an artistic lens. How does it make me feel? What does it make clearer, and what does it obfuscate? How does it change the way I see the world around me? We can look at anything through this lens, be it an album or the decision not to make one.

The act of negation can, like everything else, be viewed as an artistic act. Consider the splendor of the notes Miles Davis didn't play, the dynamic power of Marina Abramović's stoic performances, the elegant heft of the arms *Venus de Milo* doesn't have, the sheer terror of a movie

---

* Mangum performed an impromptu solo set in New Zealand in 2001 at the personal request of Tall Dwarfs' Chris Knox, a friend of and major musical influence on Jeff.

† If I learned two things, the other is that everyone involved with the Elephant 6 is still in awe of the thing. The book in your hands today was pared down from a manuscript that was once more than three times as long, but I was able to excise a pretty big portion of that just by removing all the different versions of people saying, "It was so amazing."

monster unseen, the tedium of the labor Bartleby the Scrivener would prefer not to perform and the emancipatory potential of his decision not to perform it. Good art can posit answers to the most difficult questions, but great art poses new questions, and negative space has a particular capacity for provocation. Learning is an act of continuous forgetting.

Jeff's post-*Aeroplane* absence takes the exact shape of whatever we want most from our artists. Something is "missing" only where our expectations demand any presence. It is an expanse of negative space, positively brimming with meaning, albeit opaque. A pause pregnant with pathos. It is the Grand Canyon of indie rock, a chasm whose sedimentary beauty inspires no more wonder than its emptiness. It is the evidence of a geological force so massive—hundreds of miles, millions of years—we can fathom it through only its remnants.

The one thing more difficult for the human mind to conceptualize than infinity is a pure void. No sound deafens like silence. Our imaginations rush to occupy the empty spaces, usually before we even notice there were holes. Vacuums are filled quickly with assumptions, hopes, speculation, myth.

We do not discover our heroes. We build them.

CHAPTER 1

BY THE END OF 1998, NEUTRAL MILK HOTEL WAS AMONG the most promising indie bands in the world. It had performed nearly one hundred times that year, across the United States and ten other countries. Tickets sold well, and those who stuck around long enough—Neutral Milk Hotel was not an especially punctual band and often took the stage hours after its listed set time—eventually turned what they saw into a legend: a singular band at its peak, a transcendent, you-just-had-to-be-there, too-bad-you-weren't performance. Many report having been moved to tears. A&R reps from major record labels took notice, too, and had begun sniffing around.

The band filigreed much of the North American and European maps, lingering ephemerally but leaving its marks indelibly, touring in support of a record, *In the Aeroplane Over the Sea,* which the band had released that February. Appreciation for the album has certainly grown since then. Year after year, *Aeroplane* remains one of the best-selling records of the so-called vinyl revival. *Pitchfork* counts it as the fourth-best record of the 1990s. The band is name-dropped by Grammy winners, hip TV characters, and talk show hosts. At the time of this writing, *Aeroplane*'s title track alone has been streamed more than 75 million times on Spotify and more than 10 million on YouTube, though it was released long before either digital streaming company existed, to say nothing of the counts on CD and LP spins, MP3 plays (legitimately purchased and not), and live covers. It was a hit and remains so. Today, *In the Aeroplane Over the Sea* is a capital-*I* Important record, but sold-out shows and ecstatic reviews (not to mention placement near the top of many notable year-end critics' lists) make it clear Neutral Milk Hotel had plenty of momentum even at the time.

The last true Neutral Milk Hotel show of 1998 was on October 13, in London, at the end of a month-long tour through Europe. It was the ninety-first Neutral Milk Hotel performance of the year. Jeff Mangum—the band's singer, songwriter, and guitarist—took it easy from there, playing only two sets the rest of the year, in Athens, Georgia. On December 5, at a birthday party for his friend (and *Aeroplane* art director) Chris Bilheimer, Jeff played a short solo set of just six songs. On New Year's Eve, he performed an even shorter set at the 40 Watt, only three songs this time. Julian Koster and Scott Spillane joined on saw and horn, respectively, for the first and third songs.

Over the course of barely two years, Neutral Milk Hotel had risen from house-show obscurity to widespread hype and critical acclaim, soaring to this point as the music industry itself continued to climb. Record sales peaked in 1999, so labels of all kinds still had money to burn. Neutral Milk Hotel seemed poised for whatever next step Jeff wished to pursue, though no one really expected or seemed to understand or even accept what he pursued next. The December shows—the birthday party and New Year's Eve—were attended mostly by his friends. They felt even then like precious moments, the last chances to snatch one more "before they got huge" memory. For those in attendance, it felt like the last time they'd be able to see Jeff perform in such an intimate setting. They were right, but only half-.

They would never again have the chance to see Jeff play like this, but not because he would go on to play to much bigger crowds (though he did that eventually). It was because, at least for a while, nobody would have the chance to see him play at all. Just as Neutral Milk Hotel was reaching the escape velocity necessary to ascend from indie rock success to mainstream superstardom, Jeff hit the EJECT button. After the New Year's Eve show, he called it quits. He played with other bands occasionally, but there were no more Neutral Milk Hotel shows or Jeff Mangum shows or shows under the name of any project he was leading. His bandmates all pursued other projects they'd started before joining Neutral Milk Hotel: the Music Tapes, the Gerbils, Bablicon. Jeff stopped releasing new music or even doing interviews. He never explained why, even to his own friends and colleagues. He never even really told anyone he was finished. He just stopped, or at least he didn't continue. This radical act of negation has become one of the most baffling mysteries in music history. After all, who wouldn't want to be a rock star?

For other artists, that reclusiveness could have doomed the band to nothing more than an orphaned Wikipedia page, but something strange happened. In the years following Jeff's disappearance, the few who'd been lucky enough to see Neutral Milk Hotel perform live were very vocal about what they had witnessed. Those who missed out found solace in the band's landmark album, *In the Aeroplane Over the Sea*, spinning it obsessively and hoping that Neutral Milk Hotel might one day reunite, collecting bootlegs and B sides in the meantime. A significant audience grew as well among those who could only listen to the record. Basically everyone who had heard some version of it evangelized about the music, and faced with the hopelessness of following a dead band, fans spread out into the side projects of Jeff's Neutral Milk Hotel bandmates and colleagues, namely the other members of the Elephant 6 Recording Company, the multidisciplinary collective of which Neutral Milk Hotel was a cornerstone. Jeff still had not released any new material or spoken to anyone on the record, but by the time Neutral Milk Hotel finally reunited for a world tour in 2013, after a fifteen-year hiatus, the band that had made a name for itself in dingy rock clubs at the end of the nineties was selling out four-thousand-seat theaters in minutes and headlining major festivals around the globe. Word of mouth is still the most effective form of marketing around.

The Elephant 6 Recording Company formally began as a record label in the early nineties and rapidly bloomed into something more nebulous and impactful. By the end of the decade, it had become so expansive that "Elephant 6" described not a group of bands or even a particular sound. Elephant 6 had become a movement. Aesthetically, the musicians drew heavily from psychedelic influences but also cribbed from esoteric experimental composers and recordings of antiquity from Africa, Asia, and Eastern Europe, as well as their favorite jazz, folk, and punk iconoclasts. Commercially, they mostly followed the path of that last group, pursuing their art with an aggressively DIY philosophy. They spurned major labels who showed interest, recorded exclusively in their own group houses and hovels, built treasured stage props from other people's trash, toured the country in jury-rigged junkers, and played shows with instruments that couldn't even be sold for scrap. The tight-knit nature of the collective was evident on every incestuous project they attempted. Bands went out of their way to play together and name-drop one another in interviews. They shared members onstage or lent their talents to one another's recording sessions. Hardly a set went by without folks swapping instruments between songs (or sometimes during). The whole was greater than the sum of its parts, because each part was used six or seven different ways. The bonds between them were strong enough to withstand the use.

The Elephant 6 apparatus generated dozens of works, less finished products than they are documents of messing around, dispatches from distant reaches of creative indulgence. Far from being a well-oiled machine, the collective operated like a delicate, improvised apparatus made from chicken wire, old luggage, and fifth-hand furniture, but the fragility is entirely the point. It sounds like it could come apart at any time, rickety and ramshackle by design, such that it can exist at only a human scale. Any larger and the imperfections loom too large: where duct tape and chewed gum were once sufficient to hold things together, cracks must be soldered, blemishes spackled, roughness sanded down and buffed, until the whole contraption is polished into something uncanny and without character. Simply, the Elephant 6 ethos must exist on a human scale if it is to exist at all. By its nature, it resists commodification or capitalist co-option.

How does something like the Elephant 6 come to be? How do bands like Neutral Milk Hotel, the Olivia Tremor Control, the Apples in Stereo, Of Montreal, and others emerge from it? Why did Jeff Mangum walk away from assured rock stardom—and then what happened? How did he find himself with that opportunity in the first place? What legacy does the Elephant 6 leave today?

Uncertainty and knowledge are not opposites but parallel vectors. Perhaps these questions beget only more questions, but perhaps those questions are more illuminating than any answers could be.

WE'LL START IN RUSTON, A NORTHERN LOUISIANA TOWN that's home to a university and only so much else, closer to Little Rock or Jackson than to New Orleans but hours from any of them. It is the fall of 1978, seven-year-old Robert Schneider's first day of second grade and his first at A. E. Phillips Elementary, a K–8 laboratory school affiliated with Louisiana Tech. It's exactly the sort of place you'd expect to be populated by the children of professors, with music and art classes on alternating days and its own planetarium.

Robert, the son of an architecture professor, is dressed in a Buster Brown outfit his mother picked out. Until a year ago, Robert lived in Cape Town, South Africa, where the buckled sandals he's wearing today would have looked the same as all the other kids'. Both of his parents were opposed to apartheid, so his father, Peter, had moved the family to Alabama a year earlier, taking a job at Auburn University. When the department head (who had recruited Peter to his program) left for Louisiana Tech, Peter and his family went along to Ruston.

ROBERT SCHNEIDER: I dressed in fey little British schoolchildren clothes in fucking Louisiana. I'm really hyper and weird. Even in South Africa, I was an outcast little kid. I was kicked out of kindergarten three times in three different schools and sent back to preschool. I'm a quirky person. That doesn't always hit people the right way, and I have to build up my own world that way. More than art and other things, music was a path to that.

Clothes notwithstanding, Robert had mostly adjusted to American life by then. He had tried to assimilate based on the expectations set forth by his grandfather Jack,* who had fought in World War II with the British and South African armies and spent a lot of time around Americans. He had given Robert some tips to help him blend in.

ROBERT SCHNEIDER: He had mastered how to talk like an American, which is to roll your tongue into the back of your mouth and *tawk lahk thess*. It sounded like John Wayne or something. He also told me that Americans said "oh boy" a lot, this being World War II–era slang. So I practiced saying "oh boy" with my tongue rolled back in my mouth. On the plane from South Africa to America, we took this huge two-level jumbo jet, and I remember sitting in different seats on the plane and kind of nonchalantly saying "oh boy," and to say it in the right way with my tongue rolled back in my mouth so they would be impressed with how I sounded.†

But Robert's outfit and accent didn't fit in, and so he felt like he didn't fit in. The feeling stayed with him for a long time.

ROBERT SCHNEIDER: On my first day of school in Ruston, I was called a South African freak, and I felt that. I still feel that. I think that was how I was viewed for most of my childhood in Ruston. I was happy because I'm a happy person, but I wasn't embedded in the community the way the other kids were. I was by far the least popular kid in my school. I was probably the least popular kid in my age group in the entire city.

* Technically, Jack is Robert's mother's stepdad, and Robert grew up calling him Uncle Jack.

† In the early Elephant 6 days, when the Apples in Stereo and Neutral Milk Hotel toured together, Jeff Mangum would play bass for the Apples and Robert Schneider and Hilarie Sidney would back him up in Neutral Milk Hotel. "I don't know how it happened," Schneider says, "but 'oh boy' figured into one or two prominent noise jams in my memory." Jeff would say "oh boy," and the rest of the band (which also included bassist Lisa Janssen) would erupt in cacophony behind him.

At recess that first day of second grade, "he looked all fidgety and nervous," Jeff Mangum recounted in 1998, "so I went up to him with my Wiffle bat to see if he wanted to play ball."

Robert was standing around the yard by himself while the other boys in the class assembled a game. Robert had never heard of Wiffle ball. At the behest of a teacher who noticed the new kid had been excluded, Jeff approached with a bat and invited him to join in a friendly game. Robert panicked.

"You're going to hit me with that," he said.

Jeff patiently explained to the anxious new kid that he wasn't going to hit him, that in fact he was inviting Robert to play with him. But Robert was suspicious.

"No, you're going to hit me."

Jeff explained again that he just wanted to play a game, that he had no interest in hurting or even intimidating Robert, but the new kid remained unconvinced. Fearing for his safety, he fled. Jeff ran after him. Somewhere over the course of running around the playground like Tom and Jerry, anxiety gave way to joy and Robert let his guard down. Jeff became Robert's first new friend. By the end of recess, Robert already felt silly for having doubted Jeff's sincerity.

Jeff's eighth birthday was a few weeks away. Everyone in the class had already received an invitation—except for the new kid. As the party approached, the class was abuzz with anticipation, and Robert felt left out. So after school, he called Jeff to see what the deal was.

> **ROBERT SCHNEIDER**: He was really nice about it and told me he had meant to invite me and that his mom had forgotten because there were two lists or something. He came up with something on the spot, this nice, believable story, and I remember coming out of the conversation being like, "Oh, that makes sense." It was probably my first real social interaction.

Robert went to the party. He brought Jeff a Superman Colorforms set.

A stronger connection began to form circa fifth grade as the two began obsessing about heavy metal together and bonding over their new guitars (Jeff had a Stratocaster clone and Robert a Flying V). Their relationship took another step in middle school. One of Jeff's closest friends had become Robert's nemesis.* Jeff's friend and an accomplice hatched a plot to get Robert alone in the woods under the guise of riding bikes together, with an ulterior plan to beat him up. The night before it was supposed to happen, though, Robert got a tip.

> **ROBERT SCHNEIDER:** Jeff called me up and was like, "Dude, I heard you were going with so-and-so to ride bikes, and I heard so-and-so was going to try to jump you." It was this trap that this one so-called friend had lured me into, but Jeff, being this really nice person, despite being friends with the other two bullies, had found out about it and called me. It was right after that that we started to become better friends.

As touched as Robert was by this show of kindness, it didn't work out so well for Jeff. The next day in class, Robert's would-be assailant passed a picture around class: a rat with Jeff's name on it.

The next summer, Robert's parents sent him to algebra camp to prepare him for high school. There, he finally crossed paths with Will Hart, whom he'd been hearing about from mutual friends for a year or two. Robert wanted to impress one of the girls at the camp, so he mentioned to her that he was a guitar player.† The mistake he made, of course, was saying such a thing within earshot of another teenage guitarist. Having never met either of them before, the boy interjected, proudly and confidently, "I play guitar. I can blow him out of the window." Bested, Robert didn't say another word to the girl for the rest of the summer, but he quickly befriended his interlocutor, Will.

> **ROBERT SCHNEIDER:** The irony of it is that I very quickly got much better than him at guitar. No patting myself on the back, but I got really good on the guitar really quickly. After that, I never improved at all, and I've probably regressed. But within one or two years of that story, that became a legend in our little circle because I was so much fucking better than him.

* Even decades later, Robert did not want to name names, though he still seems to hold a bit of a grudge. He has forgiven but not forgotten.

† Not that anyone would have assumed otherwise about a fourteen-year-old metalhead with hair past his shoulders.

WILL CULLEN HART:[*] I couldn't play shit. I was bravado only. I couldn't rip a solo now like he could when he was thirteen.

In May 1982, Jeff, Robert, and Will attended a Cheap Trick concert together on the Louisiana Tech campus. Neither Jeff nor Robert had ever been to a real concert before. Will had only been to a couple (Rick Springfield, Styx). The boys were ready to rock.

Before the show, Jeff and Robert stopped by the Pizza Inn to grab a quick dinner. Their slices emerged from the oven just as Jeff's mom pulled up out front to take them to the show, and though the pizza was still too hot to eat, they didn't want to make her wait. To hurry along the cooling process, they dumped a pitcher of ice water on the slices. This ruined the pizza, of course, but the boys wolfed down their soggy dinner without singeing their palates and sprinted out to the car.

Will met them at the show, where the three of them soon found themselves crammed into a dense crowd, enraptured by the rock gods onstage before them. When one of guitarist Rick Nielsen's picks ended up on the floor between Will and Robert, the boys tussled for it, with Robert emerging victorious. Years later at Jeff's house and still on a high from their first wild rock show, Jeff and Robert rocked out to the songs they had heard that night, air-guitaring with a baseball bat and a tennis racquet, respectively. Strumming the catgut with a pick Rick Nielsen had once held, Robert felt suddenly unstoppable.

ROBERT SCHNEIDER: It's exactly like the Foreigner song "Juke Box Hero." It was this magic shining golden pick that gave me these magical powers. I had the pick and the tennis racquet, and I remember thinking, *This is it. I can play guitar.* It was such magic and confidence from Rick Nielsen's pick.[†]

Will Cullen Hart was also born in Ruston, but the family moved to Dauphin Island, Alabama, shortly after his birth. That lasted about a

* Will has long included his middle name in professional references because he thinks "Will Hart" is "kind of boring."

† Robert kept the pick with him at all times. Years later, when he and Nielsen guested on the same episode of *The Colbert Report*, Robert giddily shared the story with him, but in hindsight, he thinks it mostly made Nielsen feel old.

summer. Then he was back in Ruston, but again only for a short spell. By the time Will had turned four, his mom had moved him yet again, this time to Aspen, Colorado, where they stayed another five years or so before returning once more to Ruston, at which point Will moved in with his dad. No matter where he was, though, creativity was always around him. Will's parents met in art school, and they tried to instill those aesthetic sensitivities in their son. Whenever he complained of boredom, Will's parents just told him to draw. He drew a lot.

Because Will's parents didn't work for the university (they were both interior designers), he went to a different elementary school in Ruston than Robert and Jeff. It was not until middle school that he met his eventual musical collaborators. After shuffling around the country amid shifting custody arrangements, Will was looking for some stability in his life. He went out for the seventh-grade football team with Jeff,* and though Jeff quit the team early, Will survived through the whole season.

> WILL CULLEN HART: I never hit the field until the last game. "Who hasn't played yet?" That was it. I did it to say I could stick with something. I quit almost everything.

"We'd get crushed daily," Mangum told *Magnet* in 1998. "We were always running around the field in a panic."

That stability was fleeting. Will moved again that summer, this time going with his mom to Dallas for eighth grade. They were in Carlsbad, California, by the summer. Neither was a fit for him socially. As the new kid, Will saw other students reaching out to welcome him, but he didn't feel the same connection he had felt with Jeff and Robert in Ruston.

His dad made him an offer. Will could come back to Ruston and stay with him, but he had to commit to staying there. No more moving, at least for a while. For a teenager who had been bouncing around the country for most of his childhood, it would be a change in lifestyle, but it didn't take Will long to decide. He moved in with his dad and stepmom partway

* The boys were still at different schools, but A. E. Phillips didn't have a football team, so Jeff joined the Ruston Junior High team with Will.

through ninth grade, staying in a detached guesthouse most of the time. He stuck around through high school.

ROBERT SCHNEIDER: When he came back for our sophomore year, he had gotten really punk while living in Dallas. He had gotten very Big City. His hair was spiked up, and it looked very much like Robert Smith, but blond. He dressed in a very new-wave fashion that was cool and out of place in Ruston.

Will's mom bought him his first guitar when he was eleven, but it was a little while before he really got going with it. Guitar lessons didn't really stick.

WILL CULLEN HART: I just wanted to thrash it.

So he thrashed, and in middle school he started his first band with Jeff and their friend Ty Storms. They called the band Maggott and played their best approximation of punk, which usually meant Will and Jeff plugging their guitars directly into a boombox and making as much noise as they could while Ty shouted the most absurd lyrics he could muster over the cacophony.

"It was kind of a punk band," Jeff told *San Francisco Weekly* in 1996. "We would go over to Will's house, get really stoned, make noise, scream and yell. Then we started writing pop songs."

WILL CULLEN HART: We thought we knew what punk was. A two-string guitar? That's punk. It was a lot sleazier. There was no musical sense. Robert would understand that there was actually a riff, but we were just total sonic *whatever*.

ROBERT SCHNEIDER: I remember sitting at the lunch table with Jeff and Ty, and Jeff was saying how they were philosophically opposed to having bass. That's something that was sustained through many of his recordings.

TY STORMS: We were horrible. We used a little 8-bit Casio piano with twelve keys, which was powered by two AAA batteries. Still, the tape was copied and recopied. It was extremely popular with the junior high crowd for nearly a generation.

ROBERT SCHNEIDER: It was pure teenage noise. It wasn't particularly angry. It was just absurd and clangorous. That's really it. Jeff's always been doing absurd and clangorous stuff. He continues to do that.

"My first songs were about the kinds of things you talk about when you're 13," Jeff told *Puncture* in 1996, "running away from home, defecating. I'm going to get those tapes out someday."

Maggott was mostly just a recording project, and even that is probably a grandiose label for what was really just a few bored teenagers trying to entertain themselves. Will subscribed to every punk zine he could get his hands on and read them all cover to cover. Through those, he found enough like-minded artists to begin trading his music.

WILL CULLEN HART: That changed my life, just to be able to really reach somebody.

Sophomore year of high school, spring 1987, Jeff, Robert, Will, and an older friend named Rick Metzler entered the Ruston High talent show, performing as a band called Death and Fish. Each of them set up an amp, plugged in his guitar, and began to play—together, ostensibly, but each of them played a different song. Rick played a Stones song, Robert played "Blackbird" by the Beatles, Jeff played "something clangorous," and Will played "something weird. Total noise. Bursts of noise."

ROBERT SCHNEIDER: It was a terrible racket. After a minute or two, when the faculty realized we were pulling a supposed prank, they closed the curtains, but we were still playing really loudly, and we didn't stop. They had to come to tell us to get off the stage one by one. It was really quite good. Except for our friends who were on the stage, it was probably an effect that was lost on the rest of the audience, as well as the administrators, but that was what Death and Fish was.

Bill Doss* grew up in Dubach, about ten miles north of Ruston. With a footprint of less than two square miles, Dubach's population has hov-

* Bill's full given name is Billy Don Doss, after his mother, Billie, and his father, who went by Donny. That is, "Bill" is short for "Billy."

ered between eight hundred and one thousand since the 1960s. It hosts the Louisiana Chicken Festival each September. In 1990, the Louisiana State Legislature nicknamed Dubach the "Dogtrot Capital of the World" for the town's handful of dogtrot houses, which are pairs of log cabins with a breezeway between them. As alienated as the artsy kids in Ruston may have felt from their normie counterparts, Dubach left Bill feeling mostly bored.

> **BILL DOSS:** There wasn't really anywhere to hang out in Dubach. There was one little pool hall. I'd have to drive into Ruston to go to the grocery store. Growing up in Dubach, everybody would play sports or hunt or fish. Outdoor stuff. I wasn't really into that. I wanted to come home from school and play guitar.

When Bill was eight years old, his cousin bought him his first guitar and showed him a few chords. He took to it immediately, but inspiration was tough to come by. None of his friends were into music, and he didn't even have a radio. The only music he had access to were two Beatles records he owned, and so he listened to them incessantly.

> **BILL DOSS:** When people talked about music, I really thought they meant *those two records.* People would say "I love music," and I'd be like "I do, too. I've got both of those records."

He eventually began strumming along with them. He tightened up his guitar skills and picked up bass, too. He found a record store in Monroe, about a half hour away, to flesh out his collection and started spending time at Haymaker's, a music store in nearby Ruston.

All the young musicians in Ruston cut their teeth at Haymaker's. Robert learned to play guitar there when he was twelve, and Jeff learned drums. Before ever meeting Bill, Robert had seen him in there one day, "looking like the hippest motherfucker." Bill was a couple of years older, with long red hair and big bushy sideburns. He popped in to buy guitar strings and then sped off in a seventies conversion van.

A few months later, Robert was looking to start a band and needed a bass player. He checked the bulletin board at Haymaker's and found a bassist and a drummer looking for a guitarist to start a band that sounded like Van Halen, who were at the peak of their mid-eighties heyday. Robert called the number and was excited to find the bassist was the hip redhead he had seen in the music shop earlier. Robert had a band of his own he was trying to get going, so Bill joined his and he joined Bill's. Fourteen-year-old Robert was impressed by the older kid's professionalism—he had played a couple of actual gigs already—and Bill was blown away by Robert's skills.

BILL DOSS: Robert honestly was a fucking prodigy. At fourteen years old, he was playing Bach on the guitar. He came out playing guitar. He could hear Beatles songs and hear the bass parts, so he would show me the bass parts. I learned how to play bass from him, essentially, and probably a lot of guitar stuff, too.

Robert and his friend Lee Halliburton arranged a practice at a space that belonged to the drummer they were auditioning for the band, and Bill met them there to audition as the lead singer. Robert and Bill found chemistry together right away.

ROBERT SCHNEIDER: We were like Lennon and McCartney, just much shittier. I recorded the practice, and that night, I remember staying up as long as I could to the tape of us playing "Wild Thing." It sounded like a real rock band. That feeling was incredible. The gratification of hearing the recorded band inspired me. I needed that feeling.

WILL CULLEN HART: Bill and Robert could actually play and tune instruments. Jeff and I couldn't. "Broken string? Oh well, we still got three."

Lee didn't stick around very long, but Bill took over on bass in addition to singing lead, and with Bill's encouragement, Robert took on a lot of the singing duties himself. They called the new band Fat Planet, playing mostly covers (the Velvet Underground, R.E.M., the Cure) with a drummer, another guitarist, and a flautist.

Bill was excited by more than just the band, though. Thanks as much to Robert's four-track and record collection as to anything else, Bill started hanging out at Robert's house after school almost every day to play music.

He found more to do just in Robert's bedroom than he had in all of Dubach. Will and Jeff liked to hang out there, too, and Bill was recording with them before he knew their names.

BILL DOSS: Even then, Robert was engineering us. Like Jeff wanted to record one of his songs, so Robert would set up a mic and be like, "Here, play," and then he'd put the mic on me and tell me to beat on a book or something. We were all sitting in a room playing, and I was like, "Oh, hey, by the way, I'm Bill."

ROBERT SCHNEIDER: I really saw a path to purity or something in music. This was how I started to make friends.

The four of them got along great from the start, and Bill was amazed that he had finally found some like-minded kids to jam with. But there was still a bit of culture shock.

BILL DOSS: Will, at the time, was spiking his hair straight up, was wearing a button-up shirt buttoned all the way up and Converse high-tops spray-painted silver and "Sonic Youth" written on them. I didn't know what that meant, because I had never heard the band at the time. I thought it was just like a motto or something.

John Fernandes moved to Ruston from Iowa when he was three. His father was a chemical engineering professor. John was just entering high school when Will, Jeff, and Robert graduated and started college. His older sister* once took Robert to one of the girls-ask-guys high school dances, and John got to know him, Will, and Jeff at parties his sister would throw when their parents were out of town. The older guys took a shine to him, and he to them, plying his musical skills in several configurations of their bands in Ruston.

Ruston was a challenging place to grow up for a lot of these folks. Their artistic leanings often put them at odds with their peers, and though no

* John's sister nicknamed him Mowgli at an early age—the small Indian boy resembling *The Jungle Book* protagonist—and eventually, his friends used the moniker as well, calling him Mowgli well into his twenties, though he only occasionally referred to himself that way.

one got beat up for spiking their hair or wearing the wrong shoes, it created enough distance to foster feelings of estrangement among the nascent Elephant 6 crowd. For John Fernandes, though, as a person of color, that alienation was more tangible.

> **JOHN FERNANDES:** When I was a kid in Louisiana, because my dad is from India and my mom is blind and white, a lot of people thought it was this Indian person taking advantage. She's a very strong woman. The fact that she's blind hasn't held her back from doing anything in life. She started a whole center where blind people teach other blind people how to live independently. They just assumed she's weak because she's blind and she's being taken advantage of by this Indian guy. So the Ku Klux Klan burned a cross on our yard.

It was a persistent issue for a half-Indian kid in a state that nearly elected a former KKK grand wizard to be its governor while John was in high school. The Gulf War, which began in 1991, stirred up more jingoistic hostility, as John frequently but patiently explained to classmates and friends' parents and total strangers that he was actually of Indian descent, not Iraqi, and that, no, Iraq is geographically no closer to India than it is to most countries in Europe.* In light of that ostracism, John found solace in the small community of his musical friends.

> **JOHN FERNANDES:** What we did in Ruston was band together tighter. We needed to create our own network of mutual appreciation. We were surrounded by a pretty conservative culture, so we just created our own little world.

* This sort of thing didn't exactly disappear when he eventually moved to Georgia. After 9/11, when someone asked him if he was Iraqi, he explained that he had been born in Iowa, which elicited the response: "Is that near Iraq?" In a separate incident, a racist neighbor filled his mailbox with rotting fish, which prompted him to move his family to a new house for fear their well would be poisoned.

ROBERT SCHNEIDER: It wasn't this divide between jocks and freaks, because these are the people you had grown up with. To varying degrees, you still had shreds of relationships with them. Maybe they hadn't realized yet just how weird we had become.

"In school I was surrounded by racist, sexist jocks," Jeff told *Puncture* in 1998. "From an early age, my friends and I all felt we didn't belong there. We all kind of saved ourselves from that place. . . . When I was young I must have made a conscious effort to stop talking that way, 'cause that's how those motherfuckers I hate talk. My lack of accent stems from that early rebellion."

ROBERT SCHNEIDER: It wasn't like in those movies where there's a direct tension. Our friends were all of the normal people. But as we got more weird, you start to feel the tension. It's not the tension of being at war with your colleagues and peers. It's the tension that if I continue here, I'm going to explode. I was class president my junior and senior years, and I was among the three or four least standard people in the entire school. However, to continue in that environment being that kind of person can kill your spirit. We're artists, and we needed to go somewhere.

Before they could emigrate, though, Robert and his friends (including folks who had moved to Ruston to go to college there) had to make the best of their situation. Ruston is a small town—its population has held steady around twenty thousand for a few decades now—but at least in the late eighties, anyone a little weird might feel like they were the only one. KLPI, Louisiana Tech's student radio station, offered those weirdos somewhere they could find one another.*

The radio station started up in 1966 as WLPI, a project for some electrical engineering grad students who were more interested in carrier currents than any particular genre of music. WLPI began broadcasting as an AM station from an office in downtown Ruston, but after a few years, the station moved on campus, occupying a space in the Dramatic Arts building. In 1972, the university built a new 10-watt FM station and launched KLPI from there in 1973, with the AM station going radio silent the following year. Renovations to the building forced another move, and after bouncing around a bit, the station moved off campus in 1982, where it stayed into the late nineties.

MICHEL BOULWARE: KLPI was like an oasis of awesome. It was where we could go to find out about weird music and play weird music. It was off campus, in this shitty little trailer that was stinking and gross.

ROSS BEACH: The studio was housed in a single-wide mobile home on Gilman Street in a run-down neighborhood several blocks off campus. Some people were scared to walk there at night.

For Ruston kids, KLPI offered a rare opportunity to hear music outside of the mainstream. Jeff listened to the punk show every Tuesday night, and he and Will became DJs at the station in 1987, while still in high school. They took whatever shows they could get—Will ran a Sunday-morning big band show at first—but after just a few weeks, they were hosting shows on

* Through his gig as KLPI music director, John Fernandes was able to book a lot of touring bands in Ruston, but most of them had to be house shows, as the majority of the venues that could host bands in town were less than sympathetic to their aesthetics. After one show he booked at a pool hall (headlined by a band from Austin called Pork, with John's band Sock the Monkey opening), the owner told John that "if this kind of music is going to bring these kinds of people in here, we don't want to have anything to do with it." Or as Scott Spillane put it, "The freaks showed up, and they brought their own beer."

Friday nights, playing hardcore, noise, and experimental music, as well as lots of home recordings from people like Daniel Johnston.

"All through our childhood we were completely flooded by underground music, and we were able to perceive it any way we wanted because there was no scene, no zines, no clubs, no kids," Jeff told *Tucson Weekly* in 1998. "It was just this music coming out of this crazy world that we really didn't understand, because we only had our small southern town to compare it to. We found a lot of what seemed to be missing from our daily lives, growing up in a very closed environment. So we had a deep appreciation for all kinds of music, and when we started making our own music, there was a very special, magical quality to it."

The experience proved fruitful in a lot of ways. Listening to college radio is a good way to broaden your musical horizons and hear things you would not have heard otherwise. As the children of professors, Robert and Jeff (whose father taught economics) spent a lot of time hanging out on Louisiana Tech's campus as kids.* Will often tagged along. Robert never ended up working at the station, but Will, Jeff, John, and others got started there before they finished high school, and *working* at a college radio station proved even more fruitful than listening to it.

ROSS BEACH: Many play copies went out for review and never found their way back to the music library, which bothered me, since it seemed to defeat the whole communal nature of a radio station. One time, near the end of a term, someone filled up the trunk of his car with jazz LPs from the KLPI library.

BILL DOSS: Everybody stole records. Mostly jazz stuff. There was a point where we know that just certain amounts of records were going to get destroyed, so we were just taking them. They had such a great record collection.

---

* For the first few years of MTV's existence, local cable providers refused to carry it, but Louisiana Tech's student center had satellite and a big projection TV that was usually tuned to the channel. Robert and Jeff would hang out on campus to play video games at the arcade, gorge on Coke and nachos, and watch hours and hours of *I.R.S. Records Presents: The Cutting Edge* and *120 Minutes*. "It felt like pirate radio at the time," Robert says. "MTV was like a youth culture religion for the first half of the 1980s and felt really legit and artsy, so it felt like going to a secret meeting place to worship Billy Idol."

ROSS BEACH: I never stole any physical media from the station, but I had no qualms about dubbing cassette copies of things. One time, I made a mixtape for myself by tuning a boombox to KLPI, hitting RECORD on a blank cassette, then playing all of the songs I wanted during my show. The sound quality suffered a bit with that strategy.

Free music wasn't the only valuable resource at KLPI, either. The studio had a couple of soundproof production booths, much better for recording than the typical group house bedroom. Many KLPI folks used the space to four-track. Robert used his first reel-to-reel eight-track at KLPI, the same Otari MX-5050 tape machine he'd have in his own studio years later.

ROSS BEACH: The results that I heard—or was allowed to hear—from Jeff's solo four-tracking were always incredible. It was all the more impressive because the recordings were usually two plugged-in acoustic guitar tracks, panned hard left and right, and two vocal tracks, also panned hard left and right. He did an early version of "Naomi" in this style that was one of the best things I'd ever heard at the time.

JEREMY GOSHORN: I went from seeing Jeff as a normal person to being like, *Oh crap, this guy is really amazing.*

MICHEL BOULWARE: Jeff was always silly and making jokes, but he also had a really serious and kind side to him.

J. KIRK PLEASANT: The music was so completely unique from anything anyone had ever heard. He's such a masterful performer. He's got such a gripping voice and is such a great lyric writer. Back then, we all recognized it. It's hard to hear him and not be kind of moved by it.

The KLPI DJs experimented outside the recording booth, too, exposing their weirdness to anyone who would listen.

PAIGE DEARMAN: After ten o'clock, you could do your own free-format. Sometimes during the day, you couldn't play cuss words and stuff. But after that time, KLPI was free-format and we all had our own shows. We all listened to different music, and if we liked it, we would play it.

SCOTT SPILLANE: I had a show on Saturday morning called *The Better Late Than Never Show*. I was supposed to turn on the transformer and everything, and I usually showed up just before the next guy was supposed to come on.

ROSS BEACH: At that time, we'd hook a cassette player into the board and play tapes over the air, sometimes of ourselves or our friends, things we recorded in our living rooms the night before.

BILL DOSS: Will Westbrook and I did this thing called *World of Jazz* where we would play live on the air, me and him and whoever else we could gather in. We couldn't play jazz at all, but we were trying. We would basically play what we called "free jazz," but free jazz from a bunch of white boys who didn't know how to play jazz at all and just made a bunch of noise for like two hours. Free jazz, and it's a good thing it was free, because you couldn't charge for it. It was mostly just to try to annoy people, to see how many phone calls we could get.

As a prologue to the Elephant 6 story, the most important aspect of working at KLPI* was the connections these folks were able to forge there—with one another, with other listeners, and with other bands. Working for a college radio station is Music Industry 101, an entry-level course on how to make it as an indie band.

ROSS BEACH: KLPI put Ruston on the map in a lot of ways, in the sense that it connected Louisiana Tech people with musicians, DJs, and music aficionados at other colleges who wouldn't have given north Louisiana a second thought otherwise. It was thanks to KLPI and the volunteers there that Ruston was able to host shows by bands like Beat Happening and Sebadoh.

JOHN FERNANDES: It opened up a whole world of music we might not have heard otherwise.

---

* Robert did not work at KLPI but did work at Centenary College's station, KSCL, when he was a student there. He was fired for hosting a party in the station during his show and then later rehired.

WILL CULLEN HART: We all learned a lot about indie music and putting out records without trying to get big. When we finally did those singles years later, we knew where to send them.

Scott Spillane was born in Germany, moved to Turkey when he was six or so, and then settled in Shreveport, Louisiana, around age eleven. After failing out of Northeast Louisiana University (now called University of Louisiana at Monroe), Scott took a drafting class at a vocational-technical school, but he soon decided to move to Ruston with a couple of his classmates to study engineering.

Being twenty-five years old in a town full of college students can have its drawbacks, but Scott took a positive view of things. His friend had gotten involved with KLPI, and through her, Scott knew just how to assimilate into that crowd.

SCOTT SPILLANE: I was older than everybody, luckily. Because if I was younger, I would not have been able to scheme my way into the scene. That whole thing of "If I only knew then what I know now"—I did. I saw what was happening and played it cool, because I didn't want to blow it.

ROBERT SCHNEIDER: He seemed really like a man. A really sarcastic, really brassy man.

Down the road from Robert lived a musician, the mother of Robert's sister's best friend. Interested in expanding her library, she commissioned Robert to dub her some heavy metal cassettes, paying him a dollar a tape. Thirteen-year-old Robert branded each cassette with a pair of *R*s—for Robert Records—the first of which was flipped so the letters' counters formed a heart.

As he began dubbing the cassettes on the boombox his mom had bought him for his most recent birthday, he noticed that the tapes also picked up the ambient sounds of his bedroom. So a tape he'd give to his patron might have Dio's "Holy Diver" and also the sound of a middle schooler's socks shuffling over the carpet. He retreated to his closet to record the last tape in the hope that the door and clothes would muffle the unwanted sounds, but as Robert hunkered there silently with a boombox in his lap playing

Accept's "Balls to the Wall," he had an epiphany: if he played his synthesizer (another birthday gift; thirteen brought in a good haul) during the recording, it would end up on the tape. So he included a couple of songs he had written—"Moo Says Mister Cow" and "Snot in My Jell-O"—at the end. That is how Robert Schneider discovered multi-tracking for himself. Robert spent his life savings on a red Flying V guitar just a few months later, and he began building songs by recording a synth line on a cassette with the boombox, then playing it back with a blank cassette recording in the other deck while he added a guitar track, then again to add percussion or vocals, and so on.

Will typically recorded on a two-deck boombox not unlike the one on which Robert discovered his recording technique, laying the guitar track on a cassette in one deck, then playing that back while he sang, so the second cassette would pick up both the recorded guitar and his live vocals. Then he'd play the tape back while adding another layer, like percussion or a harmony, and so on, bouncing back and forth until all the layers of his song were on one cassette. The finished product usually had about eight tracks on it. In the early nineties, Will would record his solo musical experiments under the name the Always Red Society and with Jeff as Cranberry Lifecycle, circulating the tapes among their groups of friends.

"We'd dropped out of school and had moved into a little shack of a place with this really obnoxious alcoholic slob who left smashed televisions and garbage all over the house," Jeff told *Ptolemaic Terrascope* in 1996. "We were desperate to be out on our own so we moved in there and started recording, just putting sounds together and seeing what happened."

Will would come up with a guitar riff on the spot, and then Jeff would improvise some percussion to go along with it, banging on the floor or slapping a book or doing whatever to whatever they had lying around, recording both parts within minutes of conception. They'd go off and write their lyrics on their own and then reconvene, alternating surrealistic verses about one-sided windows, backward mirrors, and women with potatoes for eyes. Sometimes, they'd do a call-and-response thing where one person would lay down a vocal track while the other was in the bathroom, singing the calls and leaving space for the responses, and upon his return, the other would sing the responses without having heard the calls.

ROBERT SCHNEIDER: I think that's where Jeff's real work was during that period, working with Will. I think that's the true birth of Neutral Milk Hotel and the Olivia Tremor Control. His singing started to sound more like how it sounded later. He would sing with a stronger tone, stronger pitch, and stuff. Higher sometimes, in higher registers, more than he did when he was younger. He used to sing much lower and more soft.

They started making twenty-minute tapes for their friends. The recordings were rough to say the least, but they included seeds of ideas that would blossom later in their careers, including the earliest version of "The Opera House," which eventually became the opening track on the Olivia Tremor Control's 1996 record *Dusk at Cubist Castle.*

BILL DOSS: Those dudes had such a spark for spontaneity. I'll stress over songs for a long, long time, but Will and Jeff have such a knack for spontaneity and just right off the cuff, making up stuff on the spot. Sometimes it's just unreal how good it is.

WILL CULLEN HART: We saw each other pretty often.

BILL DOSS: Every day after school, I'd go over to Robert's house, because he had a four-track. We'd all get together, and even though they didn't all know me very well, I felt a kinship with those guys. I went to the same school with the same thirty-some-odd people from kindergarten through graduation. When I met these guys, it was like, "Oh my god, you guys don't care about sports? You don't want to go hunting and fishing? You want to sit in your room and play guitar?" It gave me a sanctuary.

WILL CULLEN HART: It felt like the music we made didn't fit in.

Death and Fish technically played two shows, though they were years apart and with almost entirely different lineups. The band's second and final performance took place in Bill's Louisiana Tech dormitory, featuring Robert, Bill, and a drummer friend.

ROBERT SCHNEIDER: It was a totally different band, just the same band name. We played a single song. It was called "Anarchy and Cops." That was the only lyric. It was just noise. No rhythm, no chord

> structure. All the instruments were playing no notes, with "anarchy and cops" being shouted. Death and Fish was the conceptual proto–noise band, accidentally.

"Some of those early tapes are shit, but that was never the point," Jeff told *Magnet* in 1998. "The four of us existed in our insular world. We were very supportive of each other, and the love we had for each other was always really positive. I'd bang on a lamp, record my mom on an answering machine, play a tuba that I couldn't play, then give the tape a ridiculous title, and they'd go home and listen to it. The next day Will would bring in a tape with his four-year-old brother singing things like, 'I haven't found an effective way to ease my pain,' while he was pushing over a box of bottles."

Especially in places like Ruston, musicians tend to flock to other musicians. Though it might be charitable to call their social circle a "music scene," Robert, Will, Bill, and Jeff found themselves immersed in a crowd of bands by the time they had all finished high school, spending many nights either playing music themselves or listening to their friends do the same.

"There was a group of us [in Ruston] who gelled because we didn't want to be in Whitesnake," Will Cullen Hart told *SPIN* in 2006.

"When you grow up where I did," Jeff told *Puncture* in 1996, "there's not many people who share your viewpoint. You seek out freaks. You see someone walking down the street with green hair, and you're like 'Hey! Come back here!'"

Starting around age seventeen, up until he realized another band had already staked a claim to the name, Jeff recorded in Ruston under the name Milk, etching the name into the plastic of the cassettes he made for friends. He made the tapes in his closet, drumming on a set that consisted of a snare drum, a cymbal, and a bass drum turned faceup like a floor tom. Once he graduated from boombox recordings, Jeff recorded on a Vesta Fire four-track borrowed from Robert, which Robert was borrowing from another friend. Jeff would typically fill the tape with one track of drums, one track of guitar, and two tracks of vocals panned hard right and left in the stereo. On other tracks, he might play along with the TV in the background or use a multi-tracked guitar or sound effects in place of percussion.

ROBERT SCHNEIDER: It was quirky. Usually, his lyrics were good or interesting or funny. It wasn't very emotive or anything like that. What we were all doing was basically like a punk rock version of "Weird Al" Yankovic. [Jeff's] song "Snow Song," I think that song represents what his earlier music sounded like, in that it was kind of floaty, primitive. He might have recorded it in high school. I'm not sure he didn't. That first Neutral Milk seven-inch definitely feels like what Jeff's early music felt like. I think when he started recording on a four-track, it was that good right away. His songs always had a folky flare. He always had a knack for a really great melody. They were always simple, two or three chords, and they were generally more subdued than upbeat. Or they would be total noise songs with screaming and stuff like that.

ROSS BEACH: The tight-knit nature of the community was the defining characteristic of it all. The openness and the sharing of it all. Everyone was always dubbing tapes for everyone else. It had this kind of family dynamic to it. Most other music scenes I've been party to, there's always this underlying sense of "Who's going to be better than who?" In that group of people, maybe because expectations were so low in terms of quantifiable success, everyone was always promoting everyone else. There wasn't any sense of rivalry.

J. KIRK PLEASANT: We'd stay up all night long and talk about religion and music and life. One conversation was about the concept of sincerity in music, and I questioned Jeff's sincerity, and I don't know why I even would question that. He said, "No, the only thing it's about is sincerity. The most important element to it is to be honest and sincere."

SCOTT SPILLANE: I was working at Pizza Hut, assistant manager, late shift. So I'd get off work at like two thirty and show up with booze and pizza, and that's when the party started. I played numerous shows in my uniform, with the apron on as well. It was very punk rock.

Ross and his roommates frequently hosted shows in their living room, though there was more to the Ruston scene than just house shows. The Fun-O-Mat—a combination bar and laundromat—and other small venues could host local acts as well as touring bands in need of somewhere to play between Memphis and New Orleans or Dallas and Jackson. Locals were not always receptive. One of the more ambitious projects of the time, if maybe not the most accessible, was a band called Clay Bears, which was mostly Jeff's recording project but typically featured some combination of Jeff, Scott, John Fernandes, Ross Beach, and Will Westbrook in its handful of live shows. The band members traded instruments throughout the set and used the performances as a chance to experiment.

ROSS BEACH: We were just a noise ensemble, the kind of thing that would be appreciated more now than it was then. At the time, people were just turned off by it.

SCOTT SPILLANE: Each show was different, but it was mostly a bunch of detuned shit-banging, throwing cymbals around. It was the closest thing to unstructured stuff I've ever done. But it was just "let's throw some shit around." It's the seminal ultra–Elephant 6 band.

ROSS BEACH: It was kind of a free-for-all. Anybody who wanted to sit in with the band could. There was a lot of rotation. Not much in terms of structure or musicality.

At one show in particular, at a bar in Monroe, Louisiana, called Enoch's, Clay Bears attempted to play a drone piece. They made it about ten minutes before the owner cut them off.

"But it's only one note," Jeff pleaded.

"Well," the owner replied, "it wasn't a very good one."

J. KIRK PLEASANT: Jeff played this one show in Monroe, and he came back so excited because he had the tape recording of the show, and it was one note. He was just playing this one note over and over again for a long time, and this dude has a bar to run.

SCOTT SPILLANE: If you hear the recording, it's mostly a conversation between the owner trying to throw them off the stage, and the guy who owns the bar saying, "I understand what you're trying to do, but you're just not very good at it. Why don't you come back when you're better at it? You're running off the customers."

A few years later, Jeff was making his way from Denver (where he'd been living in Robert's closet) to Athens, Georgia. He stopped in Ruston for a few months and booked a show in Baton Rouge, as Neutral Milk Hotel, opening for the Jon Spencer Blues Explosion. He planned to play the set as a two-piece, but the drummer he'd lined up fell through at the last minute, so he recruited Ross Beach to play guitar instead, with Jeff sliding over to the drums. He had heard Ross playing a gospel song in the kitchen.

ROSS BEACH: I was trying to be all cool about it, like, "Sure, I'd be happy to play with you." But inside, I was like, *Oh my god.* It was pretty exciting.

They practiced twice for the show, first at Scott Spillane's house in Dubach. The next day, Ross was waiting at his house for Jeff to arrive for practice when he saw him running up the steps, out of breath by the time he reached the house. He told Ross to turn on the television.

ROSS BEACH: That's how I found out Kurt Cobain died. It was a big deal to us. He was somebody we recognized as kind of a normal person. All through our childhoods, people on the radio and MTV were so glossy and unreal, and here was this guy. He was the first one who broke through who was obviously some rural small-town kid like us who seemed normal. I have a feeling it affected Jeff. I remember him talking, before Kurt Cobain died, saying, "If he is able to do this, I don't see why anyone else couldn't also."

"Do you watch MTV?" Jeff asked rhetorically in a 1998 *New York Press* article. "I'm not being preachy, like 'MTV bad, me good.' But it scares the shit out of me. If you never watch TV and you just live inside your own head, then you turn it on, you think, 'The world is like that?'"

Bill enlisted in the Army National Guard after graduating high school in the summer of 1987.

BILL DOSS: I swear to god if anyone says they don't have any regrets in their life, they're lying. I could have spent six years better. I just joined to get money for school. I could have done something better at that time.

The First Gulf War began in August 1990. In October, Bill was activated. He was told to celebrate Christmas early, drop out of school, and show up with his bag packed at oh-six-hundred. Before he shipped off, Amy Hairston—eventually Bill's wife, but then only a friend and as-yet-unattainable crush—offered to help him hide and avoid being shipped out, but Bill balked at the prospect of spending the rest of his life in Canada. This would only be a few months of building roads and barracks, even if it was in Kuwait with Scud missiles flying past him.

Bill showed up on time and got into formation. Though his unit was overstocked by nearly one hundred people, there was still a good chance he'd be sent over. He waited by the phone each day, but the call never came. He had been designated for a slot by rank, but a first sergeant bumped Bill for the sergeant's son so they could go to Kuwait together. Bill stayed behind.

The weekend after he graduated high school, Robert set off on a choir tour of youth groups around Louisiana, playing guitar with some friends. By the time the tour ended six weeks later, both of Robert's parents had found new jobs and left Ruston: his mom and stepdad went to Little Rock, and his dad and stepmom went to Denver. Robert never moved back to Ruston. He enrolled in Centenary College in nearby Shreveport, starting there in the fall on a music scholarship, studying composition and singing in the choir. But he quit the choir because he hated having to keep his hair cut short and wear a tuxedo, and after a year of studying music, he felt like he had learned enough about theory to make the pop music he wanted to make. He changed his major to philosophy. He lost his scholarship as a result and couldn't afford to continue, so he moved into his mom's house in Paducah, Kentucky, living in the attic. He got a job at a church, which paid him thirty dollars a week.

ROBERT SCHNEIDER: I was the director for a praise choir. I'm not very religious, but I'm very philosophical, and the minister was impressed by that, and I needed a job. I never mentioned I wasn't a Christian. And he didn't ask.

His income doubled when he took a second job that also paid him thirty dollars a week, playing in a band on a riverboat dinner cruise. That gig slowed down as the weather cooled off in the fall, though. His mom told him to either find a job or go out to Denver to live with his dad and go back to school.

Robert, Will, and Jeff often ruminated on a shared fantasy of moving to the Virgin Islands together, living on the beach and supporting themselves by busking. Will went first with his partner, Shannon Willis. Meanwhile, Jeff moved to Seattle, and Robert saved up money by bagging groceries and shepherding shopping carts at a Kroger in Kentucky.

Like many of his high school classmates, Will had enrolled at Louisiana Tech after graduation, but he didn't last long before dropping out. The island lifestyle didn't work out for him much better.

> **WILL CULLEN HART**: It was cheaper to buy a bottle of rum than a bottle of water, and you couldn't drink the water.

Will and Shannon lasted four months in the Virgin Islands before moving back. Jeff and Robert never made it there. Will ended up in Athens, Georgia, and Robert went to Denver and enrolled at the University of Colorado. Jeff dropped out of Louisiana Tech after a couple of years. He went out to Denver for a while, too, and then eventually to Athens after a few other stops.

"[Where] we're from is a pretty freaky place," Jeff told the *Memphis Flyer* in 1998. "It's a very, very conservative place. And we sort of struggled to live there, I think. I mean, it was a beautiful place to grow up as children. It was just a very safe place, a very quiet place, and I think there is a certain romance that I still have for that place. There's just certain feelings that you get when you're there, just by the way the sun is hitting the trees, or the way the wind's blowing, or the way things smell. It makes you sort of feel that way. And it's good to remember, because it's such a part of you that you don't ever get to experience much anymore because you never go back."

Ruston's music scene didn't die when Will, Bill, Jeff, and Robert departed. Those who remained kept at it. Scott Spillane's first band, This Is Not Your Father's Oldsmobile (or TINYFO for short), turned into Buddha Footprint Repetition, which turned into Smilin' Joe Fission, which turned eventually into the Gerbils, featuring Scott, John d'Azzo, and Will Westbrook. After a long shift at Pizza Hut, Scott drove out to a party in nearby Minden, where John had the name ready for him.

JOHN D'AZZO: I came up with the concept for the Gerbils, and Scott agreed to it that night, but from then on, he said it wasn't a good name for a band. I gave him a choice that night. Do you like it? Great. That was it. I love it. It rhymes with "Beatles." Same amount of syllables.

SCOTT SPILLANE: We had already gone through like five names. He said "the Gerbils," and I said, "Whatever, sure." It's haunted us ever since. It's a shitty name for a band.

The Gerbils survived a move to San Francisco and eventually a move to Athens. While Scott was still in Ruston, though, Will, Bill, and Jeff returned occasionally to perform at house shows and bars, typically with Jeff playing a solo set followed by the trio performing together as Synthetic Flying Machine.

SCOTT SPILLANE: I remember from that show, Jeff had basically found his voice. It was like, *Oh my god.* And then Synthetic Flying Machine played after him, and it was over-the-top. *Wow, they actually have that shit together.*

JOHN FERNANDES: They kept switching out, do some Jeff songs, do some Will songs, do some Bill songs, and they just kept switching instruments. I was completely blown away.

SCOTT SPILLANE: My friends left town playing shabby rock and roll, and they came back playing, like, god's music.

LIKE MANY OF THE PEOPLE IN THIS BOOK, JULIAN KOSTER IS something of a nomad. He was living in Athens the first time I met him, renting a modest room from Jeremy Ayers, an old friend of his, walking distance from downtown. I met Julian in the house's detached garage, which he had repurposed as a recording studio. Before we got started, we walked to the nearby co-op so he could get his morning coffee, then returned to the house so he could prepare it just so, with a splash of soy milk and shakes from half the spice rack.

Julian speaks with a muted, almost (but not quite) patronizing affection, the way a grown-up talks to a little kid, but it's tempered with the sort of unapologetic whimsy heard only when a little kid talks to a grown-up. At separate junctures, he extolled with equal candor the virtues of hypnotic suggestion (the prevailing misconceptions of which, he says, are criminal) and rolling down hills (wistfully recalling his favorite of all time, a mossy cliff in San Francisco). Each story began as though Julian had no idea where it would end, but it was punctuated with the confident dismount of someone who has told it a thousand times. Whether his answers were spontaneous or rehearsed over countless other conversations and interviews, he always paused before speaking, considering carefully the question I posed to him.

His approach to recording is far from a well-oiled machine—he was working that day, in early 2010, on fine-tuning material that would end up on the Music Tapes' 2012 album *Mary's Voice*—and his work space resembles a Rube Goldberg contraption in some intermediate stage of construction, with homemade contrivances and objets d'arts laid about without any apparent order, but somehow still bristling with potential energy. Julian is usually here alone, so the mise en place of his worldly possessions need not make sense to anyone but him. Whenever Julian needs something, be it an instrument or a piece of recording gear or a Polynesian Christmas record or a Depression-era children's toy, he can retrieve it with minimal foraging.

These items serve as an obvious symbol for a motif that appears frequently in Julian's music and the work of many of his Elephant 6 collaborators. Each curio and tchotchke here seems in danger of being dismantled by a light draft through the window, but it all somehow holds together. Fragility is a unifying element throughout the inventory, and while the whole is no hardier than the sum of its parts, their still-functioning individual states suggest their keeper might actually know what he's doing. A mad scientist is still a scientist, after all.

This collection of knickknacks symbolizes something else about the output of the Elephant 6 at large, too: scale. Items in this space range from indivisibly simple to impossibly complicated, but even the 7-Foot-Tall Metronome has a handmade quality that indicates a human element. The music of the Elephant 6 has endured not because of its influence but in spite of it, standing tall above countless corporatized derivations exactly because of how humble it is.

Like the Rustonites and the folks they eventually found in Athens and Denver, Julian is a big part of the Elephant 6 story. His distinct style is unmistakable on *In the Aeroplane Over the Sea*, and even more so on his Music Tapes records. It was through Julian that Jeremy Barnes became the drummer for Neutral Milk Hotel, via a meeting the two had had years earlier when Jeremy's high school band opened for Julian's Chocolate USA. Eric Harris and Pete Erchick, the Olivia Tremor Control's drummer and keyboardist, came into the fold via Chocolate USA as well, joining that band before making contact with anyone else in the collective. Bill Doss played in Chocolate USA for a little while, too. Julian is also the reason Kevin Barnes got involved in the scene, after Bar/None Records signed Kevin and suggested Julian mentor them. Julian can play a lot of instruments (and draw something musical from a lot of things few people would ever refer to as instruments), but he can also play role model, muse, inspiration, catalyst. Beyond his musical and networking skills, the obsessiveness with which he pursues purity in his art is contagious.

Julian had an upbringing most musicians could only dream of. His father, Dennis, is an accomplished flamenco guitarist in his own right, who typically played close to ten hours a day back then, with musical friends passing through their New York City home constantly. To this day, Julian rarely spends time without music playing in the background. At home, it's often the same record—often just one side of the record—on repeat, nonstop, for days at a time.

But despite his dad's picking and strumming, and masters of the form like Sabicas dropping by to hang out, not to mention his mom's hiply curated record collection, Julian did not immediately fall into a musical career. For one thing, his dad was very hands-off. Fearing that he'd be the sort of parent who forced his kid to practice incessantly, he overcompensated by not even teaching his son how to play guitar. For Julian, his father's guitars were virtually off-limits.

> **JULIAN KOSTER:** They were like these living, breathing things from Spain or somewhere, and they had been passed down and all these different people had had it or it was made by all these rare people. No one was like "don't touch them," but they were definitely not like "touch them."

Both he and his father felt that, as the son of a guitar virtuoso, Julian should pursue literally anything before guitar. Writing was his first real creative outlet. Having somehow discovered and read a handful of Kurt Vonnegut novels at the age of ten or so, Julian once attempted to write a novel in Vonnegut's pithy postmodern style. But he could only resist music's pull for so long. He started out with a focus on the contemporary rock scene, about which his father—whose taste was mostly limited to flamenco and classical—knew next to nothing. Julian started hanging out at the Knitting Factory, and even as a fourteen-year-old, he never had trouble getting in (though he did bring his dad along on occasion).

Julian's parents split up when he was in third grade, though both remained in the New York area for a while. From then on, he spent most of his time at his grandmother's house in New Hyde Park, in Long Island, staying with his father on the Upper West Side on weekends and during the summer, exploring Central Park and hanging out at his uncle's house in the Village.* As he hit junior high school, Julian began to miss his father more, and he turned to music to express himself. He began writing songs a capella, and eventually his dad got him a guitar to noodle on. It was actually an old lute, but that didn't stop Julian from putting guitar strings on it.

> JULIAN KOSTER: He was not happy with me. But I was a fourteen-year-old kid playing a steel-stringed lute. It's amazing I didn't get beat up more.

Not long after, Julian had his uncle—also a musician—lobby his mother to get Julian a four-track recorder, and Julian started recording his experiments in his bedroom.

It was another musician—one he wasn't even related to—who had the biggest impact on Julian's creative development. As a kid, Julian had had a dream one night in which a handsaw waddled into the room on its wooden nubs and began to sing. It made no sense to him at the time, which is what made it memorable. Just a few years later, he watched a saw player perform, and he had an epiphany. It was the sound he'd heard in his dream.

He attempted to emulate the technique on his stepdad's tools, with varying degrees of success. Completely self-taught, the style that Julian came up with was effective to the extent that he was able to draw sound from the saw, but it was physically painful to the player and vicariously so to anyone who watched him contort himself (to say nothing for how it sounded).

One day, Julian came across an article about Moses E. Josiah, a revered saw player who had appeared on a number of Disney soundtracks and was a fixture in New York City's subway stations. Julian learned that he lived out in Brownsville, in Brooklyn. So Julian packed up his gear, hopped on the subway, and set out to learn from a legend.

> JULIAN KOSTER: The looks I got were astonishing. Brownsville was just a place where there weren't white people, and there I was traipsing through, some weird little white kid with a saw, all alone.

* Julian would eventually live in that kitchenless apartment himself with Robbie Cucchiaro and their dog and cat. Jeff Mangum and Scott Spillane lived there with them for a while, too. It was barely big enough for one person.

Julian spent only the afternoon with Josiah, but the lessons he learned from him persist to this day. Josiah taught him to extend his hand and place the saw handle where his hand fell naturally, rather than twisting his body in a way that necessitated extra effort. When the hand is at ease, the player needs to generate only enough strength to play the instrument, without having to compensate for an awkward body position.

When Julian was fifteen, his mother and stepfather moved to Seminole, Florida, and took Julian with them. A born and bred New Yorker, Julian was a fish out of water along the Gulf Coast. Up north, he had been surrounded by people with vast ranges of interests and the multicultural abundance that produces, but in Seminole, he had trouble finding people who cared about music at all. But abundance has a way of degrading power, where rarity can produce it. What was plentiful in New York was special in Florida, and something Julian had always taken for granted quickly became precious.

Any band touring the East Coast will usually find a way to pass through New York City. Seminole, however, doesn't have quite the same draw. Nestled equidistant between Clearwater and St. Petersburg, with Tampa less than an hour inland across the bay, Seminole isn't particularly remote, but Tampa Bay in general can be a little off the radar for touring musicians. So when bands did come through, Julian and the other music-obsessed Seminolians were sure to take advantage. Even the poorly attended shows were important social events for the folks who showed up.

At these shows, Julian eventually found like-minded music fans he could get along with, but his mom and stepdad did not permit him to go out all that much, so time spent with friends became precious, too. Frequently stranded home alone, Julian's only musical collaborator was a four-track recorder, on which he relied heavily as an atemporal means of communication. While his peers were gallivanting around town, he would spend evenings alone in his bedroom making cassettes to share with them later, like transmissions from a distant planet.

Given the choice, Julian would have been out with his friends, but he was trying to make the best of his situation. He created these recordings to connect with people he couldn't be with, but they were also worlds he could transport himself to, to distance himself from the real world he occupied only begrudgingly. The recordings were his imagination wrought sonically, a daydream to escape a waking nightmare of solitude.

JULIAN KOSTER: That was a way to be with them. I would be up all night making something that was going to blow their minds. It was this incredible motivation.

One of Julian's best friends at the time was a kid named Brad Truax, who befriended Julian on the bus to summer school after overhearing him rambling about his appreciation for Sonic Youth's recently released *Daydream Nation*. The pair bonded quickly over the New York bands both were obsessed with but whom only Julian had really witnessed firsthand. Brad was an eager audience for Julian's own recordings, and Julian was excited to share his music with him.

BRAD TRUAX: They were kind of weird, folky songs with sound effects in the background. He had these really catchy songs, these kind of Jonathan Richman–type songs, that kind of talking, speaking vocals, simple minimal chords, layered effects. It was just sort of like, *Oh,* we *can make this music.* And then he took it another step forward where he was doing these little concept four-track pieces, almost like radio-show style: long, experimental, but mixed with songs, mixed with skits. They were just sort of wacky, a little bit dorky, edgy. It could go anywhere from this beautiful pop song into him doing spoken word with the bathtub running.

As he got a little older, Julian's parents afforded him a bit more freedom, and he started playing music with other kids. It was rare for any of the groups to last long enough to even come up with a band name. None of them lasted long enough to perform in public until he formed a band called Chocolate USA, which survived enough practices and band meetings to start playing shows. Julian played guitar, banjo, singing saw, a fuzzed-out antique mandolin, and turntables.*

* **Julian Koster:** I got fascinated with scratching and just dropping the needle, the texture of that. I was crazy about the Public Enemy records and De La Soul to a certain extent, just the idea of hearing the texture of other recordings in a recording. In a weird way, I think that formed some of my ideas about sound recording. And then when I would go see things live like that, I was so disappointed, because all you could hear was the fucking bass and some guy talking. I was there to hear the samples, and they just never translated live. When I listened to Public Enemy on my crappy stereo, there was almost no bass.

Julian felt invigorated by the collaborative experience of being in a band. Though the recordings never came out the way he wanted them to,* the band was starting to get some attention both locally and nationally, and he began to see the project as a way out of Seminole and into a bigger world where he maybe wouldn't feel so alone. He sent Bar/None a near-finished version of *All Jets Are Gonna Fall Today*, which the label released with few changes, if any.

JULIAN KOSTER: My home life was pretty awful, and there I was, mired in Florida, which was not a place I wanted to be. Bar/None got interested in us when I was still in high school, and it just seemed like a ticket to another reality. It was partially just the fact that it felt like a dream coming through and a ticket to a different life, out of a life you didn't want.

* **Julian Koster:** They didn't sound like us, and they didn't sound like cassette recordings. I didn't quite know what they were. It became this really weird compendium of expectations, both mine and the world's for us. It proved to be vastly unhealthy for me.

IN DENVER, ROBERT COMMUTED BY BUS TO CLASSES AT THE University of Colorado Boulder and spent the rest of his time recording and working at a popcorn cart. Jim McIntyre had moved to Denver from Birmingham, Alabama, not long before. He started seeing Robert around town and wrote him off quickly.

> JIM MCINTYRE: We were behind him in line at Taco Bell once, and he took forever being neurotic about the Taco Bell staff getting his order right. He seemed like kind of a dork to me also, because he had an Abraham Lincoln beard and would always wear some kind of dashiki/poncho-type thing. I figured he was just your average Boulder neo-hippie type.

Their paths crossed daily in the spring semester of 1992, as the two took the same thirty-mile bus ride each day to and from Boulder for class. Jim wasn't much of a morning person, but Robert is constitutionally incapable of keeping to himself at any time of day, so he was happy to pick up the conversational slack. One morning, Robert asked Jim what his favorite band was. Jim responded honestly but with an answer he hoped would shut down the conversation entirely: the Beach Boys. Given how taken everyone seemed to be with the burgeoning grunge scene and hard rock, Jim thought Robert would think he was a square and leave him alone. Jim had never met anyone else who would list the Beach Boys as a favorite, so he was sure this would alienate Robert.

ROBERT SCHNEIDER: He tried it on the wrong person.

Little did Jim know that his interlocutor was a lifelong Beach Boys obsessive, and aside from his friends back home, Robert had never met any big Beach Boys fans, either. Rather than push Robert away as Jim had intended, the answer pulled him closer, which is the next best thing.

The Beach Boys' *Smile* is one of the unifying influences of the collective. When they first learned about the attempted *Pet Sounds* follow-up, they knew only that it had been abandoned and that they had no way to hear it. There are many reasons the album was left unfinished, but the one they clung to was the escalation of Brian Wilson's mental health issues. As Wilson made himself less available to the public over the years, it seemed as though the sheer ambition of the maximalist record had broken him, that he had flown too close to the sun and was still tending to his injuries and melted wings. The mythos enchanted and allured. This was a work too massive for its creator's mind to bear. As bootlegs eventually trickled out, Robert, Jim, and their friends could finally hear bits and pieces of songs as they had been conceived, filling in the gaps with imagined instrumentation based on what they'd read.

ROBERT SCHNEIDER: The legend of *Smile* embodied every aspiration that we had. We were obsessed with *Smile*, which we couldn't hear. So we dreamed what *Smile* was like. The whole philosophy was so intriguing to us. It was the holy grail of everything we wanted music to be, even though we had never heard any of it.

With the Beach Boys and *Smile* as a launch point, Jim and Robert bonded quickly over music. That night, Robert dropped by Jim's place to share some of his music with him and Jim's musical comrade and girlfriend, Hilarie Sidney. Jim and Hilarie leaned more toward experimental music at the time, but they were impressed by Robert's songwriting. Robert introduced Hilarie and Jim to *Smiley Smile* and other post-surf Beach Boys records, and they turned Robert on to Pavement.

HILARIE SIDNEY: We would see him around, but he sort of annoyed us. He was always like, "Hellooo, my friend." He seemed kind of strange and annoying. And I remember Jim came home from the bus one day, and he was like, "You know that guy with the dashiki and the Abraham Lincoln beard? Well, he talked to me today and he asked me what my favorite band is, and he seemed hell-bent on being my friend. He wants to play us some songs on his guitar."

JIM McINTYRE: He played a song about Jupiter, and I was amazed at how good it was. Robert also did a lot of four-track cassette recording, so it was awesome to meet somebody about my age who was into a lot of the same musical things I was.

HILARIE SIDNEY: We were both really taken with his songs. We were really, really pleasantly surprised.

Like Robert, Jim had taken an indirect path to Denver, and it had plenty of parallels to Robert's. Growing up in Birmingham, Alabama, Jim's adventurous music tastes made him a bit of a misfit. He started recording music around age eight and became charmed by the world of DIY music through music zines like *OP Magazine*. He and his cousin sought out spaces where they could make a lot of noise, like the deserted former headquarters of a local power company or the foreclosed-upon house his cousin had grown up in, drawing sound from whatever he could find.

JIM McINTYRE: I remember hitting the washing machine with bleach bottles or close-miking little metal measuring cups and cranking up the distortion to get a massive sound. [My cousin] Douglas was a saxophone player, and one of the cool things he would do was put his saxophone mouthpiece on a long piece of PVC plumbing pipe, maybe six feet long and two inches in diameter.

After high school, Jim enrolled at the University of Miami. He made the track team as a freshman, but his athletic career didn't last long, as his roommate was "really into starting fires," and Jim frequently went along with him. He got kicked out of school. After taking a semester off back home in Birmingham, he returned to Miami, but he got kicked out again, this time for getting into drunken fights with other students. Colorado seemed like a nice change of scenery. At the University of Colorado Boulder, he met eventual Apples in Stereo guitarist John Hill and moved out into the foothills with him and a couple of other roommates, one of whom introduced him to Hilarie Sidney, then a high school student who worked in a record store in suburban Denver. They hit it off and began playing music together almost immediately.

The next year, Jim dropped out of college again and went back to Birmingham, this time bringing Hilarie with him. They recorded a bunch and then moved back to Denver in the fall of 1989, moving in with Hilarie's parents at first, then moving into a place of their own a year later. They began playing shows around the city as Von Hemmling. Their first gig was just Jim and Hilarie, before either had met Robert. They played a few before meeting Robert, actually, including several with John Hill, before *he* had met Robert, either. John played at least one of those shows with a broken arm.

LITTLE FYODOR: John had broken his arm, but he still had to go on, so he played with a broken arm in a cast. Back then, they were kind of a noise band, so it didn't matter that much. He kind of used his cast like a violin bow and banged out noise on his guitar.

JOHN HILL: I had a drumstick in my hand, so I was fretting with a drumstick, and I could barely push down with a couple of fingers. It was very painful. We ended up playing a few shows like that as Von Hemmling. It was pretty noisy, but fairly melodic and rhythmic.

ROBERT SCHNEIDER: Probably along with Will's side projects, among the strangest things that ever happened within Elephant 6. Jim had a guitar that had no bridge on it. He had taken the bridge out and put a coat hanger on it and wrapped it through the strings a couple of times so it just went *kkkkllllccccchhhh kkkkllllccccchhhh* every time. And that was his guitar! There was no musical content. They were into very, very strange stuff.

Hilarie Sidney grew up in suburban Chicago, where she lived until she was sixteen. Her father and older siblings got her into music, playing classics by the Who and Pink Floyd and relatively modern stuff like Devo and the Cars. Her brother Andy gave her her first record, *Magical Mystery Tour*, when she was eight. She was playing in bands by middle school, albeit only as well as a middle school band typically plays.

HILARIE SIDNEY: We didn't realize we had to tune our instruments together, so it was really bad.

Hilarie's family moved to Denver when she was in high school. Working at Wax Trax, a record store in the mall, she met a lot of local musicians, which eventually led her to John Hill and Jim McIntyre. They needed a drummer for their band, so Hilarie bought a drum kit and the trio started playing together.

At Wax Trax, Hilarie noticed her coworker Lisa Janssen had selected Smog's *Julius Caesar* as her staff pick for the week and struck up a conversation.

LISA JANSSEN: We were instant best friends. When we found each other, we were like, "Oh my god, you like that, too? No one's ever heard of that but you."

At the outset, Robert had plans to start a psychedelic R&B/swing band, drawing on his time playing on the riverboat in Kentucky. Chris Parfitt had just moved to Denver, wanted to start a band of his own, and placed an ad in Denver's *Westword* looking for a bass player who was into the Beach Boys and Pavement. Robert and Chris connected immediately, but the rest of Chris's band was put off by Robert's cheerfulness. They didn't want to bring him on, and they never found their bassist. Chris eventually left the band, too, and Robert invited Chris to jam with him and Jim.

ROBERT SCHNEIDER: Chris was the most knowledgeable person about music I've ever met in my life. He made Will and me look like we were dunces. What year did this Rolling Stones album come out? Who engineered it? He could tell you. He could tell you anything about music he wasn't even interested in. He could tell you about Jackson Browne or somebody I didn't even care about at the time. He knew everything. Also, he was the best guitar player I ever heard. And I don't mean slick. He wasn't slick. He was the most raw, fucked-up, great-sounding guitar player I had ever heard in my life.

For a few months, they played together whenever they could, usually in Jim's living room, which he shared with Hilarie, who eventually joined as the band's drummer.

JIM MCINTYRE: Robert wasn't too keen on having Hil drum for us, even after we tried a few songs with her. But I was convinced she could do it, so eventually he relented.

HILARIE SIDNEY: I really wanted to play, but Chris and Robert really didn't want me to, because I wasn't very good. But I was unrelenting, begging all the time, and they finally let me. I couldn't let them do it without me because they were practicing at my house anyway.

ROBERT SCHNEIDER: The first song we learned was "Heroes and Villains." I had worked out kind of a punk rock, Ramones-y version. The thing about the Apples, when we started, our goal as a band was this: we wanted to fuse *Piper at the Gates of Dawn*, the Beach Boys, Black Sabbath, and Pavement. That was our goal for the band. It was the grunge era, so that seemed natural.

They called the band the Apples, starting as a four-piece, with Robert singing and playing rhythm guitar, Chris playing lead guitar, Jim playing bass, and Hilarie playing drums. She started out on a toy kit because they were still jamming in the apartment, and she used those same toy drums at their first performance, an open mic at a rock club called Cricket on the Hill.

HILARIE SIDNEY: It was a bunch of bikers there. Some people heard what we were doing and thought it was very different, especially because I was playing a toy drum set. But that angered a lot of people. There were these biker guys yelling at me, like, "Why don't you get a real drum set?" They were just mad.

Though the reaction wasn't exactly unanimous praise, a few people in the crowd liked the Apples enough to offer them some gigs. To prepare, they rented a practice space in an old yogurt factory. Hilarie bought a real drum kit, and their first real show came soon after, opening for Little Fyodor at Penny Lane coffee shop in Boulder on February 26, 1993.

LITTLE FYODOR: Nirvana even played there before they were famous. Anyone they booked was cool.

While Little Fyodor was into Jim's Von Hemmling stuff, he wasn't sure whether he dug the Apples yet. They seemed friendly enough, though, and so the Apples were the first of three bands on the bill that night, with the sort of crowd you'd expect for the first of three bands playing in a small Boulder coffee shop. A year or two later, Fyodor found his band opening for the Apples in Los Angeles.

ROBERT SCHNEIDER: Some kids had gotten our seven-inch and invited us to come play on the West Coast. Three shows. We piled into a minivan and Apples and Neutral Milk went out. Then we just wanted to tour. We had the bug. We managed to book a few other shows here and there. We bought a van. A really shitty van. We just wanted to play, and we just wanted go play places. Denver wasn't a very receptive scene to us musically.

HILARIE SIDNEY: Robert was working at a popcorn wagon at the time, and his boss and his boss's wife came to the show and videotaped it. Our amps were feeding back and the guy came up and put his arm around Robert and said, "Do you hear that squealing noise that's coming from your amplifier? That's called 'feedback.'"

CHRIS PARFITT: The early Apples sound that started to develop was a little different from what came later. It was a hell of a lot noisier. We were very loud. But endlessly cheery. It sounded like Sonic Youth playing Hollies covers or something.

LISA JANSSEN: I've seen like five hundred Apples shows. I've seen good ones. I've seen bad ones. I've seen people throw temper tantrums. I've seen crazy noise jams and equipment go out and fights and amazing freaking shows. It was all just Robert's crazy energy. It came together really quickly when it did.

JIM MCINTYRE: I'd never played in a real band, so it was a learning experience for me, fitting my bass parts in with other people's songs. I learned a lot from Robert in that respect, and how to put real pop songs together. It's hard to overestimate how much Robert's songwriting magic rubbed off on everyone who had a close relationship with him and his music. I'm sure the same could be said of Jeff and Will and probably Bill, too. They all became better songwriters being around Robert. Robert is such an incredible natural songwriter that absorbing his influence and wanting to reach toward his level provided great inspiration.

To fund the Apples' first seven-inch, Robert got himself a credit card.

ROBERT SCHNEIDER: They're always trying to give them to college students. I got a credit card with a $500 limit, which was exactly how much my budget was. As far as the packaging goes, I did it at Kinko's. I put the booklets together as needed. It was a twelve-page booklet and all kinds of stickers and stuff, and since we didn't do it all at once, there was always different stuff going into the records. The cassettes all had booklets made by the artists, but I would physically assemble them myself. We hit up the people at Wax Trax for advice on distributors and stuff. We pressed five hundred copies of the first Apples seven-inch, and they sold out almost instantly. We had all of these indie distributors buying them.

CHRIS PARFITT: I didn't realize at the very beginning how serious and ambitious Robert was. I just thought, *Wow, this guy is the most talented bastard I've ever met in my entire life.* Either the first or the second time I hung out with Robert, he sat down and played me a bunch of songs. They weren't songs that ended up on any of the Apples records. I remember just being floored by the melodic content of his songs. It was fairly obvious to me that this guy was a genius of sorts. He was just so friendly and so positive. It took me a little while to believe that anybody could be that positive. He was just a wiry, Big Gulp–drinkin', million-mile-an-hour-talkin' guy.

By that point, everybody had dropped out of school entirely to focus on the band, and with new gigs popping up regularly, they seemed to be on a steady upward trajectory. But rifts between band members were starting to cause trouble.

JIM MCINTYRE: One time while we were playing a gig, Chris dropped his guitar pick and asked me in the middle of a song if he could have mine—the one I was using to play the bass at the time.

The original Apples lineup didn't last long. Tensions were high from the start with Chris, whose cynical attitude never really jibed with Robert's relentless positivity and cheerfulness. At the same time, Chris was drinking a lot and having some relationship issues of his own.* The rest of the band wanted someone they could rely on. Meanwhile, Jim and Hilarie were still dating and cohabiting, but their relationship was taking a toll on each of them and on the rest of the band.

HILARIE SIDNEY: Jim and I had a really angry relationship. We always fought a lot. We had been fighting for a long time before we moved into our apartment in Denver. We were really mean to each other. Jim is one of my best friends, and we really should have just been best friends. We smothered each other.

JIM MCINTYRE: Hil and I had an extremely tumultuous relationship. We used to get in major fights at the supermarket. At the time, it seemed somehow normal, but looking back on it, I've been to supermarkets thousands of times in my life, and I've never once heard people screaming at each other like Hil and I used to do.

All of that came to a head when Chris pointed out that Robert and Hilarie seemed to be becoming more than friends.

CHRIS PARFITT: I was apparently the one who inadvertently told Jim that Robert and Hilarie were together. That pretty much sealed my fate in the band, because Hilarie then blamed all of the tension on me, because I shouldn't have said what was patently obvious to everyone.

After Chris left the band, the Apples played a few shows as a three-piece before adding John Hill to the mix as another guitarist, with Robert taking over lead duties and John playing rhythm. John had moved back home to DC for a couple of years, but the Apples were using his Tascam as a second four-track for recording, and Chris had been playing his guitar. With some of his gear in the band before he even joined, John could slip in easily, but he still felt a little out of place at first. He joined the band in November 1993, with the next show scheduled for January 10, 1994, at the Lion's Lair in Denver. The other band members went home to visit

* Since leaving the band, Chris has found himself happier and less cynical. "For the most part, I don't drink anymore. I'm married. I'm much happier. Much healthier."

their families for the holidays, but John stuck around and practiced on his own.

JOHN HILL: I played guitar eight or ten hours a day, until I gave myself carpal tunnel syndrome. I played like crazy for two or three weeks until I couldn't play. I had to take a week off because I had played too much. We reconvened in late December or early January to do two or three rehearsals, and I was ready to go at that point. We were a ramshackle bunch back then. It wasn't that we couldn't play. We'd spend more time on the recordings, and then when it came time to do a show, we just kind of gave it hell, like we were a punk rock band.

By showtime, Jim and Hilarie's relationship tension was boiling.

HILARIE SIDNEY: It's weird with Robert, because he and I were good friends, but I always thought there was a little spark there. As things were going bad with Jim, I talked to him more and more. I think we became really fond of each other.

JIM MCINTYRE: It's something that happens to young people. Young people have turmoil. They don't have reality shows about fifty-year-old people who are set in their life. There was a lot of that in the whole scene.

Robert's roommate moved out, and in his place, Hilarie moved in. Jim was under the impression she was just moving in as a friend, but it didn't take him long to figure out something else was going on, and the acrimony eventually bubbled up during a show.

JIM MCINTYRE: We had one gig where Robert and I were arguing about something onstage, and instead of saying something to me, he said something to the audience about "our bass player is pissed off," and I took my bass and picked it up over my head and slammed it on the stage and walked off.

JOHN HILL: He just stomped out, yelling and screaming and knocking stuff over. We were just like, "Fuck it. Let's just keep playing." It infuriated Jim. He expected a reaction. He was prone to throwing tantrums and stuff. The crowd was laughing.

HILARIE SIDNEY: Jim just dropped his bass in the middle of a song and went and ordered a drink at the bar. Robert just told us, "Keep playing. Keep playing. Fuck him." So we kept playing, and then Jim started heckling us from the bar, like, "Robert, you're a fucking pussy!" Stuff like that. People loved it, though.

MARTYN LEAPER: They were honestly the best pop band I had seen. It was an amazing thing, and I was sold immediately.

ROBERT SCHNEIDER: That happened a number of times, actually. Almost every show we ever played. He would get very nervous and anxious. Jim is a fantastically creative person, and that also gets wound up in him in physical stress. He's a fireball. He's one of the most creative, far-out thinkers you could ever imagine.

The Apples were gearing up for a trip to California to record *Fun Trick Noisemaker*, their first full-length album, followed by a small tour through the state and a spot at the Yoyo A Go Go festival in Olympia, Washington.* It would be a lot of time sharing such close quarters given the state of their relationships with one another. Jim quit the band, which he had done many times before, but when he asked to join again, this time Robert said no. With half of the original members now gone, the Apples' sound changed, and they changed their name as well, albeit just a little. The Apples became the Apples in Stereo.†

LISA JANSSEN: I saw one of their first shows they played with a new lineup. It was one of those moments where you knew you found your people. We all loved sixties pop. We all loved psychedelic music. At that time, not everyone was into that. Not everyone collected that or loved Brian Wilson yet. It was all kind of new,‡ and we were an exotic species.

Lisa spent a lot of time at Hilarie and Robert's apartment, listening to music and watching *90210*. Hilarie and Lisa had a specific affinity for noise

* Robert and Hilarie would also play bass and drums for Neutral Milk Hotel there.

† Or the Apples in stereo, or the Apples (in stereo), depending on which album or gig poster you think is canonical.

‡ Kind of.

music that the other Apples folks didn't share, so Hilarie helped Lisa pick out a guitar and learn how to play it, and they started a band called Secret Square, with Jeff on drums and Robert on bass for shows. Secret Square released one seven-inch and one LP, both in 1995. They're difficult to find, and few records are more sought after by Elephant 6 diehards.

> HILARIE SIDNEY: We would call out of work and she would come over to my place with her guitar. I helped her pick out her first guitar and she taught herself how to play little things. We would sit there and play and take codeine all day. The live shows were really fun. They were more improvisational than when we played as the Apples or Neutral Milk Hotel. They weren't structured. I don't think we played more than six live shows ever. I wish we had done more of it.

The project also gave Hilarie an opportunity to explore her own ideas more than she was able to do in the Apples, or at least to have those ideas taken seriously.

> HILARIE SIDNEY: That's always been one of the things that's bothered me about Elephant 6. It always has felt like a boys' club to me. A lot of those guys have a really Southern mentality about women. I don't know if they still do, but at the time, it was like girls were doing stuff and were involved, but it seemed like they were less involved. It kind of bummed me out. It was more just a general vibe, but a lot of times, if I had an idea, it was like, "Oh that's cute, she had an idea. Pat her on the head." But then someone else might come up with the same idea an hour later, and it would be brilliant.

Lisa was also impressed by Hilarie's pragmatism, which she felt was a great balance for Robert's quixotic ambitions.

> LISA JANSSEN: She kind of kept their life together, as far as making sure bills were paid and socks were picked up. They were figuring out how to be a band and how to get a record manufactured and all that stuff. Robert would have a lot of inspiration, and Hilarie would be the one who was figuring out how to do that practically.

After Hilarie moved out, Jim searched for a new place and stumbled on a musician's dream: a former fish market that had been converted into an apartment, bigger than any other place he could find in that price range, with long rooms and an addition in front. Perfect for recording. A number of Denver musicians had lived and recorded there previously.

Robert helped turn it into a studio and recorded there for about six months of the year. Jim, who had been working in the chemistry lab at a Denver utilities company full-time, switched to part-time and recorded his own material in the studio when no one else was using it. The old building had been pretty worn down, and they spent time plugging leaks and tarring the roof, along with building up the studio. They continued to augment their arsenal of gear, and they decorated the studio with a few massive wall hangings that artist Steve Keene had made for their "Tidal Wave" music video: a nature scene, a *Defender*-esque space scene, and in the studio's control room, a colorful, expressionistic rendition of a studio control room.

Perhaps the only downside was that, like many residential buildings in Denver at the time, this one didn't have air-conditioning. Denver only gets hot for a few weeks each year, but with all of the equipment running inside, the Apples spent days at a time in the control room with the temperature lingering around ninety-five degrees.

JIM MCINTYRE: The house worked great as a studio because the control room area in the front had actually been added on to the original building. So the wall between it, along with the other front room and the rest of the building, was extra thick because it had been the former outside wall. It made the control room nice and isolated from what you were recording, which is very important because you have to be able to hear what you are doing. If you can hear the loud drums or guitar in the next room, it's not possible to hear the manipulations you are making to the signal coming in. Even with the nice soundproofing from my bedroom, I could hear what was going on in the control room, because my bedroom shared a wall with the control room. Many nights I fell asleep to the sound of the Apples' or whoever's songs being played over and over.

CHAPTER 6

JIM MCINTYRE: I was introduced to [Will, Bill, and Jeff's] music before I met them. I can remember hearing Synthetic Flying Machine tapes and stuff Robert had recorded with Will. I remember hearing a song of Will's he had recorded in a commercial studio. It was an awful, bland production. Just a horrible rendition of a good song, which leached most of Will's personality out of it.* It was a stark testament to the direct communication that recording your own music provides. I was very impressed by the rest of the music I'd heard from Robert, Will, and Jeff. That definitely made me want to impress them with what I'd done.

HILARIE SIDNEY: Will came out to live with us in Denver. Robert and I had this little one-bedroom basement apartment, and then Will lived there with us, and Mike Owens, his friend from Ruston, came, and sometimes Jeff would stay with us, on and off from Seattle, where he was recording his first single for Cher Doll [Records].

LISA JANSSEN: I was always hearing about the other kids from Ruston. They would talk about Will and Jeff a lot. Eventually, all those guys came through Denver and lived there for periods of time, and that was really exciting. They had a bunch of cassettes out at that time. But it was all so completely new. I just didn't meet people who were into psychedelic music at that time. Meeting a whole clan who

* The recording sounds as if the engineer had only ever worked with bands who wanted to sound like Nirvana's *Nevermind*, which may have actually been the case. But it sounds nothing like anything Will ever released.

were into it, we were just so excited to meet each other and know each other.

On a quick jaunt to Athens, Robert was impressed by his friends' performance as Synthetic Flying Machine. This was the same trip on which he'd decided to name his own band the Apples. Back in Denver, Robert decided the best way to funnel this torrent of creative energy was a proper record label, and when Will came to Denver, they ran with it.

ROBERT SCHNEIDER: Hilarie and Jim and I had the ambition to start a small label to put out our underground music. This was just a pipe dream, just something we talked about, but we talked about it enough that we started trying to come up with a name for it.

HILARIE SIDNEY: We would just stay up all night getting high and talking about what we wanted it to be. I was really obsessed with Flying Nun and Drag City and all these little labels I really liked. Robert had all these sixties ideas and I was into the modern-day do-it-yourself stuff, and we took all these aspects of the things that we loved and decided to have a record label that was going to have a sound and a style. Aesthetically, it was going to be really uniform.

ROBERT SCHNEIDER: Will and Jeff were fairly obsessed with K Records. Jim and Hilarie were obsessed with Flying Nun Records, and they introduced me to Flying Nun. As much as I worship Phil Spector and Brian Wilson, those aren't realistic role models for young four-track record producers. But Chris Knox was producing actual records on vinyl of other bands on four-track. He was recording them as if it was a regular recording studio. So that inspired me because all I had was a four-track. I had this vision of myself as a producer. I don't have to go to a studio, because Chris Knox didn't. I *am* the studio.

To the uninitiated, a name like "Elephant 6" might conjure images of trapped miners or political prisoners rather than a collective of psychedelic musicians, but those musicians had been branding their homemade recordings with the insignia of imaginary record labels and studios for years. In 1989, for example, Will dubbed a few of his recordings over some Keith Sweat promo tapes that had been sent to KLPI. He labeled them

"Amoeba Kite," with a small drawing of someone flying an amorphous unicellular organism in the wind from a string.

Will's four-track recorder was broken, but he borrowed Robert's while he was in Denver and rediscovered his love for recording. After a couple of days of messing around, he scrawled "Elephant 6" on the cassette, a name he'd proposed to Robert on an earlier visit to Athens.

WILL CULLEN HART: It sounded cool. Max Ernst had a painting called *The Elephant Celebes,** and I was like, "Uhhhhh, Elephant 6." Couldn't really pronounce "celebes."

ROBERT SCHNEIDER: When he said it, that's it. That's the name. There was no question.

From there, Robert added "Recording Company" to make it sound official. It's unclear whether the "6" in the name was connected to anything—"Elephant" definitely was not—but six people were involved at the outset: Bill, Hilarie, Jeff, Jim, Robert, and Will.

ROBERT SCHNEIDER: Elephant 6 really was a small unit that was founded by a few specific people. There wasn't anyone else involved at first. We had friends that were part of a collective, but that wasn't Elephant 6 at first.

BILL DOSS: Back and forth, they blossomed this thing. I remember Will calling me. I was touring with Chocolate USA at the time. "Elephant 6! We're going to do it!"

HILARIE SIDNEY: We wanted to create something that was an experience from the time you open the package and put the music on. We wanted to connect to other people who loved the music that we loved and the art that we loved, and to be a part of something big and creative. We poured all of our time and all of the money we could

* *The Elephant Celebes* is an early Surrealist work from 1921 and one of Ernst's finest. The dreamlike composition features a headless mannequin wearing a surgical glove in the foreground and fish flying through a bleak but empty sky in the background, while most of the canvas is dominated by an iron, furnace-like elephant. The aesthetics of the work and the processes the artist employed to create it (Ernst made no studies, sketches, or preliminary collages in preparation, conceiving the work as he painted it through a method called automatization, making few alterations as he went) bear many similarities with the Elephant 6's eventual output, which would be less interesting if that had been intentional.

put together to make our cassettes and EPs. I remember staying up all night putting together our first EP. Coloring the first fifty covers, hand numbering, stuffing them full of little fun things to look at and experience. It was very gratifying.

Jeff made the *Everything Is* seven-inch after the label idea was conceived, but the Apples' *Tidal Wave* EP was the first release, in June 1993, to bear the Elephant 6 Recording Company logo. Will had promised Robert he would design a symbol for the label. In Denver, Will often kept to himself, drawing and painting in solitude, so Robert let him be, but less than a day before the artwork was due for the first Apples in Stereo record, Will had not yet drawn it. Robert begged him to finish and then went to sleep. Will stayed up the rest of the night. When Robert and Hilarie emerged from their bedroom the next morning, Will showed them what he came up with.

ROBERT SCHNEIDER: I have never seen anything so beautiful.
HILARIE SIDNEY: We were really excited. Will always made really cool drawings. We were just like, "Oh that's it. That's the logo. We love it." Perfect.

It bears a way-too-similar-not-to-note resemblance to the cover design of Edgar Allan Poe's *Complete Tales & Poems*, published in 1975 by Vintage Books. Robert would not say whether he owned a copy, and when I asked Will about it directly, he smirked but neither confirmed nor denied the influence. Regardless, Will's Art Nouveau–via-Haight-Ashbury logo is unapologetically handmade, particularly the typeface, the strokes and stems and bars and bowls of its letters varying from one to the next. It's messy but ornate, with loping curves and intricate serifs that distort and decay with analog reproduction. Every photocopied or rubber-stamped instance is thus unique. A logo typically communicates a cohesive brand and thus some degree of professionalism—stasis as stability. The Elephant 6 design's inexorable mutation is a fail-safe against anyone taking things so seriously, constant deviation as insurance against even the possibility of bland uniformity.

Robert overnighted the logo to the record plant to get it there in time. It has remained unchanged ever since, but it's also a little different every time.

The Elephant 6 Recording Company was founded as a record label, but from the outset, it was fated to fall far short of that ambition, while turning into something else entirely: a unifying framework for the collective creative energy of like-minded friends.

ROBERT SCHNEIDER: We conceived it as an open club that anyone could join. "If you're like us, please join our club." We anticipated that four-track kids from around the globe—we estimated there were probably ten to twenty other people like us—would find us. But there was a little more than doing it for free, because we sort of had this fantasy that maybe it was a way of bypassing the music industry and being able to be legitimate musicians and artists and songwriters without having to have demo tapes and press kits.

BILL DOSS: It was one of those things where every day you're like, "I can't believe we have this cool thing." It was almost like a dream. For me, it was inspirational, almost a competition. Every time I'd hear one of Robert's new songs, I'd say "I have to go write a new song right now."

JIM MCINTYRE: You're just really inspired. The flame is ignited. Being in the studio, I would hear people going to Athens and then coming back two years later with a new record. And they're so driven by it that it makes you feel the same way. For Robert, too. It's like a friendly competition. That, to me, was always the essence of the Elephant 6.

REBECCA COLE: You got a good feeling being around these people. They were kind. Lots of hugs and I-love-yous. It just felt really inclusive. Everyone was really supportive of everyone else doing whatever they were doing. It was such a positive, nurturing place. In retrospect, I cannot believe how lucky I was.

LISA JANSSEN: It was just really loose. Everyone's idea mattered. They were doing their own little thing, in their own insular world. Once it started seeping out into the real world, it was so different from the mood of what was going on at that time. It was so fanciful and optimistic and guileless.

MARTYN LEAPER: You had a return to this sort of dedication to an authenticity of music again. It was in the hands of people making it for themselves. It wasn't being made in these giant studios with these silly producers or big-budget disasters that didn't have any guts. To meet guys who were dedicated, and still are to this day, I was really impressed by that, and I got drawn in.

ROBERT SCHNEIDER: Before we thought of Elephant 6 as a label, I realized it was a special, unique sound that my friends were making. While the sound of the cassette tape gives a very strong sound quality to music, the content of it was a lot different. It was very psychedelic. It was a mixture of punk and indie and sixties music and some folk music and stuff like that. It had lots of bells and whistles. We tried to do lots of harmonies and horn arrangements. Even in indie bands that used horns, it wasn't common to be trying to put so much crazy fun into a recording. That was common to all of the Elephant 6 recordings. It's not that it had to have a lot of tracks. It's that it had a lot of vibe. It's your dog barking, and you're recording while your friends are in the room.

BILL DOSS: It felt like the best place in the world to be. It really did.

Another thing the Elephant 6 folks all seemed to have in common, regardless of what kind of music they listened to most, was a history of making mixtapes.

JIM MCINTYRE: That's what we all grew up doing, making mixtapes for ourselves or as gifts to our friends.

ROBERT SCHNEIDER: When you make a tape for a friend, you write on it, you draw on it, you put little pieces of collage art on it. You make it really special. That's the punk rock and friendly thing to do. That aesthetic was a big part of how we traded tapes and how we perceived the music we made and how we would share it with other people. The idea of you opening the tape up and all this stuff falling into your lap, that was something I really wanted to translate into our releases for Elephant 6. I wanted the releases to feel like you were the friend who was receiving the handmade tape. It was really important to me that they would be handmade, not printed. They should be entirely magical, but they should be something you could have done, too, at Kinko's or with some scissors and glue.

For as much as they shared, the bands of the Elephant 6 are quite different musically from one another, but one of the traits most common among their records is a self-contained stylistic eclecticism. This heterogeneous approach is rooted in their formative musical experiences, be it the free-form hours on KLPI or the song-to-song U-turns that wind across amalgamated records like the Beatles' "White Album," *The Faust Tapes, Double Nickels on the Dime,* or the *Smile* bootlegs. Perhaps most influential on this aesthetic were the mixtapes they made for one another, cassette collages abutting sixties bubblegum pop with contemporary indie rock with noisy avant-garde compositions. They followed the through lines from each track to the next, beguiling one another with high-contrast juxtapositions. Sequencing was itself a means for expression. Unintentionally, they trained their ears to not just tolerate these juxtapositions but embrace and explore them.

In addition to the tracks its curator selects, each tape carries with it the artifacts of samizdat reproduction: pre- or post-track radio DJ rambling, tape recorder clicks and hisses, environmental sounds from the room in which it was dubbed. Each incidental whorl creates a unique fingerprint and thus a handmade quality far more endearing than any shrink-wrapped official release. No two mixtapes are the same, but every one of them can expand how both the listener and the curator hear music—and how they hear each other.

They also acclimate both parties to the thrill of sharing music, which in the case of the Elephant 6 grew into starting a label to share cassettes and seven-inch records of their own music. Their experience and resources were limited, but their enthusiasm could cover any shortfalls. They distributed a catalog listing all of their upcoming releases, hoping to get people as excited about their music as they were. Which would have been fine, except many of those records were not even close to being finished when the catalog was created. Some were never completed at all.

HILARIE SIDNEY: We made a catalog before we had everything done and then stupidly started mailing it out with our seven-inches. People started ordering stuff, and we got in way over our heads.

JIM MCINTYRE: Our ideas were more ambitious than our follow-through when it came to actually producing the stuff in the catalog and getting orders out to people. A lot of that stuff was never made.

HILARIE SIDNEY: We were a little spacey. This one guy, Roger, wrote us so many nasty letters, because he ordered something so many times and sent money. We hadn't cashed his check yet, but we hadn't filled his order. So finally we got it done, and me, Jeff, and Robert recorded a song called "We're Sorry, Roger" and sent it to him along with his order. We never heard from him, but I hope he liked the song.

In 1991, alternative rock broke into the mainstream. Lollapalooza kicked off that summer, and Nirvana released its major-label debut, *Nevermind,* in the fall. The music industry's initial reaction to these commercial successes was that maybe American listeners were more open to new ideas than the labels had assumed, that there was money to be made from novelty. Spikes in profits from the introduction of the CD a few years prior meant labels had money to burn investigating this theory. Suddenly, a whole bunch of weirdos who had no business being on a major label were (briefly, in most cases) signed by major labels. From the Nirvana-adjacent Melvins and Daniel Johnston to noisier outfits like Flipper, Mr. Bungle, and the Jesus Lizard to aggressively and abrasively peculiar acts like Royal Trux and Boredoms, there was a gold rush to find the next transgressive hit. Within a few years, though, major labels decided that they just wanted to find more bands that sounded like Nirvana.

NOEL MURRAY: Everything went in a more metallic, heavy direction. After Kurt Cobain died, it made it all that much easier to begin the progression of loud, grinding bands that weren't as interesting as Nirvana or even as interesting as Soundgarden. And it got worse and worse and worse until you end up with Nickelback.

JIM DEROGATIS: The alternative thing was really weird because all of a sudden you had these people who had been doing fanzines that five hundred people read getting hired by major labels to be in the publicity department or getting jobs at *SPIN,* so bands that had previously sold three thousand records were getting signed to record deals for $350,000. When the Elephant 6 thing was coming up, the alternative thing had fallen apart, but the underground had all sold out.

STEPHEN THOMAS ERLEWINE: It seems to me that Elephant 6 has a whimsy or a lightness to it that counteracts those things. That can be why certain fans of guitar music or music that's not pop

> were drawn to it. It offered a lighter perspective or at least something a little different from what was dominating the indie scene just beforehand.

At the time, music generally progressed along a fairly linear path. Bands were influenced mostly by contemporary artists. That's what the record stores carried, that's what magazines talked about, that's what the radio played, and that's who you could go see at a rock club. It wasn't just *uncool* to be into older music—it was also exceedingly difficult. The geekiness of a hobby tends to correlate closely with how much work is involved in maintaining it. That is, the people who were most into retro stuff were the people obsessive, patient, and persistent enough to find it. And so just about any band forming at that time would end up sounding mostly like whoever else was active at the same time, especially those based (and therefore performing and recording) nearby. The aesthetics mutated organically if only from technology and other external circumstances, but those mutations tended to be incremental. Only so much music was within reach at a given time, and anything out of reach faded away.

Eventually, the limitless audio library of the internet demolished these hurdles almost entirely, but a cultural shift was in motion before a single line of Napster's code was written. In the early eighties, compact discs were introduced to the market, branded as a superior listening experience to cassette tapes or vinyl records. The technology was marketed heavily as the *true* way to listen to music, the way engineers get to hear a song before it's eroded by analog reproduction, and by the end of the decade it was poised to take over as the dominant medium for music consumption: US CD sales grew from 17.2 million in 1983 to 286.5 million in 1990 (peaking in 2000 at 942 million). Eager to hear their favorite music at a fidelity theretofore unheard by civilian ears,* people with robust record collections were quick to buy up CD versions of albums they already owned

* For recorded music, obviously, as fidelity isn't really a consideration for live music, though maybe it should be. A live performance will sound very different based on the gear used to amplify it, the acoustics of the structure inside of which it's performed, the immediate meteorological conditions and state of inebriation the listener finds themself in, the length of hairs and abundance of wax in a listener's ears, and so on. Variations in these conditions can create at least as much of a range in how the music is heard as the choice of format for a recorded version.

on other formats. CDs were not only the allegedly "best"* way to listen to music, but they also took up a lot less space than vinyl, and so people were more than happy to dump their old LPs at the nearest used-record store. In *MP3: The Meaning of a Format,* Jonathan Sterne writes:

> The record industry is prone to crisis. In the late 1970s, sagging profits were blamed on the failed promise of disco and on lost profits from home taping. Between roughly 1990 and 2000, record-industry profits were artificially elevated by format changes and resale and repackaging of back catalogues. Once LP collections were replaced by CDs this market dried up and, with it, a substantial portion of industry profits.

That is, people were only going to repurchase their old records on a new format once. But that took a few years,† and at the outset the CD looked like only progress to the average listener (that is, anybody who spent more money on music than they made from it). People could fit more music into a given physical space, and they could hear that same music more cleanly, closer to how it sounded in the studio. So albums they already owned on vinyl or cassette, they purchased again on CD, parting with the more antiquated formats cheaply. Record stores could pay lower prices for used records because the market was flooded by people upgrading their collections. Downstream, this was a boon to enterprising record-store customers who suddenly had access to a much broader set of choices. For a curious crate-digger, this was an unprecedented opportunity to discover new music, especially if that music was old. So rather than listening to only new releases from one's home country, anyone with a turntable could now explore musical output spanning decades and continents with relative ease. It was a whole lot less difficult to learn there was more to Brian Wilson than surfboards and hot rods, and so it was no longer uncool to like the Beach Boys (or at least *less* uncool). Listeners could more easily travel through time, around the globe, into the most obscure cracks and crevices. Temporal and cultural tourism became a lot more accessible via

* The scare quotes here are not to be derisive about CD technology but rather the arrogance inherent to any format being objectively better or worse than any other. Whatever you think of the resurgence in vinyl collecting, it at least demonstrates that there is a vast diversity when it comes to preferred listening experiences, and each has pros and cons that elude a linear ranking.

† We'll get to this in greater detail later.

the grooves of gently used LPs, and revivalism of abandoned, overlooked, and otherwise marginalized styles followed organically, at times culturally appropriative, often curatorial and generative. Sometimes with self-consciousness and sometimes with self-awareness, rarely with both. This had always been possible, but it had never been easier.

JIM MCINTYRE: You could go in and buy records for two or three dollars. You could take twenty-five dollars and instead of buying two CDs, you could buy ten or twelve records. That was really important in the evolution of what we wanted to do at that time. You could buy a record by the Monkees or Tommy James and the Shondells or Herman's Hermits, all these great records from the sixties. At the same time, you could buy experimental albums from the eighties. You could go to the record store and buy all these different things at once. It was really like the dawn of the information era for us.

This had a profound effect on the musical styles and aesthetics of the people buying up these once-rare finds. For home recorders, it affected their aspirations, too. "Lo-fi" was very much an aesthetic unto itself, but while the Elephant 6 folks viewed it as a certain dimension to be embraced on its own merits, it was also a challenge to be overcome.

LISA JANSSEN: The whole lo-fi thing was going on, and Robert wanted to be more than that. Even though those first records were kind of lo-fi, he already had such aspirations to make a great-sounding record with complex instrumentation and harmonies. Robert is really the linchpin that everyone else at that point revolved around. He was the one who would say "let's put out this cassette" or "let's manufacture this Neutral Milk Hotel cassette." He was the one who figured out how to put that all together. He was the one saying, "We're going to have a label and the next thing we're going to do is an Olivia Tremor Control seven-inch." He was the one that was making those practical steps, whereas at that time, it felt like everyone was still just sitting in their bedrooms with their four-track recorders going, "This is great."

Chapter 7

Jill Carnes: It was a lot smaller in population. Everyone rode their bicycle everywhere. It was easier to get a parking space downtown at night. You could go to a thrift store and buy a bag of used clothing for less than doing your laundry at the laundromat. Hardly anyone I knew had a telephone.

Andrew Rieger: Athens just kind of has a reputation for being a place that good bands come from as well as a good place to live if you're in a band. So that probably draws people to move here.

Henry Owings: When I moved here in the early nineties, this city was a fucking wasteland. Once I moved here, I was like, "What the fuck was I thinking?" Nobody who was there then who went on to become the old guard now, none of them moved here for anything other than cheap rent and to have a good time. Nobody could get a record out. There were small indie labels, but nobody was putting out records [of] the caliber that it became. All of them were just kind of struggling along.

Few towns of Athens's size boast such a vibrant cultural community. On paper, it makes sense that an artist would be comfortable there. It's home to the University of Georgia, which despite its reputation for football and fraternities brings all sorts of speakers and programming to town, not to mention lots of young people with time on their hands. It's also, even for a college town, pretty cheap. Rent, food, beer, pot: all affordable with a part-time gig. When you can live comfortably on very little income, you don't need a serious job that would interfere with the time you need to make music, and you don't need to compromise your art for the sake of money. You can wait tables or work at a call center for fifteen to twenty hours a week and, with some ingenuity and the right sort of community (and probably a few roommates) around you, be just fine. And it's Georgia, so the general vibe is pretty relaxed. Often, the only pressure anyone feels is of the barometric variety (a killer in the brothy Athenian summer). It's sleepy enough that one can live a pretty mellow lifestyle, even by Southern standards, but barely ninety minutes from Atlanta, it's not so remote as to sequester its inhabitants entirely. Whenever desired, more metropolitan trappings are a short ride away.

But there are certainly other places that fit some version of that profile, so what makes Athens unique? How did a quiet Southern college town engender such explosive creativity from the Elephant 6 Recording Company, from the B-52's and R.E.M. before them, from Pylon and Vic Chesnutt and Danger Mouse and Drive-By Truckers and countless other revered artists?*

The catalyst may have been one person in particular. Jeremy Ayers was an Athens native, born in 1948, the son of a UGA chaplain and professor of religion. He lived most of his life there, too, but sometime around 1970, he moved to New York. When he returned to Athens in the mid-seventies, he brought with him Max's Kansas City and the Velvet Underground and glam and drag and gender subversion and all the glimmering vestiges of 1970s New York underground culture. His impact was sizable. Ayers has a writing credit on "52 Girls," the B side to the first B-52's single. He may have taught Michael Stipe to dance (and he has a writing credit on at least one R.E.M. song, too). In *Cool Town: How Athens, Georgia, Launched Alternative Music and Changed American Culture*, former Athenian Grace Elizabeth Hale observes that, from his music to his personal style to his philosophizing, Jeremy Ayers was "more than a local star. He made Athens the place *to be* a star."

* It should be noted that, while Athens's indie rock reputation is well deserved, the town boasts a rich music history across many genres and demographics. When the city launched its Athens Music Walk of Fame in 2020, it included the acts mentioned here (only some of which could be classified as "indie" or "rock") as well as Black spiritual composer Hall Johnson, blues musician Neal Pattman, and jam band Widespread Panic.

Other people moved between New York and Athens, too, but Ayers's connection to that world was about as hip as it could get. Adopting the stage name Silva Thin from a cigarette ad—"Cigarettes are like women. The best ones are thin and rich"—Ayers "had been a part of the Factory, Andy Warhol's studio and bohemian hangout, a central hub of New York's underground art world," Hale writes. Though many in his Athens social circle had no idea he had been a Warhol Superstar, Ayers's return to Athens provided a blueprint for a lifestyle somewhere where it was much, much more difficult to express any kind of sexuality at all. Even heterosexuality was largely of a repressed variety. To express *queerness* could get you killed. When Ayers returned to Athens (and even before—founding B-52's members Ricky Wilson and Keith Strickland visited him at least once in New York), things began to shift. As the art school kids began to feel more empowered to experiment, new possibilities revealed themselves.

"The blurred lines between men and women, gender and sexuality, and anatomy and identity became a model for thinking about everything else, too," Hale writes. "Suddenly other seemingly opposed categories like amateur or professional, southern or avant-garde, and even making your own culture versus remaking the culture looked more permeable."

Ayers and his friends having opened the door years earlier to so much freedom to experiment, it makes sense that the folks who felt confined by Ruston's culture (and the cultures of other towns) would converge in Athens, even if they weren't yet aware of Ayers himself (and with some exceptions are themselves mostly heterosexual and cisgender).* By the time the Elephant 6 folks got to Athens, a generation or two of brilliant, transgressive artists had laid the foundation for a booming cultural community.

Years earlier, listening to Pylon together on a drive out to a water park in Shreveport, Will, Jeff, and Robert decided they'd live in Athens together someday. Of the Rustonites, Will Cullen Hart was the first to get there. After four months in the Virgin Islands, Will and his partner, Shannon, headed back to the mainland, but the only place less desirable than the Virgin Islands was Ruston. They crashed with Shannon's sister in

* They became aware of and eventually befriended him. Ayers introduced Jeff and his now-wife, Astra Taylor, to each other. When I first met Julian, he was renting a room from Ayers. And so on.

Lake City, Florida, for a little while to brainstorm their next move. Nothing seemed to hit the right note—and Lake City wasn't a fit, either—so the couple began their drive back to Ruston, defeated. On the way there, though, Will remembered that a friend of his from KLPI had moved to Athens, and they decided to take a detour to visit her.

Will never made it back to Ruston. Not only did he decide to settle in Athens, but he phoned Jeff and convinced him to come live with him and Shannon there, too. Will wanted to start a band with him.

ROBERT SCHNEIDER: Summer of 1992, I went to Athens, and I spent some weeks there, staying with Will.* During that time, Will had a paper route. He delivered newspapers. We would get done recording at four a.m., go pick up the newspapers, put them in his car, and drive around in the country, putting newspapers into people's postboxes. They had those funny little round boxes that you'd stick your paper in. We'd just listen to music until the sun rose and talk and dream about things. It was a great time. It was as fun a time as someone could possibly have.

WILL CULLEN HART: We got robbed all the time. Constantly.

Will and Jeff recorded together at home, as they had in Ruston, and eventually took their experimentation to the streets, busking on the sidewalk downtown for fun and whatever spare change ended up in their immediate vicinity, which was rarely much.

WILL CULLEN HART: One time, someone kicked over our change by accident and gave us four or five bucks.

They finished the night with eight. By performing their music in public, though, what had been a project originally meant only for friends to hear was transforming into a real band. It didn't last long. Will and Shannon broke up, so Will went to Denver for a while to stay with Robert and Hilarie,† while Jeff shipped out to Seattle. Bill got out of the National Guard in 1993, and by the

* This was the same trip on which Robert came up with the name "The Apples" and decided to start a record label called the Elephant 6 Recording Company.

† This was the aforementioned visit during which Will was driving the Apples to all their gigs.

summer, he, Will, and Jeff reconvened in Athens. The three of them inquired about living together.

"Yeah, we have a room available. It's ninety bucks," Bill remembers their first landlord telling him.

"Can we split it?"

The three of them shared the attic in a house on the corner of what is now Sunset Drive and Sunset Terrace, whose other rooms were occupied by a few other dudes around the same age. Will, Bill, and Jeff each paid thirty dollars for a third of the room. The attic had exactly enough space for three parallel sleeping bags and a turntable. The house was an A-frame, so in the attic, you could only really stand up straight in the middle of the room. You could barely kneel along the sides.

They also had to contend with the group house reliquary of possessions previous tenants had abandoned. When people moved out, they left some portion of their stuff behind the attic knee walls. This space was littered with boxes, most of which contained your standard attic fare: old clothes, books, tchotchkes of ambiguous origin. Toward the back of the space, though, there were also dozens and maybe hundreds of old soda and beer bottles, and they weren't empty. They didn't have beer or soda in them, either.

BILL DOSS: We mentioned that to one of the roommates, and they were like, "Oh, don't even go near that." Some dude used to live there, and he would stay upstairs for weeks at a time and not come down for anything.

WILL CULLEN HART: We opened the boxes, and it was just bottles of piss.

BILL DOSS: He was peeing in the bottles. I think that was the last time we went into that space.

Sharing such close quarters was manageable for a while, but when a couple of other rooms in the house opened up, Will and Bill relocated to a larger chamber while Jeff took a smaller one that doubled as a practice space for his solo work.

BILL DOSS: Every time you'd walk by, you could hear something coming out of there.

As a trio, they performed as Synthetic Flying Machine, most often at the Downstairs, a small venue located one story below street level in downtown Athens.

GORDON LAMB: That was the first time I had seen a band of guys that were my age playing this real kind of sixties-inspired pop music.

DAN GELLER: I remember my friend forcing me to go see Synthetic Flying Machine. My friend told me they sounded like the Beatles, and I remember thinking how weird that was. Little did I know we were all going to try to sound like the Beatles in two years. I remember thinking before we walked in that they'd be wearing bell-bottoms, and Bill very well could have been. I remember not really comprehending Synthetic Flying Machine. The choruses were awesome, but then they'd do their freakouts and I totally wasn't ready for it.

Synthetic Flying Machine didn't last very long. Jeff and Will bickered a lot, and Jeff had his own project he wanted to pursue.

BILL DOSS: He sat us down one day and said, "You know, I love what we're doing, but at the same time, I've got this other stuff I'm working on that I want to focus on, and is that cool that I do that instead?"

WILL CULLEN HART: It wasn't unexpected. He's Jeff.

BILL DOSS: He kind of does his own thing. At one point, he had a bunch of stuff he was working on and really wanted to focus on that. Well, that kind of sucks, because I enjoyed playing together. Who else is going to play drums with coat hangers? He wouldn't play with drumsticks. He was exhausted by the end of the night, especially, Moe Tucker style* with coat hangers.

JULIAN KOSTER: His arms would start hurting. He'd get really tired after, like, two songs. He would make up these patterns that were so physically hard, and then his arms would start aching and he'd have trouble keeping up the tempo.

BILL DOSS: He always had a thing where certain plastic coat hangers sound better than other ones. What he said at the time—and

* Like the Velvet Underground's drummer, Jeff usually played standing up with a modified, simplified drum kit. Rather than sticks—or coat hangers—Tucker usually opted for mallets.

I believed him—was that out of necessity he used them for a long time, and then he just kind of got used to them, and then he kind of liked it. And then drumsticks just didn't have the same feel.

Even with Jeff off to Seattle again, Will and Bill wanted to stick with what they had started. Jeff had taken only a few of their songs with him, too—most of them remained Synthetic Flying Machine material—but with Jeff himself gone, Will and Bill felt like a name change was in order. Moreover, they regretted the unintentional similarity to a James Taylor record titled *James Taylor and the Original Flying Machine*, plus they felt Synthetic Flying Machine was too obvious a drug reference (not that sobriety or subtlety was ever something they were passionate about). Jeff had a song titled "Olivia Tremor Control" and offered it up.

BILL DOSS: We were going over different things, and Will and I both really liked that name. And Will named Neutral Milk Hotel. They're just sort of non sequitur, Dada names that flow well when you say them. And since they don't mean anything, people can put their own meanings on them. So Will and I had a talk, and we decided, let's continue doing this. We combined a bunch of our songs together that we had been working on, kind of like what we continued to do after that.

WILL CULLEN HART: Just do a bunch of drum tracks or make a riff up, and maybe tomorrow you'll get something. "I feel like shit." Whatever. Just do something.

BILL DOSS: It was just us. We just wanted to make a record. And Jeff's on *California Demise*. He still lived in the house [at the time], so we'd just be like, "Hey, come play drums on this."

HENRY OWINGS: I just remember being absolutely, one hundred percent fucking *floored* by it. At the same time, the first Neutral Milk single came out, *Everything Is*. It's like this really crazy, hand-assembled collage sleeve he did. I remember going, "Oh my god." It sounded very similar to Synthetic Flying Machine, but they were doing their own thing. Synthetic Flying Machine, I always thought of as this beautiful, sharp, shocked version of Syd Barrett being done by the Minutemen. It was incredible, but they'd be like forty-second songs.

LANCE BANGS: Prior to the Elephant 6 stuff really kicking in, there was a reaction against the sort of melodic structure of R.E.M. songs.

In a similar wavelength to what was happening in Chicago or Minneapolis with the Amphetamine Reptile stuff, there were bands in Athens and Atlanta going in a heavier, kind of proto-grunge or parallel to what was happening in Seattle. Nobody prior to them being in town was drawing upon the Beatles or Beach Boys as a valid musical reference.

On a trip home to Louisiana, Bill bumped into John Fernandes, who was feeling a bit lost.

BILL DOSS: We were driving around in his car, and he was saying, "I'm out of school now. I don't know what I'm going to do." I said, "Why don't you move to Athens? We could use a bass player." He was like, "Well, I don't really play." At the time, I didn't realize he was so incredible on violin and clarinet and stuff. He said he didn't even know how to play bass. "Don't worry about it. I'll show you."

JOHN FERNANDES: In Olivia Tremor Control, Bill would write the bass lines on a lot of his songs, and on Will's songs, a lot of times I would write parts, but Bill showed me a lot of things on the bass. Eventually, I started getting my own sound.

BILL DOSS: At some point, I don't know when it was, but he whipped out the violin and just started going to town. He's been classically trained since he was like four.

JOHN FERNANDES: I had taken violin lessons from when I was seven years old up to junior high, and then I took saxophone lessons in junior high, so eventually playing with the Olivia Tremor Control, I started putting some violin and woodwinds into some of the songs we were doing, where for a section of a song I'd pick up a clarinet and do some stuff and then eventually someone else would play bass and I'd play violin or clarinet.

Will and Bill were both guitarists, so even with a bassist who was secretly virtuosic on several other instruments, the Olivia Tremor Control still needed a drummer. Earlier, they had met someone who wanted to manage the band, and he invited the band over to his studio to record. The management arrangement never worked out, and the "studio" was mostly just his roommate Kelly Noonan's recording rig. Kelly was also a drummer.

After Jeff left for Seattle, Kelly joined the band with one major caveat: she would only play in Athens. She'd do for now, but they'd have to find someone else if they ever wanted to tour.

John Fernandes followed Will and Bill to Athens when he was only nineteen years old, which meant he couldn't go out to bars. He spent most of his time working whatever jobs he could find: temp work, telemarketing, making sandwiches at a sub shop, driving U-Hauls, construction, and so on. Will and Bill were temps, too, and the three of them would alternate working for two weeks at a time at a local bookstore so that they could all make some money. John spent a lot of time working and very little time spending the money he made, instead saving up for the birth of his first child, Ravi, with his girlfriend, Lucy.

JOHN FERNANDES: For about two years, I pretty much just played music with Will, Bill, and Kelly, and worked, and hung out, and didn't really know anybody. I spent two years in solitude, pretty much.

Davey Wrathgabar: The ugly truth about independent music is that bands don't go on tour. They go on the *grand* tour, in that seventeenth-, eighteenth-, nineteenth-century aristocratic sense. Playing in an indie band and going on tour is, in some social circles, a rite of passage. It's part of one's education. It's what you do after college, if you're into music. You start a band and go on tour.

Andrew Rieger grew up in Greenwood, South Carolina, a smallish city in the western part of the state, but like many of the like-minded folks he'd eventually meet in Athens, his upbringing was a bit more urbane than that of most of the other kids in town. Andrew's parents were both teachers: his mother taught at the high school and college level, and his father, Branimir, was a professor of English literature at Lander University, where he taught a popular course called Madness in Literature that had a syllabus of books and plays featuring mental illness as a narrative device. Andrew himself lived in England for a bit as part of an exchange program through his dad's work.

Although Andrew began playing guitar in junior high and played in "a bunch of crappy punk bands" throughout high school, Greenwood didn't have much to offer in terms of a music scene. But it's located only eighty or so miles east of Athens, so in high school Andrew began visiting regularly to see bands like the Pixies play there. He enrolled at the University of Georgia and moved to Athens right after graduating high school in 1990.

LANCE BANGS: When you would see Andrew Rieger walking around town, he looked like a Nic Cage character. He didn't look like Nicolas Cage the actor in a restaurant in Hollywood. He looked like a character Nicolas Cage would play. It was a great, striking energy.

Of all the inner-circle Elephant 6ers, only Laura Carter grew up in Athens, moving to town at the age of two when her father got a job teaching at the University of Georgia. Though she lists a "vibrant, underground music scene" as a big part of her adolescence, Laura was a little too young to interact much with the B-52's or the R.E.M. crowds, only just starting to come of age as that stuff took off. But after high school, she stuck around Athens to attend UGA and started going to more shows. That's how she met Andrew Rieger, who was himself just starting to write his own songs. They started dating right away. A self-described "cocky youth," Laura volunteered to join his band, despite not having much in the way of musical chops.

LAURA CARTER: At the time, I was like, "Anybody can play bass, at least like the Ramones." So I borrowed my brother's bass and set out to play with Andrew.

Laura would learn how to play a lot of instruments over the years and boasts maybe the most diverse set of credits in the collective: trumpet, piano, drums, clarinet, accordion, ukulele, gourd, zanzithophone. Often, someone else would record an album on four-track, playing the instruments on different tracks on the same song, and then when it came time to start playing shows, that person would realize it wasn't possible to sing and play guitar and play drums and play trumpet and play keyboard all at the same time. So Laura filled in the gaps.

Born in 1969 and raised first in Nashville, Bryan Poole was around music a lot growing up. His mother worked in radio advertising and often brought little Bryan to the studio with her, where he hung around with some of the best country musicians who were alive in the early seventies. Chet Atkins babysat him for an hour or two when Bryan was two, while his mother was out to lunch.

When Bryan was eight, his father's new job moved the family to Columbus, Georgia, a decidedly less musical city. Still, his parents' record collections and a couple of cool older siblings turned him on to a lot of music. He wanted to play drums as early as seven, but like a lot of parents of overactive children, Bryan's denied his request, fearing for their eardrums.

In high school, his dad's job moved the family again, this time to Charlotte, North Carolina. Bryan hated it. His hobbies were of the nerdy sort—video games, phreaking,* computer hacking—and he didn't make many friends.†

> **NOEL MURRAY**: Bryan was the first person I knew who had the internet. He was telling me about getting on his computer and looking up articles about the Minutemen. I was dumbfounded.

> **BRYAN POOLE**: Big nerd. Totally. My glasses were held together by spiralbound notebook wire. Super thick. I'm totally blind. But I was still really into music, and there were some good record stores in Charlotte.

Though Bryan didn't make many friends in Charlotte, his interest in phreaking connected him with people around the globe through private online bulletin board systems, where those able to gain access could find a trove of methodologies and tricks from other phreakers and hackers. There, he discovered punk music, starting with the Dead Kennedys, and then learned everything he could from magazines and the one punk kid at school.

When another job promotion for his dad brought the family back to Columbus, Georgia, Bryan started taking music lessons, and he met other musicians he could play with. Despite the social development, though, he was struggling with depression. He still didn't have many friends, and he had stopped caring about school altogether, failing all of his classes. His school threatened expulsion. A teacher interpreted a poetry assignment as a suicide threat. A therapist told his parents to give him some time off from school, if he wanted it.

---

* Phreaking is a largely forgotten practice of using audio frequencies to manipulate phone lines in a variety of ways, often just placing long-distance calls without paying the toll. Apple founders Steve Wozniak and Steve Jobs were noted phreakers.

† Bryan wore a "High-Tech Redneck" cap regularly for years, which John Fernandes had given him, until he lost it on tour in Europe. "Some Swede absconded with that hat, and I'm sure they're living large with it now," Bryan says.

As it would be for many teenagers, this was fun at first, but it became a stressor of its own. That same year, though, Bryan's cousin moved to town to attend Columbus College (now Columbus State University) and encouraged Bryan to go with him. Bryan passed the GED exam and enrolled right away. When his cousin decided to transfer to the University of Georgia, he told Bryan he needed a roommate and asked him to transfer with him. So he did. He met Andrew Rieger at a Dinosaur Jr. show at the 40 Watt their freshman year.

> **ANDREW RIEGER**: Back then, you would just be walking across campus, and you'd see someone with a Sonic Youth T-shirt on, and you'd start talking to them. There weren't that many people into good music. There were still a lot of people into it, but not as many as today.

Bryan gave Andrew a ride back to his dorm, and they started playing music together. Bryan had met Rafael Batine in the dining hall, and Rafael had already decided to start a band with Andrew, so he recruited Bryan to play with them. Bryan had been going to shows just about every night since he moved to town, always in awe of the performers, even when there were more people onstage than in the audience. Actually playing in a band was a new horizon. The most popular band in town at the time was R.E.M., and as a reaction to their jangly pop rock, many bands in town moved in a heavier direction. Spawn—which Rafael, Bryan, and Andrew started with Raleigh Hatfield and Ginger Robinson—was in the same realm. As that band was reaching its natural end, Andrew moved in with bandmate Raleigh and their friend Davey Wrathgabar, who had just gotten a four-track recorder. The crew bought up more recording gear when a friend moved out west to study Buddhism, selling his earthly possessions before he left. Already revering home-recording pioneers like Lou Barlow, Robert Pollard, and Chris Knox, Bryan and Andrew started recording constantly between themselves and with other friends.

> **BRYAN POOLE**: I remember going over there and hearing "Temporary Arm" and going *holy shit*. Who fucking knew? I had never heard Andrew sing. The song was so fuckin' rippin', and it sounded fucking great. I was so in awe and so stoked he had had this breakthrough. Andrew basically recorded *Vainly Clutching at Phantom Limbs* on

his own, and then when I heard some of those songs, I was like, "I'll play in your band if you start a band."

ANDREW RIEGER: Before, I thought you had to form a band with a certain lineup and you had to go record in a proper studio, but then I realized you didn't have to do all that. You could write a song and record it playing all the instruments yourself, and it could sound like a band, or even cooler. That was a big realization.

They made cassettes and passed them around to whoever wanted to listen, calling themselves Elf Power, though Andrew no longer knows why.

ANDREW RIEGER: I remember it was written in the concrete downtown. Someone had scrawled it in the concrete, but when I went back to look for it, I couldn't find it again, so I'm not sure if that was true.

The first version of the live band featured Raleigh and Davey, but the first iteration of Elf Power to tour was a two-piece with Andrew and Laura, who had played drums and other instruments on the *Vainly Clutching* album. They dated for three years and remained friends after breaking up and continued playing together. The band has been active for nearly three decades now, with Laura and Andrew serving as the only constant members.

LAURA CARTER: I started playing on *Vainly Clutching at Phantom Limbs* not because we had the grandiose idea that we were a band, but because Andrew was four-tracking it and I thought it sounded rad. I just wanted to hang out at this crappy apartment. Because he made the album, we had to become a band to perform it live. We just recorded and played little shows. Some of the bars downtown, but mostly house parties and little weekend tours. We made our first record because we found someone who had a vinyl lathe and no minimum. So we just pressed fifty, thinking that was a good amount.

WILL CULLEN HART: I met those guys when they were in Spawn. I was walking past on my way to another place and I heard them playing "Lucifer Sam." Then they gave me the record they had made, which some guy in Texas had made for them. Some of [the records] wouldn't even play. But Andrew was one of the only guys around here doing four-track stuff like I was doing.

LAURA CARTER: I never had the luxury of "I'm going to learn piano." It was "We could pull this off if you can learn these two bass line parts." If you practice enough, you can memorize any line on most any instrument, which is how I learned to play so many instruments. The only reason I ever learned how to play trumpet or even sing was because Scott was like, "You're going to have to learn the horn part because I'll be in the middle of singing."

Elf Power continued to play around Athens and developed a modest following. As their prominence grew, Laura and Andrew figured the next logical step for the band was to move to New York. They crashed with Laura's brother in Brooklyn but realized within a year that Athens was a better fit for what they were trying to do, mostly because Athens was cheaper and they didn't have to spend so much time working on things that weren't music. Back in Athens, they began working on a record together as a three-piece—Bryan had rejoined the band, primarily on bass—but Laura's self-taught drumming style wasn't satisfying any of them, least of all Laura. Her technique also left her thighs with massive purple welts. She volunteered to switch to keyboard and other instruments, and Aaron Wegelin joined the band as its new drummer.

BRYAN POOLE: And then we recorded *When the Red King Comes* pretty soon after we got Aaron. We had this momentum. It was around that time that all the Ruston kids started coming to Athens.

Derek Almstead is a jack of all bands and master of none, but if a band has anything to do with Elephant 6, Derek has probably appeared onstage with it or in the liner notes of one of its records. Talk to folks in any of those bands—or anyone who was paying attention to the scene, even as an outsider—and they'll tell you the same thing: the dude can play.

DAN GELLER: He was a genius. He was the best at what he did. He was the best bass player. Still to this day. I've heard he's probably the best guitar player, too. He's just the best musician of the group. You really wanted him to play on your record, because you knew he was going to come up with a really cool part, play it flawlessly.

ROBERT SCHNEIDER: He was the rising star producer. He still is, but he was a rising star producer in our collective because of his work with Of Montreal, as an engineer. Everybody was like, "Holy shit, Derek can do everything." He can play all the instruments, and he's also a producer and engineer.

Derek spent his early years in Oklahoma and started playing piano at four years old. When he was twelve, his family moved to Manassas, Virginia, and he got into guitar within a year or two. He never found much interest in most academic subjects, but music took hold. He had a guitar in his hand for ten to twelve hours a day, from the minute he got home from school until he went to bed. At school, he spent as much time as he could in the band room, learning drums and xylophone. When he wasn't actually playing an instrument, he was studying theory or fingering a fretboard to develop his technique. His skill endeared him to bands of many genres.

DEREK ALMSTEAD: I played in this progressive metal band that I wrote all the music for. I played in a blues and classic rock band, playing Hendrix and the Stones and stuff like that, with a bunch of my stoner art-class friends. Then I played bass in a cheesy pop/funk band. I played bass in this all-Black R&B band. We'd be the guest band at a church and play some gospel songs, and then on a Saturday night we'd go to a party and play the classic hits of the day like Tony! Toni! Toné! There was this other white kid who played sax. I was in some pop bands with some good friends from high school. Those were the people I formed my musical language with.

Northern Virginia proved to be a bummer, though, and he was too far from DC to take advantage of what the city had to offer, which at the time was mostly just the waning vestiges of a once-thriving hardcore scene.* With musical ambitions bigger than their exurban surroundings could satisfy, Derek and his friend Zack Larkin moved down to Athens. Zack had visited earlier to scope things out, and when the place he lined up had space for an extra tenant,† he invited Derek to come along.

* Derek hadn't even heard of Fugazi until after he graduated high school.

† It was $125 a month for a large corner of the basement.

DEREK ALMSTEAD: We were of college age, but we weren't going to school. We really wanted to do music and party. I was twenty. April of '95. I moved down here and within a year felt this was the place for me. Within a year, I met Andrew and Bryan Poole and all those kinds of people.

Kevin Barnes was born in Ohio, just outside of Cleveland. They're still a Browns fan today.* When they were eleven, their dad got a new job in Detroit and moved the family to the suburbs out there. That's when Kevin got into music.

Kevin didn't make friends easily, and as the new kid in town, they spent a lot of time alone. Their parents bought them a drum kit when they were thirteen, but after hearing what it sounds like when a thirteen-year-old practices drumming, Kevin's parents encouraged them to play guitar instead and let them practice in the basement. As they developed their skills, Kevin would invite some friends over to jam together in the basement. Kevin and their friend Mark Tremonti even started a band, with Mark playing guitar and Kevin singing. Both were really into hair metal: Ratt, Poison, Mötley Crüe, and similar bands were a heavy influence on the teenage Barnes.

Kevin's dad moved the family again for a new job, this time to the West Palm Beach area of Florida. Kevin didn't make friends too quickly in Florida, either, but Mark's family moved to Orlando around the same time. It was about three hours away, so their parents would often meet in the middle to drop one off to spend the weekend with the other, meeting in the middle again a few days later. After a few times doing that, though, the trips became tiresome to Kevin's parents. After losing contact with Mark,† Kevin had trouble finding like-minded musicians to perform with, so rather than playing music they didn't like, they set out to build songs

* In June 2020, Kevin Barnes announced they are nonbinary and genderqueer (and, a couple of months later, that they are bisexual). Kevin uses he/him, she/her, and they/them pronouns, and so in the interest of visibility and inclusivity, I use they/them to refer to Kevin in this book. Several people, interviewed before this announcement, referred to Kevin with he/him pronouns during interviews, and some of those quotes have been revised for the same reason, with permission from the speakers.

† A few years later, Mark and his friend Scott Stapp, classmates at Florida State, started a rock band called Creed, which has sold millions of albums and gone on to become both one of the most commercially successful bands of all time while also being one of the most reviled.

by themself. In their bedroom with their four-track, they pieced the music together one instrument at a time, learning how to arrange songs as they went. But when they tried to share the music with others, that proved to be a mostly solipsistic endeavor, too.

> **KEVIN BARNES**: I'd make these cassette compilations for my brother and some of our friends, and that was about it. I played a handful of acoustic shows locally, but nobody really cared. My ten friends would come to the show, but it never turned into anything.

The few people who heard the songs seemed to like them, so Kevin put together a demo and sent it to Bar/None. Bar/None told Kevin they wanted to put out a record, but Kevin didn't know how to do that, or even what it meant. They were still a teenager, just out of high school, living at home with their parents in South Florida. They didn't know anybody even interested in a music career, so Bar/None put them in touch with another quirky Florida-reared four-tracker on their label: Julian Koster. The two of them hit it off immediately.

> **KEVIN BARNES**: He was the one that sort of encouraged me to stay on that DIY home-recording path, keeping it very intimate. He always gave me great encouragement, especially early on.
>
> **GLENN MORROW**: We recognized they were a kindred spirit to Julian. They both had something whimsical in their rock, and this sense of creating an alternate universe.

Julian also suggested that the wayward Kevin move to Athens, where they'd be around people more closely aligned to their musical tastes and worldview. He even offered them a room in his house on Sunset Street, and Kevin moved in right around the same time as Will, Bill, and Jeff.

> **KEVIN BARNES**: It was sort of transient. Nobody's name was on the lease. For a long time, we didn't have a lot of the utilities. We had running water, but we didn't have gas, and so we didn't have any heat. We could do all sorts of crazy things, because as long as we paid the rent, the landlord would never come. I think I lived there maybe six months.

Kevin then spent a few years bouncing around the country, living in Minneapolis and Seattle and occasionally their parents' house to save some money. After moving back to Athens in 1996, they met Derek at a house show, impressed by Derek's skill when he jumped onstage to play drums on a Minor Threat cover. Kevin asked Derek if he was interested in joining the band they were trying to start. Derek had moved to town with his friend to start a band of their own, but they were having trouble focusing, so Derek started playing drums with Kevin.

> **KEVIN BARNES:** All the time, I was looking for someone who played drums like Ringo, but everyone played too hard and hit the cymbals way too much and did all these cheesy fills. I wanted to find someone who played like a sixties drummer. So I met Derek and thought he could be that, but I also realized what an amazing musician he was. I gave him a copy of my demos, and he learned how to play the songs on bass really quickly. A lot of the people I tried to get in the band, I would send them the songs and they wouldn't be able to figure them out, even if they weren't super complicated. Derek was able to figure out all the songs within an hour. I was like, *Holy crap, this guy is an amazing musician.*

Kevin tried to recruit Andrew to play with them—Kevin had been playing with Elf Power, opening for the Olivias and Neutral Milk Hotel—but Andrew didn't know the names of any guitar chords, so Kevin brought Bryan into the band instead. In Elf Power, Bryan struggled with harmonies due to the unique timbre of Andrew's voice. Bryan's voice was a better match for Kevin's. They were singing Everly Brothers covers together barely an hour into hanging out for the first time.

The original Of Montreal lineup had Kevin and Bryan on guitars, Derek on drums, and Joel Evans on bass. They lined up a gig opening for Elf Power (with whom Bryan was also playing) at the 40 Watt in December 1996 and practiced daily for a month to get ready for it. But a week before the gig, Joel no-showed. He didn't show up the next day or the day after that. Four days before the show, they gave up on Joel, and Bryan moved to bass, spending the remaining time learning the bass lines. He played from crib notes he'd written for himself.

DEREK ALMSTEAD: To me, that was by far the best time for that band, when we were a three-piece. It was the only incarnation where I actually liked the songs and I liked playing them and I felt connected to it. It very quickly after that became a musical exercise. "Let's make a psychedelic song." "This one will be kind of Kinks-y." It's fun to do, but the actual connection faded very fast. Kevin's a songwriting craftsman, so contrivance is the whole purpose. But there was a time when they were writing these emotional tunes. There were times when it was a little too personal or emo for me, but I still felt the power of the music.

Kevin had a deal with Bar/None to make the first record, and the new band brought in Jeff and Julian, ostensibly as engineers, to lend more credibility to the project. The label gave Of Montreal some money to buy new recording gear.

KEVIN BARNES: Julian was actually really producing, setting up mics and teaching me different ways to do things. At that point, I had actually moved in with Derek and Bryan. Eventually it got to the point where we realized we didn't need Julian there for every song, so I think maybe two or three songs were engineered or produced by Julian, and the rest were self-engineered.

BRYAN POOLE: After maybe two or three sessions, [Kevin and Derek] kind of figured out they could do it without Julian. But Julian was a big influence on Kevin. Kevin really looked up to Julian and really admired the way he saw art and characters and music.

Growing up in Cleveland, Heather McIntosh began listening to R.E.M. when she was in middle school, and from there, she quickly fell in love with Athens. Whenever her family would drive down to Orlando to visit her grandparents, she'd insist they stop in Athens, and she found a way to visit on each of her spring and summer breaks. While Heather was a freshman in high school, a music professor from the University of Georgia reached out and encouraged her to aim her cello studies at their music program, and from then on she was singularly focused on going to school there. When she finished high school in 1993 and finally moved to Athens, though, it wasn't exactly what she expected it to be.

HEATHER MCINTOSH: I didn't realize until I got into the dorms that there was football and sororities and all the other stuff that comes along with a big state school. I kind of felt like I was the only weirdo, but I immediately found other ones.

Heather knew the folks in bands like R.E.M. and Pylon had developed their aesthetic sensibilities in the UGA art school and figured her school would have a lot of crossover with the local music scene. Instead, she found that those two worlds tended to either ignore or actively resent each other. She got to Athens through academics, but the music scene is what drew her there in the first place. It was only a matter of time before she began playing with some of the other musicians around town. Laura Carter and her Dixie Blood Mustache collaborators were the first to connect with Heather.

Dan Donahue met Ben Crum when the latter moved to Atlanta, when the pair was in high school. With a mutual interest in skateboarding, they became friends and found they shared musical tastes, too, listening heavily to bands like Teenage Fanclub, the Jesus and Mary Chain, and Spacemen 3. To pass the time, they recorded music together in Dan's basement, with one of them on guitar and the other using whatever he could find for percussion.

After high school, Dan went to Athens to attend what is now the Lamar Dodd School of Art at the University of Georgia. When Ben joined him there, Dan had already befriended Jamey Huggins, who was also from Atlanta and had been coming to Athens for shows before eventually moving there himself. The trio started a band and called themselves Great Lakes. They expected their tastes to make them outcasts, but they quickly connected with the other psychedelically inclined musicians in town. Soon enough, they found themselves hanging out regularly with the Elf Power, Of Montreal, and Olivia Tremor Control crews.

BEN CRUM: Someone took whatever tiny idea I would have had and did it times fifty. It was humbling and inspiring at the same time. Those guys were maybe four or five years older than me, but it felt like they had been out of college a long time and were developing as artists and musicians.

A friend of Ben's from Atlanta played with them, as did many of the Athens Elephant 6 folks. The band usually performed as at least a four- or five-piece, sometimes swelling to as many as twelve people onstage. But the trio of Ben, Dan, and Jamey was the core. Robert Schneider offered to mix their first album.

DAN DONAHUE: We had done initial mixes and stuff, but we wanted Robert's touches. We were at his place in Denver and basically never left the house. I remember waking up to him, he was right in my face, and he was like, "Good morning. We're going to make the best record ever." He was in your face, and he'd grab you and squeeze you and hug you. Hearing his enthusiasm for it, it's kind of nice after laboring over this forever to have this mad scientist excitedly talking about each nuance and how we're going to push it and pull it.

BEN CRUM: He woke me up the first day at like seven a.m. I could hear the water in the bong bubbling next to my ear, and he'd blow smoke in my face to wake me up. And then he'd say, "Let's go make rock history." It was a really inspiring attitude. He'd wear a white lab coat whenever he was working.

ROBERT SCHNEIDER: To me, the Great Lakes' first album was the epitome of what Elephant 6 was about. In the first crew, it's too close to me to evaluate. The Great Lakes came in along with Of Montreal and some of these other bands. The Great Lakes really impressed me as these kids that were making this perfectly ambitious thing. It was really lo-fi and home recorded, it was beautifully poppy, and it was unexpected. They came into Elephant 6 from outside. They were able to be Elephant 6–y in a more conscious way than we were. It felt more perfect to me.

When he was eighteen, Julian took a road trip with a friend up the East Coast. As they were passing through Athens, they stopped at the 40 Watt to check out a show. They had never heard of the bands on the bill, but before they left the venue, the headliner had offered to let Julian and his friend crash at their house that night. The next morning, the band members (who all lived together) left for work, but they told Julian that he and his friend could stay as long as they wanted.

JULIAN KOSTER: It created an impression of this place as somewhere people feel comfortable and trust each other. It was so lush and green and so quiet.

The impression stuck with him. He was desperate to leave Florida, and touring seemed like the best way out. He passed through Athens again with Chocolate USA, and he and the rest of the band eventually moved there.

LANCE BANGS: When they showed up in Athens, they were another thing that didn't really fit the dominant music culture of the time. The childlike thing he was going for and pulling off, it's very genuine, but when you see this band show up and they're already signed to Bar/None, there were a lot of people who were suspicious or wary of like, "What's this shtick that this kid is trying to pull off?"

In Athens, Chocolate USA had put up a flyer looking for bandmates for an upcoming tour. By the time Jeff called, they had already found somebody to fill in, but Julian and Jeff realized they had a lot in common, from favorite records to long-term ambitions, and so they decided to meet up at the Downstairs, a small café and music venue in downtown Athens. Though they had only spoken on the phone before then, the rendezvous felt like a reunion.

JULIAN KOSTER: I could just feel that level of comfort and family instantly, like, "Oh, you're one of my greatest friends and we've been friends for twenty years, except it hasn't happened yet. But it's going to." You can sense it as easily at the beginning as you could at the middle or the end. It's a strange thing to say about somebody, but Jeff's way was comforting to be around. You felt, in a weird way, that Jeff could look out for you. His presence was just really comforting. It's kind of ironic, because he's always got this intense state of trying to figure things out and being uncomfortable.

Julian and Jeff—and Will, too—exchanged mixtapes of their favorite songs and shared with one another whatever they were working on themselves. It was easy for Julian to assimilate.

JULIAN KOSTER: To me, it was like meeting your brothers. I had friends, but I felt very alien always. And I felt this sense of comfort or peace or understanding with Will and Jeff that was unrivaled in my life at that point.

GLENN MORROW: I remember Julian introducing me to Jeff once. Neutral Milk Hotel was just starting to be formed. Julian said something like, "This is our commercial artist." It was a little bit tongue-in-cheek, but I think they recognized something in him. He had a voice that people connected with, as well as the songwriting.

JULIAN KOSTER: One thing about Will and Jeff, when they made music, the spirit of what they were making and the enthusiasm with which they made it was *it*. That was what I had always felt and loved. To me, it was one of the first times where I was seeing people who had it. I had seen it in my favorite bands, but the spirit that I felt or imagined or loved, I recognized it in them, and that was really exciting.

As he got to know Will and Jeff better, Julian noticed stark differences in their approaches. In particular, Will had a confidence and an enthusiasm for his ideas from inception to completion, though it always came in bursts. Jeff was a little steadier in his output, but he created in a measured, trial-and-error sort of way that often kept him from barreling through any one piece the way Will could.

JULIAN KOSTER: He would play things for you, but it was almost like a question. "What do you think?" It was like there was a question mark in the air for some reason.

Not long after that first meeting, Jeff shipped out to Denver to live with Robert for a little while. Then, after a brief stint in LA, Jeff moved up to Seattle to be closer to a girl he was seeing. He hated his time there.

Julian moved back to New York for a bit, too. While up there, he received a nervous phone call from a kid in Ruston, identifying himself as Mowgli, the music director for KLPI. John Fernandes was calling to invite Chocolate USA to headline a small festival he was putting together at their friend Squashy's farm. By the time the band was to take the stage, it had started raining, so they set up inside a garage.

JULIAN KOSTER: There was like an inch of water coming into the garage. Someone in the band was afraid to get electrocuted.

SCOTT SPILLANE: Julian is a show-must-go-on kind of guy. They put on the best show I've ever seen in my entire life. It was raining, so the crowd was standing out in the rain while they were inside. Everyone's jumping up and down.

Eric Harris had been playing drums in a band called Swales, another band signed to Bar/None. When Chocolate USA needed a drummer, Bar/None recommended Eric. Then Chocolate USA needed a bassist, so Eric brought in his friend Pete Erchick for what started as a two-week tour. They kept booking shows, though, and Pete couldn't keep playing, so they found a new bassist, who was living at the Sunset Street house in Athens, where Will and Bill were still living and Julian and Jeff had lived previously.

On the tour, Chocolate USA had a night off between dates and stopped in Athens to play a show at the house. Will and Bill wanted to play some songs, too. Bill asked Eric to sit in on drums with them.

BILL DOSS: Eric is just a wizard, or he's from another planet or something. We went upstairs so I could show him some songs, and I was like, "Okay, the first song kind of goes like this, and 'We're in the movies / Watching people duh nuh nuh'" and he's like, "Okay, next song," and I'm like, "But then there's a chord change." "Yeah, yeah, yeah, I'm sure there is. Next song." He was just so completely flippant about it, like, "Yeah, whatever, what's the next song?" "But then there's a bridge . . ." "Yeah, yeah, I'm sure." I really was worried. Like, this guy sucks. He obviously doesn't care. We shouldn't have even asked him to do it. But then we started playing, and oh my god, if he didn't fucking lead every song and lead us into changes and stuff. He was just that good. He knew the vibe of the song, and that's all he needed to know. He heard the songs that night, upstairs, just me going through some chords. I remember looking at Will at one point in the set like, "Something is happening." I knew from that moment.

Bill considers this to be the first real Olivia Tremor Control show, though they had used the name before. Eric would eventually join the Olivia Tremor Control as its full-time drummer.

While back in Athens, the fill-in bassist decided he was done with Chocolate USA, but he agreed to play a few more shows. The next night, they played in Chapel Hill, more than three hundred miles away. Bill, Will, and Will's girlfriend, Lara Hetzler, drove up to see the show.

JULIAN KOSTER: I just remember being so moved. They drove five hours to see us, and then drove home. I remember feeling like, *This group of friends is extraordinary*. It really felt like, *Oh my god, this is special.*

BILL DOSS: We just loved them to death. Their music was great, and they were great people. We just loved hanging out with them. Everything just sort of clicked. You know when you meet someone and you feel like "I've known you forever"? It's that sort of thing.

Chocolate USA played in Atlanta as a trio after that—Julian says this tour was arranged by a "booking agent, but a fledgling booking agent"—and then on the way to a show in Florida, the band passed through Athens to drop off the departing bassist. That day, Julian dropped by the DialAmerica call center where Bill was working a telemarketing job. Julian knocked on the window and motioned for Bill to come outside for a minute. He asked Bill if he wanted to play bass for Chocolate USA for the remaining three weeks of their tour. The next show was in Pensacola, that night. Bill left the call center and got on the road that afternoon.

BILL DOSS: It was the very first time I was ever joining a band and going on the road. Before that, it had all just been talk about wanting to do stuff. So I learned the songs that day, in the van on the way to the first show. It was nerve-racking as hell.

ROBERT SCHNEIDER: Julian was more Elephant 6 than the rest of us. Whatever ideals we had written into our manifesto, he was that squared. It multiplied the collective. Part of Julian's talent is that he is this wandering, traveling organizer. He meets people, they love him, and he wraps them into his dream and pulls them in. Both Olivia Tremor Control and Neutral Milk Hotel as they came to be, they were literally formed by him, or they came from his orbit. In that way, he's the first person that came into the collective that really changed it in that way. That added the gravity to the whole thing that made it suddenly be like, *Wow, there's a lot of people in bands here, y'all.*

JOHN HILL: We played a lot of shows where we went out and did a tour and played for a hundred people total on the whole tour, spread over twelve shows. We played a lot of shows where we didn't make any money, or very little money. In the early days, Robert's dad would rent the minivans for us. We weren't taking per diems. We weren't taking salaries. It was really bare-bones.

HILARIE SIDNEY: When we put out that seven-inch, we had so many people call us. Warner Bros. called us. It was at that crazy time after Nirvana had broken, so it was like anything could happen. Pretty much for the whole first eight years of the band, we had these crazy opportunities. We got put up at nice hotels and taken out to nice dinners and got to raid CD vaults. When *Fun Trick Noisemaker* came out, we were building momentum, but looking back, it was faster than it seemed like. It was like, "God, are we ever going to play a show not in Nebraska for more than five people? Is this even worth coming here?"

Joel Morowitz, who founded spinART Records with Jeff Price in 1991, had seen an enticing description of the Apples in then-Denverite John Porcellino's zine. He put four dollars in the mail and received the Apples' first seven-inch in return a couple of weeks later.

JOEL MOROWITZ: I dropped the needle down, and from the first five seconds, my jaw was dropping. It was raw, but it was beautifully put together. I just fell in love with it.

Joel sent them a letter to let them know spinART was interested. Robert called him a few weeks later to tell him about all the other irons he had in the fire and his general ambitions for Elephant 6. Even over the phone, Joel noticed Robert's effusive positivity.

JOEL MOROWITZ: Robert is just a complete bundle of energy. His enthusiasm is really infectious.

JEFF PRICE: Just the sweetest, nicest people when you first meet them. Robert with his hugs and Hil with her smiles. Of course, if Robert ever gets pissed off, there's a whole other side to him. He was a very strong personality despite being extremely friendly.

Joel flew out to Denver to meet Robert and Hilarie. After listening to everything else they were working on and getting a better idea of who they were and what they wanted to do, he offered to help the Apples release their first full-length. Though the Apples had received interest from other labels (including some majors), they went with spinART because of the freedom the label afforded them.

ROBERT SCHNEIDER: On any of my albums that I ever released, I contractually could have turned in a tape of me farting and said, "This is my album." They would have to put it out, and they couldn't even shelve it. That was the contracts I negotiated.

HILARIE SIDNEY: They agreed to give us full creative control and a good enough art budget to do the kinds of artwork and packaging that we wanted, and they agreed to buy us equipment so that we could begin building our own studio and continue to record on our own.

ROBERT SCHNEIDER: There were a lot of major labels that started to contact us. We were punk kids living in a shitty apartment with six people in one bedroom with a bunch of cats. We'd be getting calls from Atlantic. Geffen and Reprise and all these labels were contacting us. We had these major labels offering us full-on record deals, but we didn't want that. SpinART said they would buy us an eight-track and recording gear. That's all we wanted, to record our album.

When a label gives a band some money to make an album, the band will typically spend that money on some studio time and a producer. The Apples in Stereo had a more forward-looking approach, since they'd be recording it in their own space and Robert made producing the album his full-time job anyway. Some of the money went toward offsetting his lack of income, and with the rest, they bought gear to flesh out their studio.

For an individual album, it was a wash: the label spent about the same amount of money either way. The difference was that with the traditional approach, the band would come away with little more than the master recordings and some stories. The Apples got all that, plus a burgeoning arsenal of gear with which to record any other bands they liked, and they could pad the studio with more gear each time they made a new record of their own. The band also figured out how much time they would need to work on the record—Robert did not have time to take a job on top of playing and producing, so he took a small salary while they recorded. Hilarie worked temp jobs when she wasn't playing. They managed to keep the lights on.

> **ROBERT SCHNEIDER:** The mail-order aspect of the Elephant 6 eventually collapsed. Our bands all signed to labels and stuff. We just got busy as bands. Elephant 6 at that point really morphed into a collective. It was a label that we took seriously, but it wasn't a label we were trying to commercially make a business. The label was purely an art project. We saw ourselves as a collective. But it was a collective of like six people.

One of the first bands Robert brought into the Elephant 6 from outside his existing social circle was the Minders. Martyn Leaper had moved to Colorado with his family (his father was an electronic engineer who worked for a semiconductor company in Colorado Springs) from England when he was in high school, about ten years before he met Robert. He had gone to see the Apples at the Lion's Lair,* and as a fellow devotee to the

* The show in the middle of which Jim McIntyre quit the band.

psychedelia and power pop the Apples seemed to be worshipping, Martyn approached Robert after the show.

MARTYN LEAPER: I played him my demo,* and he played me his. What he was doing in his bedroom was much better than anything I was doing.

ROBERT SCHNEIDER: We were the modern band representing what he liked in music. At that time, there had not been another band doing that. After us, there were tons of bands. We were part of the generation that did that, but we were the first one. I'm not stating that as a fact, but I wasn't aware of anyone doing that same kind of fusion. So Martyn was right when he was blown away by us.

MARTYN LEAPER: It was so good I wanted to quit, and I did. I quit for like two years. It's not jealousy. It's despair in the sense that you're searching for ways to be as relevant, but you know that you're not. It was pretty hard to bear. But I still loved it and still listened to it, even though it made me want to quit music altogether. Robert actually talked me back into it. He was like, "My man, let me help you produce your music." I thought he was having me on.

Rebecca Cole grew up in Kentucky, moved to the Virgin Islands with her mom for high school, and graduated at sixteen with no intention of going to college. Instead, she moved out to Colorado to live with her dad, taking a job in a movie theater. A few local musicians were slinging popcorn there, too, and she bonded with them over music. She felt like she could get along with Bill Doss best, because both of them had a southern accent.

REBECCA COLE: I thought he was the coolest guy I had ever met. Here's a guy who is from the South, but he's wearing this polyester paisley vintage shirt. His hair looks cool. He knows all about music. He was the first person to tell me about the 13th Floor Elevators. He was a cool guy in a band who was nice to me. It made a really big impression.

* Martyn was playing with a band called the Henrys at the time.

The theater job provided all of them a fairly laid-back source of income, not to mention a steady supply of popcorn. Among others, Hilarie, Will, eventual Apples keys player Chris McDuffie, and Martyn all worked there, too.

Rebecca went out to see the Apples and Neutral Milk Hotel one night, arriving early enough to see Martyn's band, the Minders, open. After his set, she offered Martyn some feedback: she thought his lyrics were too whiny. He complained too much.

Despite the criticism, they started hanging out. Rebecca was a classically trained pianist but had no interest in playing the piano anymore, though she didn't have another musical direction in mind. After trying the guitar first, she found her groove behind the drum kit. The Minders set out on a few tours, some with other Elephant 6 bands, and moved to Portland, Oregon, in 1998, but Martyn and the band kept close ties with the Elephant 6 through Robert in Denver.

Another Denver band brought into the Elephant 6 fold was Dressy Bessy. John Hill had met Tammy Ealom just before the Apples' tour with the Flaming Lips in 1995. Before getting on the road, he showed her a few new chords and how to use the four-track. When he returned three weeks later, she had written ten songs. Within a year, they had formed a band, playing their first show on New Year's Eve 1996 and recording their first record a month after that.

JOHN HILL: We never actively tried to get any Elephant 6 approval, because from the beginning, it was obvious that Dressy Bessy was going to be lumped into an Apples side project. Tammy didn't want that, and I didn't want it, either. It really didn't have much of a relationship to Elephant 6. It was just Tammy's band, and I just happened to be in it. The Apples were so busy back then that Robert and Hilarie weren't really digging that I was in another band. There was a little bit of tension there for some years over it. The Apples always took priority. We would plan Dressy Bessy around the Apples entirely, and not the other way around. But we had songs in the movie *But I'm a Cheerleader*, so in the early days, we had a fairly large gay and lesbian following because of that. That's where it kind of split off, and it was only like twenty percent Apples fans at our shows, and it became pretty obvious that we were our own entity.

Denverite Andy Gonzales started his first band, the Gray Parade,* in high school. At an open mic night, he met Martyn, who introduced him to Robert. Every week, seventeen-year-old Andy would play a three-hour set (mostly covers, but some originals) at Denver's Café Euphrates, and he eventually opened for the Apples there. He got to know the rest of the Elephant 6 crew when they spent time in Denver, and he was especially taken with Julian's band, Chocolate USA.

ANDY GONZALES: Julian was living with a crew from Ruston in downtown Denver. Julian and I remained friends, and he left some recording stuff at my little house, which is what I used to do the first Marshmallow Coast record. Of course, I instantly felt Julian was a special individual with a plan and like he came from another world. For a landlocked Coloradan, a person from New York City seems very alien and cool.

Many of Andy Gonzales's friends left Denver for San Francisco over the next couple of years, which coincided with an offer from Julian to join the Music Tapes, so the now-nineteen-year-old hopped on a plane to New York. He came up with the name Marshmallow Coast for his own project on the flight over. He played bass, banjo, keyboards, and various forms of percussion for Julian's band. Eventually, he made his way down to Athens. As the youngest person in that crowd (and smoking pot "like five times a day"), he was a little shy at first, but he felt comfortable.

ANDY GONZALES: When I moved out to Athens, I'd hear people say the E6 scene was kind of snobbish, but everybody was extremely warm and welcoming and they all liked my music, and it really brought me out of my shell. All of a sudden, everything I ever wanted to happen for me was happening.

---

* The name was the inspiration for the title of Of Montreal's *The Gay Parade*.

ROSS BEACH: I never really had to dub tapes for anyone, because everyone was already dubbing everything for everybody else. This one time, though, a friend of mine asked me to dub him a bunch of Jeff's early stuff, so I made him a tape of that. I think that was the only person I ever did that for. Then about six months later, probably in 1994 or early 1995, Jeff told me he didn't want any of that old stuff to get out anymore.

Jeff got to Denver in the spring of 1994. He began playing shows as Neutral Milk Hotel, with Robert, Hilarie, and Lisa serving as his backing band. They'd open for the Apples in Stereo, which made the changeover easy: John Hill was playing guitar in the Apples, but otherwise the lineups were the same. They toured together to promote the first Neutral Milk Hotel single and *Hype City Soundtrack*, the solo album Jeff had made while in Seattle.

At a show in Boulder booked by the student radio station at the University of Colorado, the bill featured Neutral Milk Hotel, Secret Square, and the Apples in Stereo. A young Conor Oberst was in attendance. Jeff, Robert, Hilarie, and Lisa all played three sets that night, trading instruments between each one. Jeff, for example, would sing and play guitar in Neutral Milk Hotel, move behind the drum kit for the Secret Square set, and then pick up the bass for the Apples in Stereo.

ROBERT SCHNEIDER: The version of Neutral Milk Hotel that had Hilarie playing drums, she is super loud and a smashing drummer.

She's smashing drums. That version of Neutral Milk Hotel, we were a loud noise band, noisier than but similar to punk rock.

The Apples were the most established band of the collective at that time, which is to say they were established at all. As such, the people who came out were mostly there to see them headline.

LISA JANSSEN: One of the little jaunts was in the spring of '94. We went to LA and stayed there for a few days. We had two shows. It was all based on the Apples, that seven-inch. No one had ever heard of Neutral Milk Hotel yet. There were huge crowds there for the Apples. The most amazing thing was that there were tons of kids there, and they all knew those Apples songs from that seven-inch. But when we played those shows, people went crazy. Jeff could pick up a guitar and be able to sit down and play any song he heard. And he had these songs pouring out of him.

Some of the people who attended those shows had labels of their own, or they knew people who did and gushed to them about what they had seen. Directly and indirectly, people wanted to be a part of what Jeff was making.

LISA JANSSEN: There were a lot of labels chasing Jeff around. The shows were really raw and punky in a way that you wouldn't expect. There were a lot of people really interested in signing him, and he had to kind of navigate that. That he came from a small town in Louisiana made that kind of difficult for him. I don't think it ever stopped being difficult for him. Having to deal with that sort of business stuff was hard, and it was hard to watch not-ethical people try to maneuver their way around in that.

ROBERT SCHNEIDER: If you're thinking of Neutral Milk Hotel as a band, that was the founding of the band Neutral Milk Hotel, the version of the band that was around on *Avery Island*.

Both Neutral Milk Hotel and the Apples were gaining steam, and by 1996, they both had their own tours and couldn't play together regularly.

When it came time to record a new album, though, Jeff relied heavily on his Apples bandmates, especially Robert.

"I've done [four-tracking] all my life," Jeff says in a 1996 *Alternative Press* interview. "All of us have: the Apples in Stereo, Olivia Tremor Control. It wasn't something we looked at as demo material. We felt like we were making our music. We used to really enjoy tape hiss. We'd smoke pot and sit around listening to tape hiss. I just want to make sure I keep it simple so it's always a pleasure. I just want to leave people with a warm feeling."

ROBERT SCHNEIDER: *On Avery Island* was a head-trip album, and it was a meditation of me and Jeff together. We were trying to make a sound that was disconnected from all other rock music with that album. For me, I was trying to make things that were both classic and different. For Jeff, it was very important that it would be completely unique.

Jeff settled on Merge to release the record and, obviously, chose to record with Robert, who also played bass and keyboard on it. Jeff used the same guitar he'd always played, and he set up his drum kit in the faceup-bass-drum-as-floor-tom configuration he'd developed in his closet as a teenager. On earlier recording projects, Jeff almost always doubled his vocals, which could hide flaws and sound more psychedelic, but for this record, he wanted a single vocal track, for a purer sound. Jeff and Robert also brought in instruments like horns,* organ, and fuzz bass to differentiate themselves from their more straightforward indie rock contemporaries.

LISA JANSSEN: Robert and Jeff are so symbiotic, just constantly coming up with crazy ideas. They had so many inside jokes from growing up together, and they spoke their own strange language between the two of them. When someone had an idea, it was never like, "What I'm trying to get at is . . ." They just got it immediately. They could be really funny and childlike together. Something about Robert, from the very beginning, he was amazing in the studio. He just had killer instincts.

* **Robert Schneider:** The reason we thought to use horns was because we had played in California with the Eggs, who were an amazing Teen-Beat band and a huge influence on us. We thought they were the coolest band in the universe, along with Pavement.

"I was very isolated in Denver, so that record was me and my vision with Robert helping me along and embellishing," Jeff told *Exclaim!* in 1998. "So I think of *On Avery Island* as more of a collaborative effort between me and Robert."

They recorded some at Robert and Hilarie's house and some at one-time Apple Kyle Jones's house, the first floor of which had been gutted and turned into a studio.

ROBERT SCHNEIDER: Jeff and I would walk over from my apartment to Kyle's studio. I didn't have a car or anything. He would smoke cigarettes and I would smoke weed as we would walk around the block and talk. It was very soul-searching. We must have been like twenty-three or twenty-four, filled with anxiety and idealism.

HILARIE SIDNEY: I was supposed to play drums on a couple of songs on that, but I didn't get to. Jeff and I got in a really big fight in the kitchen. I screamed at him. Robert spent a lot of time on it, though, and I was really stressed about it. I was working temp jobs to help pay the bills, but Robert wasn't making very much money and he was putting a lot of time into it. In the end, he was so happy. We were all so happy. But I remember it being stressful. *Are we going to be able to make it? Are we going to get our rent paid?*

Most musicians record the drum track first and then play the other parts along to that rhythm, or they'll play along to a metronome or click track to stay in time. Jeff played the guitar and drum tracks on the album himself, and he usually recorded them out of order.

ROBERT SCHNEIDER: Since Jeff would be playing both instruments and he's a drummer, he has a really good sense of timing. He could put down a rhythm guitar track and then play drums along with it, which is almost impossible usually, but because he's a drummer, he could just play the whole song through on guitar and hear the rest of it in his head.

The essential parts of each song were the vocals, guitar, and drums. They recorded on a Fostex reel-to-reel four-track, mixing down to two stereo tracks once those parts were finished. That left them with two whole tracks with which to experiment. Robert tried organ, horn, bass, guitar, sound effects. He had Jeff record other guitar parts, or he'd bring in other musicians to try things, like some gamelan players Hilarie and Lisa knew from the record store.

> **ROBERT SCHNEIDER:** Invariably, Jeff wouldn't like it.* We would experiment wildly, day after day, to try to make the songs perfect. Every single day we would record stuff on the two extra tracks and we would come back the next day, and Jeff wouldn't like it. I would just wipe the tracks clean. Gone. With some reluctance at first, but then I started to feel okay with it and almost delight in it. The thing we recorded yesterday is gone, except for the drums and the guitar. It's cool because there were so many versions of those songs that got erased. We didn't mix them down and save them. I don't know why I didn't think of that.

"Recording *Avery Island* was a learning experience for me," Jeff told *Addicted to Noise* in 1998. "For years I'd had all this music, and not knowing what to do with it, and then having to create one album and figure out what this one album's going to sound like. . . . Some of it I don't understand, I don't know what it is, but it sounds real nice. Sometimes listening to it is almost like listening to another band."

Jeff called the record *On Avery Island*, after a place he and Robert had visited on a middle school field trip. Avery Island is located a little more than two hundred miles south of Ruston. McIlhenny Company has produced Tabasco sauce on the island since the late 1800s, and Tabasco production used to take up a big swath of the island: in addition to the factory, they used to grow all of their peppers there, too. (Today, they raise the seeds and ship them to growers in Central and South America.) It's a local landmark and a source of pride for native Louisianians.

About two hundred of the island's twenty-two hundred acres are an aviary called Bird City, which was established in the late nineteenth century by Tabasco heir Edward Avery McIlhenny as a refuge for the snowy egret. Jeff's class visited this part of the island, too.

---

* A gamelan piece did make it in, though, on a drone that closes album.

ROBERT SCHNEIDER: It's an incredible floral park that looks like you're somewhere between the Amazon rain forest and India. It's so tropical and beautiful. There's a pond there, and they have alligators. They would let you feed marshmallows to the alligators.*

The kids were let loose in the bird sanctuary for an hour. What stuck with Jeff was a Buddha statue, encased in glass and supposedly nine hundred years old. "It made a huge impression on me as a kid, and I guess there's a spiritual aspect to the record because of it," he told the *Chicago Tribune* in 1997. "The album is a story but it doesn't have a beginning, a middle or an end. It's more like a little film in my head."

ROBERT SCHNEIDER: The experience of seeing the Buddha and the tropical paradise, as little kids from Louisiana, it was so solemn and profound. At the same time, it came from one of the most innocent childhood experiences that both of us shared. It was the perfect emotional and visual overlay for the two of us. Nobody else could know that. Jeff named the album, but that was the imagery, the overlay of personal imagery that he and I both shared that gave the finishing layer of meaning to the album. It wasn't controlling the theme, but the album came out of the era that began there, on Avery Island.

CHRIS PARFITT: In 1996, I was living in Manchester, New Hampshire, and I turned on the college radio station for a college that no longer exists. I heard "Song Against Sex" by Neutral Milk Hotel. At this point, I did not know that *On Avery Island* was out. I met Jeff back in '93 when he came through town right after he recorded the *Everything Is* seven-inch, because I remember him playing that. He was very quiet. But once you hear Jeff's voice, you don't forget it. So when I heard that, I knew who that was. "Oh my god. What the fuck?"

On Avery Island sold a modest five thousand copies or so in its first year, but the tastemakers took notice. It garnered decent reviews in some major publications, and the *Village Voice* ranked it thirty-fifth in its year-end critics' poll.

* Mercifully, this practice seems to have ended.

"I had a little bed, my turntable, and some Coltrane records, so I was happy," Jeff told *Alternative Press* in 1998. In other interviews, he noted that the closet he inhabited was haunted.

"I moved into a friend's house and was living in a closet and it was cold, not only because of the weather but because it was a haunted house," he told *Ptolemaic Terrascope* in 1996. "The closet I was living in was haunted. The person that lived in the house kept having dreams of people having cocktail parties in my closet. There would always be these really beautiful women in really tacky fur coats drinking champagne and telling my friend that we should get the fuck out of their party because we were really pissing them off."

> **LISA JANSSEN**: One thing that's funny is that when you read old interviews from that time, he always says, "I lived in a closet when I was recording *On Avery Island*." That is not true. He lived in my apartment with me for at least six months of that. Not in a closet. Our relationship didn't last, and he ended up moving into an apartment. It was like eight people living in this place, and at that point, I think he did occupy a closet for a little while. But it certainly wasn't the whole time he was recording it.

Throughout the interviews Jeff participated in before he stopped speaking with anyone on the record, he talks often about dreams. He went into the most detail about it with *New York Press* in 1998, describing how he typically wakes up in a state of shock, "freaked out" that he's in his body, and how he sleepwalks and hallucinates in that state:

> I open my eyes and I see things. I've seen like spirits moving through the walls. I've seen a vortex coming through the wall. I've seen amorphous little balls of light bouncing all around in the front yard through the window. I've seen giant bugs on the floor. I was in a hotel room in Amarillo, TX, and all I remember is standing on the bed and seeing the whole wall in front of me filled with lights that were popping like popcorn out of the wall.

Meanwhile, Bill found himself losing interest in playing with Chocolate USA. He dug the music and enjoyed the company of his bandmates, but his heart just wasn't in it. He had music of his own that he wanted to pursue, but he was in New York, and Will was nearly two thousand miles away in Denver.

With his nose in a book one afternoon, Bill had a revelation. He was reading *On the Road* and got to a passage in which Jack Kerouac is trying to get from New York to Denver to see Allen Ginsberg, who was living there on Grant Street.

> **BILL DOSS:** I remember reading that and saying, "Oh my fucking god, this is crazy. *Will* is living on Grant Street, and I'm trying to figure out how I'm going to get to Denver so we can continue doing the Olivia thing." It was just one of those moments where it's like, *Something's happening that's bigger than me,* like there was a force pushing me similar to what was pushing the Beats. Sitting on the floor in the apartment, it was just one of those jaw-dropping moments. You look at another group of people, like the Surrealists or the Beats or anybody that had a "movement" or any group of like-minded people who were all friends, who were creative and were doing something, and of course you want to liken yourself to them, because you want to feel that cool about what you're doing. But you don't *really*. It's just a romanticized idea you have of another group of people. But then you read something like that, and it's *so* similar, and you're like, "We really could be doing something as cool as the Beats."

He met Will back in Athens, and then the two of them loaded a drive-away car* full of music—some reels of material they had already recorded for the album, plus a big pile of cassettes to score the drive—picking up Eric Harris in Austin on the way to Colorado. John Fernandes joined them in Denver after the rest of the band had begun working.

> **BILL DOSS:** Eric was living in Austin at the time because he had wanted to leave Jersey and go somewhere, but he didn't know where.

* If you need to move your car a long distance but don't want to drive it there yourself, you can hire someone to drive it there for you. And if you need to travel a long distance yourself for cheap, driving such a car is a pretty good option, since someone is paying you to get there. This time, someone needed a car to get from Atlanta to Fort Collins, which covered almost the entire distance.

He was working at Kinko's in Austin, and he actually printed out a bunch of the *California Demise* EP covers while he was working there, probably on the sly. He offered to do it, so we sent him the artwork for him to print out, and when he sent the covers back, he had put a little picture of himself in one of the collages.

HILARIE SIDNEY: They wanted Robert to do things that Robert's good at, like helping record vocals and drums. There was a lot of cool creative stuff going on. Will made this little shoebox, and you would pull something out and it would tell you something to do, just to do it. It was a surrealist game. Will's always really creative. He's insane, but he's always so much fun and such a positive person.

WILL CULLEN HART: For *Dusk at Cubist Castle,* I was adamant that we do a double album, present everything we can do, with ridiculous psychedelic packaging that stands out.

BILL DOSS: That says a lot about Elephant 6 right there. Trying to make something beautiful instead of just making a song. Instead of downplaying it, playing it up and trying to make it grand, especially on limited budgets.

WILL CULLEN HART: We would throw ideas around and hint at them. The continuity would add up to things. We started getting too convoluted. It's unrealized. It's supposed to be dream music for your mind.

The full name of the album, *Music from the Unrealized Film Script: Dusk at Cubist Castle,* suggests it's the score to an abandoned movie project, but despite cryptic comments to the contrary, such a script never really existed, let alone even one frame of footage. But the cinematic imagery the title conjures is a good match for the synesthetic qualities of the music, which tend to provoke all sorts of visual stimuli between its listeners' ears.

When shopping around for labels, they eschewed the normal protocol of sending out demo versions of what they wanted on the album, opting instead to share the *California Demise* and *The Giant Day* seven-inch records they had already produced. They sent packages to twenty different labels. Flydaddy was the only one that responded positively.

Will brought with him to Denver a whole bunch of four-track recordings he had compiled over the years. Synthetic Flying Machine stuff, Always Red Society stuff, Cranberry Lifecycle stuff, and so on. Many of those recordings ended up on the final version of the album *Dusk* (with some overdubs and other additions and revisions). Bill's ideas were mostly in his head, and he recorded them in Denver from scratch.

BILL DOSS: We spent several weeks actually making *Dusk*, compiling everything and getting everything together. Some of it we considered demos and we would start from scratch, and some of it had the right feel, so you just wanted to add bigger drums or a fatter bass or eighteen vocal tracks. A lot of Will's stuff came in from four-track, and we just dumped it onto eight-track. A lot of mine we recorded there from the ground up, and [Robert] blended all that stuff.

WILL CULLEN HART: Eric wrote "Frosted Ambassador" in like five minutes, while Bill was mixing "Jumping Fences" or something. With everyone around, there was this excitement. I like that energy.

ROBERT SCHNEIDER: Will is just a pure artist. He's just pure expression. If you can't catch it in one take, he's like, "Too bad. You lost it." I agree with that. If you can't capture Will in one take, you have lost it. He is the art form. But I didn't know that then, and I wasn't good enough then at setting up the sounds to capture everything in one take. In the first take, I'd still be setting the compression, and then he's like, "I'm done," and I'm like, "Will, I wasn't even recording." He's like, "Fuck you, I'm out of here, Robert." Then Bill's like, "I'll just play the part."

BILL DOSS: When you're working with Robert as a producer, it's almost like he's in the band.* As an eighth member, he's such an integral part of how things are coming together.

WILL CULLEN HART: Probably for Jeff as well. Definitely. All of us.

* Bill meant this figuratively, but Robert also contributed piano, organ, percussion, acoustic guitar, harmonies, and "Tibeten prayer bowl" to the album. Quaint as it often seems, the misspellings on Elephant 6 album covers and in liner notes are rarely intentional. The Olivia track "Hideaway" is missing an *a* on the original *Black Foliage* pressings. The first *e* and the *i* in Robert Schneider's last name are transposed in both instances where his name appears in the *On Avery Island* liner notes. The title of Elf Power's 2004 album *Walking with the Beggar Boys* is misspelled ("*Wallking*") on its cover. Nobody listens to the music of the Elephant 6 for its technical precision, and one should probably apply the same suspension of punctiliousness to its packaging.

MEANWHILE, JULIAN HAD BECOME COMPLETELY DISILLUSIONED with Chocolate USA. He loved the spirit of the band but didn't feel like they were capturing it on their records. Feeling "super freaked out and lost," Julian called Jeff from his grandmother's house for some guidance.

JULIAN KOSTER: We had this really great conversation, and he told me to stick my finger in my nose, and then he said, "Is your finger in your nose now? All right. Now say 'I believe in the brother pickers. I believe in the brother pickers.'" Which was, I guess, us.

Jeff was in a state of existential confusion as well. He had finished recording *On Avery Island* in Denver and was unsure of where to go from there. To tour, he needed to get a real band together, since the folks in Denver he had been playing with had their own projects. As the frontman in Chocolate USA, Julian had felt singed by the spotlight and saw this as an opportunity to play music without having to be the center of attention. They decided to go into it together, with Jeff as the band leader and Julian as the sidekick.

In June 1995, Jeremy Barnes's band had opened for Chocolate USA in Albuquerque, weeks after Jeremy had graduated high school.

JEREMY BARNES: I met Eric Harris and Julian out in front and helped them load in. They had an ancient, extremely heavy television that was part of the act. It broke during the first song. But the band was so amazing. Bill Doss on bass, Eric Harris on drums, Pete Erchick playing electric piano, and Andrew Hawthorne and Julian playing accordions, banjos, guitars, and saws. On top of that, the incredible violinist Liza Wakeman. They were a great live band. The songs were super weird and confusing—in a good way—and also charming. It was a ray of sunshine at a time when I really needed it.*

JULIAN KOSTER: From the first time I saw him play, I had an idea of what kind of drummer he was, this kind of crazy, bombastic, amazing drummer, with this really childish energy. It was like Bamm-Bamm from *The Flintstones.* So skinny but so strong, and he didn't know how strong he was most of the time. You'd be play fighting with him, and all of a sudden he'd pick you up and throw you five feet.

They stayed in touch, and Jeremy had recently sent Julian a letter expressing his uneasiness about the prescribed path he was on, wondering whether he should or even could drop out of school to focus on playing music. On Julian's trip out to Denver to meet up with Jeff, he made a brief stop in Chicago to see Jeremy, who had just moved there to attend DePaul University.

JEREMY BARNES: When I arrived and first walked around the campus, I thought to myself, *I need to find a band and drop out of college by the end of the year.*

They stayed up all night talking in Jeremy's dorm, and Julian continued on to Denver the next day. In Denver, Julian and Jeff played with a drummer who both thought would be fine for the band. But as they were migrating back to New York, Julian convinced Jeff to stop in Chicago to meet Jeremy, who he thought would be an even better fit.

They played *On Avery Island* for Jeremy in his dorm room to give him an idea of what he'd be in for. They found a practice space for Jeremy to audition, and he began to show them what he could do. Just two songs in, though, Jeff shut down the audition. He'd heard enough. Jeremy was

* At the same show, Julian mentioned to Jeremy that he knew a songwriter in need of a drummer. He introduced Jeremy to Kevin Barnes, the two exchanged letters, and Kevin sent Jeremy a tape of their songs, but nothing came of it.

distraught, frustrated that he had been written off so quickly. Jeff needed only two songs from Jeremy to make his decision, but it was because Jeremy had impressed him enough already. As the plan for the band came together over the next few weeks, Jeff invited Jeremy into the band.

> **JEREMY BARNES:** When he asked me to join them, it was a shock, a huge joy. I loved the way he played drums on the first record. *On Avery Island* is still my favorite Neutral Milk Hotel release. Jeff and I shared a specific philosophy about drumming, which did make me feel like I could donate something to the band. From the moment I called my family to say I was leaving college, moving to New York, I became totally devoted to that band and those songs, to that little group of people. All I wanted to do was play in Neutral Milk Hotel. I was nineteen and had been out of high school for less than a year. In the end, I left DePaul before the end of the year.

Jeremy followed Jeff and Julian to New York so they could begin practicing for the upcoming tour. On the way, Jeff made a quick detour to Austin* to visit his friend Scott Spillane, who was working the late shift at a Gumby's,† living out of his van, and playing no music but for the occasional open mic. On his way out of town, Jeff popped into Gumby's to say goodbye to Scott.

Jeff recounted their exchange to *Magnet* in 1998: "He told me, 'Man, I get this flour up my nose and I start bleeding everywhere. And I can't sing anymore.' I felt I had to rescue him. Then it dawned on me. 'You wanna come to New York with us?'"

> **SCOTT SPILLANE:** He was looking for someone else to play rhythm guitar and that sort of thing. It was two o'clock in the morning when he came by, and that's when all the drunks order pizza. I was the guy who made the pizzas, and I had about five hundred pizzas to make, so I told him, "Come back here and sauce some pizzas." I had him

* It'll help if you just don't look at a map.

† If you've never eaten Gumby's pizza, you've probably never been broke and hungry (and probably drunk and/or high) in a college town after midnight, and you're probably the better for it. Even for cheap, shitty pizza, it's really shitty (but it's really cheap).

> saucing pizzas. After the rush was finished, we were standing outside smoking a cigarette, and he said, "This job sucks." I said, "Yeah."

Jeff asked him if he might be interested in joining him in New York, and Scott put in his notice the next day.

JULIAN KOSTER: I was a little afraid of Scott, because I was really super sensitive and super fragile, and Scott has always been the kind of person who will play the devil's advocate in any conversation. He loves to get in phony screaming matches that aren't even arguments. I was always afraid that Scott would say something that would just destroy me. He felt like the kind of person who would see what you were most insecure about and just blurt that thing out, and you'd fall apart into this little pile of neuroses and insecurity, which I was always about to do anyway—and this was just my perception. It wasn't exactly right. It was off by some very important, fascinating degrees. I was scared of him, but I liked him.

ROBERT SCHNEIDER: He's like social glue to everybody. He's just so solid and kind, yet in the collective, he's the person who shoots from the hip. He's really blunt. I think that when I was younger, I would have thought of him as being acidic in his harshness, and I think that he is, but there's nobody else in the collective like that.

JAMEY HUGGINS: I can tell you the story of the first day Neutral Milk Hotel came to Athens officially. It was one of these potluck situations. Scott pulls up, and I don't know what I was expecting, but whatever you imagine, you can never be prepared for Scott Spillane. He shows up and he's this loud, crazy, slightly older dude with a beard. I thought, you know, Julian and Will and Bill were sort of stylish and cool-looking, in striped shirts and thrift-store clothes, and Scott pulls up with his shirt tucked into khaki shorts, a peace sign tattoo on his ankle, and a big-ass beard. He just busts into the party like, "Where the fuck is the fucking food? Who's got a fucking beer? Where's the fucking pot?"* Within five minutes,

* Anytime Scott's name came up in an interview, the interviewee leapt reflexively at the opportunity to do an impression. Pretty much without exception. When quoting anyone else in conversation, folks tend to speak in the generic, slightly slower, slightly deeper voice that people affect when they want to convey they're impersonating someone without actually

> he's got a plate, a joint, and a beer and was kind of like, "Who the fuck are you?" I fell in love with him instantly, but I was definitely terrified of him.

Settling in New York as a quartet, the new lineup—Jeff, Julian, Jeremy, and Scott—alchemically altered Neutral Milk Hotel's energy onstage and in the studio. Jeff had only improved as a frontman over the years, and his new bandmates each brought something unique to flesh out the band into what it became.

"None of us had ever played together, not as a band or as two people, or anyone," Jeff told *Stomp and Stammer* in 1998. "Because we had a month and a half before we were going on tour, I just thought that all of us would click really well together. For me, it's been more like a friendship through people that really love each other, even though we yell at each other all the time."

> **JULIAN KOSTER:** It was really spastic. There was a lot of intensity from every angle. We were all just shooting this intensity we had, and it all mushed up and made this weird compound or something.

The band split time in New York between Julian's apartment and his grandmother's house, but space was tight in both homes. The apartment,

---

trying to mimic them, which is typically more than enough to demonstrate they're speaking within quotation marks, which is especially helpful for phone interviews when air quotes are invisible to the interviewer and the verbalized prelude of actually saying "quote unquote" aloud is so clumsy-sounding that I can't even be bothered to transcribe it. With Scott, though—not unlike Christopher Walken, Jay Leno, most US presidents since the advent of recorded audio, and any other celebrities with conspicuously distinct speaking patterns—the mere mention of his name summons impressions from even the least mimetically inclined subjects. Scott's voice, especially when he's animated, is nasal, burly, brusque, and disarmingly aggressive, and he tends to speak much more candidly than Southern manners usually dictate. The other important thing to note here is that just about every impression of him was punctuated with a disclaimer that the impersonator actually thinks very highly of Scott. Part of this is because, though accurate, the impression casts Scott as something of a bully (in what they say as much as how they say it) when he's not nearly that mean. "Teddy bear" was by far the most frequent characterization raised in these disclaimers, and in my own interactions with Scott, he was nothing but perfectly nice. The other reason for these postscripts is that impersonations, by nature of their reductiveness, tend to imply a certain amount of derision toward the impersonated party, and in these cases, any derision was exclusively of the good-natured ribbing sort.

which Julian shared with Robbie Cucchiaro on Charles Street in Greenwich Village, had a dog and a cat but no kitchen. There was barely enough floor space for everyone to fit when sleeping, and there certainly wasn't any room to walk in that configuration. Scott, who is a carpenter by trade, estimates it was ten feet by ten feet, if that. Grandma's house, located out between Nassau and Queens, served as more of a practice space.

JEREMY BARNES: Our lives in New York City were pretty rough. I had no bed. I had no money. My experience of Manhattan was walking around the streets, often eating only a couple dollar-fifty slices of pizza a day. I hung out in parks. I knew what cafés had public restrooms. I could not find a normal job. My job was playing in Neutral Milk Hotel. It just didn't pay anything. While we were developing our sound, there was Julian saying, "Play like Moe Tucker: super simple, floor tom and snare." And on the other hand, I had Jeff and Scott saying, "Beat the crap out of the drums. Don't play the hi-hat. Smash the cymbals." That direction fit me better. I started the rehearsals playing fairly quietly. The louder I got, the happier Jeff became.

When he recruited Scott for the band, Jeff was looking for a second guitar player. Once they got to Julian's grandmother's house to start rehearsing, though, Scott revealed he could play some brass as well.

"Next thing you know he started blasting all over the place, and it sounded pretty good," Jeff told *Stomp and Stammer.*

JULIAN KOSTER: Scott's playing tone is so unique and so special. It's like a high-wire act, too, because he could just miss it entirely. Instead of Rick Benjamin,* who's kind of a pro, you had Scott, who's all passion and madness.

JEREMY BARNES: Scott had arrived as a rhythm guitarist, and in about a month, he was playing horn, and then, after practicing in the furnace closet in the basement for hours and hours each day, he came up with "The Fool." What the hell?

* Benjamin supplied the trombone on *On Avery Island.*

Jeff had handled percussion duties on *Avery Island*, but writing and playing so many other tracks on a given song compromised his ability to really let loose.

> ROBERT SCHNEIDER: When they went to the Julian, Jeremy, and Scott version of Neutral Milk Hotel, they abandoned there being a connection to rock. There was not really a rock instrument in the band anymore. There wasn't an electric guitar. There wasn't necessarily a bass. It's disconnected from the rock genre anymore. The closest thing you have to rock is that you have kind of a rock star–looking lead singer who's emoting, but the songs are really weird. Jeremy was able to pull off the energy that Jeff has as a drummer, which is very primitive. It was like having Keith Moon and Mitch Mitchell crammed into Jeff's drums, and then exploding out of them at like double time. I think it set the tone and made possible that version of Neutral Milk Hotel.

The first Neutral Milk Hotel gig with this lineup took place at Brownies, a skinny, sweltering little bar in the East Village, on April 28, 1997. Though his bandmates didn't know it at the time, Jeff had arranged the show as a sort of audition for booking agent Jim Romeo. When Romeo had asked Jeff to play the show, Jeff asked who else would be on the bill. "Richard Davies,"* Romeo told him, "and a band called the Olivia Tremor Control."

"Oh," Jeff replied flatly. "They're our best friends."

Eventually, Romeo became the de facto booking agent for much of the collective, but despite booking them for the same show himself, Romeo didn't get a chance to check out the Olivias that night.

> JIM ROMEO: I was so blown away by Neutral Milk's set that I walked out of the club and walked around for a while. It was only a couple months later that I saw Olivia for the first time, and somewhere in there the Apples got brought up, and then suddenly I was in the middle of this Elephant 6 thing, which I didn't really know much about.

* Davies is one half of Cardinal, the Olivias' Flydaddy labelmates.

That reaction—feeling compelled to leave the venue entirely after a Neutral Milk Hotel set—was not uncommon. Julian's friend Andrew Hawthorne went through the same thing at the Brownies performance.

> **JULIAN KOSTER:** Andrew had come to the show, and he left after we played, and then he showed up again half an hour later, and I was like, "Well, did you like it?" And he was just kind of like, "Oh, yeah, I just had to leave. I just saw that and I was like, *That's it. I gotta leave. I gotta take a walk. A long walk.*"

Music critic Neil Strauss* was there, too, and while he doesn't mention having to leave in his *New York Times* review, he was impressed, comparing the Neutral Milk Hotel and Olivia Tremor Control sets favorably to both *Pet Sounds* and *Sgt. Pepper's* right in the lede paragraph, and later listing Albert Ayler, Soft Machine, and Iannis Xenakis as likely influences. Strauss also highlights both bands' frequent habit of swapping instruments between and often during songs and the generally eclectic instrumentation, noting that the stage during the Olivias' set "looked like a messy bedroom studio, cluttered with wires, mixers, a four-track recorder and dozens of instruments, from a xylophone with half its keys missing to a beat-up Tibetan prayer board."

Strauss mentions Neutral Milk Hotel's instrumentation, too, characterizing the arrangements as "eccentric—sparser songs consisted of just an acoustic guitar accompanied by a musical saw, a melodica, a French horn or a banjo played with a violin bow." But as many have pointed out since, Jeff's voice pierces that wild cacophony from the first words he sings. In Strauss's estimation, "Jeff Mangum's lyrics, which he bawled as much as sang, ricocheted between surreal images, stream-of-conscious psychoanalysis and deep reflection."

* Improbably, this is the same Neil Strauss who wrote *The Game* and other seminal works in the field of Pickup Artistry and under the pseudonym Style became a prominent member of the "seduction community," awash in all the misogyny that comes with spending so much time around people—so-called pickup artists—who view women as nothing more than sexual objects and disposable trial-and-usually-error sociology experiments, which factoid this author does not have the slightest idea how to process or even contextualize, but it feels worth mentioning.

Neutral Milk Hotel's set consisted of songs from *On Avery Island*—adapted for and twisted by the new lineup—and early versions of tracks that would end up on *In the Aeroplane Over the Sea*. The foursome had been practicing for months in Julian's grandma's house at this point, but this was the first time they shared with the outside world. For Julian, he finally felt like the music he was making sounded the way he wanted it to sound.

> **JULIAN KOSTER**: We were doing what we were doing in my grandma's basement at that point, and we knew we could do that well, whatever the hell that was. So we just kind of did it.

Scott was just as positive, though a bit less romantic. He was originally brought into the picture to play guitar (and bass, sort of),* but early on, he decided he wanted to play the bugle, too. Scott had played baritone horn in high school and college, but his lips hadn't touched a brass instrument in more than a decade.

> **SCOTT SPILLANE**: The first time I tried to play it, Jeff was like, "Aw, man, no." It's a little two-valve with a tiny little mouthpiece. I was like, "Fuck this."

But every free second Scott had, he spent it in Grandma's basement, practicing on the bugle (after working out how to mute it, so as not to wake her). He was amazed by his bandmates and even more by the material, and he felt like he had to do it justice.

> **SCOTT SPILLANE**: "As long as I can do my part, there's no way this can fail." I hate to sound like that, but that's what it was. This is the best shit ever, so I've got to learn this goddamn horn part. That's what it was the whole time. I've got to learn this goddamn horn part.

* The band didn't have a bass player or even an actual bass. Just a guitar they had made "bassy as hell," in Julian's words, as much from incidental mutilation as intentional manipulation. They played it with a drumstick.

LAURA CARTER: I think for years all of us played very out of tune without knowing it. We just thought we were nailing it. Slaying every moment. Maybe we were, but I tend to guess that probably we weren't, because we didn't ever have tuners on the horns. Tune schmune. In the beginning, the crowds were tiny and you were expected to have had eight beers before you played, because that's all you were getting paid.

CHAPTER 12

ROBERT SCHNEIDER: People didn't like us in general in Denver. There's this music industry aspect to music that's repulsive to everybody in Elephant 6, which dominates the music scenes in most cities. It's an uphill climb to be a great band in an environment where there's money flying around your band as soon as you have your first practice. That ambition overshadows any possibility of seeing real art. If you're going to make art, you have to go against what's popular, at least at the beginning, to find your own way. Denver's music scene had a lot of places to play and a lot of bands but generally sucked. I think we were resented at first, because we were this really shitty band that could barely make our way through all of our songs. To do home-recording was a joke, something you did when you were fifteen.

JOHN HILL: The Flaming Lips asked us to go out in 1995. That's when people started to be like, "Oh. Maybe they are interesting." *Fun Trick Noisemaker* was out. That was really something else. We played in New York, and the guys from Jane's Addiction came to the show. Somebody took a photo with most of the Apples, a couple of the guys from Jane's Addiction, a couple of the guys from the Flaming Lips, and somehow, somebody back in Denver got ahold of it and ran it in something, and so everybody was like, "Whoa, they're hanging out with Jane's Addiction and the Flaming Lips. They must be doing something." That was the first time we ever played for real crowds. It seemed like a sea of people. It felt like we were playing stadiums.

They were playing rooms with capacities between five hundred and one thousand people. They were finding an audience, often in spite of themselves.

ROBERT SCHNEIDER: It felt like we just wanted to play for these people and then we started to do it. It was very small. A tour of like three shows over a ten-day period. It felt somewhere between kids just taking a road trip and going and playing music shows. It morphed naturally from kids who were just taking road trips in college to being that those road trips where we would play to being suddenly we're opening for the Flaming Lips. It felt like little steps every time.

HILARIE SIDNEY: When we were going on tour with the Flaming Lips, [spinART was] really worried because Robert always played this old Silvertone guitar that never stayed in tune, and this was our first big tour, so they bought us all new guitars. They wanted us to be a little more professional, or at least stay in tune.

JEFF PRICE: Robert doesn't do well with outside input into his projects, which I thought could have helped their production and songwriting. But he didn't want it.

ROBERT SCHNEIDER: I remember seeing the Flaming Lips had setlists, and I remember thinking how cheesy that was, to have a written setlist. Who told them to do that? We didn't even use tuners. To see a tuner onstage, I felt like that was a little slick.

JEFF PRICE: You would book things for them, in-stores, and they just wouldn't show up, or something would happen. The challenge when you're dealing with an extremely creative person who's new to the business side of stuff, they don't understand that we laid out a lot of money. We ran print advertisements in newspapers. You get the record store to buy extra copies of the record. The publicist is promoting it and the radio station is pushing it. If the band doesn't show up, it's a bit of a shitstorm. And that happened a lot, and it never quite registered with them.

JOEL MOROWITZ: I always wished they would take it more seriously. We talked about it. For them, they wanted to make it a career, but I think they realized, "This is who we are. This is the kind of band we are. We're not really going to change." On some level, I respected that.

JEFF PRICE: There was a press interview, and Robert was supposed to do it. And he didn't do it. These are opportunities that most bands don't get. The least you can do is show up and make the phone call, and he didn't make the phone call. "Why didn't you call him?" He was like, "I had written it down on my hand, but then I took a shower and it washed off." But that sort of shit would happen all the time.

Though they got to Athens eventually, the Neutral Milk Hotel lineup Jeff assembled to tour and record *Aeroplane* landed first in New York, in 1997, and remained there for a little while, bouncing between Julian and Robbie's place, Jeff's girlfriend's place, and Julian's grandma's house.

JULIAN KOSTER: It almost felt like we were becoming a beloved New York City band. New York is home for me, but it felt like home for the band, to me. There more so than Athens; that was the first place people were getting really, really excited about what we were doing as a group. We'd start playing shows and there'd be this palpable excitement.

ROBBIE CUCCHIARO: After they had done that tour, Giuliani had gotten into office the year before, and the rent-controlled situation, the rules were being bent a bit. We looked for another place, but everything was too expensive to live this bohemian life, not making much money. A bunch of people moved to Athens, so we decided that would be a good place to go.

JULIAN KOSTER: We really didn't play in Athens that much, because when we started, we were living at my grandma's, and then we were living at that apartment in the West Village. Then we all kind of came to Athens. The [Grady Avenue] house was so beautiful. Really high ceilings, really beautiful wood floors. It was a Victorian house, but it was crumbly and stuff. Infinitely cheaper than it was to live in New York, but it was how rich people lived.

GARY OLSON: I mostly remember Jeff playing songs and people actually stopping and listening. I was impressed with how disciplined he seemed about writing the songs. We stayed in Athens sometime in 1997 in one of the houses he was living in, and we could hear him playing songs in the next room to himself, just trying to work stuff out.

Lance Bangs: There wasn't a regular TV with cable. There was just tinfoil and art projects and dogs and great window coverings of fabrics that would change the color of everything in the room. You could walk or bike anywhere from there. Jeff would walk around town from there. It was a great place for writing. It was very conducive to spending the day with the light coming through the window and not hearing any street noise.

Dan Donahue: Some of my favorite memories of Neutral Milk Hotel weren't the shows. I remember being over at the house where Julian and Laura and Jeff all lived and Jeff would be singing. I still have these haunting thoughts. Jeff would be singing in his room, and you could hear through the walls. That's really loud. It wasn't like you were faintly hearing it. I still remember melodies and stuff that I've never heard on records. That used to always give me chills, knowing that something in that room was happening. It was a force. It always felt like it was in him and would have to get out.

Bryan Poole: We lived together in that house for about three years. I remember Jeff playing guitar and singing songs throughout the house. I had Jeff on one side, singing at the top of his lungs, belting songs that would eventually be on *In the Aeroplane Over the Sea*. At full volume. Jeff would never do anything half-assed or without full effort. When he would sing, he wouldn't sing partway. He would really belt it out. And then Julian on the other side was working on his album *1st Imaginary Symphony for Nomad*. He would record the same things over and over and over and over again. Julian's technique of layering things so much that it becomes so worn, in that it has a different quality or texture to it. He would bounce a kickball for percussion. He would stomp the floor. When I left, it was like I had to leave for my own sanity. With Jeff on one side and Julian on the other, I developed a bit of an inferiority complex.

Jeremy Barnes: When I lived at the Landfill, Will would work all night on a small piece of music, emerging from his room in the morning to get a cup of coffee and then head back in to work on something else. Robert Schneider was just relentlessly working on multiple things, and then reading physics books to relax. Jeff would sing "Ghost" over and over and over and then move on to another song. He'd be in the bathroom for hours, singing. Kevin was essentially exiled in his house, recording constantly. It was very inspiring. Bill had his home studio, and he was involved in all aspects of Olivia. I rarely saw him except when we were on tour. One Sunday, he showed up to a potluck, and we were all standing around talking about each other's music. Bill said, "Great, we're in a mutual admiration society. Can we now please get to work?"

With its new lineup in place, Neutral Milk Hotel toured aggressively, building chemistry with one another onstage and working out the material for *Aeroplane.* In July 1997, they played a few dates in California, Seattle, and Portland, with the Supreme Dicks opening for them, then spent the rest of the month traversing the Midwest and Northeast, playing twelve shows in fourteen nights opening for Merge labelmate Butterglory.

At the start, Neutral Milk Hotel was a fairly conventional band with a conventional approach to touring. For a ragtag indie band, controlled chaos is one such convention. In *Our Noise: The Story of Merge Records, the Indie Label That Got Big and Stayed Small,* Matt Suggs of Butterglory recalls their disarray.

"They had this Bad News Bears quality," Suggs says. "They never had any information or anything. 'Uh, where are we playing tomorrow night?' It's a wonder that they even made it to the gigs. Most bands who tour have a method of loading the van where everything just kind of fits. And with them, it always looked like a three-year-old had packed the fucking thing. They'd open the door and here would come a cymbal rolling out, and they'd go chasing it."

Onstage, though, the band had its collective shit together.

"I watched them on the first night of the tour, and they were fucking unbelievably amazing," Suggs says. "And I remember turning to Debby [Vander Wall] and saying, 'Fuck. You've got to be kidding me. We've got to follow this shit every night of this tour?'"

KEVIN BARNES: They were very destructive with their instruments. All their gear was really cheap and not in good shape. Amps were dying constantly. Drumheads were being jumped into. One of their shows, Jeff jumped into the drum kit on the first song, which is something most people would save for the last song. But he's so hyped up, he's got so much energy, and he's so excited.

JULIAN KOSTER: There was no bass, except for when I'd bow it or something. We didn't have a bass player per se, which is pretty weird. Scott's guitars are so bassy and fuzzy that that kind of created the bass, and then I would make up for it—you know, the Moog was really bassy, and the accordions were bassy, and we would have a bass around, but it was just that: there was a bass around for certain things. We weren't following the footsteps of anything that was presently a part of that moment in time. There's always that feeling of "Well, what are people going to make of this?"

JIM DEROGATIS: I only saw Neutral Milk Hotel once, but what struck me was that Jeff was a riveting personality. It certainly wasn't performing in a flamboyant way, but there was something about him you couldn't take your eyes off.

LANCE BANGS: There's something definitely going on with this guy that's reaching this fervor of intensity. It's almost like Jack Nicholson in *The Shining*. His eyes seem like they're rolling back in his head, and it may or may not be affected. It may be a stage move, or it may be this completely genuine sense of throwing himself and abandoning control and presence of where he is and his eyes are genuinely rolling back in his head. He's flopping side to side and strumming his guitar really intensely.

JULIAN KOSTER: The "Jesus Christ" song or whatever,* no one in those days sang about something that could be interpreted as religious or Christian. I think he tried to answer that question in the liner

* "The King of Carrot Flowers, Pts. Two & Three," the second track on *Aeroplane*, jars and in some cases drives away first-time listeners with its opening couplet of "I love you, Jesus Christ / Jesus Christ, I love you," which Jeff repeats over the minimal strumming of his guitar in a booming, obstreperous wail, sounding like unbridled spiritual mania, whether you interpret "Jesus Christ" in those lyrics as the object of the speaker's love or merely an expletive to convey the intensity of the speaker's love for whoever else is the antecedent of "you." Typically, even oblique references to anything religious will relegate a song (and with it, its creator and their entire body of work) into an artistically marginal Christian music subgenre, so to mention Jesus by name, even with ambiguous meaning, and still be taken seriously by the secular music world is very much an achievement.

notes in some way, with the "endless endless" stuff.* Jeff had really lovely experiences as a kid at a bible camp that I think stuck with him as one of the few clear positive things done in the name of something spiritual. So I always felt like the simple embodiment of faith that existed among those kids in that camp stuck with him as a really special experience. I think Jeff was always searching with this kind of really intense honesty. At the time, it was hard to interpret rationally, and I don't think I tried.

If the "Jesus Christ" song or whatever is hard to interpret, it's as much from Jeff's spirituality as from his music. Jeff's parents raised him in the Episcopal Church, but a version of it he's described as "weird" and "hippie." From age eleven to seventeen, he spent summers at a "crazy church camp" in rural central Louisiana, albeit a fairly liberal one where people would "listen to this meditative music and weep and sing about God and stuff like that." He explained the camp's vibe to *Mommy and I Are One* in 1997: "'Hey, God's groovy! Have a smoke, and like, let's listen to Cat Stevens, and get all freaked out.' But it was like a good freaked out. It was really amazing.

"Marijuana and Jesus Christ and the Minutemen were, like, my childhood. That was me growin' up."

Audiences stayed small for only so long, and as the band's relentless touring continued, people took notice. In a live review for *NME*, Victoria Segal describes Neutral Milk Hotel as a "band who can induce Freudian trauma at a hundred paces. A lumbering herd of bears, euphoniums, and Aran jumpers who probably sit on the same side of the church at weddings, they barrel through experimental brass hoedowns while singer Jeff Mangum bellows in a voice that could gut a hog."

DAN DONAHUE: Neutral Milk Hotel shows weren't a crapshoot, because they were all fucking amazing, but some would be heavier

* The liner notes for *In the Aeroplane Over the Sea* are mostly an unpunctuated, uncapitalized block of text composed of the album's lyrics, but in place of the "I love you, Jesus Christ" couplet is a brief explanation, quoted here in full and [*sic*]: "a song for an old friend and a song for a new friend and now a song for jesus christ. since this seems to confuse people i'd like to simply say that i mean what i sing although the theme of endless endless on this album is not based on any religion but more in the belief that all things contain a white light within them that i see as eternal." From there, a faithful transcription of the lyrics continues mostly unabated, including lyrics to a song that didn't even make the album.

than others, or Jeff would get really taken by what he was experiencing onstage.

BEN CRUM: One amazing Neutral Milk Hotel show, Jeff went on this long, freeform—to call it a "ramble" sounds insulting, but it was a ramble in an awesome way. He used to do this thing every now and again about the colors of the rainbow. He'd do this long stream-of-consciousness thing, like, "Yellow is the color of gold and it's the color of piss," and the band would be kind of abstractly backing him. That was pretty mind-melting. It was like listening to Moses come down from the mountaintop. You wanted to know what God had told him.

WILL CULLEN HART: Jeremy's drumming propelled the whole thing.

GRIFFIN RODRIGUEZ: Right away, they had a big audience. The shows were super energetic. Jeremy's drumming was amazing and in top shape. Parts of Jeremy's drum set would be flying all over the stage. Everybody was jumping and dancing around and pogoing and freaking out.

PHIL WALDORF: Neutral Milk Hotel were one of the best live bands on the planet. They were just a force of nature when they were up there. They'd play the songs three times as fast as the record, and Jeremy was a crazy drummer. It would just be this absolute mess. I've seen thousands of bands, and I've seen very few that are that powerful. It's tough because it's one of those things where there's a perfect mixture of raw passion and emotion from the songs and then just this force of nature of the music.

LANCE BANGS: By the time Jeff started putting on more shows at the 40 Watt in '97, I became convinced that he was the closest thing we had generationally to like Van Morrison or the best sections of John Lennon. Someone who was conscious about challenging himself and where his mind was and how his brain was working, and then also tuning into some larger, semi-spiritual or "life itself" sort of resonances with his emotional antennae, and the sort of visionary language he was able to go into, and the almost trancelike state sometimes, felt completely convincing and real.

CHRIS BILHEIMER: There were two Neutral Milk Hotel shows at the 40 Watt that I went to that I just remember starting to cry during the shows, which is very out of character for me. I don't think I've ever cried at a live show out of just emotional release from the show. That's always been a very foreign concept for me, and it happened two shows in a row. There's just something about Jeff's voice that would always just crush me emotionally. I don't know if I was even paying attention to what he was singing so much as just his voice. I've never really had that reaction before or since.

JAMEY HUGGINS: Me and Dottie [Alexander] were both crying at the show we did at Maxwell's in Hoboken. I believe it was Of Montreal and Neutral Milk Hotel. I think the very first song they did was "Up and Over,"* and Jeremy knocked over his crash cymbal and his rack tom, and Scott had knocked over an amp. Within the first twenty seconds of the show. The song was over after the first verse. They had to stop, put the amps back up. Jeff had fallen back onto the drums, amps on the floor. After they did that ramshackle shit, they chilled out, and Jeff did one of those slower ones by himself. Dottie and I just kind of looked at each other, both weeping. I can't say that's happened since.

SCOTT SPILLANE: It was a reopening of Maxwell's, and they hadn't gotten their liquor license sorted out yet. It was the oddest show because no one was drunk, and after we'd play a song, it was dead silent. It's like three hundred people crammed into this tiny room. We'd finish a song, and there'd be everyone sitting there staring at us. It was very emotionally touching, but it was so strange because it was just silence. It was amazing. There was no talking because their mouths were just open.

With the Music Tapes and Gerbils often sharing the bill, most of the Neutral Milk members were playing multiple sets each show.

SCOTT SPILLANE: At that time, I was playing in at minimum two, sometimes three bands a night. One year, we played seven months out of the year, maybe eight months, and if you counted, we were

* The original title of "The King of Carrot Flowers, Pt. Three," though people tend to refer to songs by the first name they knew. It's the same primacy bias that often makes people prefer the first version of a song they heard, even if it's a cover or otherwise lesser version of the original.

playing 480 shows a year. Because there's three a night. That's the thing I liked about the Elephant 6 the most, everybody playing. Each tour was different, but we eventually ended up settling that if you were in the bus, no matter what, you played a part. Everybody got the same cut. You might have only played two songs in the opening band, but it doesn't matter. But it never worked out that way, because everyone always played.

DAN GELLER: I remember Jeff jumping into the drum kit at the end of several shows at the 40 Watt.

JULIAN KOSTER: It always felt miraculous that no one was ever hurt, because someone ought to have been. It's a fucking miracle. I always felt like it was going to end with someone getting run through with a cymbal stand. That was specifically the thing I was waiting for. Like one of those French swords. Because there was no concept of anything when that was happening. It was very joyful. It was also because you can barely contain the excitement and the feeling of what's happening. So it's nice to be able to give some sort of physical vent to all of that at the end of the show, to feel kind of bloody and crazy.

As legendary as Neutral Milk Hotel's shows have become for the raucous energy the band (and whoever else was onstage) brought every night, Jeff's frequent solo performances have a reputation of their own. He had played in numerous punk and noise bands, so it was no surprise that he could be an electric and electrifying bandleader, but playing by himself showed a different side of him, even without so much as a stage.

JAMEY HUGGINS: Robert could pick up a guitar and start playing, and it would be awesome, and probably six or seven people would gather around him in the kitchen to listen and he would be telling a joke while he played. Will could play some crazy tape loop, and the real psychedelic geeks would be all into it and check it out, but the rest of the party would be hovering around. Same with Bill. He could sit on the front porch with an acoustic guitar and do like a Byrds cover or something, and everyone would enjoy it, but somebody would be making a drink. If you saw Jeff pick up a guitar, every fucking ass was just on the floor instantly. I've never seen anyone command so much attention so subtly. As soon as he grabbed a guitar, it was just crickets. It was like that often.

PAIGE DEARMAN: Just his voice. The story that was behind the songs. It was from his heart. It wasn't from any other place. A lot of people don't understand that about Jeff. They're like, "Why don't you put out something else?" It took so much out of him to do that because it was from a real place.

JEREMY BARNES: Once, in Norway, Jeff played a show right before having a massive emergency root canal at two in the morning. I don't think anyone in the audience was aware of the pain he was in, and it didn't affect his voice. I feel bad that we all took Jeff's super-solid, incredible consistency of vocal performance for granted. I've worked with so many great vocalists—Trish Keenan from Broadcast, Zach Condon from Beirut, Michael Gira [from Swans], J. J. Light, Heather Trost. Jeff's ability to always sing at the same high level is rare.

In Athens, Neutral Milk Hotel and the Olivia Tremor Control played a number of shows in actual clubs downtown, but they and the other bands of the scene played lots of house shows, too. The most popular house was known colloquially as the Landfill. As UGA students, Phil Waldorf and his friends had been looking for a house when Waldorf found a place.

PHIL WALDORF: I stumbled across this house that was just absolutely disgusting. But it was huge. It was way too much space for three people. And it was six hundred bucks.

It's a big house for three college kids, big even for the five who eventually lived there together, but it was a tight squeeze for the hundred or so people who would cram into it for an Olivia Tremor Control or Neutral Milk Hotel show. Bands would set up just inside the front door, under the stairs, while the audience would squeeze shoulder to shoulder, only two or three people wide at the narrowest points, back through the hallway, some hanging over the railing as they stretched up the stairs, others spilling back into the den and kitchen.

The shows had a house party atmosphere, but house parties have addresses. Shows have *venues*, which is one reason show houses always end up with names.[*] Waldorf accidentally christened this house "the Landfill" while expressing his disbelief and anxiety that a roommate's parents were coming to see it one weekend, embarrassingly messy even for a college-dude group house. The name stuck. Waldorf—who now runs the record label Dead Oceans—booked local bands as well as out-of-towners he discovered as music director at WUOG, the University of Georgia's student radio station.

PHIL WALDORF: We were probably the right-size venue for a lot of these bands and able to charge the right amount of money. If a lot of these bands came through and played the 40 Watt for five dollars, twelve people would have showed up. But because it was this wild party and it was three dollars and everybody knew all their friends would be there, it actually presented an opportunity for people to come see a show.

RYAN LEWIS: The band played with their backs to what was the front door of the house. Almost every show, some random person who was not looking for a show but was looking for food or money would just open the door and walk in and show up behind the band. I remember a lot of bands looking over their shoulders and being like, "What the fuck?"

ANDY BATTAGLIA: I remember Michael Stipe coming to at least one of those. He paid us five bucks at the door. It was more or less an official venue in the city.

PHIL WALDORF: When I was thinking about moving out, I told Will Cullen Hart about it. He had always said, "Man, if you ever leave this place, it would be great. I could have a recording space and a studio space." So I told him and his girlfriend at the time, "We're thinking about moving out," and they immediately grabbed the lease from us.[†] I remember when we moved out and cleaned it, I was like, *Man, now I want to move back in*. All of a sudden you could see the potential again.

ANDY BATTAGLIA: I don't think I've ever experienced a crowd that was so swept by one person. He came out and just started, and you

* Another reason is to avoid having to list the house's address on show flyers. This can be exclusionary to people new to the community, but it also helps to keep the cops away.

† Will still lives there today with his wife, Kelly, who now owns the house.

could feel an eyelash fall to the ground in the whole place. Everyone was sort of slack-jawed. To hear Jeff sing live is quite something.

DEREK ALMSTEAD: My first time seeing Neutral Milk Hotel was the second time they ever played the Landfill. Jeremy blew my mind. He was the blazing engine back then, blowing it out.

JIM ROMEO: About the time *Aeroplane* came out, the first tour for that record after it came out, that did pretty well. They filled the Knitting Factory in New York, which is about four hundred people. Then they went out to the West Coast and we had to add a second show in San Francisco because the first one sold so well, at the Bottom of the Hill. But they weren't selling out everywhere. In the summer, that did much better. They were able to sell out the Bowery Ballroom in New York, the Middle East Downstairs, the Black Cat in DC, which are like five-hundred-, six-hundred-person venues. So they were moving up slowly, getting to that second level of clubs. They were playing at the middle-capacity clubs. They weren't playing at the larger ones yet, but they were on their way.

Of Montreal opened for Neutral Milk Hotel on the summer leg of the 1998 tour. The third show of the run was at the Middle East, in Cambridge, Massachusetts. Of Montreal had played the smaller room upstairs there but never downstairs, which could hold a couple hundred more people. It felt like a big opportunity. But they got lost on the drive from Philadelphia to Cambridge and arrived just before ten p.m. Not only had they missed sound check, but the venue had taken their name off the bill entirely. A version of the Gerbils opened instead, since Scott and Jeremy had made it on time. Of Montreal almost had to pay to get in, but Scott convinced the person at the door to waive the twelve-dollar cover for them.

JEREMY BARNES: They showed up at the first date in Kevin's parents' conversion van, with captains' chairs and a TV in the back. They were all fresh-faced, walking around with cameras around their necks and their shirts tucked in, polishing their instruments before the show. We were just the opposite. We'd park our Econoline somewhere and get the police called on us. The accordion was thrown in the back on top of the drums. Our van was breaking down here and there. And yes, we were always late. "But, Mr. Promoter, Owner, if only you knew what we went through today to get here."

A couple of nights before, the tour opened with a sold-out show at the Black Cat in Washington, DC. About eight or nine hundred people. Of Montreal had gotten there on time, scheduled to play at nine thirty. Neutral Milk Hotel was nowhere to be found, though. They hadn't been at sound check or at dinner. The venue pushed back the start time in the hope of avoiding a long break between sets, assuming Neutral Milk Hotel would arrive at all. By ten thirty, though, Neutral Milk Hotel still wasn't there.

Of Montreal took the stage and played for about forty minutes. Still no sign of the headliner. Of Montreal played a few more songs, and then took their sweet time breaking down their gear. It was almost midnight by then. Still no Jeff, no Julian, no Scott, no Jeremy, no Laura, no call from the road. The room was full, but excitement and anticipation were giving way to anxiousness. The club could only stay open until two.

Finally, around one a.m., Neutral Milk Hotel arrived.

JAMEY HUGGINS: They nudged through the crowd, directly onto the stage with saws and drums and everything. For club promoters, for sound guys, for booking agents, and for the other bands, they were a nightmare. Do not book this band. But for the audience—and I know this wasn't calculated, but if it were, it would have been genius—they had this way of building the anticipation to such a degree that by the time they started the first song, it didn't fucking matter what they were doing up there, because you couldn't believe they were actually there. A lot of times, if you go to see a band you're into and they're in the club just hanging out at the bar, there's no mystery. But they would just explode onto the stage at the absolute last minute. You would hear stories about that everywhere. It was always something stupid. They ran out of gas or they forgot something.

JEREMY BARNES: I remember arriving in a city and checking the local free paper to see where we were playing that night. The road atlas was always ripped. Someone's foot has been rubbing on it for eight hours and it's a muddy mess. Scott is yelling, "Where do I turn? Was it back there?" Jeff is fiddling with the tape player, ignoring him.

Julian is lost in his notebook. I'm not sure why, but time didn't exist in its normal way from 1996 to 1998. Neutral Milk Hotel didn't usually rush to the club for sound checks. We never discussed load-ins or what time to leave in the morning. We were very free. If we wanted to stop in a grassy field and play baseball, we would. If a town looked cool, we would stop and go to bookstores and record shops. By eleven a.m., Julian had probably spent his per diem on sweets. Scott had spent his on iced tea and cigarettes. I would save mine and buy records.

DEREK ALMSTEAD: I loved Neutral Milk Hotel, but it always sounded like shit. The balances were always weird. I think they were a very difficult band to mix. It was visceral, but it was never this fully realized, awesome-sounding thing. Julian's stuff is always like an accordion next to the loudest drummer on earth. Or horns next to the loudest drummer on earth. That was part of the magic, that it was ramshackle and amateurish. That also translated into being very random. Some nights it would sound awesome, but most it would be kind of chaotic.

LAURA CARTER: They asked me to go on tour as their sound person. Even though I hadn't run the main board a lot, I felt like we were friends, and so I knew the music well, and I knew what they were going for. That kind of overdriven fuzz, the fat guitar. And I knew the vocals, and I knew the songs well enough to know that they juggle instruments a lot. The banjo comes in here, and now it's a clarinet, and now it's this and now it's that. Even though they didn't have any sort of budget for a sound person, I loved music and wanted to go. By the end of the tours, Jeff had taught me clarinet parts, and I had this little toy horn that was actually Julian's or Robbie's to begin with, but it broke and I bought another one. I was doing sound, and then once the sound mix was up and running, for the finale I'd run up and join them and rock out. And my parts were generally just "King of Carrot Flowers," "Ghost," and—well, that was it. The bagpipe part I played live, but for the recording, we brought in a bagpipe player. I know I made tons of notes. At the beginning of the tour, I was just running sound, and it was all about how many channels could be multiuse. If you're only going to play bowed banjo, then if there's a certain order to the scheduling of things, you could reuse that channel for three other things, because you're in a club with only twelve channels. I would be the one who figured that stuff out in advance for shows. By the beginning of it, I was probably pretty bad at it and didn't know it, but a few weeks out, I was starting to send messages ahead to find out what kind of equipment the next club had and what we were working with.

A sample from one of the cheat sheets Laura would give to the sound guys at clubs:

1. **The Singing Saw**—mic needs to be hot and wet. The saw is used during quiet songs but it is a very quiet instrument and needs a lot of help.
2. **Accordion / Moog / Organ**—It is very important that this channel is prominent in the house and monitor mix it <u>must</u> be heard through the layers of guitar.
3. **We Have No Bass Guitar**—our guitars are very bassy and the "warm"er the better.
4. **Effects**—The only instrument that needs any reverb is the Singing Saw. Vocals should be free of all effects/reverb also.
5. **Trumpet**—We <u>can</u> use the vocal mic but we would prefer a seperate trumpet mic so we wont have to worry about accidentally blowing your tweeters to hell through a vocal level mic.

JULIAN KOSTER: Whenever you're on a tour, you reach the point of comfort to where you can just improvise or just completely be unconscious of what you're doing. But it took us a while, because every song, I've got to put the accordion down really fast, unplug it, plug in this, grab this, and Scott's got to do this, and there were all these switcheroos constantly in every Elephant 6 show from the beginning. Insane switcheroos and lots of instruments and things to plug in. We really wanted to keep the wave of energy moving. You didn't want to let it die by making everyone wait ten minutes for you to get ready for the next song. So you'd finish a song and you'd feel like a gymnast or something. I'm sure it came across as wildly unprofessional, but what we were achieving was pretty remarkable. Just nobody was noticing. They'd just go, "Man, that was out of tune." They wouldn't understand what it *could* have been, which was just a massive trainwreck from the beginning.

There are lots of recordings of live Neutral Milk Hotel performances available online. Many of them have ended up on YouTube, while others circulate between and within various message boards, subreddits, Facebook groups, and other internet community fora. Not one of those full-band performances has ever seen an official release, though. Eventually, recordings of some of the rarer bootlegs of both full-band and solo shows began commanding hundreds of dollars on marketplaces like eBay, including one particular performance that Jeff played by himself at a location of the Athens coffee chain Jittery Joe's that has since been converted into a bar.

In 2001, Orange Twin released *Live at Jittery Joe's* on CD and vinyl (at a much more affordable price). It's a Jeff Mangum solo show and is credited that way, eleven-ish* songs featuring just Jeff's vocals and acoustic guitar. Lance Bangs recorded the March 7, 1997, performance, as he did many at the time. Dixie Blood Mustache had put together an installation for the space, and since *In the Aeroplane Over the Sea* had not yet come out, virtually everyone in the audience—thirty-five or forty people, seated on the floor or in folding chairs—were folks Jeff knew by name. The child you can hear crying on the recording is John Fernandes's first son, Ravi.† At the time, it felt like just another show, but in hindsight it's a precious snapshot of the time just before everything blew up.

LANCE BANGS: That particular one, where maybe for the first time he was playing a lot of those songs, in different variations of lyrics and things that have kind of changed structurally before getting recorded, that was one I handed copies to Elliott Smith and Michael Stipe and Ian MacKaye and Jem Cohen, all the people I was fond of in different

* The record features twelve tracks, the first of which is an introduction, but two of the individual songs—"Jesus Christ" and "Up and Over We Go"—as listed on the record were later (that is, after the performance but before this release) combined into "The King of Carrot Flowers, Pts. Two & Three."

† Young Ravi was no stranger to the stage at that age. "One of the early times I saw them," Ryan Lewis recalls of an Olivia Tremor Control from the same time period, "Ravi was like two, I think. They had him set up onstage playing with them. He had this little section in the front of the stage where they had a bunch of toy instruments and a microphone, and he was making crazy noises into the microphone. I remember thinking, 'Wow, this is nuts.'"

parts of the country who were culturally significant to me. I'd make tapes for Laura and Julian and Jeff and most people involved. Other people who visited dubbed copies, and then it just started spreading from there. It wasn't like I was mailing tapes to people or uploading them to torrent sites. The *Jittery Joe's* tape was one where I wrote liner notes and was handing out copies to people because of how much it meant to me. And that's all pre-*Aeroplane* getting recorded. Those things got passed around and circulated, and there's plenty of others that didn't go into circulation.

JULIAN KOSTER: It was very familial. Everything felt special, so of course that felt special. It didn't feel different from all the other special things. That's just how things were. I feel like it's a little document of that time. So much of that time could have been documented that would blow people's minds if they like this stuff. It's comical. But so little was documented. There's so few shows that were filmed by anybody, so few events filmed by anybody.

ANDY BATTAGLIA: Seeing Jeff at Jittery Joe's, a lot of us were aware at the time that it was an incredibly tense experience.

JAMEY HUGGINS: I've probably seen Neutral Milk Hotel as a full-on live band thirty times, but this one stands out the most, and it was just Jeff. There was this palpable energy in the room. It was at a time where everyone had gotten to know the band. We all thought that when they came back from Denver, it was going to be this produced record, heavily orchestrated on every song. But I was shocked when I heard that the record sounded basically just like that show. It was all before anything big had happened, before anything had gotten tainted with any sense of the outside world or any sense of success or notoriety or jealousy or hang-ups about band members. It was the purest moment where everyone was in cahoots and on the same page.

A few months later, Jeff and his bandmates converged in Denver to record the follow-up to *On Avery Island*. After about a month of touring together, Neutral Milk Hotel was ready to make another record. *On Avery Island* had been a collaborative project between Jeff and Robert, but *In the Aeroplane Over the Sea* would be a full-band effort. Jeff, Jeremy, Julian, Laura, and Scott spent the summer recording in Denver, with Robert producing and playing bass and keyboard parts again. Back when Jeff still did interviews, he spoke with a number of indie publications about the new record and how it came together.

"This new album is more involved with the band that formed after *On Avery Island*," Jeff told *Exclaim!* in 1998. "There are more people, more playing live, more sharing of musical experiences with people. But, basically, I sit in the bathroom and sculpt songs in my head. Then I present them to the band and songs just converge from there. . . . I might write a 12-minute song, and that song might get broken up into different pieces. Because I'll be singing one song and then I'll be singing another song, and then realize that they fit together and get really happy. So I say, 'Okay, this is how it's supposed to be.' That song becomes that and other songs take on shapes; some get left by the wayside because different songs take on different themes. Certain themes work together. I'll struggle with these different parts and songs and take them to the band and ask them what they think works."

"Ninety-five percent of the album is either experiences that I've had or experiences that friends have had, or historical figures—it's all real stuff. I mean, I could write a song where I'm just farting images all over the place, but I don't think I'd be very satisfied with that," Jeff told the *Boston Phoenix* in 1998.

"The songs sort of come out spontaneously," Jeff told *Puncture* in 1998. "It'll take me a while to figure out what exactly is happening lyrically, what kind of story I'm telling. Then I start building little bridges—word-bridges—to make everything go from one point to the next to the next, till it reaches the end. A stream of words keeps coming out like little blobs, in some sort of order. Like with 'Two-headed Boy,' each section sort of came out at a different time, so many I've forgotten most of them by now. None of the editing happens on paper: it goes on in my little computer-storage brain."

"When I wrote [*Aeroplane*], I finally had a room of my own to work in at all hours of the day with the door shut. I'd sit there listening to shortwave radio and my records—Captain Beefheart, this French composer Pierre Henry, Bulgarian music, Hungarian gypsy music," Jeff told *Alternative Press* in 1998. "The stability let me go deeper into my head and let the subconscious take over. There's such an obsessive nature to these new songs—a few of them really freaked me out. It took my housemates to say, 'That's not too strange.'"

"Some of the songs really scared me when I first wrote them," Jeff told *Magnet* in 1998. "They were so intense I wasn't sure I even wanted them on the album until I got to Denver. I let my subconscious take over. When I moved to Athens, it was the first time in five years I'd been completely settled down. I was so used to being on people's couches and writing songs in other people's bathrooms. It was a real struggle to try to include the more beautiful aspects of life. I find being here to be a very beautiful thing, and I wanted as much beauty as possible to come across."

ROBERT SCHNEIDER: My role was that I was like Jeff's friend and coach. I was encouraging him throughout the whole thing. He was really worried about it. These are painful songs he's pulling out. What are people going to think? Is this too dark? He wanted it to be great. We all did. Our entire social scene was based around the myth of things like *Smile,* this kind of greatness that was unachieved. We believed that going at it our way, maybe we could hit it. I would wake him up every morning. He was sleeping on a mattress in one of the rooms in our house in Denver. I would go in and be like, "Jeff, my man, hey, it's time to go to the studio." He would wake up and I would say, "Hey, good morning, my friend, we're going to go make a classic album." It became a refrain for the album. He'd be like, "Are we?" At first. But then he'd be like, as it was going on, "We are." I don't mean to sound cocky about it. You can do stuff like that on accident, but you can also do it on purpose.

Before he went to Denver to record *On Avery Island,* Jeff had decided he should learn more about history, though he wasn't sure whether it would help him understand the world more clearly or less. At a used bookstore in Athens, he picked up a copy of *The Diary of a Young Girl* by Anne Frank. He spent two days reading it and three days crying.

"While I was reading the book, she was completely alive to me," Jeff told *Puncture* in 1998. "I pretty much knew what was going to happen. But that's the thing: you love people because you know their story. You have sympathy for people even when they do stupid things because you know where they're coming from, you understand where they're at in their head. So here I am as deep as you can go in someone's head, in some ways deeper than you can go with someone you know in the flesh. And then at the end, she gets disposed of like a piece of trash. I would go to bed every night and have dreams about having a time machine, having the ability to move through time and space freely, and save Anne Frank."

"The lyrical content was more important this time than messing with things sonically, even though I still felt strongly about not making a straight record," Jeff told *Alternative Press* in 1998. "About half of the record is based on [*The Diary of a Young Girl*], about realizing how horrible the world can be. You want to save someone, but there are certain restraints—like time and space. I used to have recurring dreams of time travel. There was a lot of music in my dreams. I can't help but think the dreams have something to do with my songs. This record has more to do with my subconscious than the workings of everyday life. I don't necessarily think everyday life is reality, anyway. But there's only so much you can say about that without sounding like a cheeseball."

JULIAN KOSTER: It felt like we were capturing all the experiences we had being in a band, traveling, in front of all those audiences. This was going to be the document of that. It felt special and emotional. We wanted to capture all of those moments and magic. We wanted the summation of those experiences that were really special to be present in the record. It was weird to feel responsible to something abstract that not a lot of folks would even understand. And I think Robert had his own job and his own idea of what to do and I'm sure thought we were nuts, in a good way, but at the same time trying to reel it all in.

ROBERT SCHNEIDER: My goal was to capture every aspect of the musicians, and not just the sound, but to capture more than that, to capture all of our friendship and all of our punk rock-ness of our generation and all of this chaos and all of the fun-ness and the discord. I really felt like my goal was to capture human feelings on tape. I believe you can hear those. It was really like a religious belief to me. I'm not some scientist here, even though I'm a mathematician now. I'm not like a scientific person. I'm a mystic.

"One thing that was different for this album was that we performed a lot of these songs live in front of people before we recorded them, which is really nice," Jeff told *Exclaim!* in 1998. "When I write a song, I know what

I'm saying and what I'm feeling when it arrives, but I'm not sure if other people will get the same emotional impact. So getting that feedback from an audience helps me gauge what's coming across and re-evaluate what I'm doing and saying. Because of that, the record has taken on a really different shape, which is really exciting for me. It's fun to be working with three other guys, and recording with Robert. Every song that we do, we always try to find what magic it holds for us. Try our best to convey beauty as much as we possibly can."

ROBERT SCHNEIDER: Every single day, I on purpose said, "We're going to make a classic record, and it's going to be different." It wasn't any sort of an accident. It was on purpose, but so much of it was magical that it turned out to be an accident anyway.

SCOTT SPILLANE: That was my first real recording experience. It was relaxing. We lived in the studio, practically. If not there, we slept at [Robert's] house. That's the only time I've ever done a lot of recording with someone other than someone in the band pushing the buttons. But I also have to give [Robert] credit for writing most of the horn parts. I didn't write them. At first I was like, "Why are you telling me what to play?" Oh, that sounds awesome. I didn't read music, so he couldn't write it out. He had to play it on the keyboard, and then I would learn it. We tried to do most of the stuff on that record in one take. A lot of the horn parts we played with everybody in the same room at the same time.

JULIAN KOSTER: The day we recorded "The Fool" was really special. I lobbied for us to do it live, all at once. Robert got this great sound. It sounded like a jazz record to me. It had that really great sound that jazz records have. It was just me and Scott and Jeff and Jeremy. Just the four of us. Jeff was playing guitar. Maybe he just did a *boom chk chk* along with Jeremy, or sleigh bells or something. It was a big open room, and Robert made us stand really far away from each other. I don't think I could even see Jeremy. Lots of different mics. [It felt like] Robert was really looking for control, which I realize now was partially because we were so out of control. It was really exciting, because it felt like a really wonderful compromise, because we did get to all play live, and it just had this really silky wonderful sound that was immediately exciting. And there was a hailstorm, which was just incredible. We were recording something, and suddenly there was this insane sound. The roofs were tin. We all got scared. What's happening? We went outside and there were ice cubes falling out of the sky. I had never seen anything like it previous or since. It felt like something biblical. I would have felt no different if it had been frogs or locusts.

The longest and probably most melancholy song on the record is "Oh Comely," which is almost entirely just Jeff and a guitar for eight minutes and eighteen seconds. At the very end of the track, distant and faint, you can hear someone blurt out an incredulous "Holy shit!" in the background. There's a popular story that Robert had asked Jeff to start playing just to set the levels on his recording rig, then Jeff played the song all the way through on the first try, and Robert was so blown away by the take that he couldn't keep from barking "Holy shit!" at the end of it. It's not clear how spontaneous the performance was or how much it surprised Robert, but the outburst wasn't Robert's.

SCOTT SPILLANE: It was because I finally hit the notes on the horn line. I saw it written someplace that it was someone saying it after Jeff had finished the song, but no, no. It was because I got the trumpet part. Yes, I got it! And I don't know why it was in there. They could easily tamp it out and save a lot of grief. At least I think it was me. I'm 99.9 percent sure that it was. This is a small detail or whatever, and I can't even say the horn parts are that complicated, but I didn't want to do any punches during the recordings, because the timbre of the horn changes every time I play it. Once you start, that's where it is. If it's real brassy one time and it's not the next time you play it, then you can't really fix it in the mix. So when I got that, I was like, "Yeah! I did the whole thing at once!" I was very excitable at the time.

"All the recording sound is intentional," Jeff told *Puncture* in 1998. "There's a certain way we've gotten used to things sounding, after recording on four-track for years. There are certain sounds we love to hear. All the heavy distortion stuff is intentional. When we did *On Avery Island* and this record, we did the best-sounding record we could possibly make. We used as much old-timey equipment on *Aeroplane* as we could. I have a very limited knowledge of recording, but the miracle of being able to capture sounds on magnetic tape—of electricity and these little magnetic particles—is amazing to me."

ROBERT SCHNEIDER: The image when musicians say "studios" to people who are out there in the world that are non-musicians, I think they—largely accurately—get the idea of a recording studio. But when anyone says "studio" in our scene, they mean a junky art room in a house, or a bedroom. It never means a recording studio. We're talking about a mental space, not a physical space. You're in the studio when you have the headphones on and you're with your friends. I don't remember where the rooms were, or even if we were indoors or outdoors. I remember the headphones and the friends.

SCOTT SPILLANE: Overall feelings of excitement, mixed with poverty. None of us had jobs, so we were scraping by, but we were all very excited to be working. Me and Jeremy ended up getting jobs with temp agencies. We'd do day labor type of stuff just to get a little cash in our pockets. We were pretty broke but very happy and excited to be working on a record.

JULIAN KOSTER: We were existing on an extraordinarily small amount of money. We were getting this really crazy Kung Pao tofu every day from some Chinese delivery restaurant, and the people who were sleeping at Robert's house were eating him out of house and home.

"Sometimes the other guys would send me off into the other room [while recording]," Jeff told *Ray Gun* in 1998, "and I'm sitting there eating Chinese food hearing all these little 'boops.' Then I'd come back in and they'd ask, 'Whaddaya think of this?' and I'd totally freak out. 'Yes! That's it!' . . . We trusted our instincts on this one. It was all very spontaneous."

ROBERT SCHNEIDER: It was really a magical time. Jeff's very sociable, and he had made lots of friends in different cities. He had lots of friends growing up. He had pen pals and stuff. While we were recording, there were always people coming through town who were either on tour or just on some sort of a road trip. They would come in and play on the record. It really was the kind of colorful, wild, surrealist circus that one would imagine it was, inside the studio environment. Every room, there were hippies and punks recording on four-tracks. It was to the point where you really had to walk out of the house to get a clear head, because there was no room that you could walk into where it wasn't people making noise.

Reviews for *Aeroplane* were mostly positive but not overwhelmingly so. In *Rolling Stone,* Ben Ratliff noted that "Rock's been crippled by narcissistic irony, and it needs re-greening by exactly Mangum's type: naive transcendentalists who pop out of nowheresville" but characterized the music as "scant and drab, with flat-footed rhythms and chord changes strictly out of the beginner's folk songbook." In *SPIN,* Erik Himmelsbach described it as sounding as if Jeff "concocted the whole thing alone in his car, in the middle of nowhere, his connection to the outside world limited to faraway oldies, Paul Harvey, and a bunch of old-time religion on AM radio." In *CMJ New Music Monthly,* though, it was listed in March 1998's "Best New Music" section, with Matt Ashare describing Jeff as a "visionary poet." In the *San Francisco Bay Guardian,* John Paczkowski writes that the album is "a wonderfully dense collision of disarming reverie and uproarious, symphonic pop songs," and in the *New Haven Advocate,* Josh Westlund opines, "The old idea that *amor vincit omnia* is back in vogue, and you know what? Mangum makes me buy it."

"*Aeroplane* is an attempt to make a lot of what is perceived to be negative and turn it into something positive without ignoring the ugly shit," Jeff told *Addicted to Noise* in 1998.

ROBERT SCHNEIDER: I believed it was going to be a classic record. Of course it's a classic record. It was made to be that way. It's fucking awesome. "Young people at their prime with no money, pouring their hearts, with no oversight from any business interest, into a work of pure art" is the ideal scenario for making something classic. Every time that's carried out, it's classic. If that formula is a hit, over and over and over again, that's classic. Of course it's classic. I knew it was going to be.

CHAPTER 13

THE FIRST TIME I'M INVITED TO WILL CULLEN HART'S PLACE, I'm told to look for a blue-and-white house with a porch, and what I find when I get there is just that: a half-blue, half-white A-frame, stuck in dichromatic limbo, either blue being painted white or white being painted blue, and at any rate the project seems to have been abandoned a while ago. Both colors are peeling with equivalent ardor. With no painting supplies in sight, it is unclear for how long the house has been like this. It has a porch, but then so does nearly every house in Athens.

Around back, where I've been told to enter, I find a patio strewn with firewood, a weight bench in the driveway, and an inflatable raft in a patch of bamboo—despite no fire pit, weights, or pool in sight—plus a large number of feral cats.* Inside the house, I find more clutter: Will's paintings and posters line the walls, and floors and shelves are covered with musical instruments and old cassette tapes, mechanical typewriters, wooden orange crates, children's toys, and possibly a totem pole. Plus a half-dozen more cats.† Though the house is still known as "the Landfill," today it looks more like three or four simultaneous garage sales.

Up the stairs (each of whose balusters is painted a different color), I find Will in his studio, the upstairs back room, surrounded by not just more physical stuff but a sonic maelstrom, too, a musique concrète sound collage by French avant-gardist Alain Savouret. From Will's monaural jambox, a door creaks, a man chops wood, a flock of birds dissi-

* At least fourteen of them, most of them less than two years old, though counting cats is not much different than herding them.

† At least. See supra.

pates. All the while, Will is enraptured by the sounds he hears. I would come to find out that this was a rather pedestrian listening session for him: in a feature I later discovered in the March 1999 issue of *Ray Gun*, Hart is interviewed while listening simultaneously to Karlheinz Stockhausen's electro-experimental *Hymnen* and the soundtrack to Disney's *Mary Poppins*.

"It helps you get a different perspective," Will says in the interview. "They both have thick orchestration, but Stockhausen has these barreling electronic sounds while *Poppins* has these la-de-da choruses."

With his bands Circulatory System and the Olivia Tremor Control, and even as a teenager with Cranberry Lifecycle and the Always Red Society and many other recording projects whose names have been forgotten if they were ever created in the first place, the abutment of incongruous influences is evident throughout Will's work. A soaring pop melody will bump up against an awning of bleeps and bloops, and it's as likely to be cut off by a nasal clarinet drone as by buzzing chain saws of guitar feedback.

Though I'll eventually conduct many interviews with Will, I'm not here today to speak with him on the record. He and I have met only twice before, both times briefly and in noisy bars, after one show in Pittsburgh and before another one in Philadelphia, but I resolved from those discussions that I would need to get to know him well before sitting down for any real interviews. His deep and mostly justified suspicion of and cynicism toward music journalists at large (not remotely unique to Will, of course) meant I would have to work to establish trust if I wanted him to open up to me. Moreover, multiple sclerosis coupled with a history of drug use sometimes makes conversing difficult for Will and any new interlocutor. So my mission today is mostly just to hang out so we can feel comfortable around each other. I want for both of us to let our guard down so I can ask him the important questions, so he can answer them with candor and reflection, and so I can understand what he's talking about. This is my plan of action with a lot of the folks you see in this book—namely, to spend time building trust toward and comfort around me and allowing me to dispense with any prejudices I have coming in—but it's especially paramount with Will.

Fortunately for me, Will is easy to get to. No, he has neither an email address nor a cell phone at this time, and he won't answer the house phone if he doesn't recognize the number (and even then, it's a toss-up), so most correspondence is done with his then girlfriend (now wife) and de facto manager Kelly acting as liaison. Living with MS means Will has good and bad days, so it's best not to make plans more than a day or two ahead of time, but you can generally count on him being around. Will doesn't leave the house much save for the occasional local gig and sporadic band practices. Sometimes weeks go by without him going anywhere but the gas station at the end of the block, for wine. So I end up spending as much time with Will as I do with anyone else in Athens.

It is mid-March, which in northeast Georgia means it's just barely too chilly to want to do much of anything outside. I'll meet Will at his house a few more times for off-the-record conversations before diving into interviews, whose only distinction from the other meetings is the Olympus WS-321M recording almost* every word from atop a stack of books or the ledge of an electric piano. In August 2010, I'll take up residence in the alcove of his studio for a few weeks.† For another couple of months, though, Will's dreadlocked nineteen-year-old nephew, who joins us later in the afternoon, occupies that space.

I arrive around two p.m. and find Will in his studio taking the last sip from a glass of beer, leaving the foam wraith of a dark stout around the inside and a ring of condensation on the only part of the desk not tableclothed by unlabeled CD-Rs. I doubt this is his first drink today, and he will have several more before I leave, four hours later.‡

Will has been awake for thirty-six consecutive hours when I find him, and he has the lucidity of a somniloquist. Neither of these things is uncommon for him. Going days without slumber has been a regular event for Will for as long as anyone can remember,§ and these sleepless stints are, in his opinion, often coupled with unbridled creativity, and anyway,

* Often during interviews, Will leaves the room in the middle of a sentence without even excusing himself, and it's not until he returns that I realize he's continued the conversation without me and is now five or six excursive tangents away from where we were when he left.

† And when I move back to Athens in November 2015, I'll rent the downstairs bedroom for another nine months.

‡ Will's drinking habits have become more healthful recently. In the years between being diagnosed with MS and deciding to treat himself for it, he estimates he was drinking one or two bottles of scotch per day.

§ Following these bouts of insomniac productivity, Will usually catches up by sleeping for about sixteen hours straight, waking up to watch some DVDs (music documentaries or old sketch-comedy shows, mostly), and then going back to sleep again for the night.

when Will is awake, he's either making music or has a paintbrush or pencil in his hand. But toward the end of these runs (he'll be asleep soon after my departure today), he sometimes has trouble connecting his thoughts.

Like his music, Will's paintings cull from a variety of influences: Italian Futurism, proto-Cubism, Surrealism, Dadaism.* Really, this is the pastiche worldview by which Will lives his entire life, and naturally, this includes our conversation today. It's a rawer, vaster experience than your typical tête-à-tête. Today's discussion meanders from Frank Zappa to oral sex to amateur music reviews to color field painting to the subtler differences between tape and digital recording. Only not so linearly.

Rather than trying to follow Will's stream of logic from one sentence to the next, I let the conversation wash over me and try to glean meaning from the whole, and I learn a lot about Will today. I learn that even after an all-nighter, he's got the sugar-rush fervor of a child. I learn that, in addition to the straw hat he is wearing, he has no fewer than three others, all of them identical, and while he's rarely seen these days without one on his head, it's not always the same one. I learn that he focuses much better with something going on in the background, be it a Merzbow record or a *Monty Python* box set. And I learn how best to converse with him, which is what I wanted most of all from this meeting. In most interviews, I want my subject to pour their thoughts out to me in torrents, so I can collect them in buckets like rainwater and analyze them. But with Will, it's folly to wait for the rain at all. His thoughts are cumulous, and one must be content to lie back in the grass and watch the clouds as they pass overhead. Sporadic comprehensible raindrops are a bonus, and the forms of the clouds themselves are always open to interpretation.

"Elephant 6 is a group of people that I love very much," Jeff says in the April 2006 edition of *SPIN*, "and without them I would be lost."

The second half of the nineties was perhaps the most creatively arable time period for the Elephant 6. The Olivia Tremor Control released both of its big albums, *Dusk* and *Black Foliage*, in that span, and Neutral Milk Hotel released *On Avery Island* and *In the Aeroplane Over the Sea* in the same window. The Apples in Stereo released four albums between 1995 and the end of the decade, and Elf Power and Of Montreal released three

* The very name of the Elephant 6 Recording Company is partially drawn from Will's mispronunciation of Max Ernst's *The Elephant Celebes*, remember.

apiece. At least fifteen other acts associated with the collective released full-length albums then, too. Plenty of bands kept at it after their Y2K jitters had subsided, and plenty of others started only after the ball dropped on 1/1/00, but the five-year period that preceded the turn of the millennium was about as lush as it gets.

"Everyone is recording all the time," Jeff told *Ray Gun* in 1998. "If I'm not doing something personally, somebody somewhere is doing something you can play on."

ANDY GONZALES: It was just a very thriving music scene, there were tons of bands, and everybody seemed to be on the verge of cutting a cool deal.

BRYAN POOLE: It takes a while to find people on your same wavelength. Luckily, in Athens, people came that were on the same wavelength. I think that's still why people come here. Most people are stuck in towns where you're stuck with the guy who likes Metallica playing double kick drum or something.

DAVEY WRATHGABAR: *The Red and Black*, the student newspaper, and *Flagpole* both ran articles within a week of each other on "Is the Athens music scene dead?" It was the most hilarious thing to me, because from my perspective, the Athens music scene had not been so alive ever.

ANDY BATTAGLIA: Athens didn't feel like a museum of itself. Those bands were being covered in magazines, and people were talking about Athens. It was exciting to be there.

JAMEY HUGGINS: It felt like the audience was the scene. If those local people were coming out and enthusiastic about it, you probably knew their name. Every single one of them. So it wasn't a lot of university students or frat kids. It was more artists and collaborators. The whole audience was probably doing something as interesting as what was going on onstage. They really weren't that big of audiences. Now it's gone around the bend back to the point of legend, so people all want to say, "Oh, I was there." Whether they were or weren't.

JIM MCINTYRE: One great thing about Elephant 6, and nobody planned this at all, when it originally started, if an article was written in some magazine, you'd get some magazine writing about the Apples, and they'd mention Neutral Milk Hotel or the Olivia Tremor

Control. It was really good for all the bands, because you were getting that much more press. It was a multiplier.

ANDREW RIEGER: It was just something for fans to identify that if they became a fan of one band, they could say, well, these people played on this other record. If they like Neutral Milk, they could see Julian had the Music Tapes, so they could check that out. That's the big part of why being a music fan is fun, seeing the links between bands.

STEPHEN THOMAS ERLEWINE: There can be an aspect of Elephant 6 that can be alienating to people, because it is creating its own world, if you're not part of it. In terms of being an outsider, you start to sort of unravel a ball of yarn along those lines. You use one thing as your entry point and then you discover this whole different world. With the Elephant 6 in particular, you get one of the bands to hook you in there, and then you realize all this interconnection, that there is this whole world to be discovered. That's exciting when you're discovering something.

SCOTT SPILLANE: People would just say, "Hey, do you want to play on this?" And I would. There are certainly a lot of people who can play horns better than me.

JAMEY HUGGINS: It was more exciting the more people you had onstage. Often, it wasn't organized. Sometimes it was, but a lot of times it would be random, like a gospel service. I'd just run up onstage in the middle of "Jumping Fences" and grab a tambourine. And it was cool.

DAN GELLER: None of us thought we were big enough to play the 40 Watt, so the Atomic was this great little club that held 120 people, maybe. If you had 50 people there, it felt crowded. Everything started there. It was the first time I saw the Olivias and the first time I saw Neutral Milk Hotel. We saw them there a bunch.

KEVIN BARNES: For the first time in my life, I was around all these like-minded people, and everybody was doing the same sort of thing. Everyone had a four-track and everyone was freaking out over sixties psych pop and trying to make something that sounded like *Pet Sounds* or *Sgt. Pepper's* on four-track. Which wasn't an easy task. But we were all so obsessed with that goal, trying to make something that was really interesting and in no way sounding like the stuff you hear on the radio.

HENRY OWINGS: I think when Jeff moved to town, that was a big deal, because he kind of became this creative lightning rod. Will is kind of a shut-in, and Bill is, too, but I think Jeff was always kind of a social, out-and-about-type guy, always hugging people and smiling. But I really think the catalyst was the out-of-Athens press attention. But even with Jeff coming to town, none of those guys were big or famous. They were still just playing to eighty people at Cicero's in St. Louis on a Tuesday.

To be sure, the local press was sleeping on the Elephant 6 scene in Athens. National publications, niche though they were, had begun to name-drop Elephant 6 bands in their reviews and rundowns, but Athens was asleep at the wheel. Athens, quite obviously, is not the media hub that New York or Los Angeles is. The only publication that would have been keen on the burgeoning Elephant 6 scene would have been *Flagpole*, an Athens alt weekly founded in 1987. But like all alt weeklies, its music coverage has always been capricious, confined to the whims of whoever is editing its music section at a given time. It's not hard to imagine fawning praise seeping out of the tabloid had its music editor been simpatico with psych pop in general or with the individuals who were making it. But even if those in the *Flagpole* offices weren't into the Elephant 6 sound, comrades and cohorts were popping up around the world, and it was only a matter of time before some of them would have king-making media jobs.

ANDREW RIEGER: At first, it seemed like it was more accepted out of town than it was in town. *Rolling Stone* wrote that article on Elephant 6 before *Flagpole* ever wrote an article about Elephant 6. People were somewhat oblivious. I remember the early Olivia and Neutral Milk and Elf Power shows, and it wasn't like the place was packed. The crowds out of town were better than the ones in Athens early on.

JULIAN KOSTER: The local awareness is so just "whatever's going on around town." We laughed about that. *Rolling Stone* came to Athens to write about Elephant 6 before *Flagpole* ever did. That was hilarious. But at the same time, it felt cool. It was weird in that we really felt we got someplace by some crazy, roundabout route. The fact that people liked us in all these places was crazy and fun and extraordinary. The way people in Athens became aware that people in other parts of the world really loved what we were doing and then became more curious about it was kind of weird.

GORDON LAMB: *Rolling Stone* scooped *Flagpole* on a lot of that scene. They certainly did get written about in *Flagpole* before they got written about in *Rolling Stone*, but *Flagpole* was really behind the curve. *Rolling Stone* didn't scoop them, but they might as well have. The writers at *Flagpole* didn't catch on for a long time. It wasn't ignoring it. It was not knowing about it. The writers that did know about it either didn't see it as important or they thought of it as amateurish. I think it was seen as child's play.

HENRY OWINGS: I will guaran-goddamn-tee you—I will debate them publicly—the local press, under no circumstances, was supportive of any of those bands. It was all revisionist history. I remember writing about Synthetic Flying Machine. It never ceased to amaze me how, especially at the apex, like '97, '98, '99, how the *Flagpole* was championing it. All right, *Flagpole*? *Rolling Stone* beat you to the punch. How much of an asshole do you look like when you're a local goddamn paper, and the biggest shitheel music mag on the planet beat you to a local story. You're an *idiot.*

The *Rolling Stone* feature, dated April 2, 1998, is the first piece Will Hermes wrote for the publication. By that point, the Apples and Neutral Milk Hotel had released a couple of albums apiece, and the Olivia Tremor Control had released *Dusk* and was hard at work on *Black Foliage.* Though Robert and many of his compatriots were still in Denver, Hermes went to Athens to scope things out (checking in with Robert over the phone). He had an idea of what he'd find, and what he found wasn't far off from what he and a lot of others pictured when they listened to the aforementioned records:

> The man in the bed is half-naked and dozing, curled up alongside a battered trombone. It's not clear exactly who he is. But like the other twenty-odd people who crash at, create in and otherwise float through this perpetual house party in Athens, Georgia, he fits somewhere into the complex family tree of the Elephant 6 collective—a growing network of young, psychedelic-minded bands that may represent the most compelling warp in current rock & roll.

WILL HERMES: I went to this house, which was presented as where everybody lived. It was pretty clear after I had been there for a few minutes that this was sort of set up like a funhouse performance piece for my benefit.* I could have looked at it like they were trying to send up the clueless *Rolling Stone* journalist, or just that they were trying to make this piece a performance, and I went with the latter interpretation because I thought that was cool and smart and fun. I remember Bill Doss teaching me how to play a theremin. They had a theremin that was turned on because in this particular performance piece, the theremin is never turned off, because you never know when you need to [*makes a theremin-esque squeal*] to drive a point home.

JOHN FERNANDES: A big thing for us, as we started getting more exposure, we wanted to not just keep all the exposure for ourselves. We wanted to help other bands get exposed, too. So when *Rolling Stone* called to say, "Hey, we want to take a picture for this article we're doing," we called everyone we knew from all the other bands and tried to get a big photo together and get everyone we knew in there. Any exposure we got, we wanted to help share the light with others. Let's just call a bunch of our friends and make it this big crazy movement, which it was in a way.

"Sometimes I'll be here playing music with someone," Will Cullen Hart says in the piece, "and I'll realize suddenly that I have no idea who they are. I just love that!" Hermes continues:

> It's impossible not to be touched by E6's utopian ambition, the way a group of friends have tailed one another around the country and created a collective muse as a reason to stay together. And it's sad to think that one day, like most inseparable post-college crews, the collective will probably splinter. But for now the family seems intact, and the music hasn't lost any of its hand-cobbled beauty. And Hart doesn't see any

* As it turns out, *none* of the people Hermes interviewed for the piece did live in the house. They had convened there for the exact reason Hermes suspected: a performative scheme to play up the collective's communal reputation. Bill Doss ended up moving in a few months later, but neither his habitation there nor its presence in the *Rolling Stone* piece are the dwelling's biggest claim to fame: two decades earlier, the B-52's played their very first show there.

limits to the power of collective thinking. "I'd like to get to a point where every band we like is an Elephant 6 band," he says only half-facetiously. "The more the merrier."

In the same piece, Jeff sums up the collective's ambition thus: "I try hard to make people feel things." Hermes spent the afternoon in the house and sat down for a formal interview with only Will and Bill. But he had a brief chat with Jeff in passing, and that's the memory that stands out most prominently for him two decades later.

WILL HERMES: In retrospect, Jeff Mangum is the guy who ultimately had cultural staying power, because of what that record became for subsequent generations of indie rockers and songwriters. At the time, though, Robert Schneider was kind of the head dude, but he was living in Colorado. The Olivia Tremor Control guys had just put out this amazing record, and *Aeroplane* had just come out, so those were the three top groups, and Jeff wasn't necessarily the man. But I remember vividly the first time I met him. He just had this presence. I remember him wearing a coat that was way too warm for the weather, and I have a memory of him giving me this big bear hug. He had this magnetism as this big, loving oaf of a dude who just had this vibe.

CHAPTER 14

ERIC HARRIS AND PETE ERCHICK GREW UP IN THE SAME town in New Jersey, but Pete went to Catholic school a few miles away, so they didn't really meet until they began working together at a Hardee's. When they both ended up at Seton Hall for college, they started hanging out, which quickly led to playing music together.

When Bill's old roommate quit Chocolate USA, Julian needed a keyboardist and—through Eric, who was drumming for Chocolate USA—recruited Pete for a tour that was supposed to last just two weeks but stretched for quite a bit longer. In 1995, the Olivia Tremor Control was in New York to play the Pyramid Club for the CMJ music festival. Missing from the lineup was John Fernandes, who stuck around Athens to witness the birth of his first son, Ravi. But Eric knew someone who could play from his Jersey days. Pete filled in on bass this time, learning John's parts the day of the show.

Over the following year, the Olivias crashed at Pete's house in Jersey City whenever they were passing through. During a stay in the summer of 1996, Pete got to hear the soon-to-be-but-not-yet-released *Dusk at Cubist Castle.* Though he had played with the Olivias a year earlier, Pete hadn't met John yet and so felt uncomfortable asking to play bass in a band that already had a bassist. But that fall, not long after *Dusk* was released, the band needed a keyboard player and asked Pete to tickle the ivory-colored polystyrene for a few shows, then a few tours, and soon enough, he was a member of the Olivias. He moved to Athens, too. In the fall of 1996, the Olivia Tremor Control settled on the five-piece lineup of Pete on keys,

Will and Bill on guitars, Eric on drums, and John on bass, violin, clarinet, and whatever else.

Prior to fleshing out the lineup, the Olivias booked a gig at the 40 Watt, just Will, Bill, and John. After countless shows at houses around Athens and small clubs like the Atomic, not to mention a few successful tours, the Olivia Tremor Control had lined up its first big hometown show. They knew they'd be seeing some new faces in the crowd, people who had heard about them but never heard them live. The band had developed a strong reputation among the small group of people who had attended their smaller shows in Athens, and as those people preached about what they had seen, hype and mystique began to develop around the band. Newcomers were ready to see whether any of it was justified, and those who had seen the band in dingy basements and dives wanted to see how the act would translate to a bigger setting. The band performed as a trio that night, as they had many times before, but when they took the stage, their usual instruments were nowhere to be found. No guitars, no drums, no clarinets or violins, not even a mic stand. They sat down on the bare stage in a triangle, each of them equidistant from the other two, all facing the expectant crowd.

JOHN FERNANDES: For our debut 40 Watt performance, we just brought some sitars and some chord organs out there. We just decided, "Our big 40 Watt debut, let's just drone for forty-five minutes."

BILL DOSS: Let's see if we can run everybody out.

JOHN FERNANDES: We sat there with our sitars and chord organs in a little semicircle, and people were like, "So this is the Olivia Tremor Control."

BILL DOSS: Keep 'em guessing. Sometimes we'd try to get a sense of the audience. "Oh, these guys are a bunch of frat guys. They definitely want to hear some pop songs. We're going to drone."

WILL CULLEN HART: We really practiced the voices. We really got the harmonics.

JOHN FERNANDES: For a while, at the 40 Watt shows, we started seeing more and more people that weren't people we already knew, more college guys. I don't know if they were in fraternities, but kind of in that vein, wearing the baseball cap or whatever. Around that same time, we started getting more and more experimental. I don't know if one had to do with the other.

Derek Almstead: They sort of established early on that they're not going to be your hipster band for you. If you're going to come to the show, they might do something that you're going to get pissed off about. That was more of a selling point to me.

Bill Doss: It wasn't necessarily to annoy people. It was more to push the audience into how much weirdness they could take.

Pete Erchick: I never felt like it was spiteful. There may have been one time, but they turned our power off.

Derek Almstead: They were my favorite live. They were more balanced and sounded like a huge band sounding fucking great every night. They were my favorite live band in the country at that time. It was psychedelic as shit. It could swing from super visceral to really tender and intellectual. It was really all over the map. That's what I liked about it. It was *everything* I liked, wrapped up in one package.

Bill Doss: It was always a matter of when we could afford to have more people on a tour and when they were available to do it. Julian and Scott and Heather always had their own projects they were doing. So there was a lot of times we'd have a tour booked and they couldn't go because they had stuff they were doing, so we'd go as a five-piece. If it worked out where we had the money to bring more people and they were available, it was a circus. But it was actually more fun to play as a five-piece, because after the circus of having eight or nine people onstage, it was fun to pare it down to the five-piece, and then you really had to play better. You couldn't hide in the cacophony.

Henry Owings: I remember the Olivias playing as a three-piece—and I say this over and over and over again and no one ever believes me—the shows I saw with them as a three- or a four-piece blew away [the shows with five or more people onstage]. Those shows where it was really stripped down, where it was exclusively about the songs, they were electric. They were phenomenal.

Andy Battaglia: Phil used to have parties at the Landfill. I remember one party where Olivia played more or less, but it was more boomboxes in different corners of the room. It was an installation as much as a concert. That was very early.

Gary Olson: Someone from Olivia had called and wanted to know if they could borrow a snare drum from us one night. I heard later on they were playing it with a frying pan. Things were happening in every corner of the stage.

GORDON LAMB: I remember the very first Olivia Tremor Control show I saw. The hallmark of that whole show was they carved up and gave out grapefruit the whole time. The flyers for that show just said, "I only came here to eat grapefruit."* It was just the spontaneity of it all, like, "We're doing this because we *can* do this." It was never "We're doing this because the clubs won't have us" or "Because we hate that tough-guy rock and roll." It was "We're doing this because this is what we do."

BILL DOSS: With Olivia, we would always go out with as many people as we could afford to bring. We did have the core group of people that, if the tour was going to be very meager and frugal and streamlined, we could just take out five people. A lot of times, we'd go out and just play with another band and open for them. And then sometimes we would be able to book a tour where it was Olivia and Music Tapes and Neutral Milk. So then the whole sharing members thing would happen. The whole night would be ours, essentially.

JOHN FERNANDES: I think we got pretty professional about it where everyone got the flow. It came naturally.

JIM ROMEO: They wouldn't be a twelve-piece band. It was three bands contained within twelve people. They'd have the Gerbils or Elf Power opening, and they'd incorporate those members. They got resourceful in that regard and realized they couldn't carry all these members. They had to have this caravan. The way they toured and where they lived, they were able to maintain for a while. Certainly, none of them got rich. People sold records back then, too, so it also wasn't the only thing. They always wanted to make money, but it was never like, "We can't go on tour unless we get this much or that much." They all slept on floors, wherever they could.

PETE ERCHICK: It was funny because we were sloppy or good. One or the other would happen. But there were never more than three practices for anything, and when we only practiced three times before my first tour with the band, I didn't know the names of the songs.

* The Olivias got the idea for this from Yoko Ono's *Grapefruit*, her 1964 book of "event scores," which are basically loose instructions for performance art pieces.

We practiced three times. "We're done?" "Yeah, we're done." Everyone agreed. I'm like, "Hey, can we do tomorrow?" "No, let's take tomorrow off."

WILL CULLEN HART: When we were making *Black Foliage*, I had amassed all these tapes. Then I realized I could just get it all on a sound effects disc. You're building up all this stuff and you don't do any work on the pop songs.

BILL DOSS: When you record it yourself, you get the joy of being outside.

JOHN FERNANDES: We amassed a lot of stuff and went to Denver to start recording. We actually started in Athens and then went to Denver to mix some stuff, and then it wasn't done yet, so we did some mixing in Jeff's bedroom on Grady Avenue.

BILL DOSS: We had a two-record deal, so we knew we were going to have to make another record. And we had tons of songs. We just did it. The first record's done, so let's start working on the second one. It took like three years to make. Will was trying to find a sound. It was one of those things where you don't know what you're looking for, but you know it when you find it. So it took him a long, long time to find the sound he was trying to find.

For their next album, the Olivias had gotten the same eight-track tape machine that Robert had and did lots of recording on their own in Athens, then brought those recordings to Denver. There, they did some additional recording with Robert (who plays on a few songs himself), and then Robert mixed everything down to four tracks: generally one mono track for drums and other percussion, one mono track for bass, and everything else—guitars, keyboards, harmonies, additional percussion, and other submixes—mixed in stereo on two other tracks. That left four open tracks on which the band could add lead vocals, guitar solos, and, crucially, sound effects, most of which they handled back in Athens.

ROBERT SCHNEIDER: The final overdubs could be twelve instruments on one track. You're hearing regular music, and then you're hearing the swirl of bizarreness in front of it. In the foreground, you have the sound effects. And then you have the band, but they're playing behind the glass screen of sound effects. You also have a lot of sound effects in the background.

JOHN FERNANDES: We really labored over it. It took a really long time. We'd work on it in spurts, just try to do it at a natural pace.

PETE ERCHICK: It's also good because you're dealing with several submixes at various phases, and however that submix turns out, *that's it*. That's where it is. There were many phases of trying to be finished with *Black Foliage*.

BILL DOSS: It wasn't super high-fidelity. It wasn't an $8,000 machine or a $50,000 machine.*

JOHN FERNANDES: When you listen to *Black Foliage*, I think it's pretty amazing that we did all that stuff on eight-track. All of us would have to have our hands on the mixing board, and as the song was going along, everyone would be in charge of certain tracks, like when the track reaches this time, you've got to pull in those tracks, and pan them left and right, make sure they're pulled back out by this time, then the accordions are going to pop in a little later, so you've got to readjust the volume, and make sure that they're popped back in, and re-EQ by the time those pop in.

PETE ERCHICK: We would rehearse. There were five of us, each of us using both hands, tweaking an EQ or moving a fader, all five of us on the same board at the same time, each of us with two or three jobs to do. We did it until we got it.

BILL DOSS: It was a dance, and every single mix was different, because you could never do the same moves exactly the same way. You'd get done, and then someone would be like, "Ah, I forgot to pull the fader up at this one part," so we'd run it again, and then somebody else would forget to turn an EQ thing. You've got so many different things you've got to do and so many people doing them.

JOHN FERNANDES: Eric was the sync master. Will would take mixes home and do a lot of electronic stuff, and I would take mixes home and do a lot of string and reed stuff, and then Eric would sync it up to the mix. So you would have a lot more than just four tracks. We'd do

* They used an Otari MX5050 MK-III eight-track, which the local repairperson lovingly referred to as the "Blow-tari" for its propensity to break.

an eight-track mix and then bounce it down to one track. We ended up, through ingenuity, using a lot more than eight tracks. Sometimes probably up to thirty on some songs.

BEN CRUM: That syncing technique was something that Eric Harris clued me in to. I'd never heard of anybody doing that, but he just did it. In the mix-down, Eric would have to memorize the lag time of the PLAY buttons on both machines and get them to sync up right. Or close to right. No machine is perfect, though, and if it was anything more than a three-minute song—and most of them are, on that album—sometimes you'd begin to hear certain things peeling off from the dominant rhythm. If there was a big psychedelic flourish at the end of a song, that could end up really enhancing that effect.

BILL DOSS: I think *Black Foliage* was more coherent as an album. Will had more of a vision that he was trying to get to for *Black Foliage.* Will really had a thing he wanted to do sonically with *Black Foliage.*

WILL CULLEN HART: I was exploring that shit. I just didn't feel like it was quite ready. Everything was moving so fast.

PETE ERCHICK: Just the way that record was recorded, on so many different machines in so many different homes, in Denver and in Athens, different groups of people. There's one song that I know three of us played bass on, and I'm one of them. Can I tell you what I play? I absolutely can't. John was able to identify his part, and Eric is the other bass player. That would have been "The Sylvan Screen."

BILL DOSS: I can remember hearing something on a song and being like, "God, that's a great part," and Will going, "You played that." No wonder I like it.

The single for "The Opera House," the first track on *Dusk at Cubist Castle,* was released in two versions, with a different B side on each: "Black Swan Network (with Capillary Radar)" and "Black Swan Network (with Enveloping Bicycle Folds)." When played together, the two tracks create a quadraphonic piece.

JOHN FERNANDES: Will brought me into his room, and he had tape decks all around the room. He said, "Come sit down right here. You ready?" And he turned them all on, and it was just exploding, all this cut-up stuff he was doing, pulling things in and out on all these four-track tapes. Quick blasts of sound.

When the band released *Dusk*, they included in each copy a solicitation for listeners to record themselves describing dreams they had had and mailing the cassettes to the band. Some of those cassettes were chopped up into bits for *Black Foliage* (you can hear them most obviously on the album's closing track, "Hilltop Procession"), and many of them ended up on an Olivia Tremor Control release publicly known as *The Olivia Tremor Control vs. Black Swan Network*, but referred to by the band as "the color squares EP" due to its geometric cover art.

JOHN FERNANDES: In the early days, we would just do an Olivia show where it was me, Bill, and Will on chord organs with tape players all around the audience, and we'd call it Olivia. But then at some point, as we were doing lots of touring and recording, we decided we wanted to do a whole record of just experimental stuff, and we called it Black Swan Network.

BILL DOSS: Will is recording sound-collage stuff always, so a lot of that stuff worked its way into the Olivia recordings, but he had so much of it that he wanted to do something that focused on it. We're all on that stuff, but it's really more of Will's project. One of my favorite things that we did was that color squares EP. Of course, I call it an EP, but it's really like forty minutes long.

JOHN FERNANDES: When we played live, we would do a thing where I'd hide tape decks all around the club, run them with extension cords all into a power strip that was right by my foot. It was like cut-up explosive sound effects. We'd hide them under chairs or in the bathroom or behind things in the club. So we'd hit a part of the song in the Olivia set, and all the tape decks were turned on PLAY, but I'd have the power strip that they were all plugged into turned off, and that was right by my foot. So it was like I was hitting an effects pedal, and then all of a sudden, all around the club, these tape decks would come on. Someone would be sitting there, and all of a sudden they'd hear a *blemp-blooooo* and they'd be like, "Where did that come from?" So you'd just be sitting there, watching the band, and all of a sudden, from all around you, you're surrounded by these electronics.

CHAPTER 15

ONE OF THE IRON LAWS OF ART HISTORY—ALL HISTORY, really, and a whole lot of the present—is that if you look closely enough at any community, scene, or movement, you'll find women who have been marginalized, if not entirely ignored. The Elephant 6 is no exception, and while the collective as a whole hasn't gotten the attention it warrants—thus the impetus for this book—the contributions of the women involved have been almost completely overlooked in some major ways.

First, as modest as their lifestyles were, many of the men who could spend all their time on music were able to do so in part because they had girlfriends and wives who were working to make a little money. The more one person spent weeks at a time experimenting with a four-track, the more his partner had to wait tables or answer phones to keep a roof over their head.

These women's contributions are notable not just in the context of their male counterparts' creative output, of course. Many, like Hilarie Sidney and Lisa Janssen with Secret Square and Tammy Ealom with Dressy Bessy, have been bandleaders themselves, and though very little of its work was recorded—and even less of it distributed outside of one Athenian circle of friends—Dixie Blood Mustache was at least as artistically ambitious as any of the other groups affiliated with the Elephant 6, poking and prodding beyond the world of sound to create installations that stimulated all five senses. In many ways, Dixie Blood Mustache (operating more like a collective-within-the-collective, made up mostly and often entirely of women) was the Elephant 6's quintessential project, and like the rest of the collective, it was inspired by and inspiring to everyone else.

You can find a few tracks under the name on assorted compilations, but the group never released an album. To even call it a band would be inaccurate, or at least insufficient. Dixie Blood Mustache's members were more visually oriented than aurally (and their pieces included smells and tastes and tactile sensations as well). Most of its output was in the form of installations and immersive performances drawing from the group members' interest in musique concrète and the idea that enriching listening experiences could exist far outside the limited scope of what we typically call "music."

LAURA CARTER: That was Barbara Denvir, Laura Glenn, Beth Sale, Roxanne Martin, Lucy Calhoun, Lara Hetzler, [and me]. That was the core. We all were very creative, and a little bit of it was we were all dating guys in Elephant 6, and they were all making experimental music, and we felt that we wanted to make our own experimental music.

BARBARA DENVIR: We just started getting together whenever, sitting around drinking wine and making plans for shows and stuff. It just grew and grew and eventually there were like a million people in the band.

LULU SHIMEK:* It was very different from the other Elephant 6 music or stuff going on, which we loved. We were really the only all-women project that was doing something that was really making the statement. For us and for Elephant 6 in general, creating the music in a way that was all of the senses combined, that was really what we were doing with Dixie Blood Mustache. We wanted to do it from more of a female perspective.

BETH SALE: We'd get all excited about crazy possibilities and then actually do it.

LAURA CARTER: Our statement was that with common appliances and everyday things, even if you're just doing mundane tasks, if you listen to it correctly, then you can appreciate it in a way that you

* Since leaving Athens, Lara Hetzler has gotten married (and become a naturopathic doctor). She now goes by LuLu Shimek, so her quotes are attributed to that name, while other people refer to her as Lara.

could appreciate experimental music, in the sense that life is a very musical process. Sometimes the rhythm of sheets in the dryer might be a great rhythm, but you have to be able to hear it as music. We set out to kind of reconjure those things in those performances.

LULU SHIMEK: Thrifting was our thing. Let's go to the thrift store. Let's find crazy stuff at the junkyard. How could we then take those found objects, no matter what it was, and then create music from it? We would use beaters and all kinds of things miked up to make different sounds, and then we would use different voices through different types of machines to then create different sounds with the voice as well.

DEREK ALMSTEAD: All of the women involved with that were these crazy magical beings that had all these amazing ideas. Every idea was magic.

LAURA CARTER: We were the women who were maybe more in the role of keeping the food on the table and keeping the bills paid.

WILL CULLEN HART: They had an interest in "new music," but they brought it in a great way, without thinking about it.

BRYAN POOLE: They took household appliances and figured them all out. What makes this weird sound? Then they orchestrated live events. The first one was, like, the course of a day. It's the morning. Using vacuum cleaners and stuff, but it's birds chirping, the sun coming in. Then it's the middle of the day: working. All these other things. This whole arc of things. With modern dance stuff happening and these crazy surrealist theatrical things happening.

ROBBIE CUCCHIARO: One was like, we've conjured up this big brain through making soup, and so you're making soup, which is all these kitchen appliances, and you're describing this mystical soup and all of a sudden this brain is in our midst, and the brain needs to be soothed or connected. So coming off the brain would be clear tubes with Christmas lights in them, to these helmets, and when you place the helmet on, you would get a signal from the brain, so it would be like the brain to a body. It would be playing something. And each person would be playing, so it would be getting layered and layered upon itself. And this was a time when thrift stores weren't as picked over, so you found the neatest stuff. A lot of it was found objects.

HEATHER MCINTOSH: They played at Jittery Joe's and had these contact mics on washbasins, washcloths hung from wire hangers with water dripping down, and alarm clocks going off in an aleatoric fashion. All these blenders and just great sounds applied in this sort of Fluxus way. When I talked to Roxanne about it, I was like, "How did you construct this piece? Did you roll a die? Did you have a structured score?" I'm a composition music nerd. She was like, "Oh, no, we were just making sounds of the day." I immediately wanted to be involved, because it was such a pure place that it came from. It was exactly as John Cage–y as she could get. It was totally of that whole Fluxus world. It was clear there was influence there, but the essence of it was a more gut way to get there. It was so unlabored and perfect.

DEREK ALMSTEAD: Dixie Blood Mustache shows were a really cool thing. I remember there was one show at the 40 Watt. The Olivia Tremor Control was playing, and maybe Neutral Milk Hotel, and maybe Of Montreal, too. Dixie Blood Mustache had set up this weird thing on the side of the stage. You'd go in, and there were all these lights and rooms you could go into. It was this weird funhouse carnival kind of world. It must have taken a shit ton of work. I remember being blown away by that. It was an experimental noise band. Laura Glenn was in it, and she would do dancing. There would be a tin drum with a contact microphone in it, pouring water on top of it, with someone dancing around and electronic noises and some crazy display and a giant dragon's head.

JOHN FERNANDES: There was one at the 40 Watt where they set up an installation in the middle, where you kind of had to crawl through all this fabric and stuff. You go in this little fabric igloo, and there's people in there playing weird instruments, dressed up in crazy costumes.

LULU SHIMEK: There were walls we made that were this see-through fabric, but you couldn't see through it. There were all these heads of babies mixed in. As you would walk through the installation, there would be different sounds we had recorded or we would play live. You couldn't see us, but then you could see us. *What are they playing? What are they doing?*

WILL CULLEN HART: They did one at the Morton Theatre. They had this huge parachute over the crowd. They had all these cut-up noises and stuff. It was fucking perfect. I wish somebody had taped it.

BARBARA DENVIR: The biggest one and my favorite one was the rock art show at the Morton Theatre. There was a show at the gallery, and we made an installation for that. We got a grant, so we all came up with a little piece for the thing. Somebody built a giant radio and had Will Westbrook in there making all kinds of electronic noises. We had $150, and we spent it all on what I wanted to do, which was a little movie. It was only one part of a huge show. At the end, at the finale, we were all dressed up like appliances. Say I was the vacuum. I'd go after the popcorn maker and clean it up, and they would play the appropriate noises. At the end, a teakettle, which was Heather McIntosh, fell in love with the popcorn machine, which was Robbie, and we just made this mass exit down the aisle. Robbie was throwing popcorn everywhere.

ROBBIE CUCCHIARO: Dixie Blood Mustache was really the first band I was ever in. I was the first guy that was allowed in the band. We had a show where we just built this crazy labyrinth of booths and doors and windows. You'd stick your hand in and there'd be some kind of tactile thing. You'd look through a window and there'd be a cow beating a pig with a rubber bat, or there'd be a film thing with sonic qualities going on. That was all coming from these ladies. They really inspired everybody with that. There were a lot of shows paired up with Dixie Blood, Olivia, and Neutral Milk. All those guys were into the idea of it being an experience. We're going to blow your mind. Eric got involved in it. Jeff and Julian played roles in it. Will Cullen Hart participated in his way.

ANDY BATTAGLIA: There was this one great outdoor concert-happening-event that was outside behind the Grit in the empty lot behind there. I think it was Bryan, driving around and screaming out of a megaphone with a cowboy hat on. I remember when Dixie Blood was playing, there was this incredibly entrancing meditative sort of noise, and there was this giant ring of birds flying overhead. We slowly started noticing that these birds were flying in this huge circular pattern above us.

BRYAN POOLE: The Grit used to have shows every year. Dixie Blood Mustache played there, and my job was, at a certain point in the thing, I leaned out of a car with a big bullhorn blabbering nonsense and throwing things at the crowd. And then we used to have talent shows on Friday the thirteenth. We did two of them. They were kind of like a surrealist talent show. I was the emcee for those. Dixie Blood Mustache were great, and they kind of summed up the utopian vision that we all had for a couple of years there.

LULU SHIMEK: We were all super into artwork and creating different ways for people to actually feel the textures of things and hear the music. We would do a lot of walks through town. I learned how to stilt-walk.

LAURA CARTER: We did these Dixie Blood Mustache talent shows, and people were encouraged to be as weird as they could possibly be.

At one such talent show, a local performer and entomologist named Irene Moon stood silently onstage for the full fifteen minutes she was allotted, dressed as a dominatrix schoolteacher with a beehive wig, holding a tray covered in snails bearing photocopied images of various US presidents' heads on their shells, slinking slowly and slimily about the tray for the duration of the performance. LuLu Shimek took the stage on stilts beneath her oversize hoop skirt, singing operatic tones through a contact microphone embedded in a choker she was wearing, then run through a bunch of effects. Laura Carter appeared dressed in orchestra black from head to toe, holding a violin she had borrowed from John Fernandes for the occasion and mercifully mummified in plastic wrap beneath the strings. She reached into her pockets—which each contained a pound or two of freshly diced onions—and then wiped her eyes to summon tears. She began to play the violin as she sobbed, but before she could get to a second note, Jeff Mangum entered dressed in a full-body cereal box costume with a boombox protruding from his belly, blaring all sorts of abrasive sounds to drown out Laura's fiddle, while he hurled handfuls of chocolate pudding at her.

CHAPTER 16

Externally, the heyday of the Elephant 6 is characterized by the most notable albums those bands made, especially those released in the late nineties. Before then, no one really knew anything about these bands, and after, many of them went quiet or gave way to side projects. It's no coincidence that this time period—it's blurry, but let's say the summer of 1996 into the first few months of 1999—coincided with the greatest concentration of involved musicians in Athens and Denver (after they had descended on these cities from Ruston, New York, and elsewhere, and before they started spreading to various others) and thus the fertility of tightly knit collaboration.

When outsiders think of that era of the Elephant 6, they think of *Dusk at Cubist Castle* and *Aeroplane* or maybe some shows they attended. When the Athenian contingent of the Elephant 6 thinks of that era, they think of their weekly potlucks.

The potlucks were equal parts French salon, Greek symposium, and kibbutznik house party where they would trade bons mots, philosophize, and share whatever they could: obscure band recommendations, home-recording tricks, snacks. They were the biggest event of the week, every week, with alternating hosts. Every Sunday evening for a year or two, Athens Elephant 6 folks and their collaborators came together ostensibly to stretch their meager budgets a little further into an otherwise unaffordable feast, and they departed with full stomachs, open minds, and more inspiration than could fit in a Tupperware container. For a few hours each week, instead of being starving artists, they got to just be artists.

WILL CULLEN HART: We made so many friends, and it was all so intense for a while.

DAN DONAHUE: At that time, everything was so new, and there was nothing to lose. There's no sense of an end to any of it. None of it was ever serious. There was no goal. It just seemed like, for a while, everyone was very at peace with what was happening. And it lasted for a little while, that peace.

JILL CARNES: It seemed like every time, it was somebody's birthday.

JAMEY HUGGINS: You did not want to miss potlucks. That was more important than a show. If you have to go out of town, and Neutral Milk Hotel is playing on Thursday and the potluck is on Sunday, you would rather go out of town on that Thursday and miss the show than miss the potluck. It was like a caucus.

LANCE BANGS: A lot of not using overhead lighting. Lamps on tables in the room, fabric tossed on top of the lamps to cut the light and change the color. The sun going down. Dogs walking through, in and out. People playing music and making stuff together.

LAURA CARTER: Real loose. There's always somebody bringing Dunkin' Donuts because they didn't have time. But then there's usually people who go way out on their food. We have always leaned toward people who grow their food or knowing where the food comes from. Often when we have potlucks, people will say, "This squash came from here." We're conscious about how special it is when you're eating local food.

JOHN FERNANDES: Scott brought Cheetos with Peanut M&M's in it. That was one of his specialties.

SCOTT SPILLANE: I had an amazing dish I stole from somebody. It was angel hair pasta with a garlic tomato sauce. Raleigh Hatfield brought this amazing bean casserole. Jeff would always bring Dunkin' Donuts. There'd be mostly prepared stuff and then one box of Dunkin' Donuts. And it was mostly Lara Hetzler bringing two or three large containers of food, and then sprinklings of stuff here and there. Everybody that was in Dixie Blood Mustache was a really good cook, so they'd always be cooking tofu and shit like that. They would always bring more food than anyone else.

BARBARA DENVIR: John d'Azzo had just graduated from architecture school and we made him this giant geodesic dome cake.

JULIAN KOSTER: They were pretty unassuming. Big groups of friends. Very warm. There were great cooks, and then a bunch of us bums who would just bring Dunkin' Donuts or something. Me, Jeff, Scott, Will Westbrook, Will Cullen Hart, Andrew Rieger, we would all bring a bag of cookies or something ridiculous. Or a two-liter thing of Mountain Dew.

DAVEY WRATHGABAR: Laura Carter made this great landscape out of brown rice and this lake made out of yeast gravy. A whole forest made of broccoli. And a couple little action figures.

SCOTT SPILLANE: You give it to the people, because they only got one good meal a week. The rest of the time they were eating shit.

DAN DONAHUE: You're poor and you don't eat well. You eat a Taco Stand burrito or a Subway sandwich every day. At the potluck, anything decadent was such a strange thing back then. Everyone just made what they had. It was everyone throwing their part into a whole and it being better for it. It was as close to communal as you can come in this day and age, people sharing all their food or weed or beer. Whatever you had, you brought. You'd know Scott was there because, before you even opened the door, you'd hear him saying, "Who's got the Grinch?"* Someone would have to fess up at that point, and the weed would come out. The food was always great. It felt decadent because you'd walk in and there'd be dessert. Dessert was not something you had. No one was making cakes at my house. We were eating Taco Bell sauce on crackers.

JOHN D'AZZO: If it's at your house, you don't necessarily have to cook, because everyone is bringing the food. But you have to do the dishes. It's like the Danish cohousing principle. Villages where they have community dinners two or three times a week. Two people prepare the meals for the whole group, and it rotates. The week after you prepare the meal, you do the dishes. And then you're good for a couple months, eating homemade food other people are making. But once every two months, it's like, "Ah, fuck, I gotta cook for ten

* Every group of friends seems to develop its own argot for drug discussion, and even when it's derived from paranoia, it typically persists mostly out of the same in-joke connectivity as any cliquey slang. In the Elephant 6 community, "Grinch" means pot (it's green and furry), as does "Merv" (stemming from someone mishearing the word "herb"). "Full meal deal" is when you accidentally inhale still-cherrying ash through the stem of a pipe. I am not a narc.

people." It was sort of like that. And then you got all the leftovers if it was at your house.

BRYAN POOLE: A lot of people do that, definitely in a town like ours, where people are poor and living as cheaply as possible to pursue our art. You put something together and someone else puts something together, and all of a sudden, you have a very rich meal and a rich experience. People have been doing it for centuries.

ROBBIE CUCCHIARO: That's the thing. Elephant 6 really wasn't anything that new. Jazz musicians have been doing that for ages. Artists do that. They form communities and play off each other, and that's what makes it fuller and richer and really a beautiful thing. It would be boring if it was just musicians. You want it to be mixed up with writers and visual artists. Especially with music being a kind of art that's taking all these forms and putting it all together.

JULIAN KOSTER: Will Cullen Hart's girlfriend at the time, Lara Hetzler, was an amazing cook.

LULU SHIMEK: I was really into baking. I would always make cakes for parties and things like that.

BETH SALE: She made some amazing vegan cakes.

BRYAN POOLE: Lara loved to cook, and when she left Athens, she left to go to culinary school in New York. It was something she really liked doing. Lara was one of the instigators of the potlucks, because she provided probably half of the food. I have to credit her for me being a vegetarian today. She'd make casseroles or cakes or whatever, and she had a super positive go-getter vibe. She has a lot of drive.

BARBARA DENVIR: Lara Hetzler would always make hundred-dollar cakes. She was really into organic vegetarian food, too. She made lots of good dishes. She was probably the guiding energy for the whole group.

LULU SHIMEK: My passion for vegetarian, healthy cooking ran deep. Food to me is how everybody gets together and gets to know each other and enjoys company. That's just how we nurtured each other.

SCOTT SPILLANE: These big pots of garbanzo beans and all kinds of spices. Practically anything you'd get at a Hare Krishna food thing. You don't have to sit through a presentation. There'd be vegetarian chili and garbanzo beans and lentils of some sort. Breads. It was a feast, so it was hard to pinpoint anything. You never knew what was going to be served. [The potlucks] were in different places, shuffled around, but she usually brought ten times as much food as anyone else, and she orchestrated a lot of them. That's the sort of thing that kept the whole thing rolling for as long as it did. That's what made it all happen.

DAVEY WRATHGABAR: Lara Hetzler would make phenomenal cakes. The creative spirit definitely came to the potlucks. Visually, very appealing, and usually pretty tasty, too. I know there were some anthropomorphic animal cakes.

LAURA CARTER: We played music sometimes afterward and just ate a lot of good food. I remember fresh-baked strawberry shortcakes. I remember Lara Hetzler once made a pumpkin soup where the soup was inside the pumpkin, cooked, so you lifted the lid off the pumpkin, and there's hot pumpkin soup inside, and as you scoop the soup, you would scoop a little of the cooked pumpkin flesh, shaving it into the soup.

ROBBIE CUCCHIARO: It was really gourmet, really creative. Lara Hetzler would find these neat recipes, and you'd eat it, and you would be totally satiated but feel lighter than when you started.

BETH SALE: We would just make a decision about whose house it would be at, and then that week, whenever you'd see people out at shows—there was usually a show on Friday or Saturday—you'd just be like, "It's at this place this week."

JULIAN KOSTER: It was all vegetarian and super healthy. Most of us were vegetarian. I think I was first, and then Robbie followed pretty quickly, and then Jeff was almost instantly after that. As soon as one of us saw the other doing it, it was like, "Oh, you can do that? Is it working out? Okay, I'll do that."

ROBBIE CUCCHIARO: It was great, because there were some really good cooks, and there was a whole new cuisine open to us. Stuff I had never tried before and wasn't really interested in trying.

BRYAN POOLE: I was finally eating food at these places that were better than Wendy's drive-thru. I would bring something from working at Gumby's, but that's probably where I was introduced to vegetarian cuisine and a vegetarian diet for the first time. There were a bunch of people who would bring only veggie stuff, and I learned to develop a taste for it. I was a definite fast-food junkie that was converted toward a healthier lifestyle in part thanks to the Elephant 6 and all the vegetarians that happened to be around me at that point.

LAURA CARTER: Generally, it's a very vegetarian crowd, although some of us eat meat. I eat meat and our group out at Orange Twin eats meat, but we eat roadkill and meat farmed very close to here. We're picky meat-eaters. For the most part, in the nineties, the potlucks were all vegetarian, super healthy, and fun.

JAMEY HUGGINS: It was mostly vegetarian, because it felt like if you brought meat, you were *that* guy. It was almost offensive. Not everyone was vegetarian, but most of the potlucks were. And then you'd find people after the potluck eating a hamburger or something.

BRYAN POOLE: We just had good communal energy. We'd talk about music and art. The kind of a feeling of a utopian, idyllic mind would all come together for us there. We had all kind of lived together in various forms, but for those Sunday potlucks, everybody would get together and you'd have fifteen to thirty people show up, and everybody was welcome.

DAVEY WRATHGABAR: Maybe the Elephant 6 was a potluck. Every Sunday, we'd watch *The Simpsons*, and if you weren't into that, dinner was after. I remember one potluck was out where most of the Of Montreal guys were living, because they needed a big group vocal. They lived kind of out of town. Not far by anyone else's standards. It was a hassle to have the potluck out there, but they needed a big group vocal, and they had a sweet recording rig. Let's do it.

KEVIN BARNES: It was just about everyone getting together and listening to music and hanging out. It was also good in a way because if you were hosting a potluck, you could also say, "Oh, I've got this song that I want to have a group sing-along, so after dinner, everyone has to go in the studio and sing in front of the mic."

JOHN FERNANDES: Whenever we got together for the potlucks, it seemed like someone would always say, "Hey, I'm almost done with this. Why don't you come by and add something." It would be "Hey, why don't you come over and do an overdub on this Elf Power song." There was a lot of networking going on.

JAMEY HUGGINS: It would be Jeff outside smoking, talking to somebody about a book, and then Will actively playing something on the four-track, playing you what he was working on. Eric and Pete were always talking about what music they discovered. You would just go for two or three hours, and you'd come home with this wealth of inspiration. You'd have written down like five albums you had to check out, you would have heard the newest sound collage that Will was working on, you would have picked up some kind of technique about miking something.

ROBBIE CUCCHIARO: People were getting together and talking about their passions, which was music and the new thing they discovered this week, or their new video. A lot of those guys are really like professors about it. They know dates and connections and look at this whole movement of artistry. It wasn't just music, but it was also Surrealism and Dada.

DAVEY WRATHGABAR: When Jeff got back from Denver, this potluck was over at the house where they had taken the photos for *Rolling Stone*. There's people in there that I haven't seen since. Jeff had just gotten back. "Let's listen to it." "Well, it's on DAT tape." So I got in my car, went home, and got my DAT deck, and we sat in somebody's bedroom and listened to that fucking record. It was jaw-dropping.

DEREK ALMSTEAD: I was in the room when *Aeroplane* was first played for all of us. We were all huddled around the room. It was the time that I'm sure some people would consider the height, in between *Dusk* and *Black Foliage* and in between *Avery Island* and *Aeroplane*. Kind of the golden summer where everybody was friends, before anything got complicated.

BRYAN POOLE: That was a great place for us all to get together, talk, and exchange ideas. Just talk about music and art and whatever else. It really created a family, community vibe, even though it'd be like thirty people. You felt close to all these people. You felt like something special was in the air.

JULIAN KOSTER: There was a really nice togetherness at that time. There was never much of a sense of competition among people. We wanted to blow each other's minds. It was all so natural. You weren't even really conscious of it. And it was super supportive, in that everyone valued and was excited about what you were making, and you were excited about what everyone else was making.

Chapter 17

Neutral Milk Hotel spent much of their 1998 tour of Europe with Sparklehorse, opening for the band in England, Belgium, the Netherlands, Sweden, Norway, Germany, France, and Scotland.

JULIAN KOSTER: That was a weird scene. We were being held in restraint the whole time by their people. I think they regretted bringing us on the tour, and they realized that pretty soon. But then they were into it for six weeks, so they were putting up with us, but they were making our lives pretty miserable. We'd get to these places where we had been before and filled the room with excited people, and we were playing the same room, but a lot of the people who wanted to see us couldn't get in because it was full of their crowd. And we had to play a half hour and would get yelled at if we went crazy at all, which we did always. Every time we played a really good show, they'd yell at us for something and threaten to kick us off the tour.

They had gotten a bus to drive them around, which sounds glamorous until you consider that the bus is in lieu of not just the van, but lodging, too. They'd sleep on the bus while traveling between cities, groggily slamming into walls as the bus rounded corners at speed. They'd shower at truck stops or not at all.

JULIAN KOSTER: The bus driver was really great, though. [He told us that he] had killed a man and had been in prison for it. He had thrown a man out of a window. He caught someone with his wife. Of course, he could have made all this up. This is what he told us. But he would yell at us. Just the most trivial stuff. But then he'd get really sentimental. There was a little place you could cook, and he'd cook us these awesome omelets and be like, "You all are the best group of blokes I ever drove. Ever!" And he didn't need to cook for us. That wasn't his job. It was just a special gesture. There's this rock classism in Europe, where it's like if you're a rock star you can get away with anything. He'd yell at us for these tiny infractions, and then with a gleam and a tear in his eye, tell us stories of how [a famous but litigious British musician] used to pee in drink bottles to see if he could catch the bus driver drinking his pee. Good to be [said British musician], I guess.

Neutral Milk Hotel had another date lined up for Ireland, but when that got canceled, the band landed a headlining gig at the Underworld in London on October 13, 1998.

JULIAN KOSTER: We knew we'd be letting off steam, because it had been such a frustrating tour. That was really joyful. We were headlining and it was our crowd. It was a room that was perfect for us. Intimate but packed full of people. We had a ball. We went crazy that night.

SCOTT SPILLANE: I don't remember that sort of stuff that much. It was just a tour. There are these pointillist moments from playing and stuff, but there was never a discussion of what's going on.

They knew they had no more shows booked after that, but they didn't know they wouldn't be booking any others for a long time. It would be the last full-band Neutral Milk Hotel performance for nearly fifteen years.

When Neutral Milk Hotel returned to Athens from having spent most of the previous two months playing shows in Europe, they were exhausted. The band scheduled no more shows for the rest of the year, but Jeff squeezed in a couple of short, mostly solo local performances.

Synthetic Flying Machine, the Fun-O-Mat, Ruston, Louisiana, 1991. *Left to right:* Bill Doss, Will Cullen Hart, and Jeff Mangum. *Photo by Amy Hairston.*

Bill Doss and Jeff Mangum, Monroe Street House, Ruston, Louisiana, July 1993. *Photo by Ross Beach.*

Will Cullen Hart. Virgin Islands, 1991. *Photo courtesy of Robert Schneider.*

Jeff Mangum and Julian Koster. *Photo by Chris Bilheimer.*

Hilarie Sidney, Robert Schneider, and John Hill inspect rare United States of America album. Denver, Colorado, 1996. *Photo courtesy of Robert Schneider.*

Will Cullen Hart, Robert Schneider, and Jeff Mangum record instrumental parts for *Dusk at Cubist Castle.* Denver, Colorado, 1995. *Photo by Bill Doss, courtesy of Amy Hairston.*

The Apples in Stereo, 21 Bernice Space, San Francisco, California, May 1994. *Left to right:* John Hill, Hilarie Sidney, Jeff Mangum, and Robert Schneider. *Photo by Lisa Janssen.*

John Hill, Robert Schneider, Hilarie Sidney, and Jim McIntyre. Apples in Stereo practice space, Denver, Colorado, 1994. *Photo by Lisa Janssen.*

Hilarie Sidney, Robert Schneider, John Hill, and Jeff Mangum on tour. California, 1993. *Photo by Lisa Janssen, courtesy of Robert Schneider.*

Robert Schneider, Derek Almstead, and Jamey Huggins. Pet Sounds Studio, Denver, Colorado, March 2001. *Photo by Dottie Alexander, courtesy of Derek Almstead.*

Neutral Milk Hotel. *Left to right:* Scott Spillane, Jeff Mangum, Jeremy Barnes, and Julian Koster. *Photo by Chris Bilheimer.*

Neutral Milk Hotel and Supreme Dicks, EJ's, Portland, Oregon, July 7, 1996. *Back row:* Scott Spillane, Jon Shere, Tim Wilson, and Danny Oxenberg. *Middle row:* Jeremy Barnes and Julian Koster. *Front row:* Dan Kapelovitz and Jeff Mangum. *Photo courtesy of Tim Wilson.*

Of Montreal, SXSW Bar/None Showcase, Austin, Texas, March 1997. *Left to right:* Bryan Poole, Derek Almstead, and Kevin Barnes. *Photo by Niki Bhattacharya, courtesy of Derek Almstead.*

Jeff Mangum and Scott Spillane in tour van, 1997. *Photo by Laura Carter, courtesy of Bryan Poole.*

Neutral Milk Hotel performance, either Bottom of the Hill, San Francisco, California, or Satyricon, Portland, Oregon, 1998. *Left to right:* Robbie Cucchiaro, Will Westbrook, John d'Azzo, Scott Spillane, and Julian Koster. *Photo by Lance Bangs.*

Jeff Mangum on tour. Portland, Oregon, April 16, 1998. *Photo by Lance Bangs.*

Neutral Milk Hotel, Satyricon, Portland, Oregon, April 15, 1998. *Pictured:* Jeff Mangum. *Photo by Lance Bangs.*

Will Cullen Hart and Jeff Mangum backstage after a show at Sloss Furnaces, Birmingham, Alabama, 1999. *Photo by Henry Owings.*

Jeff Mangum in tour van. San Francisco, California, 1998. *Photo by Lance Bangs.*

Neutral Milk Hotel. *Left to right:* Scott Spillane, Jeremy Barnes, Jeff Mangum, and Julian Koster. *Photo by Chris Bilheimer.*

The Olivia Tremor Control. Athens, Georgia, 1995. *Photo by Amy Hairston.*

Dixie Blood Mustache. Athens, Georgia, 1997. *Left to right:* Beth Sale, Laura Carter, LuLu Shimek, Roxanne Martin, Laura Glenn, and Lucy Calhoun. *Photo courtesy of Laura Carter and Bryan Poole.*

Andrew Rieger. The 40 Watt, Athens, Georgia, late 1990s. *Photo by Kristine Potter.*

Preparation for Dixie Blood Mustache installation. Athens, Georgia, late 1990s. *Photo by Kristine Potter.*

Andy Gonzales and Dottie Alexander. Of Montreal practice session, New York City, New York, late 1990s. *Photo by Kristine Potter.*

Bryan Poole. Athens, Georgia, 2004. *Photo by Kristine Potter.*

Laura Carter. Athens, Georgia. *Photo by Kristine Potter.*

The Gerbils. Athens, Georgia, late 1990s. *Pictured:* Will Westbrook. *Photo by Kristine Potter.*

Laura Carter and Laura Glenn. Potluck at the Landfill. Athens, Georgia. *Photo by Kristine Potter.*

Neutral Milk Hotel. *Left to right:* Jeremy Barnes, Jeff Mangum, Julian Koster, and Scott Spillane. *Photo by Chris Bilheimer*

The first was a show at an apartment that Lance Bangs, Dan Donahue, and Chris Bilheimer* shared on Meigs Street just a few blocks from downtown Athens. It had been an old high school gymnasium, but after the high school was torn down, artist James Herbert—who had directed many of R.E.M.'s music videos and was a UGA professor who had taught both Bangs and Bilheimer—purchased the gym and converted the basketball court into a studio for his massive paintings. One end of the building had two stories of classrooms, and the upper floor has been converted into a two-bedroom loft (which these tenants had turned into a three-bedroom by cordoning off an eight-foot-by-eight-foot space with corrugated tin).

The December 5, 1998, show was staged for Chris Bilheimer's birthday party. They strung Christmas lights between two arcade cabinets—*Asteroids* and *Wizard of Wor*—to create a makeshift stage. The show was entirely acoustic, with no amplification so as not to disturb the neighbors. Elf Power played a short set (with Aaron Wegelin playing the drum kit with brushes) and then Jeff played by himself, seated with his guitar, with Scott joining in with an occasional horn. The show wasn't advertised anywhere, so the crowd was just the rest of the people there to celebrate Chris's birthday, basically the same group who might be at a typical potluck, or at one of Jeff's performances a year or two earlier, before Neutral Milk Hotel had really made a name for itself.

LANCE BANGS: We all loved that album and presumed that Jeff would go off and write a new batch of songs, and they would tour again in that configuration. There was a sense among most people that what Jeff was doing was singular and intense and to kind of focus and pay attention and not just talk over it. Most people sat on the hardwood floor with their legs crossed.

CHRIS BILHEIMER: Scott Spillane, when his horn parts came in, they were so loud that you couldn't hear Jeff at all, so he'd actually go walk into the bathroom and play in there. Every time a horn part would be coming up, Scott would get up and walk into the other room, play his parts, and then come back and sit down.

* Bilheimer was the in-house graphic designer for R.E.M. for much of the band's existence, and the art director for *In the Aeroplane Over the Sea*, among dozens of other albums in his portfolio.

DAN GELLER: The best part of it is when Scott went back into one of the bedrooms. I didn't notice he went back there. All of a sudden, the horn comes muted out of the back of the house, right in time with Jeff's playing. It was absolutely magic. I was at the Jittery Joe's acoustic thing, too. That was good, but this was better.

There are bootleg recordings of dozens of Neutral Milk Hotel and Jeff Mangum shows bouncing around online, but the recording of this show is prized for being the only one that features a song Jeff wrote after *Aeroplane* was released. He played six songs that night: in addition to four tracks from *Aeroplane* and old favorite "Everything Is," he debuted an in-progress song called "Little Birds." The lyrics are heavy and dark, abstract but inspired by the story of Matthew Shepard, a gay man who had been savagely beaten to death in Wyoming a couple of months earlier. It's the first song of the set. As he warms up, Jeff pauses to think. "I'll try this song," he says with some hesitation. "This is a new song, which is kind of twisted, and I'm sorry, but there are really sick parts. I'm going to work that all out." He hedges again and reminds the other partygoers that because it's new, he was "probably going to fuck it up" and also that it's still not finished.

LANCE BANGS: Instantly, I was conscious that this is much more fucked up, and he's dealing with heavier, more disturbing imagery, and this is not playful psychedelia. It was so striking and so intense, and you can see the strain in his facial expressions as he's delivering the lines. It was so moving and so intense, and having lived through experiences like that myself, it was really striking and upsetting and triggering. It was such a powerful song, and it goes into that drone at the end, and then it's done. I was shaken.

JAMEY HUGGINS: I remember looking over at Kevin Barnes, who was weeping. Tears streaming down his face. All of us were moved. We all just shut up.

DAN DONAHUE: The stuff that was memorable with Jeff were those very personal moments where he's playing in a living room. I remember Kevin Barnes just sort of crying on the couch while Jeff was playing. That happened to me once just hearing it on the radio one time.

Jeff played one more time that year, at a New Year's Eve show at the 40 Watt, sharing the bill with Julian Koster, Jill Carnes, and Corin Tucker. Jeff performed three songs that night—"Engine" with Julian on singing saw, "Oh Sister"* by himself, and "In the Aeroplane Over the Sea" with Julian on saw again and Scott on trumpet—seated once more with his acoustic guitar.

No one knew it at the time, but it was the last show Jeff would play for a few years. When he packed up his gear at the end of the set, Neutral Milk Hotel's unofficial hiatus began. They didn't release a statement announcing anything, and to be sure, none of the band members discussed anything formal. But they all had projects besides Neutral Milk Hotel, and after a long and intense bout of touring, each decided to focus on something else for a bit.

JEREMY BARNES: We came back to Athens after a long European tour. Jeff was constantly talking about dropping out. No one took him seriously at first.

JULIAN KOSTER: I know we were all awful busy, but we always kind of were. In between tours, we'd always have so many projects going on. At no time was there ever a breakup discussion or a meeting where that possibility was raised. Scott has this comedic line that he's the only one who never quit Neutral Milk Hotel. He claims I said I was too busy and had all this Music Tapes stuff to do, but I think probably what I said was "I'm glad we're not doing anything, because I have all this stuff to do." All these tours to do and things to make.

SCOTT SPILLANE: The way I saw it, we were taking a break. It was basically "Let's take a break for a while," and then Jeremy said he had a couple things he wanted to do, Julian said he had a couple things he wanted to do. I was like, "All right, I'm going to go dig some more ditches, nail together some more houses. Give me a call." And the call never came.

JAMEY HUGGINS: You either saw it or you didn't. It's a shame it wasn't filmed more, but goddamn it, you can't sustain that.

* The liner notes for *Aeroplane* actually include the lyrics for this song, too, even though it was not included on the album. Before playing the song, Jeff tells the audience that it "didn't make the last record and won't ever be heard again."

JIM ROMEO: They would have kept going up and up and up.

NESEY GALLONS: I got the impression that in one way or another Jeff would have kept going, but everyone else for various reasons was pulled in various directions. That's what made the hiatus go on indefinitely. I didn't get here until spring 2000. The Major Organ [and the Adding Machine] record was just coming out when I moved here. The first Circulatory System record was just coming out. *The Battle of Electricity* came out not long after that. So there was definitely a lot of activity. It was just shape-shifting. I think a lot of it was organic. I think some of it was an organic response to types of anxiety or fear or just kind of freaking out about things that seemed like they weren't going as hoped, so that might have prompted some of the changes.

DEREK ALMSTEAD: There's something incredibly intoxicating about success, but there's also something incredibly intoxicating about autonomy.

JULIAN KOSTER: I was excited about everything because it seemed like a really exciting time. Things with Neutral Milk Hotel had gotten to such a point that it was certainly uncharted territory. And Elephant 6 in general. Olivia was so popular. I was really excited because *1st Imaginary Symphony* was coming out. I had started that before *Avery Island* came out, maybe before Jeff recorded it. When we got home from England, I think we were just really excited about that record coming out and Music Tapes stuff. So I was distracted, in the context of Neutral Milk Hotel. And Bablicon was doing stuff. And we were all involved in Olivia to whatever extent as well. But it just felt like a productive, busy time, with everybody working on these projects. It didn't feel like anything bad was happening. The fact that Neutral Milk wasn't doing something just felt natural, because so much else was happening, and we had just done so much. It didn't feel unusual at all. I suspected nothing.

CHAPTER 18

WITH A SIMILAR AFFINITY FOR THE BEATLES-Y POP ROCK the Minders were drawing from, Elliott Smith came to a few of their shows in Portland, where he was living at the time, and asked them to open for him on his 2000 tour supporting *Figure 8.*

MARTYN LEAPER: That was a coach tour at the height of his fame, and we toured on the coach with him. He would close out our set, and we would close out his set. That was intense. Elephant 6 tours were equally as cool, because that was our world. We were in our territory, playing to our audiences. But there were still people who knew about Elephant 6 and stuff. There was a like-minded crowd, except more of them. Instead of being maybe three hundred or five hundred at a show, there were fifteen hundred to two thousand people at a show.

The Elephant 6 was gathering other bands out west, too, like Beulah from San Francisco, drawn into the fold by the Denver contingent.

MILES KUROSKY: A friend of mine gave Robert and Hilarie a cassette with some of my songs after an Apples show in NYC. Apparently Robert listened to it in the van that night.* Lo and behold, Robert called me later that week and told me he wanted to put out my record. That modest tin can recording would eventually be released as *Handsome Western States.* He was incredibly sincere and energetic.

* Robert recalls Hilarie having listened to it first and then excitedly sharing it with him, listening to it in the van together.

LISA JANSSEN: Everyone hears about Athens, Athens, Athens, but I really do feel like what happened in Denver made Athens possible. What Robert sort of started made all that other stuff possible. Robert was the one trying to sign other bands and seeing other groups and widening the circle. It was such a wide-open, new frontier. There wasn't really a big music scene in Denver. The Apples were like the first big band to come out of there. There was something really freeing about not having a lot of competition and playing a show and having an audience filled with your friends.

"*When Your Heartstrings Break* [Beulah's second album] got panned by a lot of people because it was being compared to Neutral Milk Hotel and Olivia Tremor Control," Miles says in a 2003 *Creative Loafing* piece. "I think that's odd, because we weren't a part of the collective ever. Nor did we ever say we were. For us, Elephant 6 was always just a record label, that's all. I don't know those people in Athens at all."*

There was a growing perception, among the Elephant 6 crew and externally, that there was a geographic split between two factions of the collective. Not a schism in philosophy, just different approaches. Elephant 6 East, the folks in Athens, were doing their best to live out a certain artistic utopia, communal in spirit, experimental in both composition and general lifestyle, and weird for weirdness's sake. Their records seemed almost an accidental by-product of their neo-hippie lifestyle. Elephant 6 West, the Denver cohort, had a more methodical approach, relatively. Whereas the Athens crew was a bunch of friends who happened to play music together, the Denverites came together foremost because Robert wanted to record and release their albums. Beulah and the Minders (plus New York bands the Ladybug Transistor and the Essex Green, whom Robert had also brought into the fold) were ostensibly labelmates first, though friendships arose due to proximity and similar tastes. Bands like Dressy Bessy and Secret Square shared members with the Apples, and Robert had a few of his own side projects, but the overall vibe in Denver was a lot more "pro."

* It's worth noting that I pulled this from a photocopy of the article, in whose margin someone had scrawled "You weren't fighting it when the '6' was on TOP Baybee." I have an idea of who wrote this, but no one I asked accepted responsibility for it.

In both towns, music was the gravitational force that pulled everyone together, but the groups had different goals.

> **MARTYN LEAPER:** Denver in the early, mid-nineties was still a little beaten up. Where we lived was always kind of a bit rough. We were poor, so we paid low rent and lived in low-rent places. Then you'd go to Athens, and they were living in a college town. Athens is very cozy. It was mellow and the rent was like four times cheaper than what we were paying. Everybody got to spend more time being creative.

> **HILARIE SIDNEY:** Miles came out first. Miles and Robert would go to the studio every day, and we took lots of walks. Miles thought it was stupid hype. I think with Elephant 6, it was weird, because it was obscure and nobody knew about it, but then all of a sudden it became this really big deal for a little while, and *Rolling Stone* wrote about it, and I think those guys always felt slighted by the Athens people. Like they weren't good enough or something. The Minders and Beulah both told me at different times that they felt snubbed by the Athens people. For a while, people were saying, "Elephant 6 East" and "Elephant 6 West." I always thought that was really stupid, but I guess at the time, it was necessary for them to distance themselves because they felt like second-class citizens.

Even with some of the Elephant 6's flagship bands going quiet, the collective was producing more than ever, expanding not just in number of people and amount of musical output but geographically, too.

As the core bands of the collective split apart into side projects, members recruited new people, often whole bands, to the scene from its periphery.

Two such bands were up in Brooklyn, the Essex Green and the Ladybug Transistor, which shared a lot of members between them and were already up and running when they got involved in the Elephant 6. While breaking down their gear after an Essex Green set at NYU, Jeff Baron (a member of both bands) got to talking to Jeff Mangum and Robert Schneider, who had been in attendance. Lost in the conversation, Baron ended up reassembling the Wurlitzer he was taking apart.

JEFF BARON: We weren't a really great live band, but we had a great set. They both said, "We want to start a label, and we want to put out your record."

SASHA BELL: When you find your kin, it's really inspirational. These guys are doing it, too. It's like you're evolving simultaneously. It's not like we heard the Apples and were like, "We gotta do that!" We were all simultaneously evolving in different parts of the country, so when we discovered each other, it's a revelation.

JEFF BARON: We formed the Essex Green in '96. We were fans, but we were up in Vermont, and we knew they were all the way down in Athens, and I had this romantic idea of what Athens was like. We finally got to go down there and play when I was playing in the Ladybug Transistor. We stayed at Jeff's house. They were building the set for what would be onstage for the *Aeroplane* tour. There was artwork everywhere. We slept in the living room, and in the middle of the night, we heard Jeff singing what would become "King of Carrot Flowers." We heard that "I love you, Jesus Christ" part coming super loud. It was filling the entire house.

GARY OLSON: We never had the stamp on our records, but we knew all those people. It was a nice umbrella to stand under. We never presented ourselves as an Elephant 6 band, but it always wound up in something somebody wrote somewhere. So it did follow us around for a while. I don't know if it helped us, but it was something for people to write about if we were coming to town.

SASHA BELL: I started playing with the Ladybug Transistor back in '95. For a long time, both bands functioned, touring. Both bands became Merge bands. Jeff [Baron] and I straddled those bands for a long time. It was totally psychotic. I would never do that again. When you're involving ten, twelve, fifteen people, you don't know the egos at stake. Even the audience was not appreciating three sets with overlapping people. I got a lot of negative feedback about that. "Why should I come to see you play three times?" To my face.

JAMEY HUGGINS: There used to be this division between the Denver Elephant 6 and the Athens Elephant 6, and as close as we were to the Athens one, it was Robert who really pulled the Great Lakes in. He was the one who made it his business to make our record. It was his approval that then came back through to Will and Bill and Jeff. I'm sure we were all friendly and like-minded enough at that point, but I did feel like we were auditioning, like, "Is this cool enough?"

BEN CRUM: It was a really fun experience for all of us. I feel lucky to have had the chance to work with [Robert]. Great Lakes went out to Denver in November 1999. We worked on the record at his Pet Sounds Studio. The place was just a cinder-block building. A few cats running around, and instruments and amps everywhere. He had what I still think was an amazing amount of focus and stamina, and he was incredibly cheerful throughout the process. All the while, he operated with basically an "another day at the office" type attitude.

MILES KUROSKY: I don't think we tried to distance ourselves from it. We just changed record labels. I admire a lot of the E6 stuff. To say my involvement was minimal would be an overstatement. I got to know the Apples and Dressy Bessy pretty well, but we didn't have much contact with the folks in Athens. Our first show was with the Olivia Tremor Control, and we did a very small West Coast tour with Of Montreal, but that was about it. Obviously, the cons are easier to pinpoint. Once you're attached to a "movement," you tend to get pigeonholed or worse yet, bogged down by others' expectations. I can't really say the association ever hurt us. I'd like to think the association helped us, but that's impossible to quantify or even prove for that matter. I can say, however, that Robert Schneider was directly responsible for giving us our start, and for that I am eternally grateful.

JOHN HILL: With Elephant 6, there were no board meetings. Those guys out there did their thing and added bands and put together releases, and we did the same thing. It didn't always seem like everybody agreed on everything. The principals all felt like they didn't have to get approval from everybody. I wouldn't call it animosity or anything like that. Beulah was a good example of Elephant 6 West, and the Elephant 6 East people, they were more hippie, super psychedelic, and so when the Beulah thing came out, I think it seemed to them that maybe it didn't fit.

HILARIE SIDNEY: They were more about the collective than Robert and I were. Robert and I were more about the label. We wanted to keep putting stuff out, and they were more like a hippie collective. It wasn't like anything where anyone said, "You can't do that." But there were some differences of opinions. It could have gotten confrontational, but everyone in that crowd tends to be afraid to say what they really think, so they tend to run a little passive-aggressive.

ANDREW RIEGER: I love the Apples records and the Minders records, and whenever we were out there, we would stay at Robert's house and hang out with him. I didn't grow up with Robert like Will and Bill and Jeff and all them, so I got to know him later. We've gotten to be friends over the years. I never really listened to Beulah. I met that guy Miles once at a show, but I never really knew them.

DEREK ALMSTEAD: We didn't have any musical connection other than the Elephant 6 name. I love the people in the Minders. I thought their records were great. But they all lived in Denver. If we saw each other, it was for one afternoon. On one hand, we're doing all this weird shit, and on the other, they're *bands.* It was maybe less crazy and chaotic over there. Athens encourages that kind of thing because you have so much downtime to come up with weird shit.

SASHA BELL: At the time, I never really considered the fact that we were in New York and everyone else was elsewhere. It felt like our family was all over the place. We happened to be living in New York, but we couldn't have survived there if we were living there all the time.

JAMEY HUGGINS: Sometimes people in Athens were very standoffish and kind of confused by the choices of including bands that were outside of Athens who Robert would choose, like Essex Green and even the Minders at first. We were suspicious of it. Definitely Beulah. Suddenly there's bands in Brooklyn and bands in California. Who are these people? When we got in, we made the rounds and did the penance and paid the piper. We went around and *asked,* sheepishly. Point-blank, but sheepishly. To Will. And Bill. And Jeff. "Can we do this?" Only asking that after we had months of attending every possible gathering, recording at every possible session. So then when you have someone who is living in Brooklyn who already had a record deal with Merge just kind of slipping in the back door, going, "Oh, we just finished our new album that none of you had anything to do with or have ever heard. Can we just slap it on there, too?" It was kind of offensive to us. We had felt like we somewhat worked for it.

JIM MCINTYRE: Robert wanted to have more of a real, tangible record label. Elephant 6 is like herding cats. For me, Elephant 6 was being inspired by mainly Robert, Jeff, Will, and Bill, these like-minded bandleaders. I wanted to impress them and I wanted them to impress me. It wasn't really like a scene.

REBECCA COLE: There was a sense of not necessarily division, but just diversification. It's going to mean this, and it's also going to mean that. I always felt really accepted by the Athens crew.

HILARIE SIDNEY: As it grew, there became a bit of a rift for a while when Will and Jeff moved back to Athens, because there became the Athens E6 movement where people just began to say they were part of E6, while the actual recording company and the original idea of actually releasing things was still happening in Denver with Robert. The two factions were not communicating very well and things got a bit messy and misunderstood at times, but in the end it all worked out okay. It became more of a concept or movement maybe than what was originally intended.

Chapter 19

SCOTT DEVOTED THE TIME HE WOULD HAVE BEEN SPENDING with Neutral Milk Hotel to the Gerbils. The band re-released its first album, *Are You Sleepy?*, with Jeremy adding a new layer of drums.

JEREMY BARNES: When they were reissuing it on vinyl, they asked me to overdub drums. I did it because I love them, but the original tape is much better. I was never a member of the Gerbils. I played with them because I loved them and needed to play drums as much as possible. Same goes for playing with the Music Tapes in the fall of '97 when we opened for Olivia on the West Coast.

SCOTT SPILLANE: Jeremy did something unique on the records he played on. He played only a snare and a floor tom and a cymbal. That was all. One take. One of the sound-collage segue pieces, he did like ten takes, but the rest of it is all one take with nothing but a floor tom, a snare, and a cymbal. Usually one microphone. Eric played drums for us for a while. John d'Azzo did most of the drums before that.

JAMEY HUGGINS: So often overlooked, it's ridiculous. When you think about Neutral Milk Hotel, you always think about Gerbils. That's a hell of a shadow to walk out from behind. For Scott to come up and sing—I think his challenge was to sing as loud and as emotive as Jeff, and he did, every breath as loud and every note as interesting. But for some reason, he was second fiddle because of the nature of the whole thing. But whenever Scott got up there and sang, people paid attention. He was great. He was like this enigma, because he looks like this old Santa Claus character with his big beard and big belly. One moment he's back there playing the horn and the next he's up there singing. I think Gerbils represent some kind of purity of the essence of the whole thing, and also some kind of steadfast, old-school, friendly rooted connection. They were Ruston.

DAN DONAHUE: I think Scott is misunderstood. I think Elephant 6 can be a blessing or a curse, and I think it was a curse for the Gerbils. They were overshadowed, but meanly. They would contrast it with Neutral Milk Hotel. Of course Jeff is this entity, but as a band and a whole unit, Scott adds so much to the sound of those records. I wouldn't imagine it without Scott.

"After playing with Jeff, there was no point in exploring a band with a vocalist," Jeremy Barnes told *Magnet* in 2000. "I can't really top that and it's easier to get the point across musically than it is lyrically. . . . I've always felt liberated playing the drums, even when I'm playing straight four-four. But I'm more interested in building textures with Bablicon than following a beat. One thing I learned from everybody in Athens was to keep your ears open."

JEREMY BARNES: The end of [Neutral Milk Hotel] was an extremely difficult time for me. I worked with other people and there were many things I wanted to do, but Neutral Milk Hotel was a very special focus. I always believed that the third album would be the one. I still do. Jeff's songs and what we created as a group through his vision, in spite of much difficulty, was truly unique. And I felt like we had just started. When it became obvious that it was over, I went through a rough depression. The only way out of that was music, to just continue playing, no matter what. I'm thankful that we never had a blowup. We just sort of disintegrated.

At eighteen, Jeremy had just moved to Chicago to begin his studies at DePaul University. During a summer orientation program in 1995, he met Griffin Rodriguez (a native Chicagoan who was there to study recording) in a Sikh temple after a performance of classical Indian music. When school started up, Griffin would bring his bass over to Jeremy's dorm room, where Jeremy had his drum kit set up. The pair would jam together, somehow evading the ire of the other students on the floor, who no doubt heard (and probably felt) Jeremy's tectonic drumming through the walls.

GRIFFIN RODRIGUEZ: He was very, very, very loud. I don't know how we managed to do it without getting in trouble, but we did.

Jeremy left school in early 1996 to join Neutral Milk Hotel and returned to DePaul that fall. He and Griffin wanted to add a third member to the group—anything but a guitarist, basically—and Griffin had seen a saxophone player with big red hair named Dave McDonnell around the music school. They got to talking one day, and after an enthusiastic discussion about the sax on Captain Beefheart's *Trout Mask Replica,* Griffin welcomed Dave into the new band. They called the trio Bablicon and started playing around Chicago in early 1997.

DAVE MCDONNELL: Playing with Jeremy the first time, I had never played with a drummer that played that loud. I played with a lot of drummers, and in high school, I had been in plenty of situations where a bunch of guitars, a bunch of drums, they're playing so loud that I can't even hear my saxophone in my skull. I've played with really loud volumes before. Jeremy was the first real rocker that I played with. I had played with people who were technically more skilled than him, but there's a way that a real musician plays, something in the way that they're playing their instrument. He had that. He could focus his energy. There was a confidence to what he was doing and a willingness to experiment.

GRIFFIN RODRIGUEZ: I knew he was an incredible drummer just from jamming with him in the dorm room. We had a great relationship right away. I liked jazz and all these things that he wasn't as familiar with, and he was showing me the Beach Boys and stuff like that that I was not as familiar with.

DAVE MCDONNELL: The first real Bablicon song we did was in two time signatures. It was in 7/8, and then it went to 5/4. He didn't need to be told that it was in 7/8 or 5/4. He just listened to the riff that I was doing and played along to the time. He just said, "How does it go?" and he just started playing to it. That had never happened before. It was always, "What is it doing? How is it counted? This doesn't make sense." He didn't do that. He could just execute.

Within a year of starting the band, though, Jeremy dropped out of school again for Neutral Milk Hotel, recording *Aeroplane* in Denver, rehearsing in New York, and heading out on tour. But even from afar, he had plans for Bablicon, emailing Griffin and Dave from the road about getting the band together once Neutral Milk Hotel slowed down. During a winter break at DePaul (1998 into '99), Dave and Griffin came to Athens to hang out and meet everyone, and the following spring Jeremy spent a week in Chicago to record Bablicon's *A Flat Inside a Fog/The Cat That Was a Dog.* The trip to Athens had left a big mark on both Griffin and Dave.

GRIFFIN RODRIGUEZ: We would go over to people's houses, and everybody had little four-track setups with microphones, or even a reel-to-reel setup, and they would just bring tapes from one house to the other, because everyone has a similar machine. You could bring a tape from Julian's over to Kevin's. Everybody had a similar recording format, so they could move around with tapes from house to house. I thought that was amazing. I was in school for recording, but I feel like I learned a lot of what I still do today recording-wise from those guys.

DAVE MCDONNELL: Wow, they just make music all the time. Some of them have day jobs. Some of them don't even have jobs. They're artists. That was striking to me, too. They're just jumping off the deep edge and doing what they want to do because that's what's important to them. That's what I ended up doing in my twenties.

GRIFFIN RODRIGUEZ: The way they recorded was one of my biggest influences right away. I really loved how you could just go and visit your friend's house. "We're going over to John Fernandes's to record clarinet today." You could just go to your friend's house and do overdubs, or John would come over to do clarinet in the afternoon. All of our recording, everyone was doing overdubs on everybody else's album all the time. A typical day would be wake up, get coffee, and then go to people's houses. It was just recording all day, every day.

DAVE MCDONNELL: Meeting those people totally changed my life. I wouldn't be doing what I'm doing now if I hadn't met those people.

GRIFFIN RODRIGUEZ: Going to recording school, I was learning more from the Elephant 6 guys. Making records is what I do, and that has definitely followed me. One of the first things that I still employ to this day is how the Elephant 6 guys were able to use a room. They were very into room dynamics and how different rooms sounded. At a time when no one was using room mics. It really gave the recordings a sense of space and a sense of place. Every single track would have so much character because of how it was recorded.

Jeremy eventually left Athens, spending his time in Albuquerque and Eastern Europe with a new band he'd started with his now-wife, violinist Heather Trost, called A Hawk and a Hacksaw.*

Julian had started recording the Music Tapes' first record when he was still living in New York, but he put it on hold when he got involved with Neutral Milk Hotel. When Neutral Milk finished touring in the fall of 1998, Julian refocused his efforts on his Music Tapes project and released *1st Imaginary Symphony for Nomad* in July 1999.

ROBBIE CUCCHIARO: The music was always around me, so we would have our philosophical whatevers about it. It's definitely born of Julian. We were together for six years, in an intimate relationship. That changed around 2001 or 2002. When we were living together in New York is when the Music Tapes were born, in our apartment on Charles Street. I think I was part of that birth, because a lot of the subject material of the first album is inspired by what we lived through and what we were able to talk about from living through that. We were trying to understand our growing up through that album. There's a lot of parallels in that for both of us.

* What makes a band an Elephant 6 band? Some of the core bands (Neutral Milk Hotel, the Olivia Tremor Control, the Apples in Stereo) obviously are, but there are also bands like Of Montreal, who recorded some albums as part of the collective and some decidedly not. There are bands like the Lilys, who released a record on the Elephant 6 label but are not considered part of the collective. There are musicians like John Fernandes, who plays with some Elephant 6 bands and some non-, and people like Jeremy Barnes, whose Bablicon and A Hawk and a Hacksaw work seems to fall outside of the collective. It's blurry, more spectrum than binary, but it's also basically meaningless. The Elephant 6 itself lacks a clear definition. I've heard it described as a record label, an art collective, a fraternity, a potluck, a cult, a commune, a co-op, and probably fifty other things, none of which is quite accurate on its own.

JEREMY BARNES: His goal was to get the Music Tapes on the radio. Not college radio, but at every level. Julian was singing through a broken window fan into a wire recorder in a closet and talking about how his songs will be on the Billboard charts. It had been obvious since before the Denver *Aeroplane* recordings that he was not happy in Neutral Milk Hotel. Jeff had a very distinct vision of what he wanted. If he didn't like what one of us were doing, he would tell us. What you hear on *Aeroplane* is his vision. What you hear on Music Tapes records is Julian's vision. It can be hard to allow someone else to lead, and it can be hard when your ideas get shot down. And we were playing at an extremely loud level. Even Jeff alone with an acoustic guitar was very loud. Once we were back from that tour and in Athens, Julian put it out there that he would become an auxiliary member, like he was for Olivia, and we would find someone else to be there all the time. Neutral Milk Hotel was never his main thing, and in late 1998, he had a record contract of his own.

Killing some time in Europe together after an Olivia Tremor Control tour had ended and before a Neutral Milk Hotel tour began, Julian and Robbie stayed in England with a friend. While there, they made time to master *1st Imaginary Symphony* at Abbey Road Studios in London. They pulled an all-nighter before their appointment, sequencing the album in a frenzy. As a sign of goodwill in the hope of signing the band, Sub Pop Records paid for the mastering session without hearing a second of it.

ROBBIE CUCCHIARO: That was just the strength of what was going on around us.

The Music Tapes ended up signing with Merge to release the album. Julian approached the first Music Tapes album with the same sense of exploration characteristic of everything else he'd done to that point. Recording gear included a wire recorder from the 1940s and an Edison wax cylinder from the nineteenth century, lending *1st Imaginary Symphony* a weathered, fragile quality. Even on a brand-new CD, it sounds like one more spin could tatter it, but the layers of experiments—in production, structure, instrumentation—overlap to keep it from coming apart. It's an album that wants badly for you to love it but has no fear about offering something you might hate.

Reviewers, when they noticed the record at all, fell mostly into two camps. Some guarded their appraisals with "not for everyone" disclaimers but acknowledged that it's originality-above-all ambition succeeded on its own merits. The *CMJ New Music Report* describes it as "perfect for adventurous, non-commercial radio programmers." In the *Calgary Straight*, Elizabeth Chorney describes the first third of the album as "spooky, noise-ridden tracks that are virtually unlistenable," but overall, it's "a nice, albeit sometimes difficult, slice of [Julian's] daydreams." In *The A.V. Club*, Keith Phipps writes, "Connoisseurs of violently fragmented pop will find a lot to like here," but the record "should prove rough going for anyone else."

What's original and creative to one pair of ears, though, can sound pretentious and weird-for-the-sake-of-being-weird to another. *Pitchfork*'s Brent DiCrescenzo, for example, called *1st Imaginary Symphony* an "overwrought beast nobody has been waiting for . . . a fitting album to close out this selfish decade."

In the Elephant 6 era of Neutral Milk Hotel and the Olivia Tremor Control, those bands fostered critical affection in part because of how strange and new they seemed in the context of indie music more broadly at the time. The next wave of releases was judged against the Elephant 6 output that preceded it.

JULIAN KOSTER: They tried to make it about sixties pop or something, but nobody was trying to make sixties pop, and nothing that was being made—if you listen to it in any sane, rational way—has much of anything to do with sixties pop. But that was really important. The stuff that Kevin and Of Montreal were doing was in a different universe from what Olivia was doing, which was in a different universe from what Neutral Milk was doing, which was a different universe from what the Music Tapes were doing, which was a different universe from what the Gerbils or Elf Power were doing. All these things were like coexistent universes. So it made it really cool and exciting to peer into that. Everyone's excited, and then you're excited to go into your room and work on what you're making. But that feeling is something deeper than thought. Its presence gives energy to whatever you're doing, and its radiance is warming. I do feel like in periods of time when that's especially present among groups of people in my life, the things that get made are very generous in spirit. They're different from the things people might make in isolation.

As Julian and others—empowered by the support they'd received, cheered for their idiosyncrasies—leaned harder into the tendencies that so many had found appealing the first time, some sort of a backlash against the Elephant 6 had begun.

As his Neutral Milk Hotel bandmates released records from their own projects, Jeff stayed out of the public eye. No one was really sure why, but neither did anyone have any reason to suspect it was more than a post-tour breather. After the *Aeroplane* tour concluded, Jeff turned his attention to a tape-collage project under the name Korena Pang. He never released it, but those who have heard the album describe it as very different from anything Neutral Milk Hotel released.

GRIFFIN RODRIGUEZ: Jeff basically moved to Chicago for a month or two. We did a little playing and recording, but not much. It never really happened that we would end up playing with Jeff so much as just hanging out with him a bunch.

DAVE MCDONNELL: Jeff had this amazing collage record. Digital was brand-new back then. We were all working with tape. Jeff had this Fostex digital eight-track. It's laughable now what he had to do to make these edits. There's this tiny little LED window, and you'd have this little scrub wheel that would move you fractions of a second closer to some edit point.

ROBERT SCHNEIDER: Jeff's been interested in that sort of stuff for years. He never outgrew it. He's always pursued this separate angle of doing noise music and musique concréte.

GRIFFIN RODRIGUEZ: There were some pop songs, too. There were a couple pop songs with mostly cut-up stuff. We loved that record. It's such a weird, amazing follow-up to *In the Aeroplane Over the Sea*. It wasn't going to be called Neutral Milk Hotel. But it never happened.

DAVE MCDONNELL: He was obviously burned on being on the road, and I think he was burned on people approaching him to make more money with his music. I think Jeff felt straitjacketed into being this song guy, and so he pushed back. It was like he was daring people: "Try and still like me now that I have this weird interest." Korena Pang was this absolute masterpiece of him totally pushing all the buttons. I absolutely loved it. We all thought it was a work of genius.

ROBERT SCHNEIDER: Jeff would have his life as a lo-fi folk singer, folk-pop guy, and then separately he'd be doing some project like Clay Bears that was more purely experimental.

DAVE MCDONNELL: We were going to do a record together in Chicago, summer of 2000. There was this week where Jeff was up there, but Jeff didn't want to do it with just Jeremy and me. It had to be all of us. Griffin had to finish something, but we were like, "Dude, you don't understand, he's going to get bored and leave." And he did, abruptly. He was so tired of it that he left his eight-track at my apartment, and I'm so pissed I didn't copy that stuff. I haven't heard Korena Pang in years.

Jeff's musical interests extended well beyond noisy folk rock. *Aeroplane* and *Avery Island* are rife with flourishes of those vast and varied tastes, but they were only keyhole views, and though Jeff felt comfortable writing and playing some version of rock music, he had other ambitions as well. He chose a different name for more experimental pursuits, perhaps to insulate the work from the rockist expectations it would command under the name Neutral Milk Hotel.

Korena Pang wasn't a new thing, exactly. Jeff had been recording experimental work for years, accumulating boxes and boxes of tapes. Even before he took a break from Neutral Milk Hotel, he spoke openly about wanting to explore that world further. "I'm probably gonna put out a lot of the really weird, experimental records under a different name for a while," he told *Stomp and Stammer* in 1998. "Stuff like that's sorta fun to get lost in for a while, to really sort of free your mind of everything and just sort of go for it. I'd like to make a record of a hundred little five-second songs. That's the kind of thing this summer, I wanna get a lot of people together and recording and having fun and not taking it too seriously.

"I think that's what's important."

Jeff would appear onstage once in a while behind a friend's band, or people would spot him in the crowd at shows, usually in New York. But he didn't perform anymore, never released any new music, turned down or usually just ignored interview requests, and generally stayed out of the public eye.

In the Aeroplane Over the Sea has the following it has in large part due to its uniqueness as a record, but Jeff Mangum is not without his influences, and among the easiest to hear is Tall Dwarfs. Give one of the earlier Tall Dwarfs records a spin and you'll hear the well-worn instruments, lyrics that blend the whimsical with the devastating, and many familiar tones and artifacts of analog recording and production. Mangum's signature sound (not to mention his DIY sensibility) owes a great deal to the New Zealand lo-fi pop band, and the Elephant 6 as a whole was conceived with Flying Nun (the aggressively indie label that released all six Tall Dwarfs albums along with seven EPs and two compilation records) as a reference point. So it's no wonder he felt compelled to play a show in Auckland with Tall Dwarfs singer-songwriter Chris Knox.

Jeff and Laura spent most of January 2001 on vacation in New Zealand, with Knox showing them around. Knox took them to Goat Island, a deceivingly named fish sanctuary where they snorkeled with thousands of finned friends. They stayed at Knox's family's beach house for a week. When a neighbor put his Corolla up for sale, Jeff and Laura bought it on the spot for $200 and drove it around the islands. They checked out the glaciers. They drove up to the top of the North Island and then took a ferry down to the bottom of the South Island. They saw hot springs and ice caves. They slathered themselves in sunscreen and bodysurfed.

At the end of the trip, on February 4, 2001, Jeff, Laura, and Knox played a show together at Kings Arms, a small bar in Auckland. All three were barefoot. Probably seventy-five people in the crowd, maybe only fifty, all of them sitting cross-legged on the floor. Chris played some of his songs, and then Jeff played a bunch of his. Laura provided accordion and clarinet. Jeff's set lasted just over fifty minutes, featuring a bunch of songs from *Aeroplane*, a few from *Avery Island*, a couple of covers (John Lennon's "Mother" and the Paris Sisters' "I Love How You Love Me"), and "Everything Is."

LAURA CARTER: Jeff and I tend to be hypercritical. If I fuck up, I'm like, *Damn it, I blew it.* That show, I thought we slayed. I thought it was a special, flawless show. We had such a special time.

You'd never guess he hadn't had a public performance in more than two years. The show wasn't even advertised as a Jeff Mangum or Neutral Milk Hotel performance. It was billed as Walking Wall of Beards Inc., which Jeff explains during the set was the name of a company in the early 1900s that manufactured devices that would produce an inaudible sound that caused all of the loose hairs in the vicinity—beard hairs, pubic hairs, "if you lived near a barber shop, you were really doing good"—to form a wall and walk around.

"One day, we will all look like fools for not having beard walls to walk around with, because in the future, it's going to be really hip."

Early in the set, between "Song Against Sex" and "The King of Carrot Flowers," Jeff takes a moment to address the crowd. He tells them he hasn't played a show in a while and has no immediate plans to play another, and he reveals that he's had "a little bit of a nervous breakdown."

"But it was a very wonderful thing to have happen to me," he continues with some hesitation, "and I mean that sincerely. It was really a good thing after a while. At first, it was a real drag, but then I learned a lot."

From the audience, someone barks, "Where can I get one?"

"I'll let you borrow mine," Jeff responds with a laugh. "I think I'm about done with it, so I'll let you have it."

A year later, Jeff's performance in New Zealand went from being his first show in two years to the only one he had done in three, and he had done exactly zero interviews over the same span. But after declining request after request, he sat down for a conversation with Marci Fierman for *Pitchfork* in January 2002. Fierman's interview with Jeff feels breezy from familiarity (they met in a yoga class, before she even knew he was a musician). She writes of his absence: "Those of us here in Athens, Georgia, knew he was hanging out with friends, shooting the shit and pursuing odd and sundry projects the way most of us do," but their conversation yields some specificity on what he had been up to.

His most recent activity at the time was a collage of field recordings he had compiled on a jaunt to a folk music festival in Bulgaria. He hadn't traveled there with any intent to make a record, but he brought his field recorder with him so he could share some of the experience with his friends. Upon his return, he spent a couple of days cobbling together the pieces that he found most moving. The people he shared it with encouraged him to release it, and so Orange Twin put it out, donating the proceeds to

Bulgarian charities. Released in June 2001, it's the second-to-last record credited to Jeff, with the final being *Live at Jittery Joe's*, released about two months later but recorded years earlier.*

While in Europe, Jeff also spent time collecting sounds in France and Spain for a new tape-collage project, different from Korena Pang. He described the Korena Pang record as a collage of about twenty different home recordings he had made throughout the nineties, but he abandoned it because "it turned into a mishmash that I wasn't totally in love with." The new project, by contrast, was "like a thousand sounds in one minute. Now I'm able to go out into the world with my field recorder, record sounds, and bring them home to collage on the computer. The raw sounds can really move and come alive that way. I love the idea of a record containing an entire universe; where the sounds span decades of recording from all over the world and all sorts of different sources. . . . I wish I could work on it all the time, but if I work on it for more than a few hours a day I start going insane. It can take an entire week to make twenty seconds of music."

Fierman describes Jeff as "incapable of hiding his internal state of being: emotions skitter across his face like rapid weather fronts beating their way to the coast." Throughout the interview, even though it's text-only and published as a straight Q&A without any descriptive interjection from the writer, a reader can easily ascertain Jeff's emotional state, which vacillates through the conversation. Though he's excited about his current projects, he's bearish on ever recording as Neutral Milk Hotel again. The songs he wrote in that vein, after *Aeroplane*, he says, were too linear.† He rejects the idea that it had anything to do with pressure from the success of *Aeroplane* or the increased attention he was receiving. Instead, it was the fact that the album had reached so many people and didn't do what he wanted it to do.

> I went through a period, after *Aeroplane*, when a lot of the basic assumptions I held about reality started crumbling. I think that before

* Later records from other bands like the Apples in Stereo would include parts played by Jeff, and he recorded a Tall Dwarfs cover that was included on a compilation released to raise money for Chris Knox after Chris suffered a stroke, but *Orange Twin Field Works: Volume I* and *Live at Jittery Joe's* were the last two actual albums listing Jeff as the primary artist.

† Fierman characterizes Mangum's description of the songs' creation as a "long farting noise."

then, I had an intuitive innocence that guided me and that was a very good thing to a certain point. But then I realized that, to a large degree, I had kept my rational mind at bay my whole life. I just acted on intuition in terms of how I related to life. At some point, my rational mind started creeping in, and it would not shut up. I finally had to address it and confront it . . .

The songs were what I stood for. It was a representation of the platform of my mind that I stood on. And if the platform of the mind is crumbling . . . then the songs go with it. Also, I think that the difficult thing after *Aeroplane* was that, when we started doing the Elephant 6 thing, we had a very utopian vision that we could overcome anything through music. The music wasn't just there for entertainment: we were trying to create some sort of change. We had a desire to transform our lives, and the listeners' lives. . . . So when so many of our dreams had come true and yet I still saw that so many of my friends were in a lot of pain . . . I saw their pain from a different perspective and realized that I can't just sing my way out of all this suffering. I have to try to understand human nature and myself and the nature of suffering and a lot of these other issues on a deeper level.

Jeff continued to look inward. The tape collages and other projects he mentioned in the interview were never released.

As he retreated further from public view, Jeff found some creative release with an overnight show on north Jersey radio station WFMU, DJing under the name "Jefferson." He hosted a three-hour show nine times over the ten Mondays from October 14 to December 16, 2002. A typical playlist would include free jazz, tape collages, avant-garde compositions, spoken word, antique folk and religious music, and any number of other pieces not so easily classifiable.

Lance Bangs: One of the times I felt happiest for Jeff was when he started DJing on WFMU. Just going in and playing long chunks of interesting music. You found a steady activity to go do that's going back to when he was a college radio DJ when he was younger. I'm sure there was a community of supportive friends at the station. That's a cool, semi-structured thing to do.

Jeff is nomadic by his nature. In the old interviews I came across while researching this book, he seemed to be speaking with the writer from a different location every time, even when he wasn't touring. Often, when he mentioned where he was, he would add that he was on his way out, with a different destination in mind each time, be it a small town in Arizona, back to Louisiana, or a shack in the Ozarks. When I began searching for him myself, his oldest friends seemed to all have a different guess as to where he was living at the time. I heard Oakland. I heard Toronto. New York was the second-most common response, but even then I heard a mix of in the city, just outside of it, and hours upstate. The most common response was "I'm not really sure, to be honest."

Jeff didn't disappear, exactly. He just kept doing what he always did, which was move around. His friends were not surprised, and even distant admirers could have seen it coming. An incomplete list of relevant quotes published before the end of 1998 follows:

> "I just want to end up in a basement with my 8-track making tapes."

> "We're always moving somewhere. We tend to find ourselves leaving places more than coming to places. Typically, I'm more comfortable packing my things in a box than having them sit all folded on a shelf. That's too properly arranged."

> "Being in different places has been really good for me. But now I'm getting to where I want to settle down and live in the forest. I don't like the way we're so disconnected from nature. I'm going to move up to the Ozarks, and not have a telephone, or computer, or television, or newspapers. I never felt like I was part of the music scene world, but I definitely think that dropping out is something I'm going to have to do. I think I'd be happier that way."

> "And now, the songs and the band are getting attention and that's really cool, but I know it's only temporary. It's something I would never try to hold on to. My music can only handle so much attention before it

eventually retreats . . . I'm getting more and more mentally detached from the way the quote-unquote real world works. At this point, I have to accept the fact that I'm caught up in living in a world where you have to eat and get in a car and put on clothes and stuff. I just want to make music with my friends and have that communal experience."

"I think this is about as well known as we'll ever be. I can pretty much guarantee it."

CHAPTER 20

IT TAKES A LONG TIME TO INTERVIEW ROBERT SCHNEIDER. A *long* time. As you've no doubt noticed by now, he's a big part of this story, from start to wherever it ends, which means he and I had a lot of ground to cover. But he takes a long, *long* time to cover that ground.

Today, we're starting at his house in Decatur, just outside Atlanta. He has lived here while pursuing his PhD in mathematics at Emory University, studying under decorated number theorist Ken Ono. He was up early. Demolition on the house next door began at seven a.m., and the din woke him up. His house will face the same fate when they move out, he says, and a shitty McMansion will be erected in its place. His house as it still stands is orderly but overrun by old science books. A large poster displays dozens of minerals and taxonomizes their physical properties.

After a long chat with his wife, Marci, Robert decides he'll be able to concentrate better if we take our conversation to a nearby coffee shop. He delays our departure to give his son, Max, an extended farewell, as if he's heading off to sea and doesn't know when or whether he'll return. In a teal bucket hat and a tight, fuchsia-striped T-shirt, Robert has the look of a fisherman drawn by a child who has already exhausted their primary- and secondary-color crayons and moved on to the colors of scarcer application.

When we finally get outside, Robert stops to talk to his neighbor. In the half mile or so to the coffee shop, Robert runs into another few people he has to say hello to, and then he catches up with two folks behind the counter at the coffee shop. He's apparently a regular here. After microwaving his breakfast burrito, we go to a table outside, but a few passersby catch his attention out there, too. It takes us a while to get going.

The interview itself isn't much smoother.* Robert is a natural storyteller, with the familiar oratory style of a professor accustomed to teaching sleepy undergrads but wanting so badly to get them *excited* about logarithms. The stories progress on his terms, so when I ask a simple question expecting a straightforward answer, it takes him an awful long while to get to the point. Each part of the narrative has its own little backstory, and each of those has a backstory, and the whole fractal will collapse in on itself if I don't sort of twist his arm about moving along. It once took him about ten minutes to answer "What was your paternal grandfather's first name?"

We spend a few hours at the coffee shop together, but Robert doesn't stop once to eat his food. When it's time to leave, he swallows his nearly full cup of now lukewarm coffee in a few rushed gulps, and he brings the burrito home with him. We're heading back to his house because it's beginning to rain, and as we walk through the neighborhood, he protects my recorder with his hat so we can keep talking. Every minute counts. Back at his house, we settle into a back room. His cat, Odd, enters and settles against the leg of a desk. Robert is eager to show me his son's new instrument, a contrabass clarinet. It's about eight feet long, and Robert had never heard of it before Max first mentioned it to him, which has Robert just giddy. Max, still in high school, has also enrolled in some college courses and built his own computer. Robert is effusively proud.

Before each interview I conducted with Robert, he told me (with an uncharacteristic concision that suggested he had given the spiel to many interviewers before me) to interject if I ever felt he was getting off topic, that he would take no offense if I forcefully directed the conversation to keep his penchant for tangents from sabotaging my interrogative efforts. Even with his explicit permission, this proved awfully difficult.

For one thing, Robert goes on a *lot* of tangents, but they only count as tangential because I didn't know to ask about them. Even when they're not

* Like all of my interviews with Robert, just setting it up was a challenge, though this one was particularly slippery. In December, he had suggested a weekend in March for me to fly down to Atlanta and spend some time together. I purchased my plane ticket that day. In the time between booking the trip and the day of the flight, Robert went dark on me. He didn't respond to any of my texts or emails or phone calls. His voicemail inbox was full, so I couldn't leave a message there. It was only when I was sitting in the terminal at Philadelphia International Airport, forty-five minutes before boarding the plane to Atlanta, that he called me and suggested we get coffee the following day.

relevant, they're always compelling (and it takes a while before a story's relevance is clear). The guy knows how to tell a story, and he tells stories with a masterful command of suspense. Cutting off a subject before you know where their story is going is generally not a good investigative tactic. With Robert, I know he's going *somewhere*, so I usually just let him roll.

The other challenge with interviewing Robert is that he talks so damn *fast*, and I lack the conversational ferocity to shunt his train of thought.* On this particular day, my recorder ran for nearly five hours, and he was actually able to keep things relatively linear. We covered from about 1983 to about 1987 in terms of his life story. Conversations with Robert move in several directions at once, but he never loses the thread.

None of this should sound like a complaint. Robert's natural state is one most people would require a quadruple espresso and maybe a B_{12} shot to attain, and it is infectious. Within a few minutes of talking to him, even on the phone, I feel like I could lift a car over my head. Whenever I spoke to anyone else about Robert, they would inevitably mention what a catalyst he's been for the collective, how he radiates enthusiasm and makes them feel motivated. He's not the only person in the collective with this quality, but he's probably the most intensely positive person among them. I've experienced this myself every time we've interacted in person, over the phone, and even in some extended iMessage exchanges.

One more example. In the early days of the COVID-19 pandemic, we arranged for another chat. I figured we'd talk over the phone, or maybe a video call, as had become de rigueur during the quarantine. Instead, he had me download *Second Life*, a somewhat dated online "virtual world" in

* It's worth mentioning here that this also makes Robert's interviews a pain in the ass to transcribe. Transcription is always tedious, but it's especially so with people who speak quickly. The key to transcribing efficiently is getting into a rhythm where you can type along at the same rate as the playback, especially when you can sort of anticipate what's coming next. (This makes it much easier to transcribe interviews you've conducted versus conversations you're hearing for the first time, and the sooner you transcribe relative to when you conducted it, the faster you can go.) I'm a pretty fast typist, but I can't usually type along in real time. To get into the rhythm, I'll usually slow most interviews down to ninety or maybe eighty-five percent of their original speed, allowing me to type along without having to constantly pause and rewind and start again. With Robert, though, I sometimes have to slow him way down to about fifty percent if I want to keep up. I honestly don't stand a chance otherwise. And slowing it down to half speed actually takes more than twice as long to transcribe, because in addition to the speed decrease, it also makes us both sound kind of drunk, which means I end up taking breaks to laugh every so often.

which users create an avatar, design their environments, and walk around and interact with one another. It looks like if *The Sims* were also a chatroom. Robert, now a math professor, had been teaching classes at the University of Georgia. Once those classes shifted online in response to quarantine guidelines, most instructors just set up Zoom meetings in place of classroom interactions, but Robert moved his classes into *Second Life*.

When I met him there, his avatar was clad in dark jeans, a red hoodie, and a few long, beaded necklaces. But for the periwinkle skin, the avatar looked a lot like his real-life physical form, down to the round-framed glasses, bushy beard, and avuncular baldness. Robert led me to the office he had created for meetings with his students, proudly showing off the digital sound sculptures they'd made in there. Then he showed me his second, secret office, accessed through a waterfall. We flew there. He told me he had built this office pretty much from scratch, deleting everything that was in there when he arrived except for the ducks that were swimming in a small pond inside. The polygonal mallards seemed to have some form of sentience, he supposed, so it seemed karmically risky to remove them. They weren't causing any trouble anyway.

Without access to a physical classroom, Robert wanted to give his students an immersive experience. He treated this virtual world as if it were his physical-world classroom. Only once they were inside could students access the "coordinates" for that day's class, that is, the Zoom meeting URL. To quote a review from one of his former students on the website Rate My Professors: "Robert Schneider is one of the kindest people I have ever had the blessing to know. As an education major, his drive for teaching is inspiring, as he is the epitome of who a teacher should be. He is kind, flexible, understanding, hilarious, knowledgable and insightful."*

"SpinART loves us," Hilarie told the *Denver Post* in 1999. "They'd do anything for us. They understand where we're coming from creatively, and they encourage that . . . and we have an agreement with spinART that allows us to make a lot more money [per record sold] than we can make on a major label. The real reward is that we're living it now. I work a part-time job, and I'm pretty happy with that. We live pretty hand to mouth, and sometimes the bills don't get paid on time, but it's cool, because we

* Robert is rated a healthy 4.6 out of 5 overall and twenty out of twenty-one students say they would take a course with him again.

have a lot of free time to work on our band, and that's all I want—free time to do music."

The Apples got along well with spinART for a while, but certain tensions were too much to bear forever.

> HILARIE SIDNEY: Joel was the sweetest guy in the whole world, but he would forget things and mess things up and give us his word about something without talking to Jeff, the other guy. Jeff ended up being the main guy for spinART by default, even though it was Joel originally, just because Jeff was more responsible. Jeff was constantly mad at Joel for promising us stuff Jeff thought was crazy. So I think Jeff thought we were asking and asking and asking for things without giving them what they wanted.
>
> JOEL MOROWITZ: Jeff is very forthright and gruff, and he often rubbed people the wrong way.
>
> HILARIE SIDNEY: He said weird things sometimes that pissed us off, like we should dress up more. One time, after I had had Max and I was probably at the heaviest I've ever been, he told me I should really lose weight and no one is going to like me if I'm fat. He doesn't have a lot of tact. He and Robert fought a lot over money.

Hilarie and Robert started dating in 1992. They married in 1999, and had their son, Max, in 2000. That's around when both the Olivia Tremor Control and Neutral Milk Hotel stopped playing. Given that both of those bands were on an upward trajectory when they slammed on the brakes, it's easy to imagine how much bigger they could have gotten keeping a foot on the gas pedal instead. But consider the Apples in Stereo, who were having relatively similar success at the time and only coasted from there. Perhaps the Olivias or Neutral Milk would have continued to accelerate, but perhaps their hiatus was a big reason for their popularity. Perhaps all three bands were mutually dependent on one another—given that they all took every chance they could to talk up the projects of their friends in interviews, and any press any of them got usually mentioned the Elephant 6 as a whole—and a one-legged stool cannot stand on its own.

At any rate, Denver was beginning to feel a bit isolated. No longer did the Apples have friends passing through so frequently. Their earlier guests were mostly settled in Athens now and didn't have much to justify a trip out to Denver to record, now that they were touring less frequently. The city wasn't offering much for Robert and Hilarie, either. In the summer of 2002, after they sent the masters of *Velocity of Sound* to their label but before it was released, Hilarie and Robert left Denver and moved to Lexington, Kentucky, to be a bit closer to their families and friends.

HILARIE SIDNEY: I sort of dragged Robert here. He did not want to move. But rent kept going up in Denver, and we had tried to buy a house, and we couldn't qualify for anything that we could afford. And my parents moved here, and I wanted to be close to them because they were getting older. Geographically, it's closer to Chicago, it's closer to Athens, it's closer to a lot of places we like to visit. Robert does not like change, and he doesn't like to move. He collects a lot of things. When we moved from Denver, every single friend we had helped us move. We were packing boxes up until we drove away.

ROBERT SCHNEIDER: Our music life and having a studio and a label was so intertwined with our personal relationship that they had never been separated. The marriage aspect kind of fell apart. When we moved to Kentucky, I had just finished *Velocity of Sound*. We finished recording the album as we were packing the studio up and loading it into a moving truck. We recorded it on the eight-track, and I had sent the tapes off to get mixed by Bryce Goggin, who had done Pavement's *Crooked Rain, Crooked Rain*, which is one of my favorite records. As we were moving into the new house in Kentucky, I would be getting mixes and reviewing them and sending back mix notes. We went on tour for the album soon after that.

HILARIE SIDNEY: There was a lot of tension with us playing together. It was hard. It was still fun, but it was hard. It's all really good now. We get along really well, and I really like his wife, Marci. I think she's great for him. She's really organized. I was never organized like her. She's really good at keeping his shit together, and he needs someone to keep his shit together. I'm not very good at keeping my *own* shit together.

Robert and Hilarie split up in 2003. The following year, Hilarie married Per Ole Bratset, whom she'd met on the tour supporting *Velocity of Sound*.

He moved to Lexington, and they started a band together called the High Water Marks and released their first album, *Songs About the Ocean*, also in 2004. They had a son together, Anders, in 2005.

Now based in Norway, the High Water Marks have since released a few more full-length records and shorter works. Hilarie remained in the Apples for one more album, 2007's *New Magnetic Wonder*. She went back to school and got her nursing degree, then moved to Norway in 2014.

HILARIE SIDNEY: We started writing songs together through the mail. [Per Ole] would send me tracks and then I'd get them and transfer them from the four-track to my laptop, and then I'd record some more parts, and then when we had about eight songs, I bought a ticket to go out there and finish recording. I went out there in March and we recorded the record and some extra songs in my hotel room. I don't see us hitting the road anytime soon. I'm just not into that anymore. I love music and I'll always record music, but I just don't give a shit if anybody hears it.

JOHN HILL: The Apples are two distinct entities. There's the Apples with Hilarie and the Apples without Hilarie. Hilarie had an underground approach to it, and she kept us grounded in that way. There was no possibility of anything sounding cheesy. And then the second she leaves, we break wide open with the cheese. *New Magnetic Wonder* kind of started it, because that's when she was breaking off and wasn't paying attention as much. Then we come in with *Travellers in Space and Time*. I always try to imagine Hilarie listening to that record, and I imagine her cringing the whole time.

HILARIE SIDNEY: I asked Robert not to say this, but when he announced I was leaving the Apples, they had all the press say I was leaving the band to focus on the High Water Marks, which was really not true. I guess they didn't want to say why I was leaving the band because they didn't want to make it seem scandalous.

ROBERT SCHNEIDER: Everybody in Elephant 6 rubbed up in different ways with the popular culture and that scene. It might shock you out of making music, like with Jeff. Everybody treats it in different ways. I always looked at it as sort of a game. I loved records from the time I was a little kid. I loved the music industry. I loved MTV. I was like, *We're just going to play this like a game.* They covered one of my songs on *American Idol*[*] and shit. Even so, it didn't feel important, but my mom called me and was proud because she saw it on TV. That's what matters to mainstream people. If you're going to be in the public eye, it's because you've done something either so shocking or something so poppy that it's become available to the public. So the impression the Apples make [on the mainstream] is *Powerpuff Girls* and "Energy." Us doing sound collages or something that sounds like an LSD trip isn't part of that image, even though it's part of who you are as a band. TV presents the line. If you're on it, you're a simplified cartoon character. You're not the subtle artist anymore, regardless of who you really are.

* "Energy" was performed by the remaining five contestants in 2009 in the show's weekly car commercial/music video.

IT TOOK ME A LITTLE WHILE TO FIND ORANGE TWIN WHEN I came out to talk to Laura Carter today. Fewer than five miles north of downtown Athens, things are a bit more spread out and rural up here. The community was founded in part to provide a way for people to live off the grid, and while it still draws electricity and running water from civilized society, the site is at least a bit of a counterpoint to Google Maps' omniscience. The GPS I used to navigate here led me to a totally separate subdivision, and when I tried to figure out the route the old-fashioned way, I ran into some analog confusion: the sign for the street Orange Twin sits on had been knocked over, so I didn't even notice it until my third time passing by.

When I finally found the compound, I was greeted by Laura's two hounds, Alice and Gertrude. Mountain curs, both of them. "The most versatile hunting dog known to man," Laura told me in an affected Southern accent (which is to say, a cartoonishly exaggerated version of her own inflection, which is noticeably, hospitably Georgian). Neither Laura nor anybody else who lives here hunts, but the dogs at least keep the indigenous coyotes at bay.* Alice brought Laura a squirrel just yesterday. The dogs were the first to greet me when I arrived at Orange Twin, which made my approach down the winding dirt road to the main house that much slower: as they vetted my car, they kept crisscrossing in front of it, and I rode the brake the entire time to keep from flattening them.

* Or at least they're supposed to. Orange Twin had a half-dozen egg-laying chickens up until a week ago, when Alice and Gertrude were apparently sleeping on the job.

Laura was there to greet me when I finally arrived at the house, but before we dove into an interview, she had to feed the braying "chew crew," the ten or so goats (most of them just a few weeks old) she deploys to help clear the land via their grazing. Some of them produce milk, which saves Orange Twin's residents a trip to Kroger. After their dinner, the goats mellowed out quite a bit, but it still ended up being one of the noisier interviews I conducted. Instead of the typical clatter and clang of a coffee shop in the background, though, today's conversation contended with birds chirping above us, twigs and fallen branches snapping beneath our feet, a creek babbling and spitting nearby, and, still, goats hollering in the distance. Lots more animals than humans out here.

I was here around what my dad used to call the shank of the day, the soothingly liminal time before dusk, early enough that there was still sunlight (dappled though it was by the deciduous trees in their hypnopompic early-spring state of undress) but late enough that we could amble about the 155-acre tract without sweating profusely. It was warm, but Laura wore her grandmother's heavy wool cardigan. Regardless of the topic at hand, she spoke with an iceberg of a smile, the kind that usually creeps across a person's face right before they deliver a killer punch line.

Laura is, in the parlance of folks I've talked to about her, a doer, a go-getter, a catalyst, an ass-kicker, a dynamo. Among a crowd of artists who like to move at their own pace when they move at all, she's one of the few who really makes things happen. Her contributions to the Elephant 6 are as much logistical as they are musical, and her organizational aptitude is every bit as remarkable as the vastness of her pan-instrumental skills. There's not a lot of folks who would or could play trumpet and drums and clarinet and keyboard and zanzithophone all in one set, but at least among the E6 crew, there's even fewer who can organize a tour, pack a van, and keep everyone moving in the same direction.

Laura has been a member of Elf Power basically since its inception and has contributed to a number of other Elephant 6 projects, with credits on Neutral Milk Hotel, Olivia Tremor Control, Of Montreal, and Circulatory System records, to name just a handful. But she's never really been a bandleader. Even Dixie Blood Mustache was fairly horizontal and anti-hierarchical. But while Orange Twin involves a lot of people—a half-dozen residents, another twenty or so community members, and countless volunteers over the years, only some of them musicians—this one is her project. And it's a big one.

LAURA CARTER: We were looking for thirty acres for us, because it was the only way we felt like we would have a home, for each of us to split it up together.

ANDREW RIEGER: I think Jeff Mangum came up with that name. I think it was from a package of Little Debbie's or something, like two of them in a pack, something orange-flavored. Taken out of that context, it sounds kind of cool and psychedelic.

As the Elephant 6 grew in popularity, many of the folks involved came to value privacy, anonymity, and seclusion. Interactions with particularly intense fans made them feel overexposed and vulnerable, feelings heightened by the turn of the millennium.

"Eventually our plan is to start a commune in the middle of nowhere," Jeff told *Ray Gun* in 1998, "because we want to drop out of society as much as we can. [Robert's] into geodesic domes and Buckminster Fuller, so he wants to initiate some of that thinking. We want to build giant waterwheels for electricity . . . We're piecing [the idea] together bit by bit. Will wants to set up speakers all throughout the woods and have random noises come out at random times. I'd be the activity guy and read Zen to everybody, trying to bring people together. . . . Maybe it seems ridiculous. But we're all used to being together all the time."

LANCE BANGS: Laura was aware of this chunk of area out by the woods. Everyone was having some pre-millennial tension. There was an anxiety in the late nineties among some people about 1999 and the end of the world and Y2K and all that. There was a sense of like, we should have someplace out in the woods to get away when society collapses and everything goes wrong. And also with the Bush election cycle in 2000, there was a sense of where things were headed, and if things were going to get worse, having an escape hatch. And then also, as things had risen attention-wise around some of the people in that music scene, the idea of having a place to go get away from all of that into a more agrarian thing, not that Athens was some thriving cityscape.

Athens was still relatively sleepy, but not as sleepy as it once felt. They started searching for a parcel of land a bit outside of town that they could develop together and reserve as their own fortress of solitude, or an emergency Walden. In the process of trying to find the land, they accidentally started a record label, also called Orange Twin. To raise funds for the property, they put together an online store and let everyone involved sell their wares through it, sharing the cost of the credit-card processing service.

LAURA CARTER: We were predominantly musicians, so for every one piece of artwork, we had ten albums.

One of the first items in the store was *Live at Jittery Joe's*, the Jeff Mangum set Lance Bangs had recorded in 1997. Lance donated all of his proceeds from the release to the land trust.

LANCE BANGS: I was happy that record got out there and that people saw these earlier incarnations of those songs, these really staggering performances shot from three or four feet away in the back room of this coffee shop one night. Jeff talked to me a couple times about different iterations of going through the audio and finding some stuff he was willing to put out on CD to help them and raise money for them, and then would alternately decide against that and kill that idea and kind of disappear for a while, and then resurface with a different version. He was in Spain, he was in Bulgaria, and then he went upstate. I think he visited friends in Chicago. He was sort of popping around. It started to sink in that Neutral Milk Hotel was not an active, going concern. They won't be doing a fall tour. The rest of the guys will have to figure out something to do.

In addition to their own work, Orange Twin wanted to reissue sixties folk rocker Elyse Weinberg's overlooked debut album (for which the masters had been destroyed, so the Orange Twin release was taken from the best-condition LP they could find). It turned into a record label from there, releasing reissues and new material from Elephant 6 musicians, other Athens bands, and artists from all over. The label still operates, with a portion of the profit from every sale going toward the land project.

Laura continued to keep an eye out for the right parcel. In 2001, she came across one that not only fit their price range, it exceeded the size they were looking for: at 155 acres, the former Girl Scout camp was more than five times the area they had originally agreed upon. Laura decided to purchase the then-uninhabited plot with Laura Glenn and Barbara Denvir.

They needed $1,000 to hold the property, which they didn't have. Laura cut a check knowing it would bounce. The worthless check didn't buy them any land, but it bought them some time, and that allowed the three of them to each cobble together their share of the payment. By closing time, they had found another ten investors and had gotten a nice fat loan (which, at the time of this writing, is nearly paid off).

There are six full-time residents today, including Laura. They live in a farmhouse at the northeast end of the property. The house itself once sat downtown, but when it was set to be demolished, Laura purchased it for a dollar and dropped everything to focus on moving it to Orange Twin.

> LAURA CARTER: We had two weeks to move the house to Orange Twin. I had to break out of the music scene. I was getting construction loans. I was basically the contractor for the project. It was one story, but we added a second story just because of a coding thing. They wouldn't let us use the roof lumber because it wasn't graded, so we had to buy all new lumber and it made sense to just pop it up another level. My life just changed instantly to full-on construction-dude mode. I had to sit out of tours, but it's nice that we have a good relationship and can get back together and make music when it works.

About two-thirds of Orange Twin has a conservation easement on it, and the other fifty acres are mostly still undeveloped. A few dwellings sit near the main house, allocated for short-term rentals, along with an old school bus Laura is converting into a livable space. On a hillier tract about a quarter mile into the woods, they've etched an amphitheater into the earth, surrounding a stage Scott Spillane constructed. Orange Twin hosts shows there sporadically but momentously, hosting avant-garde legends like dissonance maestro Jandek (who despite decades as a vegan allegedly couldn't turn down Orange Twin's farm-fresh eggs) and Krautrock pioneer Faust, not to mention a few Elephant 6 acts.

As well, the Orange Twin crew raises some food on the land, which they sell to local restaurants. They also run a business called the Hungry Gnomes, planting edible native perennials in yards around town. There have been chicken coops and apiaries, and Laura is trying to get a goat club off the ground, where volunteers would each milk does once a week and share the spoils. A hundred-year master plan for the site involves the construction of more homes, studios, offices, and the like, with the ambition of making the Orange Twin community as self-sustaining as possible.

Today, Athens is a music town because Athens is a music town. Decades after the B-52's and R.E.M. put it on the map, Athens has the infrastructure (studios, venues, shops) to support a thriving music scene, not to mention a community of people who come out for shows. It's still relatively cheap to live there, which means someone can live much more comfortably off the wages of a part-time job than they could in a major city, leaving plenty of time to focus on art. And with countless bands having called it home over the years (not to mention evangelizing for it on the road and in interviews), it has a strong reputation for being a music town, and because of all the people making music there, it's very easy to find a supportive community. Aspiring musicians still flock there from all over the world to pursue their art, and it's a can't-miss stop for touring bands, so there's more cross-pollination than you might expect from a town of its scale, and since so much of the local scene is made up of transplants, there isn't that protective insularity you often find in other scenes.

To those who lived in Athens in the nineties, the turn of the millennium brought with it a feeling that there was a bit of a lull. R.E.M. was still living in town, but given their massive international profile, they were hardly a local band anymore. The local music scene seemed unspectacular, a shadow of former glory. The emergence of the Elephant 6 helped to breathe life back into the scene, but not everyone enjoyed the attention it attracted.

Henry Owings: We all just kind of accepted each other for who we were. I'm certainly not trying to make it seem like it's miserable now, but I do think that there's a certain level of starfucking that goes on.

Jim McIntyre: When Jeff was finishing his second record, people showed up to those gigs that would not be at other sorts of Elephant 6 gigs. Scenesters and hipsters who would just glom on to whatever was hip. The Olivia Tremor Control was attracting a hacky sack–playing, dreadlock-wearing hippie crowd. The Apples were drawing girls and their boyfriends who didn't want to be there.

JULIAN KOSTER: Towards the end, there'd be kids that would come from around the South to see shows here. And then there were some kids that you became aware of later who moved here because they liked Elephant 6 bands. And that's obviously still happening. Once they're here, they're really shy about it. When you get here, it's not like you're not going to see us every day and end up playing Wiffle ball with us. It almost gets embarrassing for some folks that we had anything to do with their coming. Because we're just a bunch of whatever we are. You see us constantly and everyone gets to know who everyone is. It feels really weird when that doesn't happen, too. There's been a couple of situations where I've felt roughly like a human baseball card.

ROBERT SCHNEIDER: I don't think that was desirable to [Jeff]. I don't think that that was something he was striving for. Everybody in our collective felt and feels skeptical of that kind of attention. That's the same time we all observed him stop playing shows and stuff. I can't say if it was that or not.

In their earliest days in Athens, the Elephant 6 thrived under obscurity. Increased attention didn't ruin things exactly, but it definitely changed the dynamics at play. As the 1990s came to a close, a major transition was underway for the collective.

The last thing the Olivia Tremor Control recorded together, in 2000, was an EP with Kahimi Karie, entitled *Once Upon a Time*. She had reached out to them about a collaboration (her boyfriend at the time, musician Cornelius, had previously worked with Robert), and they recorded some tracks for her to lend vocals to. The band recorded them fresh, but the songs themselves were mostly leftovers, old Olivia or Synthetic Flying Machine material. Though Karie's are the only vocals, and the production is a lot slicker than other Olivia releases, it's not unrecognizable. At a tight fifteen minutes in duration, there's not a lot of room for instrumental suites or loping soundscapes, but each of the five songs on the EP is rife with the Olivia Tremor Control's sonic hallmarks and psychedelic flourishes. Still, after two maximalist, hallucinogenic double albums, *Once Upon a Time* is a relatively restrained record, and Kahimi Karie's plushy, whispered lyrics make it feel like a denouement.

The Olivias stopped playing shows or jamming together or hanging out with one another. Their website was updated to display only: "trying to break out of a state of exegesis. please check back later." There had been no public feuds or tell-all interviews or a press release announcing a breakup. Much like Neutral Milk Hotel little more than a year earlier, they just stopped.

LANCE BANGS: Until people really took in and processed *Aeroplane* and embraced it as strong as they did, there was a sense that Olivia seemed like the more functional band to sign to a label or promote. They were catchier and more likely to end up on the radio or a film soundtrack.

BRIAN MCPHERSON: There was a time when Olivia Tremor Control was in a position to probably capitalize on their success and make some significant deals, but I just don't think they were in a position to make decisions amongst themselves. I think this ultimately led to their demise.

BILL DOSS: We weren't communicating, and we weren't talking. It wasn't any one particular person's fault. There was just not any communication happening. Because of the confusion and the lack of communication, I don't think anybody really knew what was going to happen. I don't think anybody had a plan. I know I didn't.

WILL CULLEN HART: Over those years, we all changed. We couldn't talk. I didn't want to have to constantly argue.

PETE ERCHICK: The last show we played, at the 40 Watt, was in February of 2000. After that show, I came home, and I knew we weren't going to play again for a long time. My mother had just died, and I was still reeling from that. You don't have a job. You don't have a band. You don't have any money. You don't know how you're paying rent this month, and it's a shitty house you live in. I walked in the house that night and I stand there. It's just a dead silence. I felt like a suction, and there was nothing.

BILL DOSS: There was a huge void for me, too. The thing you had put every thought into for the last ten years was now just completely stopped. It didn't even trickle out. It was just boom, gone. It was confusing and heartbreaking, and you're just like, "What happened? Where'd everybody go?" I didn't talk to Will for a while, because I was mad. I was mad at everybody. I was mad at myself. I was mad at the world.

Flydaddy declared bankruptcy. The Olivia Tremor Control got a tip that the bankruptcy sale was proceeding and that among the assets up for purchase were the masters to their own records.

JOHN FERNANDES: They sold about forty thousand records, but they never gave us any money. They had given some advances for recording and helped pay for us to do some traveling, but at the same time, they got a big deal from V2 Music. Both Flydaddy and our European label, Blue Rose, were bought out by V2. They got a lot of money, and we only saw a little of it. And then they ended up filing for bankruptcy, and we never saw any money from all our album sales.

BRIAN MCPHERSON: They owed the band a substantial amount of money, and it's an unfortunate situation. That's one of the downsides of dealing with an independent label. They might be cool and their heart's in the right place, but sometimes you just don't get paid.

BILL DOSS: I was mad at Flydaddy for a while, but then I dealt with spinART and it was even worse. Then I realized it's just labels. You love them when they're good to you, and you hate them when they don't want to do what you want them to do. They were good to us up until the end. To this day, I can't believe that they owed us money but were selling our masters instead of giving them to us or even contacting us to see if we wanted to buy them.

WILL CULLEN HART: Sometimes people flew here to take us out. I know now not to take them to bars we usually go to. We didn't mean it like, "Look at us, we've got this guy here," but I can see that now.

BILL DOSS: We talked with Elektra, with Warner Bros., with DreamWorks. It always seemed like one of those creepy, weird major-label talks.

PETE ERCHICK: We were meeting with this guy from Elektra. He was real enthusiastic about the band. He would take us out to dinner when we toured through LA, which was like, *Oh, free meal.* And then finally we got a proposal. I forget how much money it was for, but it was exciting to get it. But some of the terms were they had the right to put together greatest-hits packages, to refuse a master and reproduce it themselves. They could demand that we record it in their studio.

JOHN FERNANDES: Or make us use their producer, even.

BILL DOSS: Or they could refuse what we turn in as an album.

PETE ERCHICK: This is where you start to play ball. You say, "Okay, less money, these terms." This happened a couple times, where we said we don't like these clauses, we don't need that much money. That went to Elektra, and then something came back as a counter. We really were just hemming and hawing about the compilations and the production.

BILL DOSS: It always happens where labels will like a band and really be excited about them and want to sign them, but immediately want to change them. I never understood that.

PETE ERCHICK: The second counter from us just never got a response back. At that point, the guy who was in our court at Elektra works for another label. No one there gives a damn. This is done. Maybe we seemed like prima donnas, but would it have been right to sign the deal giving them whatever rules they wanted? We would have hated ourselves.

BILL DOSS: We got two or three different offers from major labels that if you looked at the money that was offered up at first, they were million-dollar deals. You just look at it and *cha-ching*. But then you start looking at everything they want to do, and it's like they basically want to control everything. The more control you get back, the less money. It's exciting to think about what could have happened, but nothing ever panned out.

DEREK ALMSTEAD: I think it was a "too much, too fast" situation. They were getting offers from Warner Bros. and crazy shit. Some of them were all for it, and some of them balked. I think it was a punk rock versus pragmatic argument. People develop animosities toward each other in bands. Especially when it's really tied together.

BILL DOSS: It was just a bad year for everybody. Not just band-wise, but personally. There were so many variables that everyone was going through, not only on their own but just in the band. There was so much stuff that it was almost inevitable. Unless we were like

Metallica and brought in a band therapist or something. It seemed like it would be easier to just go off and do other stuff for a while.

If you talk to five people about why the Olivia Tremor Control broke up, you'll get fifty different answers. When you talk to a few dozen people, you start to realize none of those answers is any more valid than any other. There's not any one money squabble or drug habit or creative disagreement to point to. But listening to all the different reasons people have—far too many to print here, without even considering the varying levels of verity—accentuates certain patterns among them, through lines that turned into fault lines along which the band cleaved.

An offer to contribute to a *Powerpuff Girls* music compilation is certainly not *the* reason the Olivia Tremor Control split up, but it's a good example of the tensions at play. There was a lot of bitterness in the air on the Olivias' last tour. They headlined most of it with Bablicon opening for them, until they reached the West Coast, where they played eight shows opening for Stereolab.

BEN CRUM: I came along to sell merch and be a roadie on the Olivia Tremor Control "farewell tour," as they jokingly started calling it part of the way through. They were all really cynical about the E6 thing by then. It had been hyped to death and the backlash was coming, and the whole thing just seemed to annoy everybody at that time. I picked up on this attitude and just jokingly started telling people the E6 was really just a T-shirt design. That was callous and obnoxious of me, but they all thought it was pretty funny. The air in that van was rife with cynicism.

The Powerpuff Girls was an animated TV show about three young superheroes named Blossom, Buttercup, and Bubbles. It originally ran for six seasons on Cartoon Network (plus a movie) and garnered plenty of awards and acclaim in its time, not to mention all sorts of licensed merchandise and a three-season reboot in 2016. Early in its first run, creator Craig McCracken was tasked with compiling an album to release under the *Powerpuff Girls* banner, something appropriate for kids that stayed in line with the bright colors and positive themes that were the hallmarks of the show. Naturally, McCracken went for artists he liked. Mark Mothersbaugh mixed the comp, and Devo and Frank Black contributed tracks, as did Elephant 6 siblings the Apples in Stereo and Dressy Bessy. McCracken reached out to the Olivia Tremor Control as well. The offer reached the band while they were on tour.

Not familiar with the show, the Olivias popped a tape into the VCR in their hotel room after a show, to see what they'd be associating themselves with. The more pride-aphagic members of the band mocked it, and as a group, they decided it was too commercial an enterprise to involve themselves with. But Bill didn't think the endeavor would be so toxic, and because the band was going through sort of a rough patch anyway, he stayed in touch with McCracken. Bill wanted to contribute something to the project, and since the rest of the band had passed, he figured no one would mind if he went ahead and recorded something on his own.

Since the song wouldn't be an Olivia Tremor Control work, Bill offered up the Sunshine Fix moniker he'd used for his solo material before, but it was rejected for sounding too much like a drug reference. This was a children's album, after all. So he submitted a track as "The Bill Doss."

> **BILL DOSS**: I talked to Will, and he was just like, "Whatever. I don't care." I told Will, "I want to do this." And he said, "I don't want to do that. I don't want any part of that. I want to paint." I think, because of all the things that were happening, he just wanted to isolate himself from it.

A couple of days after the tour ended, the band had a meeting, and Will suggested they take a break.

> **BILL DOSS**: What can you say to that except "Okay." If we need that, we need that. And then the *Powerpuff Girls* thing was still there, so I was like, I'm not just going to let this go away. As the band was dissolving, I was like, *I've got these recordings and I want to release them and do something with them.*

So on *The Powerpuff Girls: Heroes & Villains: Music Inspired by* The Powerpuff Girls, The Bill Doss has the twelfth track, a two-and-a-half-minute piano-driven pop tune that wouldn't have been out of place on a Sunshine Fix record but for name-dropping *Powerpuff Girls'* villain Mojo

Jojo. And though the song is ostensibly about the cartoon, it's hard not to read a little into the chorus:

He'll only win
Win in the end
When he can begin
Begin to be friends.

ROBERT SCHNEIDER: Jeff moving away from Athens in 1993 and leaving the Olivia Tremor Control was a source of acrimony. You're going solo? What? Similarly, [the Olivias'] splitting up and having different projects around 2000, that was a source of acrimony in the band. It's a collective where everyone is doing different things, but there's a certain sense of allegiance to your main project. You don't split off from your main project and try to have your side project happen on that scale. Marbles isn't trying to replace the Apples on the touring bill. It was some band the Apples don't want to play with. The idea is you have your main band that everyone is pooling into, and you all are benefiting from, and then you have your side project that everyone is supporting. That's the unspoken rule of being in an indie collective.

The Olivia Tremor Control was to some extent a synecdoche of the entire scene. A lot of roads passed through the band, sharing members with others and relationships with so many more. So when the band fell apart, it seemed like everything else might, too. Folks kept at it, and the Olivias spun off into several bands, but while there was more activity, suddenly everything seemed secondary, after the fact, doomed to be a side project.

Chapter 22

Even with Neutral Milk Hotel and the Olivia Tremor Control now on hiatus, the Elephant 6 was still making music. The ingredients just got a little shuffled around. Still brimming with creative energy, members of those bands found other outlets for their experimentation. Nearly all of them had another band of their own, and they still found time to contribute to one another's projects.

One of the zanier things that grew out of this period was Major Organ and the Adding Machine. The entity produced one self-titled album, though it's not entirely clear who that self is. It was created with no intention to release the album to the public, though that happened long after it was finished. The album is also not the most highly regarded in the E6 catalog. It's easily one of the weirdest, though, and given how it came together, it serves as a remarkable document of the time period and community, like some kind of Dadaist Polaroid. The stream of unselfconscious is evidence that even without commercial ambitions of any kind, folks were still doing their thing, trying to entertain themselves and one another.

The project began a cover of "What a Wonderful World" that Julian, Jeff, and Jill Carnes recorded together for a Kindercore compilation of Christmas music released in 1997. The Louis Armstrong original is a song most people have heard so many times that it's basically white noise, but the Elephant 6 rendition has its own feel. Of the trio's contributions to the song, Jill's vocal melody hews closest to the familiar, but her creaky timbre weaves in and out of Julian's ethereal saw like a frog clambering through a thicket of swaying cattails. Jeff's verse in the middle is modulated just to the point of peculiarity, and a haunting tape loop from his homemade sound effects library undergirds the entirety of the two-minute track.

Julian submitted the track under the name Major Organ and the Adding Machine and then lent the name to the project that emerged next, a bunch of songs that came together via an exquisite corpse–style sharing of tape. No one seems able to recall the exact origins, but it basically came about like this: one person would compose the beginnings of a song and put it to tape—maybe a fractured, looping guitar riff or a surreal lyric—and pass it off to someone else, who would then add sound effects or some percussive toy piano and pass it to someone else, who might add a bass line or instead decide to cut the whole thing up and rearrange it. Each person would add bits and pieces and then pass it to the next person, until a song was ready to collapse under its own weight. The tapes were passed around for years, each song swelling into maximalist oblivion as much from divination as from intentional composition, without anyone guiding the process or even keeping track of it. Eventually, there was an album's worth of material.

JULIAN KOSTER: It sort of happened on its own. That was what was so fun about it. It really was like Major Organ was a real person, like we weren't directing the record. It was just happening.

DAVE MCDONNELL: It was a real fertile time for them because people were putting out their music and requesting their stuff. It's a perfect aural snapshot of that moment.

GRIFFIN RODRIGUEZ: When we did the recordings for Major Organ, it was just like any other day. "We're going over to Julian's to do some recording. Julian has a track for you to play on. Bring your bass." It was always very impromptu and in the same spirit as all the other records. They would just invite you over and you'd play an overdub.

JOHN FERNANDES: Everyone kind of inspired each other. On the Major Organ project, everyone would kind of bring in things, and someone would say, "Hey, I've got a bass line for that." We've never really talked about it. I'm not even sure if we're supposed to be talking about how "we" did it.

KEVIN BARNES: In the best way, it was a collaborative project. Everybody seemed to be contributing equally and making everything better. It was never getting worse because somebody laid some stupid tracks on it. It was like, "Whoa, this song is so much cooler now, and it was already cool." I wrote that song "Madam Truffle." I don't remember who got it, but they sped it up really fast, and there's this extra cool stuff Eric added.

JULIAN KOSTER: But we weren't doing it to put it out. That was the thing. It entertained us to no end. It made us all laugh when we listened to it. It was just so funny and weird and fun. We all loved the Boredoms and Faust and Stockhausen.

JOHN FERNANDES: When it was put out, it was supposed to be an anonymous tape found in a thrift store. Eric kind of said, "Okay, I'm going to finish this. This thing's done and I'm going to sequence these things."

ANDREW RIEGER: It took a while, from what I remember. I can't even remember who all was involved in that.

BILL DOSS: There was probably something on there that I contributed that got turned around.

JILL CARNES: If I'm on it, I have no idea. I was never told if I was. A lot of times, things have been recorded, and people don't remember who was there at the time. Or people don't remember if they were there at the time. Or maybe people didn't know if it was being recorded.

SCOTT SPILLANE: I know I recorded some stuff, but I don't know if I made the cut or not. There's lots of stuff I've listened to that's like, "Am I even on that?" I can't even tell.

Even with the heavy use of effects, certain contributors are identifiable by their vocals—Jeff, Bill, Kevin—but the record was released without proper credits, and a whole lot of people are genuinely unsure whether they recorded anything for it in the first place. Those who are certain they did something are often unsure about what they played specifically. The album is almost as much of a mystery to its creators as it is to listeners.

Most of the recording happened in 1998 or thereabouts, and the album was released to the public in 2001. The finished product is every bit as eclectic and bizarre as anything else in the Elephant 6 catalog, and even more opaque. The lyrics are nonsensical even with the context of the film it eventually scored.* No two consecutive songs have the same vocalist, and most of the vocals are heavily modulated anyway. Instrumentation varies from track to track, and the actual songs (using that term fairly loosely, though most of the pieces have a recognizable structure to them) are intermitted by tight little instrumental freakouts. Contributing musicians were free to indulge in whatever sort of experimentation they could conceive, and since the intended audience was originally just their own friends and collaborators, their weirdest tendencies sharpened into one-upmanship. Absolutely nothing had to be distilled into something accessible, because no one expected it to have an audience that wasn't in on the joke. No one expected it to have an audience at all, beyond the people who made it. If the spirit of their weekly potlucks could be transposed into a record, it would be *Major Organ and the Adding Machine.*

Bruce Miller wrote in *Magnet* that the album is "best listened to while standing on your head," describing *Major Organ* as "a sound collage where the slightest audible pin prick might signal a funeral march played by dwarf clown wrestlers. Sounding at times like a more sugary *Meet the Residents* or a less menacing Caroliner Rainbow, this loose concept album manages to be the most avant of any E6 release without losing that penchant for melodic focus."

Generally speaking, critics didn't really know what to make of the record, but they certainly weren't impressed. It received 1.5 stars out of 5 in *AllMusic,* where Ari Wiznitzer calls it a "jumbled mess of lo-fi production tricks." *Pitchfork,* historically sympathetic to Elephant 6 projects, gave it a 4.5 out of 10, with Matt LeMay writing, "Alternating between vaguely interesting and flat-out fucking annoying, *Major Organ* is a tragically anticlimactic release by a group of immensely talented luminaries of late '90s indie rock." Manhattan record store Other Music, in a description ostensibly written to encourage people to buy the album, described it as

* Debuted on the first Holiday Surprise tour in 2008, the *Major Organ and the Adding Machine* film contains no dialogue, only the album's instrumental pieces as its score. It stars Sophie and Jeremy Kiran Fernandes (two of John's kids) in a series of vignettes acting out the album's surrealist lyrics, centered around the bakery of Madam Truffle. Jeff appears in a lobster costume, and dozens of Elephant 6 folks and other Athens scenesters appear in the short film. Joey Foreman and Eric Harris wrote, directed, and edited the film.

"a bit self-indulgent, with its cluttered and chaotic pop approach" and "not bound by a need for even underground commercial viability."

ANDREW RIEGER: It was something we talked about for a long time. I think it's a really cool, great album. Some people like it and some people don't.

JILL CARNES: I think it was stepping into another area of the already interesting realm. It was keeping curiosity alive.

JULIAN KOSTER: That was a little bit more like what we did at home for fun. Jeff made all kinds of completely insane recordings all the time, things that were never considered to be shared, especially as Jeff became aware of the sorts of people who were into the band recordings and realized a lot of those people would hate it or just not understand, which came to be true. Some people's reactions to the Major Organ record were just mind-boggling. People were just more conservative then. Underground music culture has actually gotten infinitely more broad-minded since then. Back then, it was really conservative. It might as well have been mainstream top 40 music. People were like, *Underground music has to be this, this, and this*, and we already majorly were *not* that, that, and that, so it was a miracle that we weren't getting our heads kicked in, although we started to get our heads kicked in, culturally, because we weren't doing the next thing people expected. We were just getting weirder. We were supposed to get progressively less weird and we were seeming to get progressively more weird.

* * *

HEATHER MCINTOSH: The Instruments started around 2000-ish, like two blocks away from where Laura and Jeff and Robbie lived, on Grady, and I became fast friends with those guys. I got a guitar my mom gave me and started playing around the house, but I was terrified of it. But I had all these songs, and then Jeremy was like, "You should make a record."

Jeremy Barnes paid for Heather to record the first Instruments album at a studio in town. In addition to Heather's cello, guitar, and vocals, the album includes contributions from the other three core members of Neutral

Milk Hotel, four of the five core members of the Olivia Tremor Control (everyone but Bill), Andy Gonzales, Derek Almstead, and John d'Azzo. The other two Instruments albums feature similar ensembles. While still living in Athens, Heather founded AUX Fest, a music festival showcasing a wide range of experimental artists at venues around Athens, and the Instruments provided the score for Astra Taylor's 2008 documentary, *Examined Life*, on modern philosophy, featuring Judith Butler, Cornel West, and other notable philosophers.

On an Instruments tour opening for Elf Power, Brian Burton—known better as Danger Mouse, an accomplished musician and producer who as a UGA student had worked at Wuxtry Records in Athens with John Fernandes—attended a couple of shows and reconnected with Heather. A few months later, while tour-managing for the Clientele, Heather invited Brian to come to a show and hang out. He invited her to join his band, which turned into touring gigs playing cello and bass for Gnarls Barkley and Lil Wayne. The experience was a lot different from the tours she'd been on with Elephant 6 bands.

HEATHER MCINTOSH: It's different anxieties. There's less connectivity. It's a different kind of thing. I have to be more professional, and I don't own it in the same way. It's like you're clocking in.

Heather returned to Athens after those tours and then moved to Los Angeles, where she's become a prolific scorer of films and TV shows, with composer credits on more than forty productions.

While living in Athens, Bill had met lots of musicians he wanted to play with, but the Olivia Tremor Control always took precedence. When the band took a break, he started making up for lost time, making good on years of no-longer-empty promises of "let's jam sometime." Through that process, he settled on a lineup for his next band, featuring him, Kevin Sweeney, Sam Mixon, and Dave Gerow. He had been using the Sunshine Fix moniker since his Ruston days, and he released a cassette under the name in the first Elephant 6 catalog, so it made sense to him to revive the project.

BILL DOSS: Some of the songs that ended up becoming Sunshine Fix songs, we had played on the last Olivia tour. But I liked the songs and wanted to do something with them, and I didn't know how long this break was going to be. I thought to myself, *What is it that I do well?* Well, I write songs, I record songs, and I play shows. I'm going to continue doing that, because otherwise I'm going to have to get a job. The only constraint I felt was having the Sunshine Fix and then being compared to Olivia. You're being compared to yourself. Obviously, it's not going to be the same thing.

WILL CULLEN HART: Why even go there? It's a different project.

BILL DOSS: But as far as being defined as "an Elephant 6 band," I didn't feel any constraint. In fact, I felt the opposite of that.

In its office, Kindercore had built a recording studio, which it was sharing with Bill around the same time. He recorded a Sunshine Fix album there and produced a few other bands' music. He usually showed up in a suit.

RYAN LEWIS: He got really excited after watching this documentary about the Beatles recording at Abbey Road, and he got really taken with the fact that the studio engineers would get dressed up to go to work. They would go to work in suits. So he started getting as many weird, flowery, psychedelic, wide-collared polyester shirts as he could find, and big ties, and he would get dressed up. We would say it was his Donovan outfit. Bill and his dandy finery.

With a bit of money coming in from the Kahimi Karie record, Will didn't feel pressured to find a job right away. He did more painting. He made music, too, but not with any specific sort of project in mind.

WILL CULLEN HART: I didn't want to *have* to make that record. I wanted to take a break, but I didn't know what I was going to do. I enjoyed making music. I didn't know how it was all going to work, but everything was changing.

JOHN FERNANDES: He had written a poem at some point that was called "Places to Be." It was on the Web, and you'd click on one thing, and it would jump to another thing. And one of the things he had as places to be was a circulatory system. I was listening to the lyrics of a lot of his songs about the system of how things are all connected, from the really large to the really small, and everything outside and everything inside, so I was like, "How about the name 'Circulatory System'?" and he liked it, so we went with that.

Circulatory System started as a three-piece with Will on guitar, Jeff on drums, and John on bass and on all the other instruments he played in the Olivia Tremor Control. That shifted after just a few shows.

DEREK ALMSTEAD: Old conflicts arose or it didn't go so well, and plus Jeff moved out of town. Will and me had kind of bonded over the years about music and production and that kind of stuff, and he asked me to come in. It was me, Will, John, Hannah Jones, Pete, and Heather McIntosh. That was the early, classic lineup that lasted until 2007 or 2008.

You can approximate what a *Black Foliage* follow-up would have sounded like had the band stayed together by sequencing the songs from the first Circulatory System album with those from the post-Olivia Sunshine Fix records, but both bands had more traditional sorts of bandleaders (Will and Bill, respectively) in comparison to the Olivias' more democratic style, which yielded a different result.

JOHN FERNANDES: With Olivia, everyone was bringing in songs, but with Circulatory System, we kind of get in a certain mood all based around Will's songs, and it kind of sustains that mood for a long time. It's more like an orchestrated drone piece.

HEATHER MCINTOSH: When I play in that band, I have parts I play. It's not experimental. There are strange parts, but they interlock, and that's the part I play every time. A lot of it was just me playing off of John and coming up with stuff that interlocks. The other half is from studio time, with Will twiddling knobs and me playing and listening and coming up with different ways to do stuff.

JOHN FERNANDES: Will was working on home recordings, and I encouraged him to keep working on them, and they started sounding really good, so I decided to borrow that money and try to get this record out. We had had some bad experiences with record labels before, so I said we've got to do this ourselves so that we don't get ripped off.

With the Flydaddy experience behind him, John didn't want to get burned again, so he decided to start a record label himself and release the Circulatory System record through that. He had some money set aside that he once planned to use for college tuition and instead used it to get Cloud Recordings off the ground. It quickly proved to be an educational experience of its own.

> **JOHN FERNANDES**: I was doing all the press stuff myself, making the callbacks from all the stuff we sent out. And I was so close to it because not only did I believe in the music with all my soul, but I had borrowed all the money I was supposed to use to go to college to put out the record. I borrowed like $8,000 from my mom and another $4,000 from my wife at the time. I had kids and all these pressures, and I just really hoped this makes it. So I was super stressed out about it, where sometimes we'd get a negative review and I'd call up the reviewer and just go off on him.

After spending a half hour on the phone with a *Magnet* writer who had panned the album—John was crying by the end of the call—he started to see the benefits of delegating. He hired an agency to handle publicity.

John didn't have to call many writers, though. The album was garnering mostly glowing coverage, but despite the otherwise consistently positive reviews, the release coincided with an industry-wide drop in record sales. The album was released in 2001, the first time CD sales had truly declined from the previous year since the format was introduced to the market in the 1980s. CD sales have continued to decline in terms of dollars almost every year since. Digital music sales and streaming have created new revenue opportunities, but not nearly enough to offset the financial decline (and with much of the new revenue captured by digital streaming platforms like Spotify anyway).

> **MARTYN LEAPER**: People stopped buying records. It didn't happen overnight. I remember my neighbor yelling out of his window, "Hey, I just ripped your last record from Napster." *Great. Thanks, man. Thanks for telling me you're a douchebag. I'm broke. I would have given you the record.* If you're already on weak footing and you're an indie band and you don't have any money and you're scratching out

> a living to begin with, then it becomes harder and harder to sell your records and to promote your record and to go out on tour. All of that stuff happening at once is kind of devastating. We didn't sell more than five thousand copies of one record or another, so it went from five thousand to maybe three thousand to one thousand. We weren't viable to begin with. Five thousand records isn't a lot, but it's just enough to get you into the game. And then the labels go out of business. What do you do?

After peaking in 1999, with total US music sales over $14 billion, revenue for recorded music began to decline, and Americans spent less money on music than they had the year before, nearly every year until 2015, when revenue was just about half of what it had been at the peak. There's been a rapid rise since then, but it still has not caught up to where it was in 1999, and of course that's an aggregate figure for the entire industry: individual musicians seem to be getting a much smaller slice of the shrunken pie, with more competition among artists and digital streaming services taking a monstrous slice of their own. The rise of music piracy is one popular explanation for the collapse, and surely that has played a role to some extent or another, but there was also a global recession in there, which is likely a big reason, too.

It should also be noted that the sharp rise in growth the music industry experienced through the eighties and nineties was heavily fed by a onetime spike in CD sales when so many people wanted to purchase CD versions of albums they already owned on vinyl, cassette, and other formats, due to the purported audio quality of the new technology. That is, because CDs were supposedly an objectively "better" listening experience, people went out and bought CD versions of albums they already owned on other formats. Recall how this led to the boom in used LP sales, which in turn shook up the once-linear path of musical development.

So why didn't this happen when CDs were edged out? Digital music, namely the MP3, was the next format frontier, but listeners could rip music files from CDs (and, with the right setup, their other physical media) right to their hard drive, and it was often easier to just download the files illegally, which many otherwise law-abiding netizens may have felt justified in doing, since they already owned the music on CD. The average iPod user is not exactly a scholar of intellectual property law anyway. So the digital revolution didn't bring about another spike in sales (though it seems to have accelerated the consumption and expanded the influence of older and otherwise more obscure music that the bear market for used LPs had set off a decade or so earlier). Basically, the advantages that digital music offered were mostly in cost and ease of acquisition, since there is no physical product: you don't have to leave your house to buy it, and you can fit a whole lot more of it in any given space. If you already own it on CD and can rip the MP3s yourself, those advantages are marginal. The music industry loved the CD, because they could charge nearly twice what they had charged for vinyl LPs, and they passed only a small portion of these new profits along to the artists.* When the labels began hemorrhaging money, of course, they were more than happy to share in the losses, cutting tons of bands from their rosters.

Moreover, because the digital marketplace made it possible (or at least easier) to purchase individual songs instead of entire albums, a person no longer had to buy a twelve-song album just because they liked the single. Sure, sometimes that album model had benefits for a listener—maybe you discovered a few other songs you like that way, or maybe the album (or double album) format is a better vessel for what the musician is going for. The three-and-a-half-minute pop song formula isn't arbitrary, but it's not one-size-fits-all, either. But when you can pay by the song instead, then any song you pay for and don't want is an economic inefficiency to some extent or another. The album model often forced music consumers to pay for music they didn't want (or just didn't know they wanted) just to have music they did want, and unbundling the songs from that format practically eliminated this inefficiency for many listeners (even if it meant they might not discover songs they could have otherwise loved).

It's likely that music piracy has negatively affected the music industry,† at least in economic terms, but there are other compounding factors: MTV's pivot to cheaply made reality shows over music-centric programming, labels' abandonment of record stores for price-slashing big-box chains like

* According to *Appetite for Self-Destruction: The Spectacular Crash of the Record Industry in the Digital Age*, "labels sold CDs for almost $8 more than LPs at stores, but typical artists made just 6 cents more per record." An LP sold for $8.98 netted an artist 75 cents, while a CD sold for $16.95 brought the average artist 81 cents.

† Much less clear, however, is to what extent it has affected music production and consumption outside of an economic framework, positively or negatively.

Walmart and Best Buy, a lack of promotional channels when "legal payola" loopholes were closed, the RIAA's strategy of suing its own customers for piracy instead of the big tech and telecom companies that enabled and encouraged it.* As early as 2000, bands like Radiohead and Dispatch were purposely "leaking" their music for free over the internet and reaping the hell out of the free publicity it generated, exploiting those demonized peer-to-peer networks to sell more records than they otherwise would have. It is impossible to quantify the positive externalities this new technology engendered, but it sure seems like it allowed more people to listen to a lot more music. The people who downloaded the most music were often the ones who spent the most money on it anyway. One 2009 study found that people who downloaded music illegally were ten times more likely to pay for songs than those who never pirate music.

Despite all this, Circulatory System's record and ticket sales were strong enough at first that neither John nor Will had to take a desk job. It was the beginning of the end for the record industry, but still just the beginning. At first, John ran the label by himself, doing all the press, promotion, and shipping. For a while, he was making multiple trips to the post office and UPS each day.

Meanwhile, Flydaddy had gone under. Olivia Tremor Control records had been out of print for a while, but now the label was bankrupt and selling off its assets, including the masters to *Dusk at Cubist Castle* and *Black Foliage*. John was offended. The whole band felt like the label owed them money, so in their eyes, giving them the masters was the least they could have done. Bankruptcy law says otherwise, though.

> **JOHN FERNANDES:** Since the Olivia Tremor Control records were out of print, I tracked down the Flydaddy guys, and they made me buy the rights to the Olivia Tremor Control records for $4,000, after not having paid us anything for forty thousand records sold.

Cloud Recordings re-released both Olivia albums on CD. John found it rewarding to be releasing his own music on his own label. He made mix CDs for people who ordered from him, both to show gratitude and to turn

* Including Sony, whose record label was fighting music piracy at the same time the company's technology division was hawking CD burners and MP3 players.

people on to new music he cared about. They included lots of free jazz and tracks from *The Secret Museum of Mankind* anthologies.

The sheer amount of labor involved in running the label by himself—not to mention working at a record store and raising his kids—began to take its toll on John. He hired an agency to help with publicity and signed a distribution deal with Secretly Canadian. It became more manageable from there.

Circulatory System and the Sunshine Fix weren't the only new projects former Olivia Tremor Control members pursued. Eric Harris released a self-titled album as the Frosted Ambassador, borrowing the name from a track he'd written for *Dusk at Cubist Castle* (and borrowing a bit of *Black Foliage*'s "Opening" for one of its songs). Kindercore released the record in 1999. It's ostensibly a solo album, and Eric never performed live under the name. Details are intentionally hard to come by. Eric stays quiet about it.

> **RYAN LEWIS:** He, for whatever reason, was unwilling to have his picture taken, do interviews, do anything. That was such a weird negotiation to put out this record. The only reason anybody would give that record the time of day was to say it was the drummer from the Olivia Tremor Control. Without doing that, it was like starting from scratch. He didn't want to do that, which we had to respect, obviously. He didn't want to put the name of the record on the packaging. And all of the songs were untitled.* As little information as possible. At one point, he made an eight-track [tape] of the album, and he wanted us to make the CD off the eight-track, which wound up being not something that we could do. He made all these weird, slightly different bios that contradicted each other about who the Frosted Ambassador was. It was frustrating, because I was running a record label and I really wanted people to hear the record, because it was amazing. That was Eric.

Pete was playing with Circulatory System and leading his own band, Pipes You See, Pipes You Don't. Its first album, *Individualized Shirts*,

* In fact, the album packaging includes blank spaces next to each of the track numbers, with instructions to name the songs yourself.

featured lots of Elephant 6 veterans, including all of the Olivia Tremor Control's core members, save for Bill. The band opened for Circulatory System on a 2002 tour.

Pete got the name from an illustration in *Childcraft Encyclopedia*, volume 9, in a chapter about plumbing. He and his brother laughed at the rendering growing up, mostly because it included a bare-assed child, a jolt to his "Victorian" upbringing. As he got older, though, the phrase took on a meaning deeper than moving water and sewage to and from the bathroom.

> **PETE ERCHICK**: Emerson thought—I can't quote it, but I can paraphrase it—a thread runs through all things. A connection between everything. Past, present, future. Whatever exists now, everything is the same. But it's not even just the Emerson quote. A lot of things I'm thinking and reading are bringing me to the same place. The thing that I found in the encyclopedia as a kid is that everything is connected, and you see some connections, but you don't see most of them.

Right around when the Olivias went on hiatus, Will started to feel shooting pains throughout his body. The pain seemed to get worse every day, but years went by before he saw someone about it. He didn't have health insurance, so he just tried to muscle through it for a while. It only got worse. In 2006, Will woke up to find he had lost most of his vision in his right eye.

He finally saw a doctor, who diagnosed him with multiple sclerosis. MS is a disease that affects everybody differently, but basically the body's immune system begins to attack its central nervous system. There are all sorts of nasty symptoms, with some people losing the ability to walk or see. Even when it's not debilitating, it's pretty scary. For Will, the symptoms were minimal at first, aside from the sudden loss of vision (from which he recovered quickly). But doctors suspected the MS had afflicted him since at least 1999, and it took Will another year before he started treating it. For a little while after the diagnosis, Will kept on fighting it, mostly hoping it would go away on its own. But that's not how MS works—there's not a cure. We don't even know the cause. But there *is* treatment, and about a year after the initial diagnosis, Will began seeing a doctor every other day to administer intramuscular shots. Other treatments exist, but given Will's drug history, his doctor was hesitant to give him anything he could potentially abuse.

WILL CULLEN HART: He asked me, "Why would you want to put that stuff in your body?" I was like, "Why wouldn't you?"

He continued the injection regimen for a few years, but when he started touring again with Circulatory System, he didn't bother bringing any of the medication along with him, and he stopped with the treatment altogether. Eventually, a pill version of the treatment became available, and with help from the National Multiple Sclerosis Society and prescription assistance programs, he was able to receive the medication without paying the thousands of dollars it would have cost him each month without health insurance.

Even with the medication, though, Will's symptoms got worse. He has trouble regulating his body temperature and his mood, and he endures intense nerve pain in his head, neck, shoulders, and upper back. Will was a creative spark plug among the Elephant 6 crowd. Even when he wasn't actively making music himself, his energy and enthusiasm were an inspiration to others. So when MS began to slow him down, many of his colleagues slowed down, but not all of them.

KEVIN BARNES: I was never extremely close with Will or Bill or Jeff. They're a little older, so they were almost like these big-brother figures. I wanted to hang out with them, but I wanted to be cool and not annoy them. I looked up to them. I really admired them. I remember talking to Will about it one time and being like, "Is it okay if I put the Elephant 6 logo on the record?" And he was basically like, "Yeah, sure, put it on! Everyone should be on Elephant 6!" It was kind of a funny endorsement, because it wasn't like, "Fuck yeah! You guys are great! I love your music! Please be a part of it!" It was more like, "Shit. Fuck it. What do I care?"

ANDY GONZALES: That was our paying-our-dues period. We worked really hard and toured quite a bit for a good five years. We were lucky. Of Montreal got a huge leg up. Neutral Milk Hotel and the Apples and the Olivias, they started from scratch, they generated this huge crowd and buzz, and we had the advantage of opening up for them. We were making money essentially right away.

KEVIN BARNES: Early on, it was really frustrating, because we weren't selling records and we weren't drawing well when we went on tour, and then to get shitty reviews on top of it, it's extremely discouraging. Nobody wants us to even do this. Go on tour and play for thirty people a night, sleep on people's floors, eating Taco Bell. Barely able to survive, but doing it because we love to do it, and not getting any sort of positive encouragement or feedback. But because I lived in this Elephant 6 bubble, I felt good about it, because I knew my friends liked it, and I knew we were doing something interesting that wasn't catering to the trend of the time.

DEREK ALMSTEAD: It started slowly becoming for me more about the technical process than the musical process, and at the same time, it was more of a business, because when we went out on the road, we would come back with more money than if we had stayed and worked our shitty jobs. It became a draw to do the work. Right in the midst of doing *Gay Parade* is when Bryan left the band. He was, point-blank, like, "I just don't like the new songwriting direction." On one level, I was like, "Yeah, I totally agree," but on the other, it's a fun exercise. Me and Kevin kept rolling with that ball and started searching for people.

When Bryan Poole left Of Montreal, Kevin solicited Jamey Huggins to join and play bass and drums, alternating with Derek on both instruments. Jamey insisted on bringing Dottie Alexander along to play keys. Andy Gonzales joined the band, too. The new lineup shook up the band's stage presence.

JAMEY HUGGINS: We instantly created this whole persona. Right out of the gate, on that first show, everyone had their personality, as far as stage dress and costumery. Even on that first show, we had [Kevin's brother] David making sculptures and paintings for the stage, and we had these kazoo apparatuses on wires. I was wearing ties and vests and shit, and Dottie was playing the clarinet wearing a little dress. It all sort of instantly clicked. Derek was always much more reserved and way more about being a musician first, and not so much into the performance element. But Kevin and Dottie and I made up for that in spades, so it balanced.

Most of the quintet moved in together (Kevin, Jamey, Dottie, and Derek, that is—Andy remained with the band but lived elsewhere) into a house a thirty-minute drive from town. That may not sound like much of a distance, but consider that the rest of the Elephant 6 crowd in Athens lived within walking (or, at most, biking) distance from one another. Comparatively speaking, it was a very isolated sort of living arrangement, and it cost them the creative pluralism they had been drawing on for years, consciously or not. But it had its benefits, too.

DEREK ALMSTEAD: We lived out fifteen miles outside of town in this big pink—which is part of what drew me to it, as a Band fan—plantation house that used to be on campus but this guy had moved out and plopped in the middle of this field. We all had our own bedrooms. There were two rooms for a studio, big kitchen. We loved it.

JAMEY HUGGINS: That was like college. That was the heyday. I used to have a marimba and an upright piano in our hallway. Kevin and I had opposing bedrooms in the back where we shared a bathroom, and between our bedrooms was a piano and a marimba. And then we had a separate control room and recording room. We had bongos and banjos and accordions and every imaginable percussion instrument and flutes and clarinets and cellos. It was just a wonderland museum of instruments. We had finally gotten some decent gear, some money from Kindercore, and we bought a decent home-recording studio. We lived there for three years, I think.

DEREK ALMSTEAD: It was kind of a fantasyland for that scenario, but it was kind of the demise of all of our personal relationships. It destroyed the democracy/equality factor.

JAMEY HUGGINS: It never occurred to us that you need personal space or downtime or mental stability. It was no big deal to us to rehearse four or five hours a day, go on tour for a month, and then come home and cook dinner and sit on the couch together for the next two weeks watching movies. The sort of things that annoy you with overfamiliarity and roommate-type situations, or any kind of environment where you get too comfortable, didn't occur to us at that point. Derek hated it and Kevin did at the end, and it was the two of them who had the real loggerheads tension, which ultimately meant Derek leaving that band while we were in that house.

KEVIN BARNES: I also wanted to have more creative control, because we had become sort of a democracy. Everybody was contributing their own parts, and Derek was sort of taking over engineering duties. He really wanted to do that, and I didn't want to give up that control, because I really like recording myself and being able to record all my own parts and write all the parts, like I had done in the past. It just became a power struggle on a certain level. I understand why it wouldn't be a lot of fun to have someone else tell you what to play all the time.

BRYAN POOLE: The funny thing is that when I quit Of Montreal in '98 or whatever, I told Kevin, "Whoever else you get into the band, you've got to make them a part of the band. You can't just have them be session people. You've got to involve them." And they did that with Dottie and Jamey and Andy. It was a very fertile period for them. They all lived in that house together. I was kind of jealous, to be honest. This is what I wanted when I was with them, but now they've got it. Well, at least they took my advice. But Derek having control over that—and Derek has a real forceful personality—Kevin all of a sudden was like, "I'm not having fun."

Around the time Derek was on his way out, Bryan was starting to feel a little stilted creatively with Elf Power. Having played on and off with them for seven years, just thinking about leaving the band was causing him some emotional tumult, but limited to playing only bass, he felt like he had been painted into a corner. Laura and new drummer Adrian Finch had locked down the other parts he might want to add—keys, drums, guitar, textural stuff—and while he was writing his own songs, he didn't think they really fit with Andrew's style. So he left Elf Power in 2001 and started hanging out more with Kevin, but things were a bit different from when they had been bandmates three years earlier.

Kevin moved back into town with their wife, Nina, which made it easier to hang out with Bryan again. Bryan built them a computer, which Kevin used to record *Satanic Panic in the Attic* mostly by themself. Up to that point, Of Montreal had gotten mostly negative reviews locally (dismissed as wimpy and overly twee by a *Flagpole* staff partial to math rock) and in the scant national press it could garner, but *Satanic Panic* got a much more positive response, validating Kevin's more independent approach. Around the same time, Kevin and Derek had a falling-out, and Derek left the band. Bryan returned in Derek's place, but in more of a supporting role than he had had before. There was less room left for Dottie's and Jamey's contributions, too. It took some getting used to.

Even in Athens, the Elephant 6 maintained a certain mystique. Kindercore—an indie label started by Dan Geller and Ryan Lewis—had more of a public face, releasing records by indie pop bands. As the label grew, it dovetailed frequently with the Elephant 6, with E6 bands like the Essex Green and Dressy Bessy releasing singles and eventually full-length albums through the label and sharing the stage with other Kindercore artists. Though Kevin was still signed to Bar/None, Bar/None hadn't been happy with how the Of Montreal records they'd released were selling, so they let Kindercore release *Coquelicot Asleep in the Poppies* and *Aldhils Arboretum* without a fuss. They didn't sell all that well, either.

Kindercore was getting big, though. *SPIN* named it a "label to watch" in 2000. It just hadn't figured out how to turn a profit. They turned to Emperor Norton for a bit as sort of a farm label: Emperor Norton gave them money to sign and develop unknown bands, with the intent to sign them themselves if they were successful. Both parties eventually ran out of money, though, and they parted ways amicably. Another deal with a company called Telegraph turned into a legal dispute that emptied out Kindercore's savings. Dan and Ryan were able to retain control of the label, but with Telegraph declaring bankruptcy, they had no way to recoup any of their losses. They closed Kindercore.

DAN GELLER: We have all this stock, no infrastructure, and no money, and I'm out $35,000 to $40,000 out of my pocket. Every cent I made went into this lawsuit just to keep it going. I'm broke, and we have this label. And then all of a sudden Of Montreal hits.

Of Montreal released *Satanic Panic* on Polyvinyl, but its success led to renewed interest in the band's back catalog, a couple of records to which Kindercore still owned the rights. The success of *Satanic Panic* and the next couple of records after it generated enough sales of *Coquelicot* and *Aldhils* that Kindercore could bring the label back online.

CHAPTER 23

Contrary to their reputation for reclusiveness, the Elephant 6 folks interviewed herein were relatively open about whatever topic came up in our conversations. There were two exceptions.

The first exception was themselves. It's not a boastful bunch, and some of them seem downright allergic to anything that might resemble self-promotion. They could share biographical details, like which instruments they played on which records or where they lived and when they lived there, but when it came to feelings or analysis or anything a bit more subjective, the conversations tended to be more fruitful when they spoke about others. Almost to a person, they'd rather say someone else was a genius or a virtuoso than that they themselves had any talent whatsoever.

The other exception is an inversion of that. On the subject of Jeff Mangum, people were more than happy to volunteer their opinions—about his singular voice, his devotion to his art, his deeply held artistic principles, the inspiration they felt just being around him—effusively and without caveat. They were much, much cagier with biographical details, however.

Derek Almstead: We all feel that way, a little bit. I can feel that even within the collective. A protection element. I was hyperconscious of backstage rules and etiquette and stuff like that. I guess if you just ask people to treat you a certain way, you'll get it, but it doesn't hurt that he legitimately has that success and cult of personality and stuff. It's weird to talk about a person in that way but also feel like they're just a big goofball. You can hold more than one thought in your head about this, but it's a weird dynamic. It's hard to talk about without feeling like

> you're revealing something private. There's always a desire to have this sort of mythological, magic person who makes music.

After Jeff went quiet, that mythos became steadily more powerful, such that it would have overshadowed most albums. That *Aeroplane* is as revered as it is on its own terms says a lot.

You can hear elements of Elephant 6 music and aesthetics in countless artists today, from open mic nights to top 40 radio, across nearly every genre and style. Take a couple of Grammy winners, for example. Arcade Fire lead singer Win Butler cites Neutral Milk Hotel as a primary reason for signing with Merge, which released Arcade Fire's first four LPs. Producer Danger Mouse worked at Wuxtry Records in Athens with John Fernandes and credits the multi-instrumentalist for helping him realize "you can make a record and have it just be good even if it's not meant for the mainstream." Indie rock heavyweights like Tame Impala, Bright Eyes, the Shins, the Decemberists, and Beirut are some obvious disciples, but even Radiohead (who shared a European booking agency with several Elephant 6 acts) and Elliott Smith (who had mutual friends keep him apprised of Jeff's post-hiatus whereabouts and mental states) seem to have drawn from the collective.

It's impossible to count the number of musicians whose work has been colored by the Elephant 6, but the collective's cultural impact goes beyond music. On the NBC sitcom *Parks and Recreation*, April Ludgate nearly leaves her boyfriend when he doesn't know that her favorite band is Neutral Milk Hotel. Writing as April, showrunner Michael Schur penned an ode to the band in *Vulture*. "After you listen to *In the Aeroplane Over the Sea*, you are never the same," Schur-as-Ludgate observes. "You'll feel like a god because you have been exposed to Jeff Mangum and his crazy brain and sometimes you'll think about the songs and, like, start crying in a grocery store because you can't take how awesome they are, but it's totally worth it."

On the final episode of *The Colbert Report*, the series finale of a show that ran for eleven seasons before host Stephen Colbert took over CBS's *The Late Show* after David Letterman's retirement, Colbert chose Neutral Milk Hotel's "Holland, 1945" to score the closing credits in lieu of the show's theme song. He told *New York Times* columnist Maureen Dowd that after his father and two of his brothers died in a plane crash and his eight other older siblings had left for college, he eventually found some solace in the "strange, sad poetry" of the song.

Aeroplane has inspired innumerable memes and works of fan art. Google "neutral milk hotel tattoo" and you'll find any body part you can think of inscribed with words and images pulled from the album's songs and packaging, some more literally than others. Tribute band Neutral Uke Hotel has toured the country performing a sing-along of the album on ukelele. Chiptune artist Doctor Octoroc raised more than $10,000 on Kickstarter to produce *In the RP2A Over the Sea,* an eight-bit cover version of *Aeroplane* made using "only the five monophonic channels available on the Nintendo Entertainment System's RP2A03 sound chip." Professional theater kid Amanda Palmer produced a musical based on the album with the drama program at Lexington High School, her alma mater, filling the one-thousand-person auditorium for three nights of performances.

As an undergraduate at Wesleyan, musician Max Heath wrote his thesis on *In the Aeroplane Over the Sea.* After listening to it in full more times than he could count, he pored over the album in ten-second segments, repeating each one until he had found every detail he could. The assignment was to write a twenty-five-page paper. Heath's came in at seventy-six. He includes the biographical details available at the time—largely drawn from Kim Cooper's 33 1/3 book about the album and a handful of shorter articles about the band—but the paper mostly focuses on the content of the album: its song structures, instrumentation, musical styles. Heath analyzes the narrative implications of alternating between single- and double-tracked vocals and speculates on the origins of simple chord patterns. A close reading of Anne Frank's diary provides additional context for lyrical themes and perspectives.

> **MAX HEATH**: I loved it more than ever afterwards. It was way deeper than I had ever imagined. Even as well as I understand it now, there's still so much mystery.

The album continued to grow in popularity in a way that sales numbers or streams fail to capture. Lots of people bought the record or listened to it through other means, but they also connected with it deeply. It was no longer just good, but canonically so. A classic, a must-listen, an Important Record. Jeff remained quiet.

ROBERT SCHNEIDER: I think it was something he noticed parallel to what was going on in his life, but I think that by the time he noticed that it was a big deal, it was already far enough from the time he had been professionally in bands. I don't think "professionally" is the right word to add to Elephant 6, because we're so unprofessional. It had been enough time that had gone by, then it was kind of like, how can you go back? All your bandmates are now leaders of other bands. I figured he would just start doing it again one day. Every few years, he would express to me that he was hoping or planning to do it sometime. It was never to me like he's totally stopped doing it. It was always just like, *Okay, he'll pull it together.*

Many others held out hope for the same change of heart. On June 6, 2006, an Elephant 6 Townhall user by the name of Nigh made the following post, entitled "news and fish and meaningful messages":

hello again.

for the past few months ive been putting together the pieces of everything ive written in the past three years and its been a revelation. whenever i had the time ive been writing melodies and keeping them in my head for later, and songs just accumulate, im not waiting as some have said. i still dont know how we're going to put it all together, the songs will have more noises and collages in them. because of that we dont know whether this will be korena pang or neutral milk hotel or michael bolton but that doesnt really matter. names are just a box we put things in to separate them, and we're figuring out what box these songs go in.

we dont have a timetable for releasing the album yet, so dont get your hopes up for new songs now. if you want more "aeroplane" just ignore all of this, the songs are songs but they're longer and more free. when jeremy came down after his tour we just spent days playing noise while screaming and it was incredibly liberating.

it has been so much fun that we will for sure be playing a show or two, probably more. freedom is a wonderful thing but at a certain point you need the routines of normal life. ive had that for a while but i realized last year at the show with the livys that the best sort of normal ive ever had was on the road with my friends. getting to gigs late with cars coughing and trombones smacking on doors, the giant egg leaks over the masses, the yolk sustains us, we eat whites for days. it can never be the same but i need to get as close as i can to that again.

so thats all. everything is happening soon, this is the year.

thanks for listening. jeff.

It was Nigh's first post on the forum, and the first post anyone had made purporting to be Jeff. But plenty of other Elephant 6 musicians had posted there before, and it made sense that someone so famously shy would make such an announcement in such a sympathetic space. People had flocked to the message board in the first place because they were so fond of Jeff's work. They wanted more of it, and so many were inclined to believe. Early responses in the thread were terse but credulous:

holy fuck. . . .

:)

this is hugely awesome

And so on for pages and pages. The prose was convincing enough that, with the sort of overeager indiscretion that inverts blustery J-school professor types' pyramids, both *Billboard* and *Pitchfork* (and countless other smaller outlets aggregating them) picked up on it, citing only the post as a source. Eventually, *Pitchfork* fleshed out the story with noncommittal speculation from some relevant insiders (John Fernandes: "Sounds like him, but you never know, probably is.").

After two days (and fifteen pages of responses), Robert Schneider chimed in on the original message board thread:

dear friends—

i had not commented on this thread because i wanted to hear back from jeff mangum directly about it—i sent jeff an email quoting the initial post on this thread yesterday, and he just replied:

hello robert-i am sorry to inform you that this is not my post. could you please inform the good people on the e6 list that this is not my writing? thank you robert. much love-j

this came directly to my email from jeff's email account—the post attributed to him is 100% FALSE, sorry to bear the disappointing news—it was a very beautifully written fake post!

you are all beautiful and brilliant kids, it would do the whole world a great deal of good if you took all this great energy and excitement you have been passing around here, rolled it up with your anger and disappointment into a big wonderful pissed-off ball, and recorded a bunch of kickass songs!!! please go right now and make something special, do something great, retaliate against the mediocrity that engulfs us!!

don't just do it for me, or jeff, or elephant 6 (although it would please us all immensely) do it because the world needs it!!

love,
*robert schneider**

Nigh's post was a hoax,† but the reaction was a real glimpse at how perceptions of Jeff and his work were changing despite his hermitage. The mainstream music press only started to acknowledge Neutral Milk Hotel when the band was active. In absentia, the band had become revered.

* "It clearly wasn't written by Jeff," Robert says. "It had his tone, but he doesn't really write that way. He's very terse. He's not all longwinded like that, ever. If it were Jeff writing, it would have been five sentences or fewer. Jeff has a lot of typos when he writes, even by hand."

† On October 22, 2008, Nigh made their second post, saying, "this wasn't really a hoax, you know. some things just take time . . ." No one took the bait that time.

Part of this was just how media had evolved, especially for music. Major music magazines did not put bands like Neutral Milk Hotel on their covers in 1998. The front of *Rolling Stone* that year included the visages of Bill Clinton, Jerry Springer, and the cast of *Seinfeld*. When it featured musicians, they included the likes of Alanis Morissette, Jewel, Marilyn Manson, and Madonna: stars as established as the magazine. Lesser-known artists (especially those without the backing of a major label that bought ad space in the magazine) could not break through that way. Magazines, labels, and other pillars of the music industry took their gatekeeping role seriously. Home-recording technology was making it easier to create an album, but discourse and distribution lagged behind.

That was starting to change, though, and just in time for a band like Neutral Milk Hotel to find a bigger audience. Absent any activity or promotion coming from the band, this happens through word of mouth, when listeners connect with a work so deeply they feel compelled to tell lots of other people about it. Word of mouth has existed since our mouths could form words, but the internet brought about the means to make those words spread faster and wider.

With vast amounts of money involved, this is by no means a meritocracy or an embodiment of the "marketplace of ideas" ideal. Lately, this has manifested as a period of major consolidation and corporatization. But especially early on—namely the late 1990s into the 2000s, before the invisible hand of the market sorted everything back into familiar, exploitative, corporate lanes—there was an explosion of hobby sites and blogs, and with information transmitted largely person-to-person (that is, by email, instant message, message board posts, and so on, without manipulation or amplification by weighted social media algorithms or "viral marketing" or marketing at all), organic spread was a real thing. It is not a coincidence that this brief period of decentralization aligned with a spike in the popularity of independent music and much wider aesthetic diversity.

Just as indie bands struggled to find coverage in the pages of the mainstream press, emerging writers publishing on personal blogs and digital zines could rarely garner the participation of mainstream artists. For a big-name musician (or more relevantly, for the people marketing and profiting from their work), a glossy print publication with circulation in the millions was a much more attractive venue than a website with a few hundred or even a few thousand monthly readers. The challenges that independent artists and independent digital publications faced were mirror images of each other. A natural partnership materialized: the blogs wrote about the artists who would talk to them, and the artists talked to the blogs that would interview them. Symbiotically, both rose in prominence. As a few of those websites got big, the bands they championed saw a bigger boost from their coverage, and as a few of those bands got big, the publications who had championed them early saw their credibility increase proportionally. Now that the major labels had lost interest in trawling for hidden talent (or maybe just lacked the resources to search so vigorously anymore), this new crop of tastemakers took on the role.

> MAURA JOHNSTON: Indie just became more of a big thing. You had this rise of the internet and more people self-publishing about music, in the demographic of people who like indie. At the same time, the ecosystems of online content evolved. Publicists for independent labels and independent publicists were a lot easier to contact. Before I got a full-time job writing, if I was going to email a publicist and say I'm writing about this for my blog, they'd be like, "Uh, sorry. We have actual people who we care about." But indie publicists were like, "Sure, yeah, whatever."

The music website exemplar of this phenomenon is *Pitchfork*. Founder Ryan Schreiber began publishing it from his Minneapolis bedroom as a teenager in 1995, with a heavy focus on indie music. Over the next quarter of a century, it exploded in popularity, influence, and scope. Operating today as a subsidiary of media giant Condé Nast (which also owns the *New Yorker*, *Vogue*, *Vanity Fair*, and countless other legacy publications) and drawing hundreds of thousands of readers each day, it is now a mainstream media brand, arguably the most influential music outlet on the planet.

It was a much, much smaller presence when it first reviewed *In the Aeroplane Over the Sea* in 1998, awarding the album a sturdy 8.7 out of 10 and a short but complimentary write-up, with M. Christian McDermott describing the record as "just as catchy as it is frightening." The whole review, published not long after the album's initial release, is only 144 words long.

When Merge reissued the album in 2005, a larger and more established *Pitchfork* reviewed it anew. The gulf between the reviews illustrates how much had changed in that time: how *Pitchfork* had developed, and how adulation of the record had grown.

> MARK RICHARDSON: It's the kind of record that *Pitchfork* championed for a long time, and I think still does to a certain extent. Small-scale, intimate, indie kind of vibe. Certainly in 2005, that was like the center of the world for *Pitchfork*. That kind of expression was very central to what *Pitchfork* was and also very central to what indie rock was then.

By 2005, both *Pitchfork* and *Aeroplane* had gotten a lot bigger in comparison to their cultural import in 1998. In his review, nearly one thousand words long, Richardson (who later became *Pitchfork*'s editor in chief and executive editor) does not purport to understand the album much better than he did when he first heard it seven years earlier, but repetition is a form of change after all: to be baffled by an album the first time you hear it is a wholly different experience than to be *still* baffled by it so many spins later. The review unpacks the compelling tension between the album's urgency ("through most of *Aeroplane* he sounds like he's running out of time and struggling to get everything said") and its abstraction ("no single word describes it so well as the beautiful and overused 'kaleidoscope'"). It's not clear what Jeff is trying to say, but Richardson has no doubt that "at the core of it all was guts."

> MARK RICHARDSON: It was definitely an indie rock classic at that point, but it's somewhat unusual in that it's an indie rock classic that's very beloved, and some people really hate it. If you think of Pavement, *Crooked Rain, Crooked Rain*, if you like indie rock, you probably like it. But I definitely knew people who were like, "Yeah, I just can't get with that guy's voice or the Jesus Christ thing. It's just too much." My memory then is it was especially true of a lot of my music-writer peers. It was harder for all the people who loved it to find each other. I feel like it's talked about a little less now, but to me it seemed very in the air then.

More reflective of how the publication and the public perception of the album had changed was *Pitchfork*'s revised numerical score for the album: a perfect 10, one of only a handful it had ever given at the time. It's not the only album the publication has re-reviewed, but it's a rare instance where the publishing of a new review coincided with the deletion of the old one.

RYAN SCHREIBER: We often reevaluate albums when they're re-released, since opinions and perspectives change in hindsight. Generally, we keep the old reviews intact. That review was originally from when the record was first released, and *Pitchfork* had been around for maybe a year or so and still trying to find its voice. It's not like embarrassing or anything. We just didn't think it was particularly useful.

MARK RICHARDSON: The context for what it meant to discover music in February of 1998, it was just completely different in every way.

Another example of how big Neutral Milk Hotel became after it had disbanded was Kim Cooper's contribution to Continuum's 33 1/3 series on notable albums, her book about *In the Aeroplane Over the Sea*. In 2005, her book was the twenty-ninth published in what is now a series of more than 150 titles. Though the books tend to be about much more popular albums—subjects include albums by the absolute biggest names in recorded music history—only the one on Céline Dion's *Let's Talk About Love* has sold better.

KIM COOPER: Maybe this is the kind of record where, unlike some of those best sellers, the record by itself isn't enough. It leaves people wanting more. They want to understand what it means and where it came from.

Cooper tried to cover a lot of ground in the book's hundred or so pages. Though the book is ostensibly about how *Aeroplane* was made, it naturally expands to cover much of what the Elephant 6 was as a whole.

KIM COOPER: It wasn't a story necessarily about a record people love as much as it was a story about an environment and a set of

> relationships that are very special and something a lot of us can aspire to. It's hard to have that environment, especially with the economic anxiety that Americans suffer now, but to have that level of support for your friends where you're competitive but you actually want them to succeed and that's why you push them, that's really special and beautiful. You can't hear about these relationships and what came out of it without thinking, *Wow, I wish everyone could have this.*

Cooper's book stands out because, aside from being the only real book written about any of this stuff (prior to this one), it's a rare instance of actual reporting on the subject, featuring interviews with a number of key players.

Generally, publications didn't run a whole lot of substantive pieces about Neutral Milk Hotel. How could they, when Jeff turned down every interview request and the whole band had gone on hiatus? But because the record continued to sell in physical units and online, there would still always be a news peg for "So what's with this whole Neutral Milk Hotel thing anyway?," even if those pieces never seemed interested in trying to answer the question so much as ask it in increasingly prolix and abstruse ways. Attention is the engine of the internet economy, and where there's interest, there's content to sell ads against.

Five years after Neutral Milk Hotel's last show as a full band, Jeff's absence had begun to seem intentional and like something more significant than post-tour rest and relaxation. In a 2003 *Creative Loafing* piece, writer Kevin Griffis set out to understand what was going on. Framed by Griffis's own feelings about his brother, who had committed suicide in 1999, the writer's search has a tragic tone, as though the answers to his questions about Neutral Milk Hotel will soothe his grief. Those answers never emerge.

"But it's so hard to stop searching for solace when you know you'll never even listen to a phone ring the same way again," Griffis writes. "I discovered, sheepishly, a human need for mythological hope that no amount of intellectual sustenance could satisfy."

Griffis turned to *Aeroplane* to help him grieve, describing the record as "the sound of transcending death." It made him feel better but left him wanting more. Of course, he didn't find anything. Not another album, certainly, or even news of what Jeff was up to. So he started looking for himself. Jeff's friends were happy to talk to him—Jeremy Barnes, Scott Spillane, Robert Schneider, Laura Carter, Will Cullen Hart, and friend Josh McKay (of Macha and eventually Deerhunter) are all quoted in the piece, as well as Jeff's father, James*—but Jeff himself declined to be interviewed and expressed his disapproval of the piece's premise:

"Please," he wrote, "I'm not an idea. I am a person, who obviously wants to be left alone. If my music has meant anything to you, then you'll respect that.

"Since it's my life and my story, I think I should have a little say as to when it's told. I haven't been given that right."

Griffis went along trying to tell as much of the story as he could without Jeff's cooperation (and with a print publication's restrictive word limit). The best answer to "Have you seen Jeff Mangum?" he could find from even Jeff's closest friends was "No, not in a little while." Jeff's current absence was becoming more notable than his earlier presence.

Meditations on his creative truancy and What It All Means would appear in publications like *Creative Loafing* frequently over the years. As often as not, the headline would ask a question that the piece couldn't answer. A 2016 *A.V. Club* piece is almost a meta-example of the genre, linking to the aforementioned *Creative Loafing* piece, a 2008 *Slate* piece ("The Salinger of Indie Rock"), a 2014 *Salon* piece ("You ruined Neutral Milk Hotel: Nostalgia, millennials and the return of Jeff Mangum"), and *Pitchfork*'s ranking revisionism. It points out that there was no flash point for *Aeroplane*'s explosion in popularity, and that unlike other reclusive musicians like Kevin Shields, Brian Wilson, and D'Angelo, Jeff's disappearance didn't seem to carry with it anything particularly dark or tragic, but the article doesn't offer any sort of explanation in its place.

Our understanding of music changes as our reality does. For example, what makes live music distinct from the recorded alternative seems obvious today, but it was not until we became familiar with recorded music that we began investigating sonic concepts like fidelity and material concepts like portability. Only when digital music emerged did the specific nuances of analog music—the presence of blemishes, the absence of compression, preciousness through scarcity—become more apparent. When we create paradigms and modalities, they do not obviate or obsolesce their

* Will had given Griffis Jeff's dad's number and now regrets having done so.

antitheses. Rather, we synthesize new with old to sophisticate our framework for moving through the world. For *Aeroplane* to grow in popularity as it did with near-frictionless inertia, almost purely by word of mouth, without its author providing any new context through interviews or new material, meant that our reality changed around it in such a way that the answers it posits and the questions it poses resonate much more deeply.

A couple of years after Jeff went quiet, in the wake of a stolen election, followed shortly by 9/11 and its limitless aftermath (to say nothing of the other catastrophes of the second Bush administration), American indie rock seemed to drop its irreverent pose and instead channel earnestness into a nihilistic garage revival, aggressively gentle twee pop, and a variety of danceable subgenres with an "electro-" prefix. Self-conscious but sincere, a generation (or at least a mostly male, mostly white cohort of that generation) searched for its voice, but artists of the time struggled to cut through the noise. How could they? The world felt too unstable to make sense of it in the present tense. When flux is the only constant, to be correct one moment is to guarantee wrongness in the next.

The more chaotic the world around us feels, the more alluring order begins to seem, and the stability of the recent past becomes a provocative model for the future. Music is typically understood as the segregation of signal from noise, but beneath that simple heuristic lies a subjective arbitrage process. Who decides which is which? *Aeroplane* takes the position that even polar opposites—signal and noise, transcendent beauty and devastating ugliness, life and death—can coexist harmoniously. Order cannot exist without disorder, and either can flourish within the other. Opposites *depend* on each other. By confronting death—dark, flat, infinite, inevitable—we can more deeply appreciate life's brightness, richness, ephemerality, and impossibility, how strange it is to be anything at all. The album offers both a multifarious past (juxtaposing styles, techniques, and narratives from different eras and cultures) and a capacious future (projecting expansiveness from a remixed history) to make sense of a present that feels increasingly urgent by the day. Flattening the universe and one's existence within it into a Möbius strip, *Aeroplane* loops the contradictory acts of looking inward and boundlessly outward into a continuous, synthesized whole.

CHAPTER 24

ROBERT SCHNEIDER: Money's bad. There's nothing good about it. The only thing good about it is having it when you don't. It's just one of the dimensions of human life. We have space, we have time, and we have money. Money is more like time. Time doesn't end well. Money's that way, too.

Kindercore, founded by Dan Geller and Ryan Lewis, had already signed a number of Elephant 6–adjacent bands. In the core of the Elephant 6, they saw a bunch of cool bands made up of cool people who weren't making much money. Their label, with support from Emperor Norton, was doing well, and they thought some kind of partnership could be beneficial to all parties. They presented Emperor Norton with a proposal to basically turn the Elephant 6 into a more traditional label, as a subsidiary of Kindercore. Emperor Norton liked the idea so much that they cut Kindercore out of the equation and made an offer directly to Robert to bring the Elephant 6 label under the Emperor Norton umbrella, independent from and equal to Kindercore.

Robert found the proposal interesting, but he wanted to keep it to himself until he could work out the details. He had a lot of demands, and if Emperor Norton couldn't meet them, Robert wouldn't even bother mentioning it to anyone else. He only wanted to share the plan if he was sure it would happen the way he thought it should. He'd have Hilarie Sidney and John Fernandes operate the label. Will Cullen Hart would be the art director. All he wanted, really, was for them to be able to convert their current lifestyles into paying gigs, with minimal adjustments. Once he got the okay, he'd share the good news with everyone else.

> **ROBERT SCHNEIDER:** If they came back with an unsatisfactory deal, I wasn't going to mention it. I'm generally kind of gentle and nice, but when it comes to a creative situation like that, I am not. If you're talking about a business situation where my creative rights are on hold, I'm polite, but I'm not flexible. It was as hippie and pro-artist as it could be. It protected every single possible entry point that they could have to have an opinion on our music or releasing our music.

Crucially, he wanted to make sure the artists of the collective maintained full creative control over anything they released. Elephant 6 as a label wouldn't push anybody around, and Emperor Norton wouldn't have a say, either. The bands could release music as they wished, and the new label (as it were) could help with promotion or arrange a meeting with one of the indie labels they were already on, like Merge or spinART. The upside to the deal was that anybody in the collective who could contribute would be entitled to health insurance at a group rate, something that seemed increasingly important as the people involved approached their thirtieth birthdays. In the proposal, Robert asked for an annual operating budget of $100,000, which would mostly cover the health insurance and salaries for Hilarie and John, plus some publicity expenses.

Somehow, Will got word of the deal, or at least a version of it: he heard that Robert was planning to sell the whole of Elephant 6 to Emperor Norton for a onetime payment of $100,000, which Robert would keep for himself. Will was angry.

> **ROBERT SCHNEIDER:** We were best friends. That was the thing that really pissed me off, that he would have believed that was happening, that I would sell Elephant 6 for $100,000. He knew me. I hate money.
>
> **WILL CULLEN HART:** I was pissed at things that I was imagining.

In April 2000, from a pay phone in Arizona between tour stops, Robert tried to hash things out with Will. It only made things worse. The call ended before the conversation did, with a "fuck you" from Robert and a receiver slammed onto the hook. When both had had some time to cool down, Robert called Will back from a cell phone in the van on the way to the next venue. He explained the details of the deal he was pursuing—which had not actually been accepted by Emperor Norton yet—but as Will came around to the idea, Robert changed his mind, too. He gave up on the deal and decided he needed to step away from the Elephant 6 concept entirely.

> **ROBERT SCHNEIDER**: I just cut myself off from caring about it. I stopped believing the ideals I had previously held, not about being all hippie and shit, but I went through a period for a few years where I had completely broken my belief in all of the ornate, psychedelic kind of frills that are such beautiful decorations for songs. Everything about Elephant 6 put a bad taste in my mouth, and it was just from the money dimension. Money ruined Elephant 6.

To be clear, no such deal was ever signed. In Robert's appraisal, it was simply the prospect of money that changed everything for the worse. He stopped recording or talking to bands about putting out their records or even giving anyone permission to use the Elephant 6 logo on their releases.

> **ROBERT SCHNEIDER**: The collective was effectively shut down. When I stopped being part of it, it instantly dissolved. I didn't make a big stink about it to everybody. I just stopped being part of it. From my perspective, there wasn't a cohesive person that was involved in everything besides me. At that point, I ceased to give attention to running it and to managing the social networking of it as well. I'm not saying it's my removing myself from that that made it fall apart. I'm saying I stopped paying attention, so I don't know why it fell apart. But it did fall apart at that exact same time. I bad-vibed everybody by dropping out. Here I am, Mr. Positive, giving them the finger. It was definitely not my fault. I was just the first person to respond viscerally. But because there was no label, suddenly there was no publicity, there was no one writing the press releases for the other bands, there

> was nobody trying to get the records going, there was nobody being available to record suddenly. It slowed things down.

Athens was changing, too. A new highway made the town more accessible, and Georgia's introduction of the HOPE Scholarship meant any student in the state who graduates high school with a B average can attend any state university for free, so long as they maintain that average through college. Suddenly, parents who had set money aside for tuition had some cash to burn. Student condos spread like kudzu. Everything got a little more expensive, a little less laid-back, and as often happens when real estate speculation spikes, a lot squarer.

The Elephant 6 community was also growing. People moved to town solely and explicitly to be part of it. Bands in other towns had found their way in, too. Perhaps the chemistry changed, or maybe it was dilution. It could have just been people getting older and less enthusiastic about their art, or some combination of these factors, or maybe something else entirely. One way or another, though, there was a lull. Neutral Milk Hotel and the Olivia Tremor Control weren't playing anymore, and many of the other Elephant 6 bands (including those that had spun off from Neutral Milk and the Olivias) had fallen by the wayside. Some people stopped making music altogether, and as folks got older, nobody recorded so prolifically or toured as incessantly as they once had. Even the Apples seemed to be taking a break. From the outside, the Elephant 6 had slowed down and barely seemed to exist anymore. Things had changed.

"There was a time when we called it the 'E6 backlash' back in '99," Will Cullen Hart told *All Songs Considered* in 2011. "It blew our minds. E6 was referenced in magazines all the time, and we thought, 'Wow, this is kind of becoming a tag word or something.' We were getting referenced way too much, and I think people started getting sick of the whole E6 idea. That's one of the reasons we decided to take our hiatus."

Around the turn of the millennium, the Elephant 6 as a whole had become a powerhouse in the indie music world. Neutral Milk Hotel was its flagship band, and barely one album cycle removed from its last release, fans had no reason to believe there wasn't more to come. The same went for the Olivia Tremor Control, who were nearly as popular then. At any given time, at least a few bands from the collective were on tour, sometimes together. After a few quick years of ascent, it felt not like a peak but like the early stages of something huge. Any of these bands could be the next Nirvana or Green Day or Radiohead or Flaming Lips, and maybe the collective as a whole could be a new model to pull the industry out of freefall.

As time went on, neither Neutral Milk Hotel nor the Olivia Tremor Control seemed anywhere close to releasing another record. The more time passed, the more desire for such a follow-up grew. Two things happened.

First, an intense devotion to these bands bloomed, on message boards and other online music communities (including the Elephant 6 Townhall forum, which members of the collective frequented with some regularity). Fans traded bootlegs and rarities along with rumors and speculation about background information and current whereabouts, plus an occasional hoax. Especially for those who discovered the bands only after they'd stopped performing, Neutral Milk Hotel and the Olivia Tremor Control took on mythological status. If you had to be there but weren't, you could at least find a group of people with whom to share your infatuation and yearning.

Second, as hope for more records from Neutral Milk Hotel and the Olivia Tremor Control morphed into canonization of their old ones, fans and critics looked toward other Elephant 6 bands to sate their hunger for new material. Aside from Jeff, every member of those bands was active in at least one still-trucking band. Perhaps the Music Tapes or Circulatory System or the Sunshine Fix could scratch an itch. No matter what those new records sounded like, though, they could never sound exactly like *Aeroplane* or *Black Foliage*. So when listeners chased the high from their first experiences with those bands, they were bound to be disappointed.

MARTYN LEAPER: I thought that was really unfair. To our minds, we were in this for good. We still do it. I don't think of it any differently than I did then, but it really hurt. I've been picking up the pieces ever since. Fads come and go. If you talk to any of the bands involved in the Elephant 6, they'll probably tell you the same thing: they don't see it as a fad.

BEN CRUM: It took us so long to get our record out that Elephant 6—there was this feeling around Athens like of "Dude, another sixties-influenced Elephant 6 record with psychedelic effects?"

RYAN LEWIS: To be totally frank, at one point, it got a little obnoxious in town, because pretty much every band was like, "Well, I want the Elephant 6 logo on the label," whether or not they had anything to do with it at all. It's a little weird to me, because obviously these were people who just wanted to do it because they thought the Elephant 6 is cool or whatever and they were friends with some people, but they knew it would sell more records if they had the Elephant 6 logo on it.

DAVEY WRATHGABAR: You'd hear things like, "The Elephant 6 is dead" or "the late Elephant 6" or whatever.

ROBBIE CUCCHIARO: There was always something going on, and there were people getting together and making stuff together and playing together. Some people moved away, some people were making families, so there were some dynamics that changed.

ANDREW RIEGER: Some people would say all the bands sounded the same, but I never thought that was the case at all. I could see some similarities in some of the early Olivia and Apples stuff, where they both were kind of influenced by Beach Boys and Beatles harmonies and arrangements, but they both did it in such an original way. All of the individual songwriters are strong and distinctive enough that the crossover was never that big.

The Elephant 6 pendulum never swung quite hard enough in any direction to experience the backlash that comes from major popularity, though. In many ways, obscurity was more powerful than criticism.

JIM DEROGATIS: I think the negative criticism came in the form of being ignored rather than being torn down. It was more that they were overlooked. What invites the pushback is when these bands are perceived to have sold out, but nobody was buying from these guys. It was encouraging to see independent labels and an independent spirit among bands after the independent underground had been coopted completely and then abandoned just as quickly for the Backstreet Boys. It would have been like shooting fish in a barrel.

JIM MCINTYRE: If you take all this energy and put it together and make this new universe and then it explodes, as it explodes it starts dissipating. When the Elephant 6 started, all this creative energy was focused into one idea. As it exploded and dissipated and people moved to different places and you got press, there were people who jumped on the bandwagon and naturally it just felt like it lost a bit of energy. Some of the second-wave bands were great, but like everything else, it got a little uncool. It wasn't as hip as it used to be. It's like everything else. It runs in a cycle. People felt like they were more than just Elephant 6 and didn't want to be lumped in with this band or that band every time an article talked about them.

MAURA JOHNSTON: I wonder how much of the backlash is just, "You can't go back to your youth." And the other thing that happens is expectations get built up, and sometimes they're unrealistic.

SCOTT SPILLANE: There was one article on Gerbils that said, "Great, another Elephant 6 band," and then started smacking our segues or something. Like all we need is some more segues in between pop songs. For our next album, we're going to put that guy's name, and then "Gerbils: Great."

JOHN FERNANDES: I have no problem with other bands taking influence, because it's something that excites us. We want to see more bands doing that. But at the same time, when you start getting criticized in reviews for doing the same old thing, for other bands having copied or picked up things from you, but when you do it, it's "Oh, they're just doing the same old thing that everybody else is doing." It's like, *Wait a minute, no!*

ROBERT SCHNEIDER: There was some sense of restlessness within the collective about Elephant 6, because the larger bands would absorb all of the attention, even for smaller bands. Like the Great Lakes, who were one of the greatest bands. They were possibly the best band in the Elephant 6. And the Minders, who were for a short period really popular in the 1990s. These are bands that deserve to be more famous. These were albums that were seminal albums within our scene. The Minders were trumped by the Apples. The Great Lakes were trumped by Of Montreal. There was always the next biggest band to squash your new record when it came out. Even if your record was better and more genius, and you're younger, there was a slightly more established band that would soak up the review. They get the first sentence. You have to name off a few people before you even get to naming this younger band. I think that's bad. I think it was good up front, and I think it's bad in the end.

JULIAN KOSTER: Irony and cynicism were embraced so orgasmically by the culture as a whole, and I swear to god if you were making anything sincerely, you were the uncoolest thing on the planet Earth. I just remember feeling like, *What have we come to that you have to either be jaded or cynical or ironic, or hide your sincerity beneath this veneer of jaded, cynical irony,* and everybody is doing it like lemmings. I hated that attitude so much. It feels like the culture is permanently cynical since then.

CHAPTER 25

Derek stuck around with Of Montreal until 2004, when the tension between the creatively agnostic production work he was doing for the band and the artistically driven music experimentation he found elsewhere reached a breaking point. Andy left the band, too.

Kevin left the house out in the country and moved closer to town. Bryan had just finished a solo album as the Late B.P. Helium, and with some time on his hands and Kevin living much closer, they started to hang out again. The Ladybug Transistor asked Kevin to open for them at a show in Athens. Kevin's wife, Nina, played bass, and Bryan was back on guitar, and Jamey and Dottie were still in the picture, but they performed as the Dutch Scrubber, a bizarre sexual joke Kevin had come up with in the van one day on an earlier tour.

After the Dutch Scrubber show, though, Bryan rejoined Of Montreal as their touring guitarist, but still not adding much on records, which Kevin was mostly making by himself now. After Derek's departure, Kevin's songwriting and recording processes became even more of a one-person operation. The next album, *Satanic Panic in the Attic,* might as well have been a solo effort. The reason *Satanic Panic in the Attic* and especially *The Sunlandic Twins* sounded so different from previous albums is how differently they were made.

Bryan Poole: I built them a computer. I kind of knew they wanted to start recording that way, so I set them up, and then they learned how to do it, for better or for worse. They started creating. The songs from *Sunlandic Twins,* a lot of them were based off of failed commercial jingles that they repurposed for songs. The songs were a little extra catchy. And then for *Hissing Fauna,* I think they almost reached their full maturation of this kind of new sound that they're working on. They allow themself to get more personal with their lyrics. Starting with *Satanic Panic in the Attic,* they started to write lyrics that maybe weren't as fantastical. They were actually writing lyrics that meant something to them.

KEVIN BARNES: I'd do what the kick drum pattern was going to be for the whole song, and then I'd do the snare drum for the whole song, and then I'd do the high hat for the whole song. It was recording drums in the way you program drums. That's around the time I started writing in the studio a lot more. Up to that point, I'd write songs on acoustic guitar or piano and have them all fleshed out before I started to record them.

JAMEY HUGGINS: That's when it was apparent that the control could be there. From then on it was like, "I can do this by myself. I don't need to spend twelve hours setting up microphones, and I enjoy doing it." We were all like, "What the fuck? What about us?" It was an uncomfortable transition. It was embarrassing and sort of annoying, because obviously we felt unnecessary. Our way of coping with that was transitioning all of our efforts to the performance. To keep our dignity and whatever creative impact, we had to focus all of our energy on the live performance.

KEVIN BARNES: The way I am, being sort of a control freak and having a really strong vision of what I want to do, I'm not really the sort of person who gets excited about having other people involved, at least on that level. It's one thing to have someone come in and play a part, but I don't really like the idea of having to make every decision by committee. I've just sort of resigned to that fact that people are going to come and go, and it's fine.

Of Montreal had ostensibly turned into a pseudonym for Kevin, at least for recording, and even the live show sounded much different. It still looked garish and trippy, but saccharine psych pop was giving way to a dancier, more electronic sound. Of Montreal was moving away from the Elephant 6, at least aesthetically, and 2004's *Satanic Panic in the Attic* was printed without the E6 logo.

BRYAN POOLE: With Kevin, two or three weeks into the *Satanic Panic* tour, they said, "Man, I thought this was going to be the last tour." Any other Of Montreal record had probably sold three thousand, maybe five thousand copies, but probably not even that much. If there was any money being made from the records, that didn't amount to many people at the shows, and so you weren't making much from the shows, sleeping on people's floors and stuff. And Kevin had a kid, so they're afraid they're going to have to go home, put on a shirt and tie, and go find a real job. That's what they thought they were going to have to do. So they were really surprised, as we all were. And we started playing all-ages venues, too, which I think helped a lot.

JAMEY HUGGINS: It was total encouragement 24/7. It was exciting to have Will or Jeff or Julian to say something encouraging about a show or a record, and it was nothing but support. There was zero competition. That's the whole thing people seem to not understand. How could you have all these bands with all these egos and all these different projects, and some people's records are selling in the tens of thousands and some people's are selling less than a thousand, and you're all still—in each other's eyes—peers? That's how it really felt. Maybe that was naive, but that's how I felt. I did feel like the little brother in a way, but not in a condescending way. It was sort of like, "You can do this, too."

BRYAN POOLE: "Wraith Pinned to the Mist," people love that video. I think a lot of kids saw that video, and all of a sudden, we became popular with high school kids. That's kind of helped sustain the band. High school kids or even younger, those are the ones who are most passionate about music. They're the ones who are exploring music and finding out about music. That's the time in your life when every little thing that you hear has a large impact on your musical growth. Of Montreal seemed to be hitting teenagers. Kevin's music was that for them, and once that happened, we had them hooked.

DAN GELLER: It's weird, because their fan base is so young, and they have to keep winning them over. You lose that fan base when they turn twenty-one. So they have to win sixteen-to-twenty-one-year-olds every time they put out a new record. They have fans that stick around, but when you go to a show, there's still sixteen- and twenty-one-year-olds, and that means they're getting new fans with every record. Their fans weren't that young the first time around. It was a very different demographic.

JAMEY HUGGINS: Why have the Apples put out ten albums and never really reached anything close to the level of record sales that Neutral Milk Hotel did? Why have the Minders put out six or seven albums, every inch as good as the records of the other Elephant 6 bands, and they can't get a room with more than a hundred people in it? To me, Martyn Leaper is one of the premiere songwriters, held up in the same esteem as Will or Bill or Jeff or Robert, but for some mystical reason, they were cursed. The Minders couldn't catch a break. Same thing with Of Montreal. We did six years of heavy touring. We put out six albums, each one we all thought was great. And then suddenly, a change of label, a change of distribution, and a change of recording technique or whatever you want to call it, and suddenly it was a legitimate thing. So with that one record, *Satanic*, that was the first record where Kevin did like ninety percent of the recording. When we talk about the record selling well and getting press reviews and stuff like that, sure it was great to be involved in that, and at that point we were genuinely, totally unembittered with Kevin and genuinely happy for him. But it was more a thing of being happy for him, not like we did it. Bittersweet. We went from this Partridge Family–type deal, happily playing for two hundred people a night on what we thought were fun tours, to doing interviews on NPR and doing Coachella and playing two-thousand-seat headlining theaters and shit, all on the spark of Kevin being this autonomous recording solo artist, essentially. But at the same time, our whole prowess was based on our live performance and its total extravagance. So that's why it's impossible to this day to quantify what happened. On one hand, the records started selling, and on the other hand, we started doing these crazy performances. Which came first, the chicken or the egg?

ANDREW RIEGER: Kevin's got a wife and kids, so I don't see them that much, but they were never, even before that, much of a person that you would see at bars and shows and stuff. They were a little more of a hermit.

ROBERT SCHNEIDER: To me, Kevin Barnes is across the map the most talented person in Elephant 6.

JAMEY HUGGINS: I remember having survivor guilt. For the previous five years, we were in awe of and enamored with the sort of older brothers that we had in Jeff and Will and Bill and Julian and Robert. And I had this realization—I think we were playing at the Bowery Ballroom—and I had remembered the only time I had been there previously was to see Neutral Milk Hotel. And we were on a tour opening for them, but we weren't booked that night. It was just them. So we had a night off and got to see Neutral Milk Hotel in Manhattan at the Bowery, and it was amazing. And then a year or two later,* we were selling out two nights at the Bowery Ballroom. It was the first time I realized we were doing shows and drawing crowds that Neutral Milk Hotel couldn't even do at that time. Or Olivia couldn't draw. Or the Apples couldn't draw. And then that got bigger and bigger, to the point we were selling out headlining, indoor, single-venue tickets, four-thousand-seat places.

Elf Power and the Apples in Stereo, in also maintaining their productivity, provide an interesting contrast to Of Montreal. All three bands have been fairly prolific over the years, shifting their lineups frequently and mutating stylistically from album to album. Of Montreal has now released seventeen full-length albums (plus nine compilations, a live record, and ten EPs), Elf Power has released sixteen (and a couple of EPs), and the Apples have released seven (plus a couple of compilation records, not to mention Robert's and Hilarie's other projects). But whereas Of Montreal's years of toil paid off in headlining tours of two-thousand-person crowds and big festival gigs, Elf Power and the Apples have hovered perpetually around the same level of notoriety they've always had.

It didn't happen right away, though. Of Montreal's sound had evolved from twee-ish indie pop that fit right in with their Elephant 6 friends to a funkier, electronic, and much more modern sound that struck a chord with the tastemakers of the time.† The tour to support 2004's *Satanic Panic*

---

* Probably more like five or six years, but still.

† *Hissing Fauna* landed at #5 on *Pitchfork*'s list of 2007's best albums. The rest of the top 10 included Panda Bear's *Person Pitch*, LCD Soundsystem's *Sound of Silver*, M.I.A.'s *Kala*, Radiohead's *In Rainbows*, Animal Collective's *Strawberry Jam*, Spoon's *Ga Ga Ga Ga Ga*, Battles's *Mirrored*, the Field's *From Here We Go Sublime*, and Burial's *Untrue*. Even among the rock bands on this list (and there's only two, maybe three), electronic stuff was de rigueur.

had been positive, but with their wife pregnant and nearing her due date, Kevin canceled a month-long European leg. Worried about money with a kid on the way, they felt like the responsible thing to do was to give up on the band thing for a while—even the successful tours weren't bringing back a lot of money, since they were spending so much on the production. They decided to focus their creative energy writing jingles for corporate advertising.

BRYAN POOLE: They never once got a jingle accepted, and they spent a month, every day, just writing jingles. They did one for like, Lay's potato chips, Coca-Cola. They did one for a mobile phone company.

KEVIN BARNES: I was thinking, *I'm a songwriter, so I should potentially be able to do that for a living, even if it's not through Of Montreal.* So I started reaching out to different agencies to try to make it happen. I got as far as being able to submit things, but I never once actually got anything into a commercial spot. It's embarrassing. I think I'm really bad at it. I think what they want is for it to not feel like a jingle. I would try to do what I imagined they wanted, but it was never right.

When they were unable to sell the jingles, Kevin converted many of them into Of Montreal songs. *Sunlandic Twins* is a remarkably catchy record, so it's not hard to hear how so many of its melodies were originally drafted for ads. If you listen closely to "So Begins Our Alabee," for example, you can make out "Hear my mobile ringing" in the backing vocals, repurposed from a jingle Kevin had written for T-Mobile.

An ad agency dug the video for "Wraith Pinned to the Mist (and Other Games)," a single off *The Sunlandic Twins*, and approached the animators about turning the cutesy video into a spot for Outback Steakhouse. Kevin had pitched plenty of actual jingles before, and occasionally someone would approach with interest. Kevin would give the okay, and then they'd never write back. Kevin figured they'd see where things led this time, but the agency changed its tune. It didn't really want to use the video concept anymore, or even the song itself, but rather the "essence" of the song. They never used the word "jingle," as far as Kevin can recall, and they told them it would just be for a radio commercial.

Kevin had just had a kid, but Of Montreal had not yet become a money-making venture. They had been able to live modestly for their whole adult life, but a baby meant some new financial pressures, and if the band didn't start bringing in some money soon, Kevin would likely have to give it up entirely and go find a steadier source of income. Though Kevin was apprehensive about the whole ordeal, they went for it.

And then they regretted it immediately.

KEVIN BARNES: I didn't trust my instincts. It seemed really fishy, but fuck it, I'll do it. I instantly felt like I had just sold my soul to the devil. I called her back like thirty minutes later, like, "Look. I've changed my mind. I don't want to do this." And she said, "What? I've already told them. I already told the client." "I don't want to do it. Just fucking cancel it. I'm not going to do it." And then she lays this guilt trip on me, like, "Look, my job's on the line. If you tell them no now, I could get fired." And I was like, *Fuck, I don't want you to get fired, but I don't want to do this.* I was definitely taken advantage of. I didn't have any representation. I didn't have any lawyer at the time or anything going for me in that way. So they send me this contract, and I didn't really read it. I just sort of signed it. That's the price of an education.

BRYAN POOLE: The next day, Kevin's late to practice. "I just signed this thing to have 'Wraith Pinned to the Mist' used for an Outback radio thing. I don't know if I should have done it." I said, "Why didn't you get a lawyer to look at this contract or ask Polyvinyl about it?" "I tried to call them, but they were busy." "Why didn't you wait?" "The woman was like, 'You have to fill this out and fax it to me by five or the deal is off.'" So they do it. Which they shouldn't have done, because they were playing them. Supposedly, Polyvinyl had a thing for a GM commercial that would have run for one month, actually used the song, and Kevin would have gotten paid three times as much money. Instead, they signed a contract for three years, for a third of the money.

The agency recorded a new version of the song, which retained the bass line and catchy melody but changed the lyrics from Kevin's "Let's pretend we don't exist / Let's pretend we're in Antarctica" to "Let's go Outback tonight / Life will still be there tomorrow" and mixed in a prominent didgeridoo.

They even hired a singer who sounded remarkably like Kevin. Versions of the ad ran for three years, on television as well as on the radio. Of Montreal was heckled mercilessly on the road for those three years.

KEVIN BARNES: That's definitely one of the most bizarre things that's ever happened to me. Up to a point, we had never been allowed to enter the mainstream world in that way. I don't know if it was just the timing of it, because people maybe felt really connected to *Hissing Fauna* on a personal level, and I sort of deprived them of the intimate connection with the thing because it was brought into the mainstream world. People were like, "Aw, you're sellouts!" Someone even came to one of our shows with Outback Steakhouse menus and put them all throughout the venue. They put a lot of effort into it. They made this big sign. It was crazy how meaningful it was for people.

BRYAN POOLE: We had this show where these quote-unquote fans brought an Outback Steakhouse banner and held it up in the middle of the crowd, and then somebody threw a piece of steak on the stage.

KEVIN BARNES: For a time period, it was really depressing for us to deal with. We couldn't play the song anymore. It took us a long time to play the song again. It was just such a thing if we started playing it. Everyone would start shouting, "Let's go Outback tonight!"

BRYAN POOLE: It's something that's personal to [the fans], so they're disappointed. It's been taken away from them. And during that time period, you're so skeptical of advertising and mass media. You're starting to see it's all a bunch of crap. You've grown up with McDonald's and Coke, and you're starting to see, *Hey, this is just psychology being thrown on me.* I don't begrudge any of the fans who were hurt by it, because I would have felt the same way. On the other side of things, they don't realize that we're broke, or we were broke. At that point in time, that was a lot of money. We'd go on tour, and maybe we'd come back with $2,000 from being on the road for a month and a half.

The ordeal inspired Kevin to write a missive for *Stereogum* explaining themself. In a piece titled "Selling Out Isn't Possible," Kevin essayed to lay out the financial difficulties facing contemporary musicians, positing that what people mean when they say "sell out" is one of the few viable ways a band can make a living off its music. They argued that virtually everyone surviving in present-day America had to sometimes do things they "might not be completely psyched about" just to keep a roof over their heads, but as long as you're not consciously changing your art to be more commercial, you're not really "selling out."

KEVIN BARNES: I hope that essay I wrote will make people realize, like, these indie bands aren't making any money, and if they get an advertisement or a TV commercial, that's more money than they probably would have made all year through record sales or whatever. What's better: for the band to have to work at Outback Steakhouse because they're not making any money, or to occasionally sell a song to them? Are you less of a sellout for working at Outback Steakhouse? Who can survive with those sorts of restrictions? What do you do if you're not independently wealthy? Everyone has to be selling out, whatever that term means, all the time.

DAVEY WRATHGABAR: Part of the environment here is that time stops. Part of it is that people are really supportive. But Andrew and Kevin are really the exceptions. They have real work ethic. Everyone else is just too precious. I think that it hurts to some degree. Everywhere else I've lived, motherfuckers are motivated by fear of sucking. So you'll have these bands, and they'll practice for three solid months for their first show. They don't want to suck in front of their friends. A lot of these same bands get into the studio and they just bust out what they played live. It's pretty easy, and not good. Here, it's the opposite. They'll just put whatever onstage.* But that recording? You have to work on that. You can't suck on the recording. You can suck live. If people are having a good time, it doesn't matter.

ANDREW RIEGER: The late nineties for sure were a really exciting time. It seems like an ongoing natural thing to me. It seems like there's as many people interested in it now as ever. The people that are involved, we don't ever really think of Elephant 6 as a tangible, real thing, so it's not something that I think about in that way. It's more just a group of friends that collaborate together. The intangibility and the vagueness of it is what makes it interesting. It's just a group of friends that collaborated together and continue to collaborate together on each other's projects.

* In the time I spent living in Athens, I lost count of how many bands would emerge after just a few practices together, play a show or two, and then disappear entirely.

LANCE BANGS: Through all of that stuff, I love that Elf Power was a fairly continuous band. It wasn't necessarily an Elephant 6 band when it started, but their own instincts for writing songs from a different perspective and a catchy structure and weird tangents happening fit well with what those guys were all doing.

The key to a band like Elf Power lasting for as long as it has is keeping the definition of "band" sort of loose. Andrew and Laura have been the only consistent members of the band since its inception (and even Laura wasn't there in the very beginning), with roughly as many lineup changes as albums in that span.

LAURA CARTER: We've had a lot of different members, but it's all kind of from the same musical family. Our musical community stays pretty much the same around here, yet we're pretty consistently switching roles. That keeps it fun, and I think that has kept it going and interesting. Certainly, we've all changed tremendously over the years, but the essence of it is still the same.

DEREK ALMSTEAD: It's extremely democratic. Everybody has a voice and weighs in, and generally the things that come out of that group are things that everybody is cool with, down to artwork and stuff. You can have a vision, and then that person can say, "Do you guys like this?" In a certain way, ideas are kind of infinite. Play me a song, and I could write you five hundred bass lines for it. You kind of just go with the flow of excitement in a group. With Andrew, he welcomes that idea, and if it's not there, it's not going to stop the ball from rolling. He's an incredibly serious self-editor. He'll write twenty songs and shoot down his own stuff really fast.

In Lexington, Robert had a new direction in mind for his band and reached out to one of his earliest collaborators to help flesh out the sound. Bill felt like he was hitting a wall with the Sunshine Fix and was ready for a new challenge with an old friend. Robert had taught Bill how to play bass when they were younger and was a positive influence on his guitar skills over the years. So naturally, when Bill joined the Apples in 2005, Robert put him on keys. The Apples hadn't released a record since 2002, but as Robert was finding his religion again, he decided he could reinvigorate the whole collective. Will and Jeff appear on 2007's *New Magnetic Wonder*, too. They had been through a lot since their high school days jamming together in Robert's bedroom, but the good feelings came back quickly.

"I must also commend Hilarie [Sidney], too," Bill Doss told *Optical Atlas* in July 2006. "Even though this is the first time she and I have sung together, it's effortless to blend voices with her. She is quite an amazing singer as well and pounding the hell out of the drums at the same time!"

Hilarie left the Apples as they were preparing for their tour in support of *New Magnetic Wonder*. Max, her and Robert's son, was in elementary school, and she had another son with her new husband, Per Ole. She was also working and going to school, so touring was just too big a burden.

> **Hilarie Sidney**: It was really painful for me. I had to beg my way in it, but I started this band with those guys. I had been with them from the very beginning, when Robert's dad was renting minivans for us and we had enough money to get one Taco Bell meal a day. We had been through so much and done so much, I felt like such a part of the whole process and where the band is today. It was my whole life for a whole decade.

Elephant 6 bands had a relationship to commercialism that fell mostly between disinterest and disgust. Of Montreal's foray into that world—via licensing a song for an Outback Steakhouse commercial—seemed to have hurt as much as it helped. Most others would reject such an opportunity out of reflex (though some of them came to regret that position, too). The Apples, however, were willing to participate, licensing their music for several ad campaigns over the years, including one deal around the turn of the millennium with an international telecom company that earned Robert and spinART about a million dollars total for both the performer's rights and songwriter's rights.

> **Jeff Price**: It gave them the ability to carpet the bedroom and get food and fix the house up for their newborn child. The timing was wonderful. Licensing became a very important income stream for the Apples in Stereo. Robert's philosophy, the way he expressed it to me, was "Look, I can go work for JCPenney. I can go work for Kohl's. What's the difference? How is this a sellout?"

A 2001 *New York Times* article notes the first Apples song licensed for a commercial was "Strawberryfire," for which an agency paid $18,000 to include it in a Sony ad, "more money than the band cleared in a year of recording and touring" at the time, even after spinART took its cut. Hilarie and Robert had agreed not to license their music for certain products and businesses—meat, leather, cigarettes, alcohol, the military—but companies like Sony, JCPenney, and Bank of America were fair game.

"You imagine that it's a crass process," Robert says in the piece. "But it's not like Sony used our song in the commercial, which is how it looks to the indie kid. It's just one guy who liked our music. . . . Radio is controlled by this huge industry. Ads are controlled by a few creative people. They probably did art in college. Maybe they were college radio programmers."

HILARIE SIDNEY: I was all for it because it's really hard to make money doing music. I was a supporter of using our songs for commercials, as long as it wasn't something gross. I guess you could say consumerism in general is kind of gross, but it was a great way for us to make money. I didn't have to work for many years and just got to be a musician. We just got offers. We were never proactive about it. But once we started getting the first couple of offers, then more started rolling in all the time. I was able to pay off debt and save money. Robert and I put together an account for Max for college.

JOEL MOROWITZ: The Apples were more open to it. Out of the big three, the Apples were the most commercial. What's not to like? You can see why maybe a TV commercial wouldn't want to use Neutral Milk Hotel, but I don't think that's something Jeff wanted anyway.

BRIAN MCPHERSON: Robert's always been okay with putting songs in TV shows and movies and ads for products, and I think the nature of his music really lends itself to certain types of ads. There are a lot of ad execs who are just very fond of Robert and his music and just always look to him if they're looking for a certain mood, whether it be psychedelic or sunny or poppy or Beach Boys–y or Zombies-y or Apples-y or whatever. He's got a unique style and an incredible knack for writing a hook. I think he sees it almost as a math equation. Whereas somebody like Jeff just isn't interested in that kind of thing. Certain artists have ideals, whether things can be unique or if they support certain causes. Sometimes that goes as deep as how their music is presented or what it's affiliated with or even the corporation behind a product or service or ad. They look very deeply at these things.

ROBERT SCHNEIDER: People that are more successful, there's some weird thing that goes on with it. I can only think of one band in Elephant 6 that's significantly more successful, and the person that is the head of that band is a mess. There's this Syd Barrett, Kurt Cobain, Brian Wilson shadow that hangs over fame in our world. It's the Icarus thing, getting burned as you get too close to the sun. I think that influenced all of us. But if you don't come into the sun, you feel resentful. Maybe if you get too much sunlight, it can turn you off. I always tried to stay just below that.

Robert had walked away from the Elephant 6 concept entirely some years earlier, feeling as though the premise had been poisoned by money. He kept making music, focusing his attention elsewhere, disillusioned by his earlier ideals.

He'd been working on a project with Andy Partridge of XTC, but it fell through when Partridge's manager pushed Robert to quickly finish some rough demos and Robert insisted on taking his time to flesh them out into album-quality tracks. Partridge had been a musical hero of Robert's, but Robert walked away from the project when he felt pressured to compromise. He'd been working with a couple of Lexington musicians on it—John Ferguson and Ben Fulton of Big Fresh—so when that fell through, the three of them started a band called Ulysses to play the new songs Robert was writing. Robert Beatty (of local noise band Hair Police and an accomplished visual designer who has done cover art for Tame Impala, the Flaming Lips, Mdou Moctar, Kesha, and lots of others) joined the band to play synthesizer, sound effects, and a spring. They recorded an album together in Robert's garage, playing every song together live into a single microphone, overdubbing just a few sound effects and vocal tracks at the end.

ROBERT SCHNEIDER: That was the apex of my interest in anti-production. It's a very meaningful record to me. Having done that, that satisfied the part of me that was rebelling against Elephant 6. My rebellion against Elephant 6 was artistic. Even though I had believed in it, had publicized it, had done everything I could to promote this

> ideal of psychedelic production mashed with lo-fi mashed with great songwriting, writing hit songs and then packaging them in a way that couldn't possibly be a hit, I suddenly felt disillusion from that. Having this band with all these young guys, it washed away that previous life and made it pure. I didn't feel like I was neglecting it anymore. Then Will called me.

Will had big news: Brian Wilson had performed *Smile* at the Royal Albert Hall in London, and Will had copped a recording. The next time Robert was in Athens, they listened to it together. Prior to this performance, they had only ever heard the cassette bootlegs of incomplete tracks. It was as if they'd been obsessed with a black-and-white photo and were suddenly seeing it in color for the first time. They hadn't even known it had vocal melodies. After exorcizing the impulse toward minimalist production on Ulysses's *010*, Robert heard *Smile* with a new vividness and was ready to swing back hard in that lush direction.

Ultimately, it was commercial dalliance that allowed Robert to rediscover his religion. Around the same time, Robert had been hired by Kohl's to write pop songs that could be used as backing tracks in their commercials. They asked for one, he wrote five, and they accepted all of them. He recorded those five at home, but the company was so pleased with the work, they told him he could record one last track anywhere he wanted. Robert chose to record with engineer Mark Linett, a frequent Brian Wilson collaborator, in the studio where *Pet Sounds* had been recorded. When it came time to mix the record he'd made as Marbles, his solo project, Robert returned to Linett, with spinART extending the budget for the album so Robert could finish it in Linett's Los Angeles home. While Robert was there, Linett happened to receive the test pressing for a forthcoming album: *Brian Wilson Presents Smile*. The record was adapted from the series of performances Wilson had done, including the one Robert had heard with Will. Those performances had themselves been adapted from the songs Wilson had abandoned back in 1967. Linett suggested they take a break from the Marbles work to listen to it.

ROBERT SCHNEIDER: It's the most beautiful, incredibly psychedelic, lyrically majestic piece of music that I've ever heard in my life. And I heard it for the first time in Mark Linett's studio, on the speakers he was mixing it on, off the vinyl. I had just had this whole experience in a few years where I broke up with Elephant 6, my marriage dissolved, and all this stuff happened. I had lost my faith in big production, everything that *Smile* represented to me as a kid. It completely re-sparked my belief in psychedelia and ornate songwriting and arrangements and vocal parts. I think it had a tragic vibe to the story before Brian finished it, but to know he finished it, he came back and went through all of that and through this mental health crisis and all of this, he got back together with his friend he had written it with, he finished *Smile* as this older guy and made it great, one of the best psychedelic records that had ever been made.

After hearing this newer, fuller version of *Smile* in 2004, Robert no longer felt like there was nothing left for the Apples to do. He viewed the five albums the band had made as a story arc, each one with its own specific ambitions. The next would encompass that whole story, with elements of each of those albums and everything else that had inspired the band since. With renewed faith in his earlier philosophy, Robert felt like it was a perfect opportunity to reignite the Elephant 6 more broadly. Jeff, Will, and Bill all played on the album, and they included the Elephant 6 logo on the record, the first album to bear that insignia in years.

Robert was late to high school more often than not, which meant he had detention more often than not, too. He enjoyed math and even tested into the advanced algebra class, but he turned in only blank assignments.

ROBERT SCHNEIDER: I was being rebellious. My friend and I were total scumbag metalheads. We decided it would be conceptually really funny if we bombed the class, having gotten into it. So we conceptually got an F that year.

When he was forced to retake it, he found the work satisfying. It felt overwhelmingly messy until the end, when everything fell into place. He finds the same sense of resolution in producing an album, moving parts around until everything finds its way into the pocket. Few things in life resolve so neatly.

Flash forward to 1998. His studio in Denver looked dilapidated from the outside, windows boarded up, tagged with graffiti. Inside, he'd built up a stockpile of recording gear, almost entirely analog and used, often partly broken. As his production work developed, he had ambitions for a higher fidelity, though he still wanted nothing to do with digital recording. After finishing *Aeroplane*, he sold his recording console and bought a big fancy Neotek machine from the seventies, for about the same price, from a local studio that had been keeping it in storage. He used it to mix the Minders' *Hooray for Tuesday* and to submix the Olivias' *Black Foliage*. For the next Apples record, *The Discovery of a World Inside the Moone*, he spent almost his entire budget on an Ampex MM1200 sixteen-track two-inch tape machine from an LA studio, a major upgrade from the eight-track half-inch tape machines he'd used most recently. The new machine was the size of a clothes dryer, weighed about one thousand pounds, and arrived in a big wooden crate.

ROBERT SCHNEIDER: I loved this tape machine. This thing was ancient-looking. It was an artifact from the past. These big VU meters that would light up. All of the circuitry was open. You had to adjust it with screwdrivers and stuff. It didn't have knobs. It was incredibly romantic to me.

Like all romances, it had its ups and downs. The first time Robert used it, the machine shut down. A studio technician came by and fixed it, but it blew out again the next day. The tech fixed it again but conceded that he didn't know what else to do to keep it running. It was unlikely that anyone else in town could fix it, either. So Robert opened up the instruction manual himself.

ROBERT SCHNEIDER: It was like two dictionaries thick, and if you opened it, it wasn't just that it was a huge, thick book, it's that all the pages folded out like centerfolds, multiple times. One, two, three, four times. There were these incredibly dense, complex schematic diagrams. It was like this act of devotion. It kept blowing out. It was elderly. I had to keep it alive. It felt really romantic in that way, like I really was personally nurturing this machine. It was like it was alive.

With the help of the manual, Robert kept the machine running but discovered its fatal flaw: the mechanism it used to transport the tape would blow out the machine's diodes. He'd need to learn more to keep this thing working.

Robert bought a book on basic electronics from RadioShack. He sat down on his studio floor, the tape machine manual splayed open, tools and wires and components strewn around him, the machine itself opened up, with its guts exposed. He cracked the new book to begin the next stage of his training and was struck by an equation on the first page.

> **ROBERT SCHNEIDER:** My memory is that the ceiling lifted up off the studio and there was light shining down from the clouds onto my studio floor, this golden light illuminating this equation. I realized that this simple equation, the simplest-possible algebra, was at play in the background of everything that was my religion.

The equation was Ohm's Law, which states that voltage (V) equals current (I) times resistance (R). $V = IR$. As voltage goes up, electric current goes up. As resistance goes up, electric current goes down. Simple enough to be the very first lesson in the most elementary electricity curriculum, but also a physical law that defines the behavior of everything in the universe. The microphone Robert sings into, the headphones on his ears, the tape machine, even his own brain—all are governed by this fundamental rule.

Because Jim McIntyre had studied physics in college, Robert leaned on him (and his library) to learn more about electricity and math more broadly. He worked out parts of trigonometry and calculus and classical number theory on his own, slowly but surely. What would have been a freshman semester in a not especially rigorous college math program took Robert about five years. He continued to teach himself by devising questions and trying to solve them, carrying a notebook with him wherever he went. He earned a bachelor's degree in mathematics from the University of Kentucky in 2012 and later that year enrolled in a graduate program at Emory University, where he earned his PhD in the same subject.

In lots of music but especially the Western varieties, there are two primary schools of thought when it comes to tuning: equal temperament and just intonation. Reductively, equal temperament splits an octave into twelve sequential steps, spaced apart equally. Modern guitars, basses, and pianos are all constructed for this sort of tuning (and cannot employ just intonation unless built specifically for that purpose). On any instrument of this sort, the difference in frequency between, say, C and C-sharp is the same as the distance between F and F-sharp.

Just intonation is a mathematically derived tuning method used primarily in classical music. Rather than splitting up the scale evenly, each interval corresponds to a specific ratio. With just intonation, most notes and chords in a given key or harmonic series will resonate well together, but certain combinations can produce dissonance (or "wolf tones") noticeable to even an untrained ear, and performers using this tuning must actively adjust their pitches to the proper ratios. A trumpeter, for example, can make fine, nuanced changes to the tuning of each note in real time, manipulating those pitches as they pertain to the key to avoid dissonance.

Equal temperament, however, allows for all notes and chords to work passably if imperfectly well together. The sound waves never quite lock in on a single key or harmonic series, but aside from the fact that many instruments are not even capable of just intonation, equal temperament makes things easier for the musicians using it. Performers don't have to adapt their notes as they play, and composers have more flexibility and freedom to change keys and introduce new chords. They just can't quite hit the same level of purity with any of them. In Western music at least, non-classical pieces are typically played with equal temperament, whose imperfections create additional sounds on top of the chords, artifacts that are generally permissible to the ear.

After moving to Lexington, Jim was developing a sensitivity to music he had not experienced before. He began noticing these artifacts in everything he listened to, "beat frequencies" resulting from the imperfect performances endemic to equal temperament tuning. These unintentional overtones became difficult for him to bear, and he began listening almost exclusively to classical music tuned in just intonation, where no such dissonance could be heard.

After a conversation with Jim about this, Robert was struck with inspiration. Tuning in equal temperament created chords that resonated with unpleasant, ugly overtones, but those overtones were predictable. He left Jim's house and sat in his car with his notebook before driving home, working out some math while the idea was fresh. He devised a new musical scale, a "non-Pythagorean" one whose chords would produce beat frequencies that were themselves notes in the same scale. He had no idea how it would sound.

The math sat in his notebook for a year before Robert used a pitch generator to create the tones of the scale. His brother-in-law, Craig Morris, offered to program these tones into a keyboard for him. Whereas performers using just intonation typically play adaptively, making changes to their notes as they play, this instrument is fixed in its intonation. But while other fixed intonation instruments might be forced into equal temperament due to their inability to produce the ratios needed for just intonation, Robert's keyboard is configured specifically for the proper ratios of the scale he designed. An instrument with fixed notes is usually incapable of just intonation, because those notes cannot be manipulated while the performer is playing them. What makes Robert's instrument unique is that the range of notes it is programmed to play is configured specifically to be in this non-Pythagorean scale, producing the chords that, much like in just intonation, do not produce dissonant artifacts.

ROBERT SCHNEIDER: I remember the first time I approached the keyboard to play it. I was so shy. What's it going to sound like? The keyboard is so familiar. When I approached it and played this scale on the keyboard, it was so weird and different from any sequence of tones I had heard before. It made my brain feel like it was stretching inside of my head. I've been playing piano to some degree as long as I can remember, going back to being a toddler. You're so familiar with that setup, with the sequence of tones that comes out when you're pressing those. Even if you don't know how to play piano, you're still familiar with that sequence of tones. It was so startling.

The music he created did not sound especially good, but it was pleasing to him mathematically. He included a few short compositions on the Apples record *New Magnetic Wonder* along with instructions and audio files for others to create their own.

ROBERT SCHNEIDER: It made my brain feel very cool. It was good for my ears. There's this promise in the scale of creating chords where the beat frequencies are also notes in the scale, and those beat frequencies are interacting, and they're making beat frequencies on a second level that will also be in the scale. All of the notes you play together and all of the overtones from the notes and all of the higher overtones will all be part of the scale. It would be this ultimate, mathematically pure, alien music. That's something I hope to work on in the future.

WILL WESTBROOK WAS BORN IN DERIDDER, LOUISIANA. He went to Louisiana Tech to study photography and then followed some of the friends he made there to Athens in the early nineties, collaborating with them on various art projects, most notably as a multi-instrumentalist in the Gerbils. He sometimes made money by buying up old Levi's and selling them through the mail to people in Japan.

Bill met him in a photography class at Louisiana Tech.

BILL DOSS: He was so dorky, and all of the cool art students kind of looked down on him a little bit, thinking, "Oh, this guy is so square." He always had his hair parted like a ten-year-old from the fifties. So I was a little afraid to get to know him. Once I got to know him, he was a super nice guy and incredibly arty. He had all this stuff going on in his head. Just as much of an artist as anyone I've ever known. Will loved to find old things. He saw the beauty in the history of things. He could look at the oil can from a 1957 Plymouth, and he'd be like, "Look at that! It's beautiful." We'd be hanging out somewhere, and we'd lose him, and he'd be over here with a magnifying glass looking at a thing of pine straw. He'd show you something you had never seen before.

They spent many nights in the darkroom together. For one assignment, they collaborated on "The Little Show": Will had devised a way to make very tiny prints, smaller than even a contact print, less than one square inch. Because the photos were so small, they bought a single sheet of the most expensive mounting paper they could find, and they made frames out of toothpicks they'd painted black. At the show, they mounted the photos about two feet off the ground, requiring a hands-and-knees approach to view them. They served tiny pieces of cheese and wine out of Dixie cups.

SCOTT SPILLANE: He was a genius. He's the best guitar player I've ever heard. He was hard to pin down. He was late all the time. He had some issues from his past that he couldn't get over. He was quite self-destructive, accidentally. Most of the time, he seemed fine. I was around him a lot, but he was one of those people, you never know what he's doing when. You didn't know where he was going when he left, and you didn't know when he was coming back. He was involved in more stuff than anybody could imagine. He also was a brilliant photographer. Musically, he played a little too much saxophone, but he was the only person that played saxophone that I liked. Clay Bears wouldn't have been Clay Bears without him. He was brilliant. He left a big hole.

BILL DOSS: You never got bored hanging out with him. There was always something to do. He was always trying to make a piece of art. He wasn't like a proficient musician. But he had a love of music where he'd like, pick up a saxophone and play it, even if he couldn't play the saxophone. He had such a passion for art and music and life in general. He would always make something.

SCOTT SPILLANE: He was pretty flighty, and you couldn't pin him down. Here's a good way to describe him: He slept about once every month and a half, and he'd sleep for two or three days, maybe longer. I'm sure some people saw him sleeping all the time.

ROSS BEACH: I remember Will Westbrook had a garage sale every week for an entire summer. I don't think he even brought stuff in from the porch. He had old furniture and old photography equipment. A lot of records. Homemade art. Framed photos. He replenished the stock just by finding stuff in his house. I bought a beat-up mandolin from him, which I still have.

Will Westbrook died on December 11, 2006.

SCOTT SPILLANE: For years, everybody that I know that knew him has a feeling of guilt of "Why didn't I see this coming? Why didn't I help? Why didn't I do this? Why didn't I do that?" But at the same time, there's nothing really that we could do. It happened so fast, and it was boom, whisked away. The funeral was in Louisiana three days later, so there's not even any closure when it comes to that. He's gone, and there's no getting him back. It's not like he moved away to Antarctica or something and one day maybe he'll get cold and come back. It's hard to even think about another Gerbils album. We'll change the name if we do, just because of that, if I can even get John to play.

When Will died, Scott and John quickly decided to retire the name of their band.

JOHN D'AZZO: It was the shittiest thing ever. I thought that was it for the Gerbils. I don't even know if we ever talked about it.

SCOTT SPILLANE: We played one show at Ciné. That was about it. How can you play after that? I could play the songs, but I couldn't call it Gerbils. I could say they're Gerbils songs and play them with a different band, which I'll have to do if I want to play music, but he's irreplaceable, especially live. Recordings capture a bit, but recording with him, we'd record his practice sessions. We'd play like ten or twelve times and record him playing along with it, and then he'd say "Okay, I think I got it," and we'd say, "Yeah, we already got it. We recorded what you've already done." His brilliance was how he corrected his own mistakes. You got to see that live. He was the master of making a mistake and then three or four notes later, that mistake is no longer a mistake. It's brilliant. If you have a bad note, what comes after that can make that the perfect note.

JAMEY HUGGINS: Everyone came together, and it was the first time that all of us realized that we're all kind of fucked up, and we're all kind of crazy, and that's why we do what we do. When he died, it had the exact same feeling as one of those original potlucks, but tainted with this morose kind of thing. In a positive way, it turned into the first—strangely organized, under terrible circumstances—gathering of something resembling a family reunion, where all of the key players were there. Just one night. People were flying in and driving in. For a brief moment in time, it felt—and I know a lot of people feel the same way—for one night like it was 1997 again. I think he would have loved that.

BILL DOSS: We had a party. It's kind of bizarre. It was the sort of thing where if you had anything of his, bring it. We put it all up and everyone got to see stuff.

WILL CULLEN HART: All kinds of people.

SCOTT SPILLANE: He was the person you wanted to impress more than anyone else. You wanted to have him involved in everything, because he was so brilliant.

"Between bits of awkward banter, the calibrating of an honest-to-God analog reel-to-reel tape recorder, and the donning of wrist bells, the most celebrated psych-pop band of the 1990s, the Olivia Tremor Control, lovably stumbled through a historic reunion gig in New York City last August," reads a 2006 *SPIN* review. "It was their fifth show in five years, and the crowd clung to every banjo pluck and detuned horn blast in the band's acid-washed oeuvre. Even Jeff Mangum, the reclusive frontman of Neutral Milk Hotel, ventured onstage, unabashedly wiping away tears. As of now, OTC don't have plans to record a new album, but perhaps the warm reception has piqued their interest. 'This is fun shit,' said cofrontman Will Cullen Hart backstage while his bandmates packed up their typewriters, singing saws, and plastic sheep. 'I think we might do this again.'"

Tensions were high when the Olivia Tremor Control took its break, but after a few years apart focusing on separate projects and just getting some time to decompress, old grudges faded, happy memories shone through their oxidized crust, and everyone began hanging out again. They reunited for a short reunion tour in 2006. It started to feel like the old days, but it was a new development that served as the real catalyst.

BILL DOSS: I remember being on the Apples tour, playing at the Sundance Film Festival, and I got the phone call saying that Will had gone to the hospital with MS.

For the duration of their hiatus, the band continued to receive offers to play various shows and festivals—like Neutral Milk Hotel, they had never formally broken up—but they were steadfast in their refusal. John would get a call and bring it to the rest of the band, and they'd agree they didn't want to do it. Offer after offer received only rejection.

In 2005, actor Vincent Gallo was curating All Tomorrow's Parties in London. Like so many before him, he extended an invitation to the Olivia Tremor Control, but Gallo's offer came at the right time. Will's diagnosis had put any disagreements in perspective, and the band started practicing together again without any shows lined up, just as an excuse to spend time with one another. By the time they received the ATP offer, they were ready.

Will and Bill didn't even need a reconciliatory conversation. They put together a tour to go along with the gig at ATP, and it proved to be their most successful as a band. They played many of the same venues they had played before, but the turnouts were better, and they sometimes played the same club on multiple nights. If you're ahead of your time, perhaps you need only to wait for your time to catch up.

JOHN FERNANDES: It seems like we took a break for a while and the legend just kind of spread or something.

JIM ROMEO: They sold out the Bowery two nights in a row, which is really good. They didn't used to do that. That was much different. They were a much tighter band and more musically together than they were back in the late nineties.

JOHN FERNANDES: There were two at the Bowery Ballroom, which were really fun. Jeff played with us at those shows. I remember Jeff freaking out at the Bowery Ballroom show, and towards the end of the set, he was grabbing people while they were playing and just shaking them around. I remember everyone ending up on the floor at some point.

WILL CULLEN HART: He actually kind of hugs you and throws you down.

JOHN FERNANDES: It looks like tumbling, but he knows what he's doing. Before you know it, there's equipment laying all over you, but I think he's careful about not hurting anybody.

WILL CULLEN HART: We didn't ever talk about it, but it's clear.

JOHN FERNANDES: I think he just gets caught up in it, especially when he hasn't been onstage in a while. He was singing some vocals, maybe playing some percussion.

WILL CULLEN HART: Bill's voice sounded great, not that it wasn't before.

BILL DOSS: When I feel the most confident in myself is when I'm in a room with those guys playing that music.

JOHN FERNANDES: When we came back together to play, everybody had improved their playing abilities. I had started playing with a lot of other bands locally, and I was practicing a lot more violin and clarinet. I was playing with Elf Power, Dark Meat, Mouser, New Sound of Numbers, the Instruments, Everybody Everybody, and Pipes You See, Pipes You Don't, and I'd sit in with lots of other bands. I started developing more techniques that I was happier with in my violin playing. I even feel like I became a stronger bass player by the time we were playing the reunion shows.

BILL DOSS: There was a period of time, early 2000s, where I felt a little disenchanted. Olivia broke up, and there were a lot of things going on. My dad passed away at some point. There was a lot of dark stuff where I felt like, *Fuck all this*. But then around the time of the reunion shows, I started coming back around to it. I was hanging out with Will again. The Elephant 6 became for me again this bright, beautiful thing that it once was. All of a sudden it felt like it was fifteen years earlier.

WILL CULLEN HART: Those years, I felt like we had forgotten.

Will's recently diagnosed MS had likely been around for a while, but with no health insurance, the pain eventually became unbearable. He medicated with scotch, sometimes a bottle or two a day. Bill told him he needed to get his drinking under control and offered to get the Olivia Tremor Control back together and record every Sunday. He was ready to play again, and Will's condition put some of the pettier issues between them in perspective, but most important, Bill didn't want his best friend to die. After reuniting to play together, the Olivia Tremor Control began working on a new record.

WILL CULLEN HART: We agreed, "Wouldn't that be fun?" It feels like it's 1996.

JOHN FERNANDES: It was slow for a while, and then it started happening more and more regularly.

BILL DOSS: We didn't really try to put the band back together so much as hang out. Before I knew it, I was over at Will's house four-tracking. I know I had been kind of wishing something would happen, but I wasn't sure how to approach it. I think other people were thinking the same thing. It just kind of fell back into place for me.

They also added Derek to the band, and his versatility allowed everyone else to do a little more.

JOHN FERNANDES: Bill was like, "How about having Derek play some stuff sometimes?" That would free me up a lot more, because a lot of times with the live show I was playing a lot of the bass stuff, so that way Derek and Eric could switch off playing drums, other people could do bass sometimes when I want to play violin and clarinet. It makes it more free for a lot more switching around. Derek plays everything. He can play guitar, organ, piano. Eric's great, too. He plays ukulele, theremin, guitars, bass. Eric can play everything, too. Plus they rhyme.

The Music Tapes released *1st Imaginary Symphony Nomad* on Merge in 1999. The band's next release came in 2002, *The 2nd Imaginary Symphony for Cloudmaking,* without label support. Julian released the album by burning it onto CD-Rs and delivering them to record stores himself. It has not yet seen an official physical release, though it was included in full on his podcast, *The Orbiting Human Circus (of the Air),* in 2017.

JULIAN KOSTER: I owed Merge a record of songs that I was also making at the time, but I spent a lot of time on this one. I hadn't told them about it because of this guilt. I also didn't know if they would want to put it out, because people didn't make records like that. But I just had to make it, I was compelled, and I loved making it.

Julian provided most of the instrumentation for the sixty-five-minute opus, but his voice is nowhere to be heard. Instead, Brian Dewan—a multimedia artist Julian had known from New York—narrates the spoken-word story of Nigh, a young boy who lives with his grandmother and discovers how clouds are made (in a nearby factory) and why (you'll have to listen yourself for that one).

At the same time he was writing and recording *2nd Imaginary Symphony*, Julian was working on a more traditional record (by his standards, at least, which is just to say it featured individual songs with recognizable structures and vocal melodies). For most of the 2000s, the Music Tapes was a relatively dormant project. Julian toured with other bands and played singing saw and other instruments on albums by Of Montreal, Circulatory System, the Instruments, They Might Be Giants, and Kevin Ayers. In his downtime, he continued to tinker with the next Music Tapes album, recruiting friends to contribute. The credits include many familiar names: Jeremy Barnes, Kevin Barnes, Laura Carter, Robbie Cucchiaro, Pete Erchick, John Fernandes, Nesey Gallons, Eric Harris, Will Cullen Hart, Heather McIntosh, Griffin Rodriguez, Scott Spillane, and others. The Music Tapes finally released *Music Tapes for Clouds and Tornadoes* in 2008.

NESEY GALLONS: Julian, when he's in the act of creating, it just flows completely purely without any thought whatsoever. But he also has this very intense hypercritical capacity, and a lot of his insecurities or doubts or whatever can be really detrimental to the things he's working on in all forms of creative existence. He'd make up something beautiful and record something beautiful and have a lot of stuff that's just perfect, but then listening to it, he'd have to keep equalizing every single thing. He'd have to really process the shit out of it. That insecure part of him would keep making him feel like it wasn't done. By 2002, it was pretty much done.

The Music Tapes hadn't played a show in nearly a decade, either. Aside from playing a little more often with friends' bands, Julian had been almost as reclusive as Jeff. After some hemming and a bit of hawing, Julian signed on to have the Music Tapes play Popfest, an Athens music festival that has featured many if not most Elephant 6 bands over the years. He assembled a band and headlined the festival at a show at the 40 Watt.

Julian was also back in the mix with the Olivias, and playing with them again gave him the itch to get back on the road.

ROBERT SCHNEIDER: He's a really beautiful person. Really pure in his idealism. One of his great talents is being able to organize people and get them together around projects, like the band Neutral Milk Hotel or like building all of those amazing devices that he has built.

JOHN FERNANDES: Julian had this idea about making it this variety show sort of thing. I think they used to do that a long time ago in the twenties. Someone plays a couple songs, sometimes it's the same backing band, but then the lead guys rotate. Or Dylan would go on tour with Joan Baez and Allen Ginsberg.

NESEY GALLONS: The fact that Neutral Milk Hotel got huge and Music Tapes would open for them and nobody gave a shit about his weird, complicated, ingenious stuff really broke his heart. He was just so heartbroken and disillusioned by the fact that he was doing really amazing things that were unappreciated. Basically, where the idea for the Holiday Surprise tour originated was kind of influenced by the fact that ultimately he was too afraid to actually just play rock clubs doing a whole Music Tapes set. It was still kind of insecurity.

ROBBIE CUCCHIARO: Julian is a really inspiring force in the whole Elephant 6 history. He had a dream that we were all playing together, and he was trying to figure out a way for the Music Tapes to go on a club tour. We have different ideas about how we like to perform and in what context. Clubs don't always work out for us. Julian is famous for his impossible ideas. But it happens.

Julian had actually had the idea for the Holiday Surprise tour—a commingled effort of different pieces of different bands alternating songs over the course of the night, the same dozen or so people jumping between Olivia songs, Music Tapes songs, Elf Power songs, and so on—years earlier, but it proved much harder to book than anything they had tried before. He couldn't find a stretch of time that would work for everybody, so instead of waiting around, he just picked a window and went for it, in the hope that it would come together as it drew closer. With few names committed, Julian had it billed initially as a Music Tapes/Circulatory System tour. The lineup didn't have the name recognition to book huge venues, so it materialized across a bunch of smallish rock clubs, none of which could hold more than a few hundred people.

Once the ambition ossified into a real itinerary, interested parties made arrangements to participate, moving around other obligations if they had to or just not making new ones. The performers built their calendars around the tour after it was announced, the same way those who bought tickets did. The lineup swelled to more than twenty people. Because Julian had to book and promote everything before most of those people were on board, though, they ended up playing smaller venues than they otherwise could have with the eventual roster.

JIM ROMEO: When I first put it out there, some people were excited about it, some people were whatever. We kept it kind of small, because there were a lot of people and there was a lot of changing of who's available when. We had to do it kind of quickly, and I was very happy with it. There was this group of people who were really into it. It's a bunch of bands who individually don't draw all that well, but together, it's an exciting package.

As more and more names got on board, excitement grew, which led to quickly sold-out venues and otherwise impossibly intimate performances therein. With some foresight and a little more coordination beforehand, they could have played bigger venues and made more money, but to hear participants talk about it after the fact, you'd never pick up on any bitterness. Only joy. If there was apprehension about the tour beforehand, it was that it had been so long since this was the norm, and so now things would be *different*. More distant. But the cozy scale provided a much more familiar setting, and fears about a hollow retread of the old days proved unfounded.

SCOTT SPILLANE: Julian had this brainchild to basically jump-start everybody back into playing music together again. We had taken a hiatus that was so long and people were kind of fading. He's the consummate optimist when it comes to music. If you want to take your time and consider it an investment and try to get money back from your investment of time, he has gotten not very much for his investment. But after fifteen, twenty years, he's still the optimist. "If we do this, it can't do anything but make our music better as it goes."

JOHN FERNANDES: A lot of times we were still crashing at people's houses. There'd be revelry into the night much of the time.

SCOTT SPILLANE: That's the way I'm used to playing music. I personally cannot imagine going, playing for forty-five minutes, and then leaving. The Elephant 6 thing, I played three shows a night, every night, for however many years. If I don't get to play for three and a half hours, why the fuck would I want to set up? If it's going to be three bands, I'll play three hours that way, or if it's going to be one big band, I'll play three hours that way. We would have to stop and change things up a bit for Music Tapes, but everybody in the first band was in the second band, so we knew exactly what to move, where to move it, where to put the sonic vibration landing unit or whatever the hell. The clapping hands. It was three hours' worth of music with eighteen freaks. Of course there's no money in it, but hey, that's just what happens.

JOHN FERNANDES: We weren't even sure when we started what it exactly was going to be. We started practicing early on, and I was trying real hard to make it to every practice, but not everyone was. It was kind of an amorphous thing. But when we started putting the actual set together, I realized, *Oh my god, I'm going to be up here for an hour and a half, two hours straight,* because I'm playing on everybody's songs, on bass or clarinet or violin. On almost everything.

ROBBIE CUCCHIARO: In some ways it was similar, because we often would do tours with, like, Elf Power, Neutral Milk, Olivia, Music Tapes. Do all kinds of conglomerations. It would be like three bands going out on the road together. So that was familiar. In some ways, it was even more of an orchestra-type setting. With those early days, you'd play three sets.

WILL CULLEN HART: Julian dragged me up here and said, "I thought you were going to die," because of drinking and all this stuff, and he wanted to help me. What do I say? I was into it. I was in a bad place.

NESEY GALLONS: Will really was having a hard time. He was still in a really difficult place. A lot of people had their doubts about if he could do it. A lot of people were really excited about it in theory, but they were afraid that it would be a trainwreck. And what a shame to do that to the memory of everything else that was lovely. As soon as we played the very first show, everybody who had their doubts were kind of like, *Wait, that was so much fun. This will work.*

One name conspicuously absent from the (admittedly scant) tour promotion was Jeff's. He was nowhere to be seen at the tour's first stop in Chapel Hill, but two nights later, on October 11, 2008, at the Knitting Factory in New York, Jeff joined his pals onstage a few times throughout the set, pounding on an extra drum kit, adding another voice to a harmony, or belting out his verse on the Olivia Tremor Control's "I Have Been Floated." All told, he was onstage for just a few minutes of an hours-long set.

JIM ROMEO: The New York show was sold out in advance. Once he started to do that, the sales [for later shows] shot up, but they didn't start from zero. There was talk. He would be like, "Maybe I'll go along and jump on for a song."

It wasn't the first time since his Neutral Milk Hotel abstention that Jeff had played a bit part in someone else's show, and since he was (reportedly) living in New York at the time, it seemed like he had just dropped in for the heck of it. He did not appear at any of the tour's stops over the following week. Seven shows in all, and he'd been seen at only the New York date. A couple of those—in Hamden, Connecticut, and Purchase, New York—were within an hour or two of New York City, and he hadn't been spotted at either.

Waiting for the doors to open in Pittsburgh,* where I caught the tour myself, I watched as each sedan and hatchback rolled up in front of the club to unload a few musicians and their gear. As each of them lugged an amp or bass drum or a seven-foot-tall metronome past me, the anticipation grew. Because no official lineup had been announced and each of the few shows before this one had featured a slightly different group of performers as folks joined and dropped off the tour, I began building a list in my head of who was here. There's Julian Koster, there's Laura Carter, there's Scott Spillane, there's Bill Doss.

* Also extremely late. By the time the doors were supposed to open, the band was only just starting to sound check.

And then there was Jeff Mangum, in the flesh. The first thing that struck me about him was his size. He's tall, a bit on the lanky side, but a healthy six foot three or so. He was the tallest member of the Elephant 6 crew that night, standing at least a head and sometimes shoulders above most of his comrades. He had the ever-so-slightly curvilinear posture of someone wont to talking to people shorter than he is, a human sunflower. It was striking to see him at all, because the only versions I had seen of him before this were blurry photos and videos with very few reference points. It felt a little like running into Bigfoot at the grocery store. Out on the sidewalk, amid cars and telephone poles and trash cans, a once-flat figure gained sharper edges and a third dimension.

All that told me was that he was here, though, and for most of the set, he was just milling about on the side of the stage. He joined in on a few songs in a supporting role, but nothing more than the ancillary parts he had added in New York. Whether he was onstage or not, every song killed. His very presence electrified the other performers as much as it did the crowd. The murmured reviews of the Knitting Factory show all had the exhausted giddiness of a cathartic experience, and my expectations for that night were set high. The first four hours of the show met every one of them.

At the tail end of the marathon set, Jeff did something he didn't do at the Knitting Factory. Something he had not done just about anywhere, in fact, in nearly a decade. For the encore, the entire group of musicians gathered onstage for a gang-vocal rendition of Circulatory System's "Forever," about two dozen voices strong, Jeff's included. By the time the song had ended, it was 1:15 a.m., and much of the crowd had left already. That's when Jeff, the plaid-clad sunflower, descended from the stage with his guitar for an encore to the encore, Julian Koster and his saw in tow. What remained of the crowd drew tight around the pair and fell completely silent. Fifty people in the crowd now, maybe forty. Maybe thirty. No soft chatter, no beer glasses clinking or sneaker soles squeaking, no rustling of flannel or corduroy. Total, complete stillness, as though time had stopped or we existed somehow external from time itself. For the few hushed minutes Jeff was playing "Engine," we were all ageless.

It was the first time Jeff had performed a song of his own in public since the Auckland show in 2001 and the first time in America since New Year's Eve in 1998, at the 40 Watt in Athens. He'd play the song another five times as the Holiday Surprise tour stretched across the Midwest: in Columbus, Pontiac, Chicago, Bloomington, and Lexington. The performance I saw was the first in a while, but it wasn't the first ever, and it wasn't the last. It was nothing approaching an Only. For about three and a half minutes, though, it felt like no other song existed anywhere, that the entire universe was contained inside Jeff's strumming and squalling. There's something about his music that fosters a feeling of prideful, alone-but-not-lonely isolation, even in a crowd.

After the Pittsburgh show ended, a few of the performers broke down the stage while a few others worked the room, graciously accepting relentless praise from concertgoers who stuck around for no reason other than to offer it. With a mix of embarrassment and confusion, a few of the musicians even signed autographs.

The Holiday Surprise performances were brief—just a taste, really—but they led to widespread speculation that Jeff's return was imminent. He'd dipped his toes in the water, so surely he was ready now to take the plunge. He would have a quick tour, and then he'd release an album, and soon enough he'd be exactly where everyone had thought he would have been ten years earlier. The success of the Olivia reunions and the Holiday Surprise tour proved there was an enthusiastic audience for this stuff, and given how those went, the rewards justified the risk. Perhaps Neutral Milk Hotel had been ahead of its time, but now its time was waiting out front, impatiently, tapping its foot, waiting for the doors to open. Any day now.

And then a month passed. No news.

And then three months passed with no news, and then eight, and quickly, a year went by.

It became obvious to all but the most naive and hopeful that the performance was merely a tease. Jeff would continue to be what he had been for so long: a curio, a conversation piece, a recluse. He would not be playing shows again.

CHAPTER 28

EVERY TIME I WENT TO BILL'S HOUSE—WHETHER WE SAT IN his living room with funk music playing softly in the background, in his upstairs studio listening to early cuts of in-progress Olivia Tremor Control songs, or on wooden stumps on his front porch as he smoked a cigarette, swatting away some of the bugs and listening to others chirp and hum—he had a bowl of fresh fruit to offer me. Fresh sour cherries or cubes of watermelon. He always offered me a drink, too. The majority of in-person interviews for this book were conducted in cafés, bars, and other neutral locations, but every time I interviewed Bill, he invited me to his home to do so. He was more comfortable there, and he wanted anyone he hosted to feel comfortable, too.

The first time we met was actually in Washington, DC, a few months prior. Though I was living in Athens, I was in DC for the weekend, to see an Apples in Stereo show at the Rock and Roll Hotel. The afternoon of the show, though, I was hit by a car while crossing the street. I made out pretty good, all things considered, with only an avulsion fracture in my right ankle and some superficial scrapes and scratches. Despite the walking boot on my foot, I schlepped to the show, but I didn't last long enough to see the Apples: the events of the day took more of a toll than I'd realized, and I fainted at some point before their set, which told me maybe I shouldn't stick around. So my memories of that day are a bit hazy, but I do vividly remember coming to (and have corroborated with others, just in case). I woke up on a couch on the venue's second floor, with Bill bringing me a cup of orange juice from the bar. It was the only time I ever took him up on a drink offer.

As the most publicly gregarious member of the Olivia Tremor Control, Bill likely logged more time with reporters than any of his bandmates, but he never treated our conversations as quotidian. I'm sure I asked him many questions he's been asked before, but he never responded with a platitude, and he never sounded like he was repeating himself. Bill reacted to every question as if it were the first time he had heard it, and he considered it deeply before answering, always with a smile on his face when he did.

Our conversations were always fruitful as a result. With his bright red sideburns and brighter grin, Bill's warmth was always at the fore. The only time he seemed uncomfortable is when I asked him about himself. He could and would talk about anything, and if you brought up any of his friends, he'd go on for days about how great they were, as musicians and as people. Ask him to talk about ol' Billy Don Doss, though, and he'd get all shy.

The last time I interviewed Bill was August 19, 2010. I was living at the Landfill, and when I mentioned to Will that I was heading over to Bill's, he gathered up an armful of art supplies—loose paper, colored pencils, magic markers—and invited himself along, following barefoot to my car. At Bill's house, I spoke with the two of them together, sitting next to each other on the couch. I'd ask a question, and they'd look at each other with knowing smirks before answering, talking more to each other than to me. Bill took the lead, though, and Will was as rapt by his answers as my recorder was, despite having himself lived through the very things I was asking about. When we got through all of my questions, I asked them if there was anything else they wanted to discuss. Bill invited me upstairs to his studio to play me the latest versions of some Olivia Tremor Control tracks they had been working on. They were recording and mixing it digitally this time, and even for an unfinished track—Bill told me it still needed a bunch of overdubs, at least—it had a polish to it that wasn't anywhere on *Black Foliage* or *Dusk*. Part of that was the production, part of that was years of practice from all the band members, and part of it was just getting older.

The songwriting dynamic between Will and Bill is most noticeable when you compare their post-Olivia projects: Bill's pop superego the Sunshine Fix and Will's psychedelic id Circulatory System.

RYAN LEWIS: We used to joke around in the Sunshine Fix that we were Bill's Wings, because we were the straight-ahead pop band that was playing much more like Wings to Circulatory System's Plastic Ono Band.

But those sensibilities were there long before the Olivia Tremor Control split up, and the Olivias' output is a synthesis of these tastes. Their varied skill sets and aesthetics complement one another well, and because the members are all hungry and intent listeners, the pieces fit together a little differently each time. But they always fit, and when the band began practicing again together weekly after the reunion, the pieces locked together as neatly as they ever had. As before, they often recorded bits and pieces independently and then brought them to the group for others to add to. Sometimes digitally, sometimes still on tape.

BILL DOSS: It's cool because Will's got songs and I've got songs that we've put together, like in the early days, but with others we got together just jamming in a room. I had these chords and a melody, but I didn't have any words.

WILL CULLEN HART: Then I was like, here, I got some words.

BILL DOSS: They fit perfectly within the melody.

DEREK ALMSTEAD: They had gotten together and experimented with the idea not too long after they did those reunion shows. Bill put it to me to get involved. It's a difficult thing because it's not a ball that's already rolling. They don't want to just haphazardly jump into it again. We're trying to make it a real thing that's prepared and ready and cool. Rather than just, here's $10,000 to play this festival, here's the old songs. I don't think anybody wants to do that. Nobody wants to be a revisionist band. It's lame. What, the best years are behind you? That's not really true.

The band wanted to keep moving forward, but only because it felt like the old days again. They toured, and then they got back to recording regularly at Bill's house, slowly but surely building up material for a new Olivia Tremor Control album. It would be another double album, of course. Their musicianship was tighter now and they were not so averse to digital recording methods—or so obsessively duty bound to analog methods—so the new work sounded slicker, but the same expansive, investigative instincts were there, because the same collective sense of trying to impress one another was there, too. No one was ready to put a hard deadline on the project, but members spoke publicly about their expectation that a new record was imminent, maybe a year away. In the meantime, they released a new track, "The Game You Play is in Your Head, Parts 1, 2 & 3," which is technically just one song, but only because they said so.

They toured again in 2011. The Music Tapes opened, so Julian and Robbie were onstage for much of the Olivias' set, too. With one exception, the performances featured songs from only *Dusk* and *Black Foliage*. The outlier that made it more than just a nostalgia trip was the inclusion of the new song. It was recorded and released a few months prior (albeit written years before that). In her review for the *Village Voice*, Maura Johnston writes:

> The warm reception for "Game," though, made me wonder if perhaps in its most useful form nostalgia can actually be a manifestation of optimism, a wish to return to a time rife with the possibility of even the most sublime moments being improved with the right song. . . . The key, I daresay, isn't to simply look backward and sigh while wishing that events that have already passed could somehow Xerox themselves onto next week's calendar, but to take those more naïve ideals from the past and apply them to the coming days—even if the end result isn't completely mapped from the outset.

Will doesn't go out much these days. If you don't count shuffling to the gas station at the end of the block to buy beer and chips, he sometimes goes weeks without leaving the house. Some days, he'll have the energy to do something creative, to paint or make music, but most of his waking hours are spent in his living room (re)watching sitcoms, sketch shows, and documentaries about bands and world affairs. He self-medicates less now that he has access to healthcare, but at home, he still drinks and smokes throughout the day.

Despite his hermitage, Will was still making music, pouring his creative energy into Circulatory System. After some down years when his health and self-medicating were at their worst, he felt motivated again to play, which gave him more energy and inspired him to play even more.

JOHN FERNANDES: We were playing tons of new songs, and they got really tight on tour. We were like, "As soon as we get home, we're going to record these and finish the record." It seemed like that was a possibility. We recorded some stuff and then recorded multiple versions of stuff, and stuff started piling up. It ended up taking a lot longer. It kept seeming like it was going to be right around the corner. So much stuff is recorded. We just have to get it together. But sometimes it would elude us a little more for another year or two or three. It always felt like, *We're so close.*

DEREK ALMSTEAD: With Circulatory System, there's no one at the helm. Will needs people to take his spark and mold it, at least as far as it comes to logistics. He's a genius, honestly. He's probably my favorite of all the Elephant 6 songwriters. But he cannot organize things, which is my strongpoint, which is Eric Harris's strongpoint, which is Bill Doss's strongpoint. He's always had people around him, and I think that was one of the reasons he brought me in, to be that person. But I got worn down in that position.

The first Circulatory System record came out in August 2001, and Will started working on the next one not long after. To the extent that *Signal Morning,* the band's second album, included recordings from as far back as the early nineties, he technically started it long before. But it took a while.

As time went on, Will liked to joke that he didn't want to release any more music while Bush was in the White House, but Will's health issues slowed him down considerably, and he had trouble focusing regardless. He continued to experiment aimlessly, but as recordings of those aimless experimentations piled up, it became harder and harder to sift through them all.

If the hardest thing about that sort of process is knowing when to call it finished and walk away, the second-hardest is knowing how far you are from walking away. John Fernandes told *Pitchfork* in March 2003, "The band has been busy recording new material at Cloud that will become the next Circulatory System album proper, with plans for a late 2003 release." Late 2003 came, went, and turned into early 2004. A *Pitchfork* headline on February 6, 2004, read, "New Circulatory System album in early summer."

Nope.

In 2006, Derek told now-defunct Elephant 6 fan blog *Optical Atlas*, "It is incredibly difficult to say 'done' with this stuff; there is just such a standard to it. We have several mixes at this point but there is definitely some back and forth (to put it mildly) to go."

DEREK ALMSTEAD: I think what we had back in 2006 was really cool. Back then, I imagined we were going to do another fill-up-the-CD kind of record. So when I made it forty songs and an hour and thirty minutes long, I figured we'd just cut off a few little pieces. Those guys have a real problem with promising things. I wish I could tell them to stop. You should not promise things that you can't fulfill. I can't believe they haven't learned that by now. For some bands, by imposing a deadline on yourself, you get the work done. But that clearly does not work in that band.

HEATHER MCINTOSH: There was a definite window where I thought it was never going to come out. Up until it came out, honestly. Derek has done runs on it, and I was such family with Will that he wouldn't believe me if I told him it sounded great. It's hard to pull a record away from anybody, but especially something that's come over so much time. You get so inside of it. There's so many versions. Will at one point gave us these box sets of tracks and parts and bits to go through. To figure out how to sieve through it was so overwhelming. It needed to go through three or four phases of people listening and extracting.

When Derek joined Circulatory System in 2002, the entire album was already written, and most of it had been recorded. *Signal Morning* was finally released in September 2009. So what took so long? Given its aural complexity and the nearly two decades between its conception and completion, not to mention Will's avowed fascination with Brian Wilson and his more avant-garde tendencies, it's tempting to think of *Signal Morning* as Will's *Smile*, a multivalent and obsessively constructed inversion of sonic exploration, probing the limits of a home studio. But whereas *Smile* is the result of a deliberate megalomaniac-as-auteur directorial rigidity, *Signal Morning*'s glacially paced production derives from the work Will's accomplices put in. Its beauty comes not just from what Will created but from what other members of the band stripped away and what they left in place. Given the sheer volume of material he generated over the years, it took a lot of time for them to winnow it down.

> ROBERT SCHNEIDER: Will does most of his work up front. He produces little soundscapes, and he writes songs, and he does it spontaneously, and then he does a lot of work on the back end, plastering sound effects, doing segues, conceptually piecing things together into a larger tapestry. His skill is anything from the original inception to the final overview, making it all fit together. Everything else is the work of everybody else. And it has to be. If you've seen Will work, like you've been around when he's trying to record a Circulatory System album, you see how he needs those people to do those things with him, but you also see that if he had someone with him for twenty-four hours a day recording him, there would be an infinite amount of music and art in the world. The fact that there's not someone just following him around all the time is sad. There's literally decades lost of genius, of great songs and great art, just by not recording Will at every moment. That was part of Bill's talent, being able to capture those moments of Will. Being able to be like, "Yes, I'm a solid enough person at this moment to know that I need to be recording you."

On the Olivia Tremor Control reunion tour, during an ambient section of the band's "Green Typewriters" suite, they would play a bunch of droning cassettes and then wander through the crowd for a bit. Rather than preparing new material for the piece, Will donated a bunch of old four-track master tapes he had recorded over a decade or two. Julian ended up in possession of them, and so for preservation purposes, Nesey Gallons digitized them.

> NESEY GALLONS: Listening to those tapes and mixing them down, there were demos where clearly he was just making the song up in recording and doing different mixes of stuff off of his digital machine onto cassette and stuff like that. So there was a weird collection of stuff that was all insanely cool.

In the summer before the first Holiday Surprise tour, in 2008, Nesey was spending a lot of time with Will, hanging out and recording whenever

Will felt up to it. Eventually, Will asked Nesey if he could finish the record for him. Derek had pared it down from the original mass of material, Charlie Johnston had tightened it up further, and now Will wanted Nesey to bring it home. Nesey made minor adjustments to what Charlie had done, which became the first side of the record. For the second side, he listened to all of the available recordings for "fifteen hours a day," aiming to build off what Charlie had started.

NESEY GALLONS: [Will] was very excited about the *Signal Morning* tour and much more in command of his powers. He still had a real problem, but it wasn't the sort of thing where you were terrified he'd be incapable of standing during a show. It was like, *Yeah, he's drunk*, but for the most part, he kept it together.

CHAPTER 29

JULIAN HAS FOND MEMORIES OF CAROLERS VISITING HIS HOME as a kid, hearing the songs in the distance, the voices gradually growing louder as they approached, the flickers of their candles brightening with each step.

> **JULIAN KOSTER:** This was no less fantastical to me than Santa Claus. In fact, it gave more credence to things like Santa Claus. The idea that these people were out there wending their way through our neighborhood, through the night.

He slept well that night, feeling cozy at the thought of the strangers bringing their mirth to all of his neighbors. As he got older, he resolved to do something like that himself. The Music Tapes Holiday Caroling Tour was born. For years now, Julian has brought the Music Tapes into actual living rooms around the country. He makes an open solicitation for hosts and then strings together a tour, setting up in volunteers' homes instead of legitimate venues. Usually two or three homes per city, a new city each night. The shows are modest by default—loading in and out of homes several times a night means you have to keep things simple—but the limitations are only logistical. He plays music but also tells stories and leads participants in games he invented.

> **JULIAN KOSTER:** There were no rules, and no one had any expectations because they honestly didn't know what to expect. We could do things that were exciting and new. We could play with things that

were hypnotic or comforting. We could be with the audience like friends or family. It wasn't about any literal holiday, but about the literal *feeling of* holiday.

Eventually, Julian expanded the premise to "lullaby tours," dropping the Christmas pretense but maintaining the barnstorming celebration, showing up on the porches of mansions and hovels and everything in between. He comes bearing banjos, singing saws, euphoniums, and Static the Television. Sometimes there are 150 people waiting there to hear his band. Sometimes it's only two or three. And the people are different every time.

JULIAN KOSTER: When you walk into a house, you're walking into the unknown. Without that, it would lose some of its magic. You're doing something scary, but it's exciting. It makes you feel like you're floating. If it's bad, you know you're going to do battle with it. You're going to try to turn the bad thing into something good. If you've got performer's blood in you at all, you relish the challenges.

In 2012, with a few caroling tours under his belt, he invited people into *his* living room, or at least some ersatz version of it: the Traveling Imaginary. A tent might seem antithetical to conjuring the idea of "home," but for the itinerant Julian, it makes sense. A road warrior throughout his career, he still regularly sleeps on sofas and floors and in vans while touring, and he's lived up and down the East Coast, from Florida to Maine. So a circus tent, avatar of the peripatetic, is a fine surrogate for any actual living room.

Julian's goal was to raise $5,000 on Kickstarter to commission a circus tent in which he could play Music Tapes shows. He raised more than three times that. A lot of the money went toward commissioning "historic tentmakers in England" to build the Traveling Imaginary's shell: a tent that could be converted to fit anywhere, whether a wide-open forty-foot-by-forty-foot space or a sixteen-foot-by-one-hundred-foot venue dotted with load-bearing columns, all while accommodating a variety of local accessibility and safety laws. Erected inside rock clubs that typically hold 500 or so people, the tent can hold no more than 120, depending on the configuration. Sometimes the capacity is as low as 75. There's less money for everyone (the band, the booker, the venue), and because the loading process is so much more complicated—eight hours to erect it and then four more to break it down and get it into the van—they can't play on consecutive nights unless the cities are close together. It is unwieldy but, like so much of what the Elephant 6 has produced, precious by design.

> JULIAN KOSTER: We're going for a situation where everyone can be at home in a very different way than we're all used to being in the audience. I want to be able to treat the people there like guests in my house. In some ways, I don't want it to be a performance at all. I want to make someone my guest and try to make them comfortable and let them have fun and have fun myself. Part of the reason I'm drawn to new or unusual or different structures is it's more about getting to the core of what's really happening, what's being shared, what's being made available, what we really all are, what the universe really is, and dispensing with all of the trappings, which are more about fashion and marketing and habit. It's something much more pure.

Julian feels at home in rock clubs, but he's never found them to be quite the right setting for a Music Tapes show, which for all its unpredictable shifts and shambolic, aleatoric imprecision is still an arrestingly intimate affair. Instead of finding somewhere else to play, though, he's fitted out music venues to better suit his vision, equal parts 3-D movie and Grandma's photo album.

The Traveling Imaginary is a concept piece, some kind of interactive psychedelic variety show. Somewhere in the middle of the tent, in the middle of the set, the Music Tapes perform. As a whole, the Traveling Imaginary is transformative in the literal sense. Before the tent was even opened at a show in DC, I overheard one of the club's employees say to another, "I feel like I'm not at the same bar anymore." When I arrived, a ticket clerk stamped my hand and gave me a blindfold without an explanation. I'd put it on later, at Julian's direction, mid-set. Inside the club, a red-and-white-striped tent engulfed the room, still closed off, while a bouzouki record and ambient bird chirps and frog croaks dripped from the PA within.

Julian's knitted scarf hung to his feet, and his gaze stayed fixed down there, too, looking up at the crowd only occasionally. To the extent that this show even had a stage, he was rarely at the center of it. His human bandmates kept a low profile, too. More prominent were the less obviously sentient members of the Music Tapes: a person-shaped phonograph, a sailor as tall as the ceiling, a decades-old CRT television, a robotic organ-playing tower capped bulbously like a Russian cathedral.

Julian looked out at the crowd only between songs, when he had an interstitial story to tell, and he began his stories as though he didn't quite know where they'd end. The enchanted crowd had a wide age range—a few spectators arrived with their parents, and it's unclear who brought whom—but ladies, gentlemen, and children of all ages were hanging on every word of Julian's yarns on this chilly January evening. They knew they were inside a tent, inside a rock club. What they didn't know was that from the minute they walked in, they'd been fully inside Julian's skull.

After an hour of games that Julian invented, awarding winners their choice of rusted skeleton keys from an antique suitcase, the crowd gathered on the floor to watch an old cartoon projected onto a hanging white sheet. Only after the cartoon concluded did Julian pull back the sheet to reveal the rest of his bandmates and their accoutrements, like a giant set of church bells and the Seven-Foot-Tall Metronome. In addition to Music Tapes songs, the set included children's stories, magic tricks, more games, and some novelty records spun on a portable turntable, evoking a traveling circus, vaudeville theater, and Southern revival, secluded from the rest of the outside world but immersive in the world it created for itself.

CHAPTER 30

NEARLY TEN YEARS SINCE HIS LAST US PERFORMANCES (IN Athens in 1998), Jeff made his return to the stage playing "Engine" at six of the Holiday Surprise shows in October 2008. He went quiet again for a while after that. About a year and a half later, he reappeared.

Chris Knox had suffered a stroke, and to raise money for his rehabilitation, an A-list lineup of indie rockers released a benefit compilation that featured thirty-six covers of Knox's work. The Mountain Goats, Bonnie "Prince" Billy, Yo La Tengo, Lou Barlow, Portastatic, Bill Callahan, and plenty of other names comprise the other credits (not to mention other New Zealand acts and Chris Knox collaborators like Alec Bathgate, the Verlaines, and the Chills). Bill Doss submitted a version of Tall Dwarfs' "Bodies" with Neil Cleary. Jeff contributed a solo cover, Tall Dwarfs' "Sign the Dotted Line."

As of that summer, the last time Jeff had played multiple songs anywhere live was the show in Auckland with Chris Knox and Laura Carter in 2001. Nine years later, on May 6, 2010, Jeff played a few songs at a benefit for Knox at Le Poisson Rouge (along with the Clean, Yo La Tengo, Sharon Van Etten, John Mulaney, and lots of others). The venue didn't charge for the night, and Kickstarter founder Yancey Strickler let them sell tickets on the platform without a commission. The seventy-five-dollar tickets sold quickly with such a stacked lineup, and all the proceeds went to Knox.

"Mangum played with his eyes mostly closed, neck vein tensed, rocking and swooping to the contours of the songs," Andrew Frisicano writes in a *Brooklyn Vegan* review of the show. "His eyelids fluttered open on the chorus of 'A Baby for Pree' to reveal eyes rolled back into his head. Between songs Mangum gulped down water and was gracious, bordering on triumphant as he popped up at the end of 'Aeroplane.' He encouraged the crowd to contribute to the encore, 'Engine.' After the set, someone caught his attention with a book to sign, which he did. Most people up front looked anxious and ready for a post-show smoke." Jeff played five songs in all.

BEN GOLDBERG: Of course, the anticipation was inevitably built up for Jeff because there was a lot of anticipation and excitement to see him, but it was pretty great to see it melt away as he played. It just became a show of someone performing and connecting with the audience.

DEREK ALMSTEAD: I was blown away that he did that. I listened to a little bit of the footage, and it's like no time has passed. It's exactly the same.

Though the performance came with a strict "no recording" policy, videos popped up on YouTube after the fact, shot surreptitiously over shoulders or between legs. The footage that emerged carried a sort of hidden-camera aesthetic as a result, making up for its lack of fidelity with a heightened sense of mystery and taboo.

BEN GOLDBERG: That was inevitable. I knew that was going to happen from the start. But what's obvious to me from something like that is that there's no way that looking at one of those crappy YouTube videos you can even think that it would re-create the experience of actually being there. We live in a world now where it is very simple for anything, any type of information to be mass-produced or distributed in a large way. For me, that difference between the quality of the YouTube footage and all of that, it seemed to say, "You had to be there," which you really did.

People would have another chance to be there just a few months later. Goldberg organized a show. He had been a publicist at Merge in the nineties, and though he wasn't involved with promoting *Aeroplane*, he got to know Jeff around then, and they remained friends. In late November 2010, they started talking about putting together another concert. Not a benefit, not even something really open to the public. Just a way for Jeff to play again. They booked a show in a Brooklyn loft called the Schoolhouse, formerly an actual schoolhouse. The show wasn't listed anywhere in advance, and every person in attendance was sworn to secrecy ahead of time. They had all been invited, mostly by either Goldberg or Jeff. Neither of them wanted any hype or scrutiny or scalpers. After his short performance at the Chris Knox benefit that summer, Jeff wanted to see how it felt to play a full set of his songs, but he didn't want to deal with the baggage that would come with announcing a return. Not everyone in the audience knew Jeff personally, but Goldberg was careful to invite only people he thought would really feel the significance of the performance.

BEN GOLDBERG: What I was amazed by was how good he sounded, how good his voice sounded. I couldn't see any difference in his voice or performance there than when I saw him fifteen years ago. It felt like time hadn't changed. It just was the same guy doing these songs. That really amazed me. He's taken care of himself so well and he's maintained his voice and he looks the same.

In May 2011, Jeff performed again, but neither solo nor with Neutral Milk Hotel. This was a performance at AUX Fest, an Athens experimental music festival curated and co-created by Heather McIntosh. At Little Kings Shuffle Club, the Soap Scums—Jeff, Laura Carter, Pete Erchick, John Fernandes, and Eric Harris, but all wearing masks to obscure their identities—took the stage. After a drum fill and a few notes on a synthesizer, all five of them collapsed to the ground. The next few minutes were little more than low-volume guitar feedback and sporadic droning notes on the synth while the band remained strewn limp on the stage. They stood up, jammed for a few minutes, and then collapsed to the floor again for another drone. About ten minutes into the set, they peeled back foil that had been covering a big pile of toast—a couple of loaves' worth—eating it together while huddled around a small television. The entire piece lasted about fifteen minutes.

LAURA CARTER: I don't know what you're talking about. That was a famous band from Austria that we hosted.

In the summer of 2011, Jeff began playing shows again. On the first leg, Julian and the Music Tapes opened with music played between magic tricks and stories about a Romanian circus family and Julian's grandfather who didn't cast a shadow, joined onstage by, among other things, the Seven-Foot-Tall Metronome and Mechanized Organ-Playing Tower. Jeff headlined by himself, with Julian joining him onstage for a song or two. He played some traditional rock venues and some churches, mostly in spaces much larger than those he'd headlined with Neutral Milk Hotel in the nineties. Each of them sold out within minutes of tickets going on sale.

ROBERT SCHNEIDER: Through all of the years, he always said he missed it. He would always come to our shows when we were in New York. He would come to all of his friends' shows. He'd play with his friends. He'd come onstage when we'd play. He loved playing. In those moments, he'd always be like, "Oh, I missed this." It's a big thing to step back into it. You're standing by the river. The water's cold. Do you really want to get back in, after you've already gotten out? How can you just step back in? I think what really made it happen was the Holiday Surprise tour. He was able to go on tour with his friends, without having to actually commit to playing. He just went along for the ride, and I think he just ended up playing sometimes. It was so unofficial. It was like dipping his toe back into it, and now it's like you're already on the road. You've already stayed at places in a hotel, and you've already had to deal with the drives. You've been around people again now. It was a rotating thing, so it didn't put the spotlight on anybody. Looking at my age group, the most painful thing is to try to be a star. It's so humiliating and embarrassing and cheesy-looking, to look like you're trying to get attention. It's so deeply ingrained in me from how horrified I was by the older musicians growing up. The Holiday Surprise tour was the opposite of that. It was a rotating lineup. There was no focus. There was no one star.

I attended two solo performances, both in Baltimore at 2640 Space at St. John's United Methodist Church. The first night, the tension in the air between the end of the Music Tapes' set and the beginning of Jeff's was real, as though Jeff might change his mind and bail. Even once he started, he could stop at any time. Nothing was taken for granted. For the majority of the relatively young crowd, tonight was the first chance any of them had had to see Jeff perform, few of them having even finished middle school by the time Neutral Milk Hotel went on its hiatus. That is, many folks in the crowd did not get into the band until long after the band stopped touring, resigned to ruefully spinning *Aeroplane* and *Avery Island* and whatever B sides and bootlegs they could drum up, wondering what it must have been like and praying it might someday happen again. Most of them, until recently, had likely assumed they would never have this opportunity. Tonight was an impossibility that just happened to come true, a collective wish fulfilled not through grassroots organizing or a social media campaign, but thanks to the whim of a man whose whims had tended, for a decade prior, away from public performance.

Expectations in the crowd were high, and for forty minutes between sets, they built to a crescendo that erupted in a roar as Jeff strolled to the middle of the stage and sat among his guitars.

The roar subsided as quickly as it rose, tranquilized by the first bars of "Oh Comely," no one wanting to miss a second of it. The crowd was reverent throughout the set, respectfully if anxiously silent right up until Jeff gave everyone explicit permission to stomp, clap, and sing along. Between songs, after Jeff conceded that he had no "witty bullshit" to say and invited questions from the audience, he seemed genuinely excited to engage with the crowd, if only to maybe humanize himself or shed the misplaced "recluse" label.* He answered disembodied questions from the crowd with candor and a smile:

> "Are you ever going to make another album?"
>
> "I've been writing songs, but I'll only put out an album if my heart tells me to and not for any other reason."
>
> "What's your favorite song?"
>
> "I've always liked 'I Am the Walrus.'"
>
> "Where was your first kiss?"

* Though if the latter was his goal, covering a Roky Erickson song this night and a Daniel Johnston song the next were not the best choices, optically speaking.

"You've got to be kidding!" He laughed. "You think I'm going to tell you that?"

"Are you happy?"

"Yeah," he said, with a brief pause. "I'm happy."

For the encore, Julian joined Jeff onstage and accompanied him with his singing saw on "Engine" and "In the Aeroplane Over the Sea," and the pair left the stage to the same roar that had welcomed Jeff barely an hour earlier.

On Friday, September 30, 2011, Manhattan organizers of the quickly growing Occupy Wall Street sent out an email blast they were sure would generate some attention for their protest against wealth inequality and the disastrous structures of US and global economies that accelerate it. The email announced that Radiohead would be playing a show in Zuccotti Park that night. The band had just played two nights at the Roseland Ballroom in Midtown, and Thom Yorke and crew seemed like they would be sympathetic to the movement.

Within a few hours, the announcement was revealed to be a hoax. Radiohead hadn't made any plans to perform at the park, but provocateurs within the protest thought such an announcement could help draw the media and reach a bigger audience. It even kind of worked. It seems unlikely to be a coincidence, though, that Jeff actually performed at the protests the following week. Playing by himself, he sang a cover of the Minutemen's "Themselves," followed by a half-dozen songs from *In the Aeroplane Over the Sea*, by request. "His Occupy Wall Street set was not a bid for new-Dylan status but a simple gesture of connection," Ann Powers writes for NPR.

The performance streamed online, drawing more viewers the longer he played. Despite no advance notice for the set, the audience swelled to more than six thousand online viewers at its peak.

"In the video, you can hear someone yell, 'Play some Dylan!' and the crowd sang along with the line 'We know who our enemies are' on 'Oh Comely,'" Stephen Deusner reports for *Salon*. "Before he left the stage, Mangum told the crowd: 'You guys have done a beautiful fucking thing.'"

In November 2011, Neutral Milk Hotel released a box set containing nearly the band's entire catalog: *Aeroplane*, *Avery Island*, *Everything Is*, an eight-song EP titled *Ferris Wheel on Fire*, and two seven-inches (along with some posters). It's ostensibly a retrospective, but a close look at the liner notes reveals a credit for Craig Morris, Robert Schneider's brother-in-law. Robert married Craig's sister, Marci, in 2004, which means at least some of the older songs had been rerecorded for this release. Jeff's voice sounds cleaner than it does on the original recordings of the songs, too, and there's no tape hiss.

Chapter 31

Bill Doss died on July 31, 2012.

JOHN FERNANDES: Everything just came to a halt. We had all this momentum going. We were going to finish the record, and then he passed away. Everyone was in shock. We had all these plans, and it all just crumbled. What are we going to do now? I've never been a drinker, but I was drinking a lot. I was feeling pretty low.

DEREK ALMSTEAD: For a lot of us at that moment, we felt like we were living the dream. For all those guys, it was their favorite band they had ever been in. The personality battles that had happened had kind of gone through to the other side. It was this joyous experience, and we were traveling the world and getting paid really well, playing big concerts and working on the new record. Everything was positive. It was a real shock. I was looking out at the next decade and a half like, "This is what we're doing now!" And it's sustainable. Everything about it just seemed like it was really going to work.

WILL CULLEN HART: We're taking over the fucking world. It was a big fucking deal. Everybody dropped just for Olivia. For a month or so after, I just kept working on it. "He went up to the mountains" is what I'd say. Still do. We had basically a double album.

ROBERT SCHNEIDER: He was someone I always tried to impress. Of all of my friends, he was always the most impressed. He was always like, "Oh my god, Robert, I can't believe you did that." It made me feel so good. I always felt competitive with Bill and like I was really trying to please him. I was making music for him. He was my biggest supporter as far as being a fan of me in our social circle. It always made me feel good. It kind of drove me a little bit. With him dying, besides being horribly depressing, it pulled out part of my wanting to record and finish music.

LAURA CARTER: He wanted to bring joy and music and art to the people. That was really his goal.

JOHN FERNANDES: Many times when we were practicing, Bill would take it upon himself to point out like, "Man, you're really rocking that bass!" He'd say it multiple times. He was really complimentary. He was just a sweet guy. He brought me into the band when I was about to have a kid with his ex-girlfriend. None of that mattered. We all lived together. We were brothers.

Bill never got to see the Neutral Milk Hotel full-band reunion, passing about a year before the first date. He saw Jeff's solo shows the year before, and he was a major part of the Holiday Surprise tours, but Bill's death may have provided some motivation for the performances that followed it. The Elephant 6 as a collective was at its most idyllic and idealistic when its world felt tiny, insular, precious. As it got bigger, everything pulled apart from its own momentum. Bill's sudden death made the world feel tiny again, and it made the Elephant 6 world feel even tinier within it, safe enough for everyone to feel like themselves.

For Neutral Milk Hotel, though, it wasn't hard to make it feel huge once more. After nearly two years of touring by himself—102 performances between August 2011 and April 2013—Jeff got the band back together. From October 2013 to June 2015, the classic Neutral Milk Hotel lineup—Jeff, Julian, Jeremy, and Scott—along with a rotating cast of supporting musicians—Elephant 6 lifers like Laura Carter and Robbie Cucchiaro, as well as some new colleagues like Jeremy Thal—played more than 160 shows in twenty months, headlining major festivals and selling out two-thousand-cap theaters in minutes. The band performed in twenty-five different countries and forty-one US states (plus DC). The schedule was as grueling as it had been in 1998, but the accommodations were cushier and the crowds were much, much bigger.

LAURA CARTER: Whole different son of a bitch. Suddenly three thousand, six thousand, all the way up to Coachella, which was eighty thousand. The bigger the show, the lonelier the experience. The crowd becomes a thing, with more separation and barriers between the band and the audience. Whereas the small shows, you come away meeting all these people. You sleep on their floor, wash their dishes. Totally different playing field.

SCOTT SPILLANE: The number of people that listen to our music and wanted tickets, that was a huge, crazy surprise. I'm basically a carpenter who plays music part-time.

JULIAN KOSTER: It was like sailing a ship around the world with a crew of old friends. It was funny for a moment seeing what rock stars' lives are like. That was never a life any of us wanted, but it was fun to visit it like astronauts and then leave. I've always enjoyed playing to big audiences. They sound like the ocean. It's very comforting.

Before Jeff even started his solo tours, he had rented a practice space in New York and gathered Scott, Julian, and Jeremy to start rehearsing together again. They played together for a day and decided they still had something. Then they all went back home. Over the next three years, they got together occasionally for a week or a month at a time to practice together in this or that rented space. Eight-hour days of practice. As the full-band tour drew nearer, Jeremy Thal (who had been a roommate of Heather's in LA) joined to play a bunch of different instruments. Elephant 6 pals usually shared the bill. On the solo tours, the Music Tapes opened one leg; a trio of Scott, Andrew, and Laura opened another; and Jeremy's A Hawk and a Hacksaw opened another. When the full band hit the road, openers included Circulatory System and Elf Power. In a lot of ways, it was just like the old days, but some things were very different.

SCOTT SPILLANE: I think there was immense pressure. Imagine going to sleep one night and you're playing a bar that has a laundromat in the back, and then you wake up and you're scheduled to play Coachella. That's a lot of heat. We wanted to make sure we trusted each other while playing music. I just wanted to do good, and I wanted my friends to think I was doing good. I'm probably the least professional of the group, so there was a lot of pressure for me to make sure that everyone else could trust my abilities in front of eighty thousand people. Practice and practice and practice and more practice.

ROBERT SCHNEIDER: Every single place you go, they're paying for it, and they expect you to be there on time. They expect you to set up and tear down at this time. You're tightly controlled. You're in the machine, and lots of people have these tightly interlocked gears to make money, and they're paying for you to do it. You have to get there on time and be out of there on time. There's no freedom in the touring life once you're beyond the level of the earliest stage of being a touring band, which is the best. It's the best to be a young band with no gigs, just out on the road, no money. It's terrible as far as your day-to-day situation goes, but it's the best situation to be a touring band, I promise you.

LAURA CARTER: We were poor back then. We were working with some pretty janky stuff. All of our horns have now been straightened and had professional work again and again. None of that existed in the beginning. If your horn sounded skronky, it was just assumed that was you. The nice equipment does make playing a lot easier. Back then, we had just made up the parts. Now you're re-creating a part that is so memorized by your audience that it's like the national anthem to them.

BRYAN POOLE: I think everyone could tell there was some sort of reverence for the music, that Jeff had thoughtfully wanted to represent the music in a way that the fans would be able to appreciate. He spent a lot of time making sure everything was played in a way that was true to what fans thought of the music. The version back in the nineties was like a rollicking ship swaying from side to side, and you thought the hull would burst at the seams at any moment, and sometimes, it would. Jeff would collapse and fall backwards into his amplifiers. I think the newer shows were impeccably played, where the brushstrokes were placed with an emotional intensity but had the right amount of touch to create a complete image for every song and every narrative that Jeff was singing.

LANCE BANGS: I had been impressed with Jeff's breath control and his ability to sustain long, droning notes in the past, but I feel like he was maybe conscious of how effective that was or went deeper into that. He was really able to do that effectively in their more recent shows in a very impressive way. Sometimes you go see someone who hasn't performed in a long time, and they deflate or downplay or take the mystique out of things. I don't think he did that. I think Astra's been really solid for him. She's able to help get him through stuff and steer him through things.

ROBERT SCHNEIDER: Jeff learned how to go [frog-like noise from deep in the vocal cords] in your throat so that it warms your vocals up without blowing up your cords. He had me doing that before some shows because I always lose my voice. Jeff coached me. He was like, "Robert, you just have to do this thing." It's like magic.

SCOTT SPILLANE: There's a tuner stuck on my horn for every song, because it's hard to hear when you're playing with a band like that. I just wanted to make sure I wasn't playing any honkers.

JULIAN KOSTER: We could get instruments that weren't broken, or get them fixed if they were, or have someone there to fix something *when* it broke while we were playing. Having a chance to try to give that many people a special memory every night was humbling. That's an entertainer's job, and it's an honor to have it. At some point, I looked out and thought of the tiny rooms I normally entertained people in, and I realized that we were playing at that moment to a number of people it would normally take me a whole tour to play to.

LAURA CARTER: It's a great honor to be brought back, so you want to rise to the occasion and deliver. Jeff and I totally disagree on this, but the trainwreck is some of what people identify with. Shows were notorious for the fact that things were almost breaking and crumbling and falling apart, but somehow Julian was able to grab that as it was falling over and then come in with this part on time, and then this would happen. There were a lot of missed parts, but when it all came together and was really on, it was a sight to behold. When you were working with nothing but bubblegum and shoestrings, MacGyvering it with this crappy stuff, then it was like we had stuck some gymnastic Olympic landing.

ROBBIE CUCCHIARO: The show that affected me the most was the first show I saw Jeff play, hearing those songs again. It was very, very composed. The lines were very clean. It was more like listening to the album. It had that kind of fidelity and tidiness. The '97 shows and whatnot were obviously sloppier, but in a holy way. There was some sort of spiritual wildness.

WILL CULLEN HART: They were a lot more together. Jeremy plays just as hard and as awesome. I would just sit behind the stage and watch that motherfucker play. He's fucking incredible. He was doing all the same stuff, but he had two less drums. People were paying money. You can't really fall off the stage and shit if you're in a huge theater. You'd be re-creating it, and that's not what he wants to do.

DAVE MCDONNELL: That was the best I had ever seen them. That being said, it's important to note, with Bablicon and I would hazard to guess Neutral Milk Hotel, we didn't know what the fuck we were doing. I don't remember thinking it was sloppy at the time, but I've heard live recordings from that period, and Scott's missing notes and things speed up and slow down, but the energy is so intense that it doesn't matter.

REBECCA COLE: There's less shit flying around onstage. I remember that band being pretty raucous at times. Just this pure explosion of emotion. At the time, they were all young dudes. We're all working at a bigger level now. The biggest show in 1997 would have been what, the Knitting Factory? Come on. We all felt like rock stars for knowing them. Flash forward twenty years, and you're doing legitimately huge rooms, selling them out every night, union productions, a whole different world. It's about doing all the shows you said you'd do, which is like three years' worth of shows. It was a more professional show, but no less passionate. I was tour-managing for the last run, and up until the last show, it was always about the show.

GARY OLSON: Less wild, but trying to find the best way to present their recordings. I understand they had a lot of rehearsals getting everything right. I even heard a rumor Scott was taking lessons to get a little bit better. Sometimes there's a fine line. Doing shows like that, it can get a little bit Broadway, if it's too staged.

DEREK ALMSTEAD: In a way, they were ten times better. The band was polished and perfect. Everything sounded great and was in tune. The band was super consistent. The first time I ever saw them was in the Landfill, in the living room, twenty people in a room, that kind of punk rock energy. It was really exciting, but from the average audience perspective, this was ten times better. It was intense to be on the side of the stage and look out at people's faces. It was a religious experience for a lot of people.

LANCE BANGS: People are still getting a lot emotionally and musically out of Jeff's work. At some of those shows, there were audiences that were a little bit precious or very reverent at the beginning, where people felt restrained, like they would get shushed for applauding. But I think Jeff was pretty good at disarming that through the show and letting people know they can sing along. The feeling of being in the room when everybody starts singing that stuff—I'm not someone who thinks I would love that idea, but it really is a powerful thing.

SCOTT SPILLANE: There were rumors that Jeff was some weird freak and you couldn't sing along or he'd get mad. But he is not. Seeing the people change from that, where no one wanted to sing, and then he'd go, "Please sing if you want"—that's one of the things he didn't like to do. He had to break that ice himself, which is a little uncomfortable for him to do, because he's not a crazy egotistical frontman. He did sneak out sometimes without signing autographs, but it wasn't because he doesn't like to hang out and talk to people. It does make him uncomfortable, because he's not that kind of guy where he wants people to kiss his ass all day. That kind of plays into the public's perceptions of what they want. They want some guy who is a freak, and I'm not saying he's not a freak in his own way, but they want to make him in their minds be more precious than he actually wants to be perceived or should be. He just doesn't want the band to not play good shows.

JEREMY BARNES: We had done some traveling in Europe on a bus back in 1998, and Jeff and I both decided that there was no way we could tour like that again. We made the choice ahead of the reunion tour to rent minivans and drive ourselves. Everyone else was on the big bus. "Okay, guys, see you in Houston!" That tour wasn't really booked with the musicians driving themselves in mind. I think our agent thought that we would give up after the first leg, or maybe he was punishing us for not playing shows for thirteen years. It was eight hours a day, driving in January and February, in a polar vortex, and then Jeff's up onstage belting it out. Maybe if the band is big enough to call their own shots, they should be in Australia in January? But what do I know? I'm just the drummer. Jeff did the whole reunion tour by minivan—Jeff, Astra, their dog Iris, and me, and then at the end, Jeff, Heather, and me. The rock 'n' roll buses are really overrated. You sleep in a casket in motion and wake up in a travel plaza. You sit in that travel plaza and wait for the driver. Sometimes for hours. You become a prisoner of your own tour, exactly where the tour managers, promoters, and agents want you to be. The minivan was sometimes late, but we only missed one sound check, in Gothenburg, Sweden.

SCOTT SPILLANE: We didn't have liquor backstage, just because we didn't want to put on a bad show and then at the end have to say, "The reason I had a bad show is because I had such a bad hangover." If it's something like the sound fell apart or something broke or you had the flu, something you couldn't control, that's one thing. But to blow a show because you had a hangover, that's just not cool. Leading up to the show, we were in New York, which is the Lyme disease capital of the world. Jeff would never walk in the tall grass. We'd be like, "Come on, let's just go have a picnic," and he'd be like, "No." *Dude, you're being really paranoid about germs and stuff.* One day, he said to me, "Look, when the tour is over, I will roll around in the grass with you if you want, but if I get sick on tour, the complications that that would cause, to shut a tour down because I got Lyme disease."

JULIAN KOSTER: At the beginning of the tour, Jeff took me aside and told me that I couldn't throw him into the drum set anymore. It was funny, because I'm pretty sure it was *he* who always threw *me* into the drum set. It was all too much fun. Somehow I just knew in the old days when I was flying through the air that I would never get hurt, that the magic that was enfolding us would keep us safe. And it did. But I didn't try to explain that to Jeff when he took me aside before the reunion. Partially because it suddenly struck me how big he is. I'd somehow never noticed before, and I thought to myself, *If the man wishes not to throw me into a drum set one hundred times over the course of the next year, why deny him the happiness?* Though, in truth, if it were up to me, poor Jeremy's drums probably would've taken an unfair beating just like the old days.

SCOTT SPILLANE: He wasn't going to take the chance. It's kind of paranoia, but at the same time, it's rational. We have literally hundreds of thousands of people that are going to be coming to our shows, and we don't want to disappoint a single one of them. We want them to walk away saying, "Holy shit. That blew my mind."

CHAPTER 32

I don't know exactly why Jeff walked away when he did, and nobody else seems to, either. He never made himself available for an on-the-record interview for this book, but I'd be shocked if he had some grand answer to reveal. I don't think it's any one big thing but rather a few smaller things.

"I may not make another record for another decade," he told *SPIN* in 1999. "There's no point in making a career out of this."

Virtually everyone in the Elephant 6 has an antagonistic relationship with fame. They didn't pursue it, and they tended to reject it whenever it fell into their laps, even when it was a lucrative recording contract or licensing offer. For Jeff specifically, even when he was actively making music, he avoided being photographed, even in the controlled environment of a photo shoot. Further, *In the Aeroplane Over the Sea* is a record that has helped countless listeners come to terms with their own grief or trauma. Many of them told Jeff as much, to his face, before or after a set, their experience with the album greasing the hinges to let them really open up to someone who was still a complete stranger. At one show in Boston, a man approached Jeff and Scott before their set to request they play "You've Passed," which opens with the line, "The lady is dying." The man's friend, who was also in attendance, had terminal cancer. They played the song that night.

Jeff has also said that he once believed he could heal himself and the world through art. He is a deeply empathetic person, and so having strangers come up to him before and after shows to unload because they felt like he understood them would weigh heavily on his shoulders. He didn't feel better, and in some ways, he felt worse. It exposed him to so much more darkness, if channeled through the people he had brightened up. Perhaps relatedly, he was apparently a bit freaked out by what Y2K might bring. He's described this period as a nervous breakdown.

> **ROBERT SCHNEIDER:** I see that he's really touched when people come talk to him and stuff like that. Like if I'm with him and a person comes up to him and talks to him, he'll draw them a little picture or something like that. He's so kind. And then afterwards, he looks all like, *That was nice.* But if it's three people, suddenly it feels like a barrage, and he's looking for the exit.

Control seems to be a part of it, too. Jeff was always very particular about the music he released. As Neutral Milk Hotel became more popular, the proliferation of bootlegs likely made him feel a bit powerless on that front. When the recording of his in-progress "Little Birds" got out, perhaps he no longer felt that he'd have the safety of anonymity to work out the kinks of the art he wanted to make. Jeff labored obsessively over what he shared with the outside world. If forced to let the world hear his songs before he felt ready, then not letting anyone hear them at all could seem like the more enticing option.

He may have also been a victim of his own success. *Aeroplane*'s warm reception could have made him feel as if he was expected to make something new that sounded like it but somehow exceeded it in some way. As it grew in popularity, that feeling would only increase. The more time passed, the better that next album would have to be to justify the wait, which makes it harder even to start, and so more time passes, and a feedback loop emerges. The same goes for performance. The longer he waited, the more scrutiny a return might bring.

If you put yourself in Jeff's shoes, it's not all that hard to imagine why it was so appealing to stay quiet. That's more than enough reason to want to take a break, and once some time has passed, it gets more difficult to step back in. His bandmates had projects of their own. Expectations for his own work had only grown, and he had developed a reputation as an inscrutable genius. To puncture that mystique could destroy something that had resonated with so many people. It seems that he didn't fully realize at first how impactful his music had been, and by the time he came to understand that, it was a lot harder to return.

It's still kind of weird that Neutral Milk Hotel has gotten so big in spite of its frontman's reluctance. If Neutral Milk Hotel had come along a bit earlier, Jeff's raw emotional expression could have been dismissed as corny and contrived, out of line with the hip slacker pose and the irony that saturated the culture of the time. If it had come along a bit later, it would have had a much harder time breaking through at all, when suddenly there were a whole lot of bands doing some version of what he was doing (albeit in part because of his influence).

Under slightly different circumstances, the Elephant 6's flagship band could have been the Olivia Tremor Control, but while Merge was making a whole big thing of re-releasing *Aeroplane* in 2005, keeping it in print to keep up with sustained demand, Flydaddy was going through bankruptcy, forcing John Fernandes to buy back their masters (for which he had a limited capacity to release himself thereafter). Perhaps it could have been the Apples in Stereo if their brand of psychedelic garage pop had been in vogue at the time, rather than the popular corners of indie folk and Americana into which Neutral Milk Hotel seeped. Of Montreal was pretty damn big itself for a little while there, too, but not really until Kevin got some separation from the collective, both socially and aesthetically. A lot of folks recognized Jeff as the Elephant 6's crown jewel before it came to be, but no one could have predicted the impact his work would make.

JEREMY BARNES: The odd thing is that it worked out in the best way possible. Julian put out many Music Tapes records. Scott has a wonderful wife, he has a daughter, he became a carpenter. Jeff met Astra, and he has found a sense of peace that he didn't have back in those days, when he would wake up yelling or fall into a depression in the middle of rehearsal. I met my wife, Heather, and my adventures as a musician are still going. I think we all, knowingly or unknowingly, had a hand in the band ending. But from the moment I joined to the end, I was completely devoted to it. If Jeff had kept going, and was now releasing records for middle-aged dads and fraternity children, I would still be there with him. I wholeheartedly believe in his vision.

In the thirteen and a half years I spent working on this book, a lot of people asked me why Jeff stopped making music. It's a fair question. More than the small-business success or the white picket fence or the 2.5 children, nothing embodies the American Dream quite like being a rock star. Who *wouldn't* want that? The fame and fortune, the freedom and fulfillment, the fun: it certainly *sounds* great. Nobody, though—not one person—ever asked why he made music in the first place. That's a more relatable question, I think, and a more urgent one. Why does anyone make anything?

There's an old joke that Scott Spillane likes to tell during shows, puncturing the extended silence between songs when something needs to be tuned or adjusted. "How do you get an indie rocker off your porch?" he'll ask.

"Pay him for the pizza."

It's never been easy to make money as an artist, and it doesn't seem to be getting any easier. To make a *living* as a musician requires a lot of luck and a lot of delusion before talent or skill or work ethic even come into the picture. Some of the musicians of the Elephant 6 have been able to make enough money through their music to support themselves for a little while, and a few have been able to do it for a long time. Many of them have not been so lucky. In a more just world, they'd all be more comfortable financially.

People have made art in every human society throughout the history of humanity, but the economics are only a part of the story. Art predates the very concept of money, so perhaps there are other ways to evaluate its purpose and measure its worth. Popularity comes up short, too. An artist's "reach" (to borrow a term from the vulgar lexicon of marketing) captures only one tiny part of their influence or impact. The most valuable things art has to offer—to both artists and their audiences—are not quantifiable. To evaluate a work of art based on its popularity is like evaluating the quality of someone's parenting based solely on how many kids they have.

What do we have to gain from making music, and what do we have to gain from hearing it? The Elephant 6 heyday coincides with the music industry's commercial peak. The bubble burst at the turn of the millennium, and the industry has still not recovered. It is harder and harder every day to make a living as a musician, and yet people keep trying, even as the pie gets smaller and more people want a piece. In the present day, we all have lots of reasons not to make art. The lesson of the Elephant 6 is to make it anyway.

> ROBERT SCHNEIDER: I'm lucky because unlike most other musicians along that path, I actually did reasonably well as a band. I had to do a lot of different things. I had to be in a good band—our records were reasonably successful—and I was writing songs that were getting licensed, and I was an engineer and producer, and I had a studio to work in that I owned, and we owned a van so we could tour. You can piece it together into something like barely making a living, without selling out. I never even one time took the thing that would have been cheesy or wrong or would have been beneficial monetarily but would have gone against my ethics. I never did it, not even one time. That's awesome to be able to look back and say I made a living, and I never did anything that went against my philosophy. I didn't have to tweak it to make it match up with events. I tweaked the events, I tweaked the scene, I tweaked *music* to make it work. You want to believe when you're young that people can do that. The whole world says, "No, you'll see when you get out there in the world. It's a great philosophy, but you're going to have to make some tweaks as you go through life." It doesn't have to be that way. It is possible to be young and idealistic and stick with those ideals and be tactful, productive, street-smart, and perfectly creative, and to sustain that through a life. I did every single cool thing that came up, and I turned my back on every uncool thing that came up. You're not going to make as much money doing that, so you have to take that out of your list of things that you care about. It's really hard, because you're poor and you're an artist and you don't have any money. I used to live off of one dollar a day when I was in my twenties. I recorded albums for bands for like fifty dollars a week. The fact is that if you delete money from your list of ambitions—you don't reject it all the time, but you delete it from your list of ambitions, and you keep all the pure ones—it's possible to live a productive and satisfactory life and to support other people and have them support your art and to be creative and free.

To quote the late anthropologist David Graeber, "The ultimate hidden truth of the world is that it is something we make, and could just as easily make differently." Or as put by the brilliant Laetitia Sadier in Stereolab's song "Crest":

> *If there's been a way to build it,*
> *There'll be a way to destroy it.*
> *Things are not all that out of control.*

In what sort of world would we like to live? The Elephant 6 offers an artistic model worth emulating. It's a model of thinking galactically but acting so locally that sometimes only your roommates will notice. It's a model of pretending to take things seriously—the Elephant 6 logo isn't even trademarked!—and taking that make-believe pretty seriously, turning impostor syndrome into a superpower. It's about letting go of where you're going but fixating on how you get there, journey over destination, process over results. It's about, whatever you're doing, doing it artistically, and it's about, whatever you care about, radiating that passion outward. It's about competing with one another solely to encourage, rivalry as collaboration. It's about sincerity and hope over snark and irony, the impulse to create rather than to destroy. It's about how community can strengthen art and how artistic expression can strengthen the members of that community and the relationships between them.

ROBERT SCHNEIDER: You don't have to starve, but it takes everybody working together to support each other to make that happen. And so it's a way that a community can exist and can live at something like a subsistence level or slightly above it and make art and be pure and be philosophical and grow old together and still be friends. That's a really good way to have an artistic community. It can happen. It's a model that's reproduceable. What this approach to creativity does is seal off expression from the cutthroat impulses that ooze in when there are only so many eyes or ears or dollars to go around. Within a zero-sum economic framework, artists operate in the realm of scarcity, and the money and attention often accrue along familiar lines of race, gender, and other extant power structures, consolidating into the hands of a select few. By imagining alternatives to this framework, though, creativity can become more expansive, space can be made for everyone, and the whole—society at large—can grow larger than the sum of its parts, because

> the bonds between those parts are so fortified. It is as difficult as it is necessary to imagine alternatives that conceive of artistic success not as a finite resource to be fought over but rather as an endless, multivalent, self-perpetuating entity, something that looks and feels and acts a lot more like love.

Many of the people involved with the Elephant 6 are the children of professors, artists, and other cultural elites. There are certainly more challenging environments in which to grow up. But nearly to a person, they grew up feeling weirder than their peers, alienated and constrained. Through music, they found one another, connected with one another, and almost by accident created a community in which they could thrive and millions of people around the world could connect with them, too.

"I love the endless possibilities of music and words and sound," Jeff told *Exclaim!* in 1998. "I think that anybody can find those possibilities, and that's exciting as hell. I love music so much."

JEREMY BARNES: To a person, I think everyone in the Elephant 6 has a heart of gold, but everyone was also dealing with their own trauma, their own flaws, and serious struggles with poverty and all the issues that go along with that. There were moments of real beauty, and there were moments of real despair. It's really strange how predators and vultures appear when you are at your lowest. The salvation, in the end, was in creativity and magical thinking.

ROBERT SCHNEIDER: You have to have a little bit of an unrealistically arrogant self-image to be able to try to do things like say, "I'm a record producer with a four-track." It's really unrealistic, and yet it happened. So you can do that. You can say it and do it. It's a little unrealistically arrogant to say that our little music scene in high school is Elephant 6. It's arrogance of youth. It's healthy arrogance. That is the arrogance that makes things happen in the world. To say that I can do the thing that's improbable. I shouldn't be able to do this thing, but I can do it even though other people can't.

JULIAN KOSTER: I believe in the magic that happens on stages, between people, the performers and the audience. They are moments of shared imagination. I think that the best moments in life are moments of shared imagination.

HILARIE SIDNEY: Remember to appreciate the people you have around you. Appreciate them while they're there and do fun stuff. If you can get a group of really special people together that get along and have the same kinds of ideas, you should definitely take advantage of that. We didn't have other things to do. We didn't have money. We didn't have TV or cable or anything like that. In some ways, you're forced to create your own fun. That's a really fun thing to do if you're creative. To put your heads together and come up with a bunch of weird shit.

SCOTT SPILLANE: One thing that people need to fulfill their greatest potential is support from their friends and family. And a lot of people don't get it from their family. Supporting your friends in whatever they're doing is what you should strive for. When you do that and do it for your entire life, you end up being fifty years old and you've got nothing. Other people have retirement funds. We end up giving our lives over to this thing, and it's kind of like you sold your soul to Satan. You could go work at a factory and have a nice house and a yard and a family, and you croak one day, and your family's like, "Yeah, he did pretty good." But if you're a musician, your family is like, "What is he doing with his life?" every year. It's a different world. Working at a coffee shop or whatever and pursuing your dreams is a hard thing to do. I don't have any regrets about it. When you're playing music, there's a point where the rest of the world disappears, kind of like meditating. You become one with the universe. It sounds very cheesy. I'm not that kind of guy. You start the show and things are weird and crazy and nervous, and then you hit that moment. That moment is addicting. You can't find it anywhere else, or at least I can't. When you involve the other people in a band, there's a point where everyone's working together and on the same thing, and I think that elevates it even higher. When everybody is really in the same place at the same time, and there's an audience and they're there with you, it's that super primitive thing that makes humans humans. Those Neutral Milk Hotel shows, when that was going on, I could kiss the face of god every night. We're just trying to make that beautiful thing happen. The more we can do it, the more enriched our lives are. It's that feeling of camaraderie, and all of that hardship and the horrors of the world fade into the background, disappear for a little while, and that's when you got it. That's what it's for.

LAURA CARTER: It's like taking walks or drinking water. We should all do more of it, because it's healthy. You have no goal but to make something beautiful. Maybe it's not always beautiful. To let out something inside you or express yourself in some way. The meaningful stuff about Elephant 6 to me is that Will made this logo to kind of say "fuck you" to the big labels. We can have our own collective and make our own brand with nothing but inspiration. They could never get acceptance from one of those brands, coming from Louisiana. So they just made their own. And then they all get behind it, and it has meaning. It has actual value. I still think that's fucking cool. More power to that kind of mentality. All you have to do is make it up.

Acknowledgments

I HAVE FAR TOO MANY PEOPLE TO THANK FOR THEIR SUPPORT toward this project over the thirteen-plus years I spent working on it, so I'll keep this brief lest anyone I've forgotten feel too left out.

First and foremost, thank you to my parents: to my dad, Marc, who taught me so much about how I view creativity and who inspired me to care about it in the first place, and to my mom, Cindy, who has provided unconditional encouragement even and especially when I couldn't explain why this was worth undertaking, for no other reason than I was the one who was undertaking it.

Thanks to David Dunton, my agent, for his belief in this story and his steady hand in finding a home for it. Thanks to my editor, Ben Schafer, and to everyone at Hachette whose hard work produced the real, actual book in your hands (or perhaps on your screen or in your earphones).

It should be obvious, but endless gratitude to everyone quoted, cited, or credited in the preceding pages; to everyone who talked to me on the record but whose quotes were cut from the final pages; and to everyone whose off-the-record conversations shaped my research and framing. Thank you all for trusting me to tell this story with empathy and accuracy. A few of the folks who went generously above and graciously beyond include Lance Bangs, John Fernandes, Kelly Hart, Will Cullen Hart,

Jim McIntyre, Henry Owings, Bryan Poole, Robert Schneider, and Davey Wrathgabar.

A special thanks to Matt Spolar, who—many times over many years—helped me shape an offhanded "someone should write a book about those folks" on a hazy State College summer night into something somebody might want to read. A cop-out, catchall thanks to all of my friends, acquaintances, and even any enemies who have listened to me blab about this story at any point in time, but especially to Ryan Jordan, Philip Levitsky, Larry Weaver, and Matt Whittle, who politely put up with way more than their fair share. Additional thanks to Stacy Adelman, Ian Brown, Julia Chapman, Allison Charles, Sean Cohen, Deven Craige, Tom Dessalet, Kevin Doran, Daniel Efram, Lauren Graham Garcia, Adrienne Hamil, Jillian Jatres, Emily Jordan, Justin Kau, Amanda Kreider, Will Leitch, Chris Lipczynski, Ryan McNally, Deidre McPhillips, Kristine Murawski, Daniel Pieczkolon, Jessie Radlow, Kate Rears, Alyssa Reuben, Derek Salazar, Dylan Scott, Chad Stockfleth, Ravi Teixeira, Laurence Vallières, Ryan White, Emily Whittle, and Alec Wooden for various forms of support, encouragement, and inspiration. I'm certain I've left off some important people here and apologize profusely to each of them.

Thanks as well to Steve Keene for the perfect cover art. It looked extremely rad when I pictured it in my head but so much better when I saw the real thing.

Thanks also to about a dozen different coffee shops in Philadelphia and Athens where I spent much time working on this and significantly more time fretting about how I can never get any work done while I shook off the cold-brew jitters.

And finally, as corny as it may sound, thank you for reading this. We've probably never met and perhaps we never will, but in some abstract way, I've been thinking about you for many years now, and I'm gratified that you've chosen to spend some of your attention this way.

Interview List

This is a comprehensive list of people interviewed on the record for this book, whether or not they are quoted herein. Musicians are listed with only one or two of their musical projects for the sake of keeping this list at a printable length. In almost all cases (including some of those not even listed here as musicians), they have a number of other bands or personae not included here. All interviews were conducted between the beginning of 2010 and the end of summer 2021.

- Kenneth Aguar (The 8-Track Gorilla)
- Derek Almstead (Elf Power)
- Lance Bangs (filmmaker)
- Jeremy Barnes (Neutral Milk Hotel, Bablicon)
- Kevin Barnes (Of Montreal)
- Jeff Baron (The Essex Green)
- Andy Battaglia (culture writer, former Athenian)
- Ross Beach (Clay Bears)
- Sasha Bell (The Ladybug Transistor)
- Chris Bilheimer (R.E.M. graphic designer, designer of Neutral Milk Hotel album art)
- Michel Boulware (hometown friend of Rustonites)

- Levi Buffum (Doctor Octoroc, released 8-bit *In the Aeroplane Over the Sea* tribute album)
- Jill Carnes (Thimble Circus)
- Laura Carter (Elf Power)
- Brian Chidester (culture writer)
- Rebecca Cole (The Minders)
- Kim Cooper (author of *Neutral Milk Hotel's* In the Aeroplane Over the Sea [33 1/3])
- Jud Cost (music writer)
- Ben Crum (Great Lakes)
- Robbie Cucchiaro (The Music Tapes)
- John d'Azzo (The Gerbils)
- Sean Davidson (Elephant 6 Townhall message board admin)
- Paige Dearman (Midget and Hairs)
- Barbara Denvir (Dixie Blood Mustache)
- Jim DeRogatis (music writer)
- Dan Donahue (Great Lakes)
- Bill Doss (The Olivia Tremor Control, The Sunshine Fix)
- Justin Emerle (Echo Orbiter, Elephant 6 fan)
- Pete Erchick (The Olivia Tremor Control; Pipes You See, Pipes You Don't)
- Stephen Thomas Erlewine (*AllMusic* senior editor)
- John Fernandes (The Olivia Tremor Control, Circulatory System)
- Shawn Fogel (Neutral Uke Hotel ukulele tribute band)
- Little Fyodor (Denver musician)
- Nesey Gallons (Circulatory System)
- Dan Geller (cofounder of Kindercore Records)
- Ben Goldberg (friend of Jeff Mangum)
- Andy Gonzales (Marshmallow Coast)
- Jeremy Goshorn (hometown friend of Rustonites)
- Kathy Harr (Elephant 6 fan)
- Will Cullen Hart (The Olivia Tremor Control, Circulatory System)
- Max Heath (author of a music school thesis on Neutral Milk Hotel)
- Jason Heller (culture writer)
- Will Hermes (music writer)
- John Hill (The Apples in Stereo, Dressy Bessy)
- Jamey Huggins (Of Montreal, Great Lakes)

- Steve Keene (visual artist, painted several E6 album covers)
- Julian Koster (Neutral Milk Hotel, The Music Tapes)
- Zak Krone (Elephant 6 fan)
- Lisa Janssen (Secret Square)
- Maura Johnston (music writer)
- Hannah Jones (Circulatory System)
- Matt Jordan (music writer)
- Missy Kulik (Elephant 6 fan)
- Gordon Lamb (Elephant 6 fan)
- Martyn Leaper (The Minders)
- Dave McDonnell (Bablicon)
- Heather McIntosh (Circulatory System, The Instruments)
- Jim McIntyre (The Apples in Stereo, Von Hemmling)
- Brian McPherson (attorney for Neutral Milk Hotel, The Olivia Tremor Control, et al.)
- Joel Morowitz (spinART Records cofounder)
- Glenn Morrow (Bar/None Records cofounder)
- Noel Murray (culture writer, former Athenian)
- Gary Olson (The Ladybug Transistor)
- Henry Owings (longtime friend of key subjects and former Athenian, released several early E6 records)
- Chris Parfitt (The Apples in Stereo)
- J. Kirk Pleasant (Calvin, Don't Jump!)
- Bryan Poole (Of Montreal, Elf Power)
- Jeff Price (spinART Records cofounder)
- Domenic Priore (music writer)
- Mark Richardson (music writer, former *Pitchfork* editor in chief)
- Andrew Rieger (Elf Power)
- Scott Reitherman (Elephant 6 fan)
- Griffin Rodriguez (Bablicon)
- Jim Romeo (booking agent for Neutral Milk Hotel, The Olivia Tremor Control, et al.)
- Beth Sale (Dixie Blood Mustache)
- Robert Schneider (The Apples in Stereo, Marbles)
- Ryan Schreiber (*Pitchfork* founder)
- Dr. LuLu Shimek (fka Lara Hetzler, Dixie Blood Mustache)
- Hilarie Sidney (The Apples in Stereo, The High Water Marks)

- Scott Spillane (Neutral Milk Hotel, Gerbils)
- Ty Storms (member of Jeff Mangum and Will Cullen Hart's middle school band)
- Brad Truax (childhood friend of Julian Koster)
- Mike Turner (founder of Happy Happy Birthday to Me Records)
- Phil Waldorf (president of Dead Oceans Records, former Athenian)
- Aaron Wegelin (Elf Power)
- Davey Wrathgabar (Elf Power, The Visitations)

ENDNOTES

INTRODUCTION

xi In a *Pitchfork* interview: Marci Fierman, "Neutral Milk Hotel," *Pitchfork*, February 1, 2002, https://pitchfork.com/features/interview/5847-neutral-milk-hotel/.

CHAPTER ONE

1 *Pitchfork* counts it: *Pitchfork* Staff, "Top 100 Albums of the 1990s," *Pitchfork*, November 17, 2003, https://pitchfork.com/features/lists-and-guides/5923-top-100-albums-of-the-1990s/.

CHAPTER TWO

7 At recess that first day: Jud Cost, "Through the Looking Glass," *Magnet*, May/June 1998.

10 "We'd get crushed daily": Cost, "Through the Looking Glass."

11 "It was kind of a punk band": James Sullivan, "Tusk: The Lo-Fi Psychedelia of Elephant 6," *San Francisco Weekly*, July 3, 1996.

12 "My first songs": Steve Tignor, "Neutral Milk Hotel," *Puncture*, Summer 1996.

CHAPTER THREE

17 "In school I was surrounded": Mike McGonigal, "Dropping in at the Neutral Milk Hotel," *Puncture*, Spring 1998.

19 "All through our childhood": Wil Gerken, "Got Milk? Welcome to the New American Musical Transcendentalism," *Tucson Weekly*, April 2, 1998.

23 "We'd dropped out": Phil McMullen, "Neutral Milk Hotel," *Ptolemaic Terrascope*, September 1996.

25 "Some of those early tapes": Cost, "Through the Looking Glass."

25 "There was a group of us": Brian Heater, "Elephant 6 Recording Company: Crash Course," *SPIN*, July 31, 2012 (originally published April 2006), https://www.spin.com/2012/07/elephant-6-recording-company-crash-course/.

25 "When you grow up where I did": Tignor, "Neutral Milk Hotel."

28 "Do you watch MTV?": Mike McGonigal, "Mangum Force," *New York Press*, February 4, 1998.

30 "a pretty freaky place": Jim Hanas, "The Persistence of Memory," *Memphis Flyer*, February 12, 1998.

CHAPTER SIX

60 US CD sales grew: Steve Knopper, *Appetite for Self-Destruction: The Spectacular Crash of the Record Industry in the Digital Age* (Berkeley, California: Soft Skull Press, 2010), 38.

61 "The record industry is prone to crisis": Jonathan Sterne, *MP3: The Meaning of a Format* (Durham, NC: Duke University Press, 2012), 185.

CHAPTER SEVEN

64 "more than a local star": Grace Elizabeth Hale, *Cool Town: How Athens, Georgia, Launched Alternative Music and Changed American Culture* (Chapel Hill, NC: The University of North Carolina Press, 2020), 16.

65 "had been a part of the Factory": Hale, *Cool Town*, 17.

65 "The blurred lines": Hale, *Cool Town*, 9.

CHAPTER TEN

97 "I've done [four-tracking] all my life": David Daley, "Neutral Milk Hotel: Mangum, Lo-Fi," *Alternative Press*, August 1996.

98 "I was very isolated": Christopher Waters, "Neutral Milk Hotel: Endless Possibilities," *Exclaim!*, 1998.

99 "Recording *Avery Island* was a learning experience": Eric Hellweg, "New & Cool: The Surreal Sound of Neutral Milk Hotel," *Addicted to Noise*, February 4, 1998.

100 "It made a huge impression": Greg Kot, "Reinvigorating Rock, from the Basement Up," *Chicago Tribune*, January 12, 1997, https://www.chicagotribune.com/news/ct-xpm-1997-01-12-9701120131-story.html.

101 "I had a little bed": Daley, "Neutral Milk Hotel: Mangum, Lo-Fi."

101 "I moved into a friend's house": McMullen, "Neutral Milk Hotel."

101 "I open my eyes": McGonigal, "Mangum Force."

CHAPTER ELEVEN

107 "He told me, 'Man'": Cost, "Through the Looking Glass."

109 "None of us had ever played together": Jeff Clark, "Neutral Milk Hotel," *Stomp and Stammer*, June 1998.

110 "Next thing you know": Clark, "Neutral Milk Hotel."

112 Music critic Neil Strauss: Neil Strauss, "Matters of Life, Death and Prevarication," *New York Times*, May 1, 1997, https://www.nytimes.com/1997/05/01/arts/matters-of-life-death-and-prevarication.html.

CHAPTER TWELVE

119 "They had this Bad News Bears quality": John Cook with Mac McCaughan and Laura Ballance, *Our Noise: The Story of Merge Records* (Chapel Hill, NC: Algonquin Books, 2009), 98.

121 He explained the camp's vibe: Dave Stacey and Julie Talon, "Neutral Milk Hotel Interview," *Mommy and I Are One*, 1997.

121 In a live review: Victoria Segal, "Sparklehorse Live Review," *NME*, October 17, 1998.

133 "This new album is more involved": Waters, "Neutral Milk Hotel: Endless Possibilities."

133 "Ninety-five percent of the album": Carly Carioli, "Magnum's Opus: Neutral Milk Hotel's Epic *Aeroplane*," *Boston Phoenix*, March 9, 1998.

133 "The songs sort of come out spontaneously": McGonigal, "Dropping in at the Neutral Milk Hotel."

133 "When I wrote [*Aeroplane*]": David Daley, "Self-Analysis: Neutral Milk Hotel," *Alternative Press*, April 1998.

134 "Some of the songs really scared me": Cost, "Through the Looking Glass."

134 "While I was reading the book": McGonigal, "Dropping in at the Neutral Milk Hotel."

135 "The lyrical content": Daley, "Self-Analysis: Neutral Milk Hotel."

135 "One thing that was different": Waters, "Neutral Milk Hotel: Endless Possibilities."

137 "All the recording sound is intentional": McGonigal, "Dropping in at the Neutral Milk Hotel."

138 "Sometimes the other guys": Bob Gulla, "Jeff Mangum's Neutral Milk Hotel Emerge from the Elephant 6 Collective with the Four-Track Odyssey *In the Aeroplane Over the Sea*," *Ray Gun*, March 1998.

139 "Rock's been crippled": Ben Ratliff, "*In the Aeroplane Over the Sea*," *Rolling Stone*, February 13, 1998, https://www.rollingstone.com/music/music-album-reviews/in-the-aeroplane-over-the-sea-112548/.

139 "concocted the whole thing": Erik Himmelsbach, "Neutral Milk Hotel, *In the Aeroplane Over the Sea*," *SPIN*, March 1998.

139 "visionary poet": Matt Ashare, "Neutral Milk Hotel, *In the Aeroplane Over the Sea*," *CMJ New Music Monthly*, March 1998.

139 "a wonderfully dense collision": John Paczkowski, "Neutral Milk Hotel, *In the Aeroplane Over the Sea*," *San Francisco Bay Guardian*, January 28, 1998.

139 "The old idea that": Josh Westlund, "Neutral Milk Hotel, *In the Aeroplane Over the Sea*," *New Haven Advocate*, February 26–March 4, 1998.

139 "*Aeroplane* is an attempt": Hellweg, "New & Cool: The Surreal Sound of Neutral Milk Hotel."

CHAPTER THIRTEEN

141 Hart is interviewed while listening: Neil Gladstone, title unknown, *Ray Gun*, March 1999.

143 "Elephant 6 is a group": Heater, "Elephant 6 Recording Company: Crash Course."

144 "Everyone is recording": Gulla, "Jeff Mangum's Neutral Milk Hotel Emerge from the Elephant 6 Collective with the Four-Track Odyssey *In the Aeroplane Over the Sea*."

147 The *Rolling Stone* feature: Will Hermes, "Psych Out," *Rolling Stone*, April 2, 1998.

CHAPTER EIGHTEEN

178 "*When Your Heartstrings Break* got panned": Nikhil Swaminathan, title unknown, *Creative Loafing*, October 9–15, 2003.

CHAPTER NINETEEN

185 "After playing with Jeff": "Ready to Rumble: Bablicon," *Magnet*, 2000.

190 "perfect for adventurous": "*1st Imaginary Symphony for Nomad*," *CMJ New Music Report*, July 26, 1999.

190 "spooky, noise-ridden tracks": Elizabeth Chorney, "*1st Imaginary Symphony for Nomad*," *Calgary Straight*, August 5–12, 1999.

190 "Connoisseurs of violently fragmented pop": Keith Phipps, "The Music Tapes: *1st Imaginary Symphony for Nomad*," *The A.V. Club*, March 29, 2002, https://music.avclub.com/the-music-tapes-1st-imaginary-symphony-for-nomad-1798193095.

190 "overwrought beast": Brent DiCrescenzo, "The Music Tapes: *1st Imaginary Symphony for Nomad*," *Pitchfork*, July 6, 1999, https://pitchfork.com/reviews/albums/5524-1st-imaginary-symphony-for-nomad/.

192 "I'm probably gonna put out": Clark, "Neutral Milk Hotel."

194 But after declining request after request: Fierman, "Neutral Milk Hotel."
197 "I just want to end up": Josh Mittleman, "Neutral Milk Hotel," *Hello, Sailor!*, Spring 1997.
197 "We're always moving": Gulla, "Jeff Mangum's Neutral Milk Hotel Emerge from the Elephant 6 Collective with the Four-Track Odyssey *In the Aeroplane Over the Sea*."
197 "Being in different places": Gerken, "Got Milk? Welcome to the New American Musical Transcendentalism."
197 "And now, the songs": John Lewis, "Escape Artists: Can Neutral Milk Hotel Get Away from It All?," *Option*, May/June 1998.
198 "I think this is about": Clark, "Neutral Milk Hotel."

CHAPTER TWENTY

202 "SpinART loves us": Jeff Stratton, "Denver Band Spearheads New Music Scene," *Denver Post*, June 6, 1999.

CHAPTER TWENTY-ONE

209 "Eventually our plan": Gulla, "Jeff Mangum's Neutral Milk Hotel Emerge from the Elephant 6 Collective with the Four-Track Odyssey *In the Aeroplane Over the Sea*."

CHAPTER TWENTY-TWO

223 "best listened to while standing": Bruce Miller, "*Major Organ and the Adding Machine*: Major Organ and the Adding Machine," *Magnet*, September/October 2001.
223 "jumbled mess": Ari Wiznitzer, "*Major Organ and the Adding Machine*," *AllMusic*, undated, https://www.allmusic.com/album/major-organ-and-the-adding-machine-mw0000012312.
223 "Alternating between vaguely interesting": Matt LeMay, "Major Organ and the Adding Machine, *Major Organ and the Adding Machine*," *Pitchfork*, 2001.
224 "a bit self-indulgent": "Other Music New Release Update," May 16, 2001, http://othermusic.com/2001may16update.html.
231 One 2009 study: Sean Michaels, "Study finds pirates 10 times more likely to buy music," *Guardian*, April 21, 2009, https://www.theguardian.com/music/2009/apr/21/study-finds-pirates-buy-more-music.

CHAPTER TWENTY-THREE

241 Producer Danger Mouse worked: Kyle Anderson, "Danger Mouse," *SPIN*, October 2005.
241 Writing as April: Michael Schur (as April Ludgate), "*Parks and Rec*'s April Ludgate Celebrates the Anniversary of Neutral Milk Hotel's Finest Work,"

Vulture, February 11, 2013, https://www.vulture.com/2013/02/april-ludgate-on-neutral-milk-hotels-in-the-aeroplane.html.

241 He told *New York Times* columnist: Maureen Dowd, "A Wit for All Seasons," *New York Times*, April 12, 2014, https://www.nytimes.com/2014/04/13/opinion/sunday/a-wit-for-all-seasons.html.

244 Eventually, *Pitchfork* fleshed out: Amy Phillips, "Jeff Mangum Returns?," *Pitchfork*, June 28, 2006.

247 "just as catchy": M. Christian McDermott, "Neutral Milk Hotel, *In the Aeroplane Over the Sea*," *Pitchfork*, 1998, http://web.archive.org/web/20030201194416/www.pitchforkmedia.com/record-reviews/n/neutral-milk-hotel/in-the-aeroplane-over-the-sea.shtml.

248 When Merge reissued the album: Mark Richardson, "Neutral Milk Hotel, *In the Aeroplane Over the Sea*," *Pitchfork*, September 26, 2005, https://pitchfork.com/reviews/albums/5758-in-the-aeroplane-over-the-sea/.

250 writer Kevin Griffis set out: Kevin Griffis, "Have you seen Jeff Mangum?," *Creative Loafing*, September 4, 2003, https://creativeloafing.com/content-184720-have-you-seen-jeff-mangum-2.

251 A 2016 *A.V. Club* piece: Luke Winkie, "How did the Neutral Milk Hotel legend get so out of hand?," *A.V. Club*, May 11, 2016, https://music.avclub.com/how-did-the-neutral-milk-hotel-legend-get-so-out-of-han-1798247155.

CHAPTER TWENTY-FOUR

256 "There was a time": Robin Hilton, "Hear The First Olivia Tremor Control Song In 10 Years," *All Songs Considered*, August 30, 2011, https://www.npr.org/sections/allsongs/2011/08/30/140043128/interview-olivia-tremor-control-returns-with-first-new-song-in-10-years.

CHAPTER TWENTY-FIVE

268 The ordeal inspired Kevin: Kevin Barnes, "Of Montreal Talk T-Mobile: 'Selling Out Isn't Possible,'" *Stereogum*, November 16, 2007.

CHAPTER TWENTY-SIX

272 "I must also commend": Jeff Kuykendall, "6 Questions with: Bill Doss," *Optical Atlas*, July 15, 2006.

273 the first Apples song licensed: John Leland, "Advertisements for Themselves," *New York Times*, March 11, 2001, https://www.nytimes.com/2001/03/11/magazine/advertisements-for-themselves.html.

CHAPTER TWENTY-SEVEN

285 "Between bits of awkward banter": Heater, "Elephant 6 Recording Company: Crash Course."

CHAPTER TWENTY-EIGHT

299 "The warm reception": Maura Johnston, "Live: Olivia Tremor Control Keep Hope Alive," *Village Voice*, September 22, 2011, https://www.villagevoice.com/2011/09/22/live-olivia-tremor-control-keep-hope-alive/.

301 In 2006, Derek told: Jeff Kuykendall, "6 Questions with: Derek Almstead," *Optical Atlas*, March 5, 2006.

CHAPTER THIRTY

308 "Mangum played with his eyes mostly closed": Andrew Frisicano, "Jeff Mangum, The Clean, Yo La Tengo, Portastatic & friends played for Chris Knox @ LPR—review, setlist, video & pic," *Brooklyn Vegan*, May 7, 2010, https://www.brooklynvegan.com/jeff-mangum-the/.

313 "His Occupy Wall Street set": Ann Powers, "21st Century Protest Music: Will There Be Another Dylan? Should There Be?," *The Record*, NPR, October 8, 2011, https://www.npr.org/sections/therecord/2011/10/16/141155461/21st-century-protest-music-will-there-be-another-dylan-should-there-be.

313 "In the video, you can hear": Stephen Deusner, "Will a new Dylan emerge from Occupy Wall Street?," *Salon*, October 15, 2011, https://www.salon.com/2011/10/15/will_a_new_dylan_emerge_from_occupy_wall_street/.

CHAPTER THIRTY-TWO

323 "I may not make": D. Strauss, "The 90 Greatest Albums of the '90s," *SPIN*, September 1999.

329 "I love the endless possibilities": Waters, "Neutral Milk Hotel: Endless Possibilities."

Index